Recovery from Stuttering

LANGUAGE AND SPEECH DISORDERS BOOK SERIES

Series Editors:

Martin J. Ball, *University of Louisiana at Lafayette*

Jack S. Damico, *University of Louisiana at Lafayette*

This new series brings together course material and new research for students, practitioners, and researchers in the various areas of language and speech disorders. Textbooks covering the basics of the discipline will be designed for courses within communication disorders programs in the English-speaking world, and monographs and edited collections will present cutting-edge research from leading scholars in the field.

PUBLISHED

Recovery from Stuttering, Howell

FORTHCOMING

Applying English Grammatical Analysis: Clinical Language Assessment and Intervention,
    Jin & Cortazzi
Handbook of Vowels and Vowel Disorders, Ball & Gibbon (Eds.)
Electropalatography for Speech Assessment and Intervention, McLeod, Wood, &
    Hardcastle

For continually updated information about published and forthcoming titles in the Language and Speech Disorders book series, please visit www.psypress.com/language-and-speech-disorders

Recovery from Stuttering

Peter Howell

Routledge
Taylor & Francis Group
NEW YORK AND LONDON

First published in 2011 by Psychology Press

Published 2016 by Routledge
711 Third Avenue,New York, NY 10017
2 Park Square,Milton Park, Abingdon,Oxfordshire OX14 4RN

First issued in paperback 2016

Routledge is an imprint of the Taylor and Francis Group, an informa business

© 2011 by Taylor and Francis Group, LLC

ISBN 13: 978-1-138-99710-3 (pbk)
ISBN 13: 978-1-84872-916-2 (hbk)

Library of Congress Cataloging-in-Publication Data

Howell, Peter, 1947-
  Recovery from stuttering / Peter Howell.
    p. ; cm. -- (Language and speech disorders)
  Includes bibliographical references and index.
  ISBN 978-1-84872-916-2 (hardcover : alk. paper)
  1. Stuttering. I. Title. II. Series: Language and speech disorders.
  [DNLM: 1. Stuttering. 2. Adolescent. 3. Child. WM 475]
  RC424.H75 2011
  616.85'54--dc22

2010032472

Visit the Taylor & Francis Web site at
http://www.taylorandfrancis.com

Dedicated to Stan and Bill Yarrow

Contents

SECTION III   Theoretical Frameworks on Developmental Stuttering

SECTION IV   Practical Issues in Developmental Stuttering

Preface

This book seeks to summarize what is known about stuttering in its early stages and, to a lesser extent, to the changes in fluency that occur when various treatments are given. These two aspects are loosely referred to when fluency improves as "recovery." I set out with the intention of establishing how these forms of stuttering contrasted with those that are less transigent (referred to as persistent). The book is written by an experimental psychologist who is not involved in delivering treatments. It seeks to provide the reader with information that will allow one to interpret the research literature and evaluate findings.

The text introduces some fundamental methodological principles needed to understand different areas of research. Studies that employ these methods are selected and examined in detail. The book does not attempt a complete coverage of everything that has been written about stuttering, as it is not a handbook; it goes for depth of understanding rather than breadth of coverage. A wide range of topics is covered in the book. The 15 chapters are ordered into four sections (general aspects of developmental stuttering, topic areas ranging from genetics through to emotional aspects affected by stuttering, theoretical frameworks, and practical issues). These topics were based on courses I have taught and a new one that is being established at University College London and will be offered in the fall of 2010. Although the topics reflect the areas I am interested in, I believe that they also may serve as the basis for other courses. Thus, courses for clinicians might use just the chapters in the first and last sections. Broader courses that take the view that stuttering is language-based or others that consider it is motor-based would select the appropriate chapters from the second and third sections as well. Courses in the psychology of language disorders could use chapters in the first three sections. The detailed examination of theory (Section III) is a novel feature of this book.

Exercises are included at the end of each chapter. The questions are provided as an invitation to consider different perspectives about stuttering. They often ask the reader to consider positions to which I do not subscribe. Also, there are no right or wrong answers to some of the questions, so arguments from opposing positions are possible. Some of the questions are invitations to make research proposals that would go beyond the literature reviewed in the text. In case it helps, I would find some of these questions hard to answer as well. Though the questions are phrased for students, I hope professionals find them inviting ways to formulate their own positions or to explore alternative points of view that they may have cherished. They also should serve as a check about what they have learned from the text.

There are many people to thank who have provided help and support that allowed me to write this book. The particular clinicians to mention are Lena Rustin (Michael Palin Centre) and Roberta Williams (City University). The Wellcome Trust has funded my research for many years and I would like to single out John Williams of the Trust for his help and guidance over the years. A number of individuals have worked with me for a long time, many of whom have shown high levels of dedication. Dr. Stephen Davis, OBE, and Stevie Sackin liaised with clinicians and families and also played significant research roles. Pippa Bark, Mike Johnson, and Karima Kadi-Hanifi worked out the coding conventions for the speech data used in our own work. Mark Huckvale has always been prepared to modify his Speech Filing System software for our particular needs. Andy Anderson brought new perspectives about measurement of motor actions in people who stutter, Katharina Dworzynski introduced a range of new ideas including genetics, Kate Watkins facilitated work on scanning, and Ceri Savage raised new ideas about testing language development in children who stutter. Helen Jefferson-Brown's support in a range of ways has been crucial. Many other students have worked with me and their contribution is gratefully acknowledged. Collaborators at University College and in Europe, the United States, Africa, China, Japan, South America, and Iran are also too many to mention individually, but thanks goes out to them all. The support of Bob Audley and all subsequent heads of departments that I have worked under is gratefully acknowledged. A special thank you is expressed to all the families who have tolerated us in their homes as regular visitors, who have traveled to our lab and elsewhere so we can conduct tests with nonportable equipment. Finally, thanks to my family who should have had a fairer share of my time than they did.

Section I

General Aspects of Developmental Stuttering

1 Definitions, Stuttering Severity, and Categorization Instruments

This book is about recovery from stuttering. Each chapter provides specific information that adds to our knowledge about this topic. The relevance of the information in each chapter is given at the beginning of each chapter. Chapter 1 provides definitions and tools that allow persistence and recovery of stuttering to be established.

1.1 INTRODUCTION

The primary goal of this book is to document how stuttering changes once it has begun (whether the individual recovers spontaneously or recovers after a treatment, or if the condition persists). Stuttering usually arises close to when a child starts to talk and if the child has not recovered by the teenage years, the chance of a full recovery dramatically reduces. Consequently, the majority of this work relates to children. The research findings on groups of children who recover or persist are examined to see what insights they can provide about the development of stuttering. There are many proposals that maintain that this or that limitation reflects the underlying cause of stuttering during development. For instance, it has been proposed that the high proportion of left-handers in the stuttering population indicates potential problems in brain lateralization that affects language performance as well as handedness. Though handedness is relatively easy to assess, other aspects of performance that are clearly affected in people who continue to stutter, such as self esteem, are difficult to measure directly with children (and usually it is less clear whether these aspects are causes or effects of stuttering). The emphasis is on language, speech motor, and sensory abilities. Information on genetics, central nervous system, and emotional and cognitive functioning are also included. The main questions are whether these abilities are involved at the time stuttering starts and whether they are implicated in changes in the patterns of stuttering over the period that stuttering resolves into persistent or recovered forms.

The words *stuttering, recover,* and *persist* need to be defined. To address the first of these terms, two widely accepted definitions of stuttering are presented in section 1.2. Following this, the standard method for assessing the severity of stuttering is described (Riley's, 1994, Stuttering Severity Instrument, SSI-3; a fourth revision, SSI-4, has recently been produced, but is not currently in widespread use). Assessment of stuttering severity is required at the outset, as it has been used to validate some of the assessment instruments used to determine persistence and recovery. Also, severity might be implicated in persistence and recovery in its own right. For example, it might be hypothesized that speakers with severe problems persist in their stuttering while those with milder problems recover. A thorough understanding of how to measure severity is essential in order to evaluate hypotheses such as this.

This chapter then examines methods and procedural problems associated with studies into the persistence and recovery of stuttering that are operationally defined (section 1.3). Generally speaking, designs of studies that track individuals over a period of time (longitudinal) and determine persistence or recovery at the end of the period are preferred over other, less robust, methods for obtaining similar information (e.g., retrospective studies). This is because there are drawbacks to retrospective studies because, although it can be verified whether a person persists in stuttering, usually it cannot be confirmed whether a "recovered" person did, in fact, stutter in the first instance. This and other issues about the various measures and designs used to investigate these phenomena are discussed. One of the problems faced by longitudinal designs is practicality. Following children for long periods of time is difficult and expensive to conduct. The problem has been made somewhat more tractable by investigating different subranges over the period that most recovery happens. The logic of such approaches and their drawbacks are considered.

As stated above, stuttering severity instruments, such as SSI-3, have been used in development and validation of methods that are used on longitudinal data to classify individuals as persistent or recovered. Two of these methods are described in section 1.4 after the essential information about severity measurement has been presented. The first of these methods, developed and described most recently by Yairi and Ambrose (2005), is appropriate for younger children who stutter (from onset of the disorder in early childhood to about age 8). The second was developed by my team (Howell, Davis, & Williams, 2008a) for use with older children who stutter (8 to teenage years). The chapter finishes with a discussion about attrition, which conceivably could be a problem if it biased the sample that is studied. Consequently, when examining longitudinal data, it is important to know what the attrition rate is and whether this might affect results. For instance, are the individuals who withdraw from an investigation different in some way from those who continue in the study? The methods used to characterize persistent and recovered stutterers allow epidemiological studies into stuttering to be described and evaluated; the epidemiological studies are discussed in Chapter 2.

1.2 DEFINITIONS OF STUTTERING

Despite many years of research, it may be surprising to learn that there is no definitive method of determining whether a child stutters or is language fluent. In most cases where a child stutters, there are indications of stuttering in the child's speech attempts. Some of these children also have problems in social or emotional adjustment. The speech symptoms and other features that may help determine whether or not a child is stuttering are shown in some of the classic definitions of stuttering, such as the following two.

The American Psychiatric Association in its *Diagnostic and Statistical Manual of Mental Disorders* (DSM) gives a definition of stuttering that emphasizes that speech is a feature of stuttering. DSM version IV Text Revision (American Psychiatric Association, 2000, p. 67) characterizes stuttering in terms of "frequent repetitions or prolongations of sounds or syllables"). DSM-IV-TR discusses the speech symptoms of stuttering, whether speakers who stutter differ in frequency and/or severity of these symptoms relative to fluent speakers and speakers with other disorders, and what happens over the period of time that speakers recover or persist in the disorder.

Caution is necessary. Although it has been stated that a child attending a clinic who is suspected of stuttering usually presents with overt speech difficulties, this is not always the case. Thus, for instance, some children who stutter avoid speaking in public. In acute cases, such children can meet all but one of the criteria for a diagnosis of selective mutism (Howell, 2007a). The one criterion they do not meet is that a child cannot be classified as a selective mute if he or she stutters (APA, 2000). This criterion is only included as a way of separating the two disorders (Howell, 2007a), not as an inherent characteristic of mutism. The example shows that different disorders can be confused to some degree with stuttering as they can have similar diagnostic profiles. As another example, Wingate (2002, p. 50) discusses the similarity between stuttering and tic disorders, although the similarity between these disorders has also been disputed.

The emphasis on speech as a defining characteristic of stuttering, which is a feature of DSM-IV, is also a feature of Wingate's well-respected "standard" definition of stuttering (Wingate, 1964, p. 488). His definition has seven separate interrelated, elements that are arranged under three headings, and is given in full below:

I. (a) Disruption in the fluency of verbal expression, which is (b) characterized by involuntary, audible or silent, repetitions or prolongations in the utterance of short speech elements, namely: sounds, syllables, and words of one syllable. These disruptions (c) usually occur frequently or are marked in character and (d) are not readily controllable.

II. Sometimes the disruptions are (e) accompanied by accessory activities involving the speech apparatus, related or unrelated body structures, or stereotyped speech utterances. These activities give the appearance of being speech-related struggle.

III. Also, there are not infrequently (f) indications or report of the presence of an emotional state, ranging from a general condition of "excitement" or "tension" to more specific emotions of a negative nature, such as fear, embarrassment, irritation, or the like. (g) The immediate source of stuttering is some incoordination expressed in the peripheral speech mechanism; the ultimate cause is presently unknown and may be complex or compound.

Although Wingate's emphasis was on speech, he also recognized "accessory activity" and problems of socioemotional adjustment. Accessory features are acts that do not necessarily involve speaking and Wingate (2002) suggests they are idiosyncratic. Wingate gives a list of accessory features (p. 46), which includes all the "physical concomitants" that Riley (1994) uses in calculating an SSI-3 score, so the two terms refer to the same features (Riley's work is considered later in this chapter). Like DSM-IV and Wingate (1964), the present book emphasizes speech–language characteristics as symptoms of stuttering. Motor coordination abilities of speakers who stutter are also documented, which appear under (g) in Wingate's scheme. In this volume, following common usage in psychology, the factors referring to the experience of emotion are termed *affect*. Although it is recognized that people who stutter may differ in affect relative to fluent speakers, these aspects are difficult to measure in children and it is not clear whether affect factors are causes or effects of stuttering. For instance, it is not apparent whether anxious people stutter or whether people are anxious because they stutter. Comparatively little will be said about affect.

1.3   RILEY'S ASSESSMENT OF SEVERITY OF STUTTERING

Riley's SSI-3 (1994) provided a measure of how seriously affected an individual is by stuttering. As mentioned, SSI-4 has recently appeared. It is beginning to be used, but no studies to date have reported results with this version. It will be used more widely in the future and Riley has ensured that SSI-4 is downward compatible with SSI-3 (so results with SSI-3 are valid). Severity estimates in the current edition of this book all refer to SSI-3. Along with its application to estimating severity of stuttering, Riley (1994) considers that SSI-3 also can be used as part of the diagnostic process as well as for estimating severity, but mentions that such decisions need to be augmented by other information. This includes in-depth interviews with the person who stutters, direct observation about the person, description of the person's speech and language, interviews with parents, reports of prior speech and language evaluations, audiological assessment, examination of medical records and reports, and interviews with teachers and other professionals who have worked with the individual. Although SSI-3 is not a diagnostic instrument per se, most peer-reviewed articles report SSI-3 estimates for participants who stutter and even for fluent controls in some cases (Davis, Shisca, & Howell, 2007). SSI-3 has been standardized for U.S. and U.K. English. It has also been translated into, although not necessarily standardized for, many other languages. An important use of SSI-3 in connection with the issue of recovery from stuttering is that it has been employed to validate instruments specifically designed to classify participants who have provided longitudinal data from age 8 to teenage years as persistent or recovered (these investigations are described later in this chapter).

1.3.1   ADMINISTRATION OF SSI-3

SSI-3 can be administered to children and adults. Assessment for adults and children who can read involves obtaining samples of elicited and read speech.

Age-appropriate texts used for reading are supplied in Riley (1994). Assessments for children who cannot read are based on elicited speech samples alone. For assessments on all individuals, scores for frequency and duration of stuttering events, and a measure of physical concomitants are obtained and used to produce an overall SSI-3 score. These three aspects are described for nonreaders. The procedures used with children and adults who can read are then presented.

Speech samples are audio- or videotaped. A videotape provides a permanent recording of body movements associated with stuttering, which allows assessment of some of the physical concomitants. When audio recordings alone are made, the examiner has to make notes about any physical concomitants at the time. (Riley provides guidelines on how these should be made with audio and video recordings, as described later.) Stimulus pictures are used to elicit speech. A picture is shown where something appears wrong or out of place or where an accident is about to occur. Leading statements about the image are made to encourage the child to engage in conversation. Questions and statements that are likely to result in one-word responses are avoided. Questions, interruptions, and mild disagreements that simulate features that occur in normal conversation are allowed. Riley recommends that several speech samples should be obtained. Each speech sample has to be at least 200 syllables long. The audio tracks from video- or audiotapes are used to determine the frequency and duration measurements of stuttering. Guidelines are given on how to translate these into scale scores.

1.3.1.1 Frequency Score

The first step in the procedure for obtaining a frequency score is to obtain the percentage of stuttered syllables (%SS). This requires separate counts of all syllables spoken and those syllables that are stuttered. Riley notes that it is difficult to make syllable counts in real time and advocates that assessors should first listen and make a dot on a piece of paper for each syllable and then count them when finished. In our research, we work on recordings after they have been transferred to a PC and make the counts with the assistance of a wave editor. The editor allows short extracts to be played, so the syllables can easily be counted and checked if necessary.

Stuttered events are then counted. Stuttered events are defined as "repetitions or prolongations of sounds or syllables (including silent prolongations)" (Riley, 1994, p. 4). The SSI-3 also notes which behaviors are not included within the definition of stuttering: "Behaviors, such as rephrasing, repetition of phrases or whole words, and pausing without tension, are not counted as stuttering. Repetition of one-syllable words may be stuttering if the word sounds abnormal (shortened, prolonged, staccato, tense, etc.); however, when these single-syllable words are repeated, but are otherwise spoken normally, they do not qualify as stuttering using the definition just stated" (p. 4).

Stuttered repetitions of a syllable count as a single stuttering event. For example, "I don't wa, wa, wa, wa, want any pepper," has seven syllables and one stuttering event. The stuttering events are expressed as a percentage of all syllables that gives %SS. When there are multiple samples, the %SS is computed for each speaking sample, then averaged, and the latter is used as the raw %SS.

The following example is used to illustrate the procedures: "I'm gonna get uhm de de de dem too. A----nd dis one. A ape. Ge ge get Ste-------vy down. You are ih, ih, ih, in de way."

Below, the example is broken up into stretches with one stuttering event per stretch. Here the individual syllables are delimited by a line placed beneath them (__) and they are numbered.

| | Stuttering event 1 | | Stuttering event 2 |
| | "I'm gonna get uhm de de de dem too | | . a----nd dis one. A ape. |

| Sylls | 1 2 3 4 5   6   7 | 8   9 10 11 12 |

| | Stuttering event 3 | Stuttering event 4 | Stuttering event 5 |
| | Ge ge get | Ste-------vy down. | You are ih, ih, ih, in de way |

| Sylls | 13 | 14   15 16 | 17 18 19   20 21 |

For this short illustrative example, the syllable count is 21 and the stuttering event count is 5. The %SS is 23.8 % (5/21 × 100). The %SS test score is converted to a scale score of 4, 6, 8, 10, 12, 14, 16, or 18 using Table 1.1. As this extract is from a nonreader, the left-hand portion of Table 1.1 is used. The value 23.8 %SS falls in the row labeled "22 & up." The frequency score for the elicited speech sample is obtained from the adjacent column. Thus, the frequency score for this example would be 18.

TABLE 1.1

The %SS Score Is Used to Obtain the Frequency Task Score

Nonreaders		Readers			
Speaking		Speaking		Reading	
%SS	Task Score	%SS	Task Score	%SS	Task Score
1	4	1	2	1	2
2	6	2	3		
3	8	3	4	2	4
4–5	10	4–5	5	3–4	5
6–7	12	6–7	6	5–7	6
8–11	14	8–11	7	8–12	7
12–21	16	12–21	8	13–20	8
22 & up	18	22 & up	9	21 & up	9

Note: The scores for children who cannot read (nonreader) are given at the left (frequency score based on elicited speech samples), and, for people who can read, at the right (frequency score based on elicited speech samples and readings of supplied text).

TABLE 1.2

The Average of the Three Longest Stutters Is Obtained and Scored on the Following Scale to Give the Duration Score

Fleeting	0.1–0.4 seconds	2 points
One-half second	0.5–0.9 seconds	4 points
One full second	1.0–1.9 seconds	6 points
2 seconds	2.0–2.9 seconds	8 points
3–5 seconds	3.0–4.9 seconds	10 points
5–9 seconds	5.0–9.9 seconds	12 points
10–29 seconds	10.0–29.9 seconds	14 points
30–59 seconds	30.0– 59.9 seconds	16 points
60 seconds or more	60.0 and up	18 points

1.3.1.2   Duration Score

The duration score is the duration, in seconds, of the three longest stuttering events in the sample. My group measures this from audio files that are transferred to a computer. A display with a traveling cursor and calibrated timeline is then used to measure duration (Riley says that a stopwatch can be used when computers are not available.). These three durations are then averaged. Once the average duration has been computed, it is converted to a scale score using Table 1.2. Durations of less than 1 sec are difficult to measure accurately by stopwatch (though not by computer). They are designated either "Fleeting" or "One-half second" and receive duration scores of 2 or 4 points, respectively.

As an example, if a child's longest stutters were 4.2, 2.6, and 7.4 sec, this gives a total of 14.2 sec, and the average duration is 4.7 sec. Using Table 1.2, this converts into a scale score of 10 points.

1.3.1.3   Physical Concomitants

The physical concomitants score is based on observations of all of the speaking samples that are scored (recorded at the time the speaker said them, or obtained from videotapes afterward). Four aspects of physical concomitants are assessed. Riley's descriptions of each of these are as follows (1994, p. 11):

Distracting sounds. This category includes any nonspeech sounds that accompany the stuttering. For example, the child may continually clear his or her throat or may swallow. Other common sounds include noisy breathing, whistling noises, sniffing, blowing, and clicking sounds. The evaluator must determine the extent to which these sounds are distracting to a listener.

Facial grimaces. Any abnormal movement or tension about the face counts in this category. Examples of abnormal facial behaviors are pressing the lips

TABLE 1.3

Auditory and Visual Physical Concomitants Associated With Stuttering Are Each Scored on the Following Scale to Give the Physical Concomitant Score

0 = None
1 = Not noticeable unless looking for it
2 = Barely noticeable to casual observer
3 = Distracting
4 = Very distracting
5 = Severe and painful-looking

together tightly, pursing the lips, tensing jaw muscles, blinking or partially closing the eyes, protruding the tongue, and uncoordinated jaw movements.

Head movements. These movements generally consist of turning the head away from the listener to avoid eye contact, looking down at the feet, scanning the room, and looking up at the ceiling.

Movements of the extremities. Any general body movement, such as shifting around in the chair, counts in this category. Other common movements include specific movement of a limb, such as foot tapping, excessive movement of the hands about the face, fidgeting with something in the hand, or swinging an arm.

A separate judgment is made for each anatomical area (face, head, extremity), and for distracting sounds. Each of the four judgments is scored between 0 and 5 using the scale in Table 1.3. The four scores are added to give an overall physical concomitant score between 0 and 20.

1.3.1.4   Total Overall Score

The total overall score is obtained by adding together the scores for the three component elements (frequency, duration, and physical concomitants). The severity of stuttering, as measured by these parameters, can be ascertained by comparing this score to the age-appropriate normative data presented in Table 1.4 (for nonreading preschool children), Table 1.5 (for children who can read), or Table 1.6 (for adults who can read). In each table, the score for a person being tested can be converted into a percentile. The percentiles are given as stanines. Stanine, which stands for "standard nine," is a method of scaling test scores to a 9-point standard scale with a mean of 5 and standard deviation of 2. Using the normal distribution, 4% of the scores go into stanine 1, 7% into stanine 2, and so on up to stanine 9 (the percentage of scores are 4, 7, 12, 17, 20, 17, 12, 7, and 4 for stanines 1 to 9, respectively). Riley also collapsed the stanines into five categories that describe the level of stuttering severity as very mild, mild, moderate, severe,

TABLE 1.4

Percentile and Severity Equivalents of SSI-3 Total Overall Scores for Nonreading Children Based on Riley (1994)

Total Overall SSI-3 Score	Percentile	Severity
0–8	1–4	Very mild
9–10	5–11	
11–12	12–23	Mild
13–16	24–40	
17–23	41–60	Moderate
24–26	61–77	
27–28	78–88	Severe
29–31	89–95	
32 and up	96–99	Very severe

Note: Results were obtained from a group of children who stutter and who could not read (N = 72).

TABLE 1.5

Percentile and Severity Equivalents of SSI-3 Total Overall Scores for Children Who Can Read Based on Riley (1994)

Total Overall Score	Percentile	Severity
6–8	1–4	Very mild
9–10	5–11	
11–15	12–23	Mild
16–20	24–40	
21–23	41–60	Moderate
24–27	61–77	
28–31	78–88	Severe
32–35	89–95	
36 and up	96–99	Very severe

Note: Results were obtained from a group of children who stutter who could read (N = 139).

or very severe. Thus, using Table 1.4, a child who cannot read who scores 14 is in stanine 4, which corresponds to percentiles 24 to 40 and can be characterized as mild severity. The fact that SSI-3 labels a person as very mild when they have no stutters, poses a problem for its use in diagnosis.

1.3.1.5 Administration of the SSI-3 to Readers

The procedure for participants who can read is similar except that there is an additional reading task. Reading materials appropriate for 8- to 9-year-olds, 10- to 11-year-olds, 12- to 13-year-olds, or adults are supplied for participants to read

TABLE 1.6

Percentile and Severity Equivalents of SSI-3 Total Overall Scores for Adults Based on Riley (1994)

Total Overall Score	Percentile	Severity
10–12	1–4	Very mild
13–17	5–11	
18–20	12–23	Mild
21–24	24–40	
25–27	41–60	Moderate
28–31	61–77	
32–34	78–88	Severe
35–36	89–95	
37–46 up	96–99	Very severe

Note: Results were obtained from a group of adults who stutter (N = 60).

(each text is approximately 200 syllables). Percentage of stuttered syllables (%SS) is computed in the manner described in section 1.3.1.1. The difference in procedure is that separate frequency scores are obtained for elicited and read materials (each of these is obtained from the appropriate columns in the right-hand section of Table 1.1). Elicited and read results are added to give the overall frequency score.

The SSI-3 can be used as part of the diagnostic evaluation. It can assist in tracking changes in severity during and following treatments. It can be used to describe severity distribution in experimental groups that include people who stutter. Most important for current concerns, it can be used to validate other stuttering measures. My own team's work, reported later in this chapter, used SSI-3 for validating child, parent, and researcher assessments that are subsequently used for classifying participants aged between 8 years and teenage as persistent or recovered and SSI-3 has similarities with Yairi and Ambrose's (2005, p. 32) Illinois Clinician Stuttering Severity Scale that is described in section 1.5.1.1.

1.3.2   STATISTICAL ASSESSMENT OF THE SSI-3

With regard to questionnaires in general, construct reliability refers to the extent to which the instrument is an effective measure, while validity is the extent to which the questionnaire is measuring what it purports to measure. If a questionnaire is unreliable, it is impossible for it to be valid; on the other hand, it is possible for a questionnaire to be reliable but invalid.

1.3.2.1   Intrajudge Reliability of the SSI-3

A satisfactory test will give similar results when the same person uses it on the same data on different occasions. There are different ways of quantifying how close the scores are when a test is repeated. Riley (1994) reported intrajudge reliability of the SSI-3. Intrajudge reliability was estimated for frequency and duration by five judges who scored 17 samples twice each. Self-agreement ranged from 75 to 100% across the two scores. All mean agreements were above 80%, which shows satisfactory reliability.

1.3.2.2 Interjudge Reliability of the SSI-3

Different judges should give similar results when assessing the same samples. Once again there are various ways of assessing this. Riley assessed interjudge reliability for frequency, duration, physical concomitants, and overall SSI-3 score using 15 students from a graduate-level class in stuttering. Agreement for frequency ranged from 94.6 to 96.8%, but was somewhat poorer for duration (58.1 to 87.2%), physical concomitants (59.8 to 97.5%), and overall SSI-3 score (71 to 100%). However, all mean agreements were again above 80%, which shows satisfactory reliability.

1.3.2.3 Criterion Validity of the SSI-3

Criterion validity is a measure of how well a set of variables predict an outcome based on information that relates to other measures known to relate to the behavior in question. Riley showed that total SSI-3 scores correlated with the %SS frequency scores (the latter has often been used as a severity measure in the past). All correlations were significant indicating good criterion reliability. It has also been reported that SSI-3 scores correlated with scores from the Stuttering Prediction Instrument (Yaruss & Conture, 1992). Both of these findings were considered to indicate adequate criterion validity.

1.3.2.4 Construct Validity of the SSI-3

It is also advisable to check the internal consistency of the components in a questionnaire (construct validity). To assess construct reliability, Riley reported how severity correlated with length of time a person stuttered for selected scores. One way in which Riley assessed construct validity was by looking at the correlations between total SSI-3 scores and its separate components (frequency, duration, and physical concomitants). All the correlations between overall scores and the components were significant, indicating good construct reliability. Intercorrelations between the subcomponents alone were much lower, which indicated none of the parameters used alone would produce the same indications about severity as the combined SSI-3 score. Thus, construct reliability was satisfactory.

1.4 METHODOLOGICAL ISSUES IN THE ASSESSMENT OF PERSISTENCE AND RECOVERY OF STUTTERING

Before the instruments developed for longitudinal data are discussed, the complete age range that needs to be assessed for persistence and recovery is considered. This is followed by a discussion of some alternative methods to the longitudinal ones.

1.4.1   AGE RANGE OVER WHICH RECOVERY SHOULD BE ASSESSED

The answer to what age range should be examined to establish persistence/recovery is, on the face of it, straightforward, that is, the range that should be covered ideally is from before stuttering starts through to when recovery is complete.

Generally speaking, it is impractical to examine in detail an unselected sample of typically developing children to pick up children who go on to stutter (for reasons given in section 1.4.3). However, one solution to the problem of obtaining information before stuttering onset that has been adopted is to examine groups who are known to have a high risk of stuttering. Kloth, Kraimaat, Janssen, and Brutten (1999) took this approach in a study that investigated stuttering in families with one parent who stuttered (see Chapter 2 for a full description of this study). It is known from other research that the children with parents who stutter (or used to stutter) have a higher risk of stuttering (Ambrose, Cox, & Yairi, 1997; Kidd, Kidd, & Records, 1978). Other high-risk groups also could be used for this purpose. Thus, incidence of stuttering in children with Down syndrome has been reported to be much higher than in a non-Down syndrome sample (Preus, 1972). A caution that should be raised about high-risk groups in general is that they may not be a representative sample of children who stutter and, if so, generalizing results from such samples would not be appropriate. For example, there are many physical aspects of the speech and hearing system in children with Down syndrome that are documented to differ from typically developing children (Howell, in press) that may potentially lead to stuttering that could arise for atypical reasons.

Valuable early findings about the range that should be covered for typically developing children was provided by Andrews and Harris (1964) who followed a large group of children from around birth through to age 15 years. They sought to establish which of them stuttered, at what ages stuttering began, the ages at which there were cases who recovered, and the age beyond which recovery was unlikely to happen. This work is discussed fully in Chapter 2 on epidemiology. For now, all that it is important to note is that stuttering was reported to start at ages from 2 years up and the age beyond which no cases were reported to recover was 12 years.

Stuttering needs to be examined as close to onset of the disorder as possible to see how stuttering starts and whether it develops in this early phase. With respect to speech, onset characteristics (repetition of whole words) and changes (the emergence of part-word repetitions) that happen in the immediate period after stuttering begins may be critical to the future path that stuttering takes (persistent or recovered). A wide range of associated behavioral issues (e.g., affect, such as temperament and emotion) may be evident near onset (which parents can report) that may not be apparent with older children (i.e., they may be masked). Thus, if speech, language, motor, and affect performance develop rapidly and investigators do not examine cases close to onset, factors that could differentiate persistent and recovered groups would be missed. It is difficult to obtain samples close to when stuttering starts because cases often go unreported for some time after onset, or there can be a delay in getting an appointment at a clinic, which delays professional assessment.

Stuttering also needs to be examined to at least the teenage years as it has been seen that recovery can occur up to this age (Andrews & Harris, 1964). If investigations stopped short of this age, recovery rate would be underestimated.

1.4.2 WHY LOOK AT SUB RANGES BETWEEN ONSET AGE AND TEENAGE IN LONGITUDINAL STUDIES?

Practically speaking, following children over the entire range from 2 years to the teens is expensive. Also, if a child withdraws from a study, the entire data set may be lost. For instance, if a child who has persisted up to age 8 withdraws, they may still recover by the teens, so persistence cannot be confirmed and the child may need to be dropped from the study. The risk of losing recovered cases is particularly acute unless precautions are taken. Children who recover (and/or their parents) may think they are not of interest to researchers as they no longer stutter. In fact, longitudinal information on recovered cases who have been followed up is rare in the literature, although these cases are equally valuable to persistent ones that have been followed up. Since the time of Andrews and Harris's work, there has been an increase in mobility of families. This further exacerbates the problems faced when working with speakers through the entire age range of 2 to teenage years (e.g., maintaining contact is more of a problem). For all of these reasons, there are attractions in subdividing the age range for study although there are drawbacks. Yairi (2007) also saw value in examining different age ranges of adults. Examination of different age ranges addresses a point raised by Ingham (1976), who argued that the focus on children ignores the phenomenon of recovery in adulthood, which is rare, but does occasionally happen.

1.4.3 UNSELECTED SAMPLES OF CHILDREN (FLUENT AND STUTTERING)

Ideally, researchers would like to record and document factors that could affect stuttering on large, unselected samples of children from an age before stuttering starts. Then they should be followed up and examined in the same way through the period of stuttering onset through to the teens to pick up cases of children who stutter and examine the recovery process. Practically this is not possible. Thus, Andrews and Harris's work (1964) relied on initial screening by parents as did a recent study from Australia discussed in Chapter 13 (Reilly et al., 2009). The reason it is impractical to examine children before stuttering begins is because the incidence of stuttering is low and such a study would require large samples to pick up sufficient numbers of children who stutter to make the study valid. Thus, if incidence is around 1 in 20, as the literature described in Chapter 2 suggests, a sample of 2,000 would be needed to obtain 100 cases.

1.4.4 EXAMINATION OF SUBRANGES OVER THE PERIOD OF RECOVERY

Researchers have tended to focus on subage ranges that either start or end at the onset, or recovery, points, respectively. For instance, a group in Illinois examined children as close to onset as possible and followed them, typically, to about age 8 (Yairi & Ambrose, 2005). My group in London studies children from around age 8 and follows them to at least their teens (Howell et al., 2008a), which is the age where it is usually considered that any recovery that is going to occur will have occurred. Of course, recovery rates up to age 8 are of interest and reports of age at onset can be obtained for speakers of any age (although it would be expected that these would be more accurate when obtained close to onset). Together, the Illinois and London studies, whose procedures for characterizing persistence and recovery are considered later in this chapter, cover the entire age range that Andrews and Harris's work suggests is necessary.

Whilst the Illinois and London studies taken together provide results that cover the span from onset to teenage, there are some disadvantages in not examining the entire range in a single study. The main one when studying the onset to 8 years age range is that some cases will recover after 8, so recovery rate may be underestimated. The main disadvantage for studies that start examination from around this age is that they cannot provide an absolute estimate of recovery.

Are there advantages to splitting the age range into two at age 8, as was effectively done in the Illinois and London studies? Splitting into subranges makes for more efficient testing than examining the full range because it reduces the dropout rate and results can be obtained quicker than for the entire age range of potential recovery. It is useful that the Illinois and London groups complement each other. That said, inclusion criteria and details about how recovery was assessed need to be fully documented so that readers know how comparable the materials are. There are several other reasons why age 8 is a suitable choice for a dividing line for the two age subranges.

First, some authors consider that children need not go to a clinic before that age (Bryngelson, 1938). Wingate (2002) mentions that this has been corroborated although he does not supply any further references. Consequently, this justification is at best debatable. If accepted, this would suggest a natural division at age 8 between those who should and those who should not attend the clinic.

Second, the sorts of tests that can be performed by a child under 8 are limited in scope. This was noted when discussing affect, which includes abilities usually tested by questionnaires filled out by parents. In the Illinois work, speech characteristics at onset are based on a parent report (although the investigators have developed a detailed probing technique to try to ensure the reports about speech are accurate). The limited scope for testing young children is more of a problem when examining speech, language, motor, and sensory abilities where a child is required to perform complex tests. Spontaneous speech can be recorded, the children can answer some queries, and tests to assess abilities at young ages have been developed and used with children who stutter (e.g., Howell, Davis, & Au-Yeung, 2003). More performance tests are needed that are suitable for testing children below age 8 in order to establish whether stuttering is due to the development of the language (Bernstein Ratner, & Wijnen, 2007) or motor system (Van Lieshout & Namasivayam, 2010), in both systems (Howell, 2004, in press), or is due to some different aspect of behavior entirely (e.g., anxiety changes with age). Age 8 is a suitable age to divide children who will mainly be assessed by questioning them and their parents and those who may be able to provide experimental data.

Finally, recovery rates of around 50% occur from about age 8 onward (Fritzell, 1976; Howell et al., 2008). Recovery rates higher than this are usually reported with children under age 8. Recovery rates around 50% are suitable for certain analyses where other rates are not (see Chapter 13 for examples). Examples are multivariate analyses and learning algorithms, which do not work well when there is a big imbalance in sample sizes. For example, discriminant function analysis is a multivariate test that classifies cases into discrete classes based on the optimum solution from a set of supplied variables. If 80% of cases fall into one group (e.g., children who recover before age 8, Yairi & Ambrose, 2005), discriminant function analysis would achieve this level of accuracy by placing all cases in the recovered group. Rates of persistence and recovery closer to 50/50 occur past age 8 and are more suitable for such forms of statistical analysis than the rates at younger ages, which show large imbalances.

There are other ways in which information about persistence and recovery rates have been obtained, but these have employed less robust methods for collecting data. The principal alternative methods are (1) informal report of cases observed in clinics over a period of time, and (2) retrospective studies that involve speakers who are fluent and self-reporting that they had a stutter in the past. When clinical reports are used, there are no guarantees that information was collected systematically. Problems with self-report methods are discussed below.

1.4.5 SELF-REPORT METHODS USED TO ASSESS PERSISTENCE AND RECOVERY

Generally speaking, longitudinal work, even over a subrange, such as that of the Illinois and London groups, is preferable to cross-sectional work and is highly desirable when determining persistence or recovery. Thus, although recovered cases can be classified using self-, or parental-nominations, such report data are subject to memory limitations, so parents and children may not recall that a child stuttered (e.g., parents sometimes try to play down the problem hoping it will go away and do not speak about it to the child). Inclusion of only those cases where stuttering was recalled in later life may result in a biased sample. Some potential respondents may not be aware they had a problem or, more generally, will fail to respond (see Yairi & Ambrose, 2005, p. 273). With retrospective reports, unless a clinic or health professional was consulted in early life, there is no record against which the claim that a person stuttered can be checked and there are not likely to be recorded samples that can be reexamined. Stuttering must have been self-diagnosed in cases where treatment was not sought (see Bloodstein & Bernstein Ratner, 2007, pp. 85–88 for a discussion of problems with self-diagnosis).

There is evidence that the children who stutter evaluate the problem in different ways than their parents. This was shown in part of a recent study by Howell,

Davis, and Williams (2008b), discussed later in section 1.5.2. They reported a factor analysis of child and parent forms of a questionnaire. Factor analysis is a statistical method used to describe variability among observed variables in terms of fewer unobserved variables called factors. The factor analysis produced different solutions (two factors were required to explain the child data, but only one to explain the adult data) (see below for further description and an interpretation of these results).

A further problem with self-report arises because stuttering is difficult to diagnose by professionals (Kully & Boberg, 1988). Self-reported diagnoses by children who stutter or their parents, both of whom are not experts, is potentially even more problematic.

1.4.6 ARCHIVED SPEECH SAMPLES FOR ANALYSIS

Some longitudinal studies into recovery are based on systematic clinical judgments, but lack reference recordings (Mannson, 2000). Yairi has emphasized in his writings over the years that recorded samples should be made for reference and in-depth analysis (Yairi & Ambrose, 2005, p. 36). Then the recordings can be reexamined if necessary to check details. With the current rapid advancement in assessment methods, reassessment of old data will be increasingly essential and digital archiving is preferred (see Chapter 15, section 15.1.4 for further discussion).

A feature of the London team's work is that they digitally archive the speech samples they obtain and the analyses they perform and, where possible, make them publicly available in several formats that allow further speech and language analysis (Howell, Davis, & Bartrip, 2009; Howell & Huckvale, 2004). Language analyses for some of the software packages are linked in time so that they point to the appropriate position in the speech sample, which makes measurement of speech timing and relating fluency performance to linguistic structure easy and objective. The results also can be independently checked by other researchers. Examples of analyses would be measuring the duration of different symptom types, relating stuttering to language forms available in transcription, etc. So, for example, transcriptions with stuttering marked are aligned in time against the audio record, and utilities can be employed to display and analyze results. Software can be written that allows a speech sample to be analyzed so that the three longest stuttering events can be located and their average obtained, which, it will be recalled, is a step required when obtaining an SSI-3 score. As new algorithms become available for speech analysis or if procedures for estimating duration scores are changed, results can be recomputed. Results for new analyses on these speech samples can be compared against similar earlier analyses made on the same material to see whether the new algorithms represent an advance over previous ones. All of these factors commend recording speech and filing these analyses with the speech. Professional associations should provide guidelines about how such samples are recorded for different purposes.

1.5 LONGITUDINAL ASSESSMENT OF PERSISTENCE/RECOVERY

Two procedures are now considered that process the data from children who have been diagnosed as stutterers. Both procedures have explicit inclusion criteria for entry into the study that cover complementary age ranges. After a follow-up period, the same children are classified into (1) those who persist and (2) those who recover in their stuttering. Sets of assessment instruments for carrying out the classification are available for the two age ranges indicated earlier (the Illinois group focuses on the age range from onset of stuttering to about age 8, and the London group focuses on the age range from 8 to teens). The procedures of the Illinois and London group differ according to what is best suited to the age range examined. A further reason for examining the work of these groups in detail is that they have assessed the instruments they use statistically and have shown them to be robust.

Generally, the assessment instruments used to determine persistence/recovery should not be based on analyses of language, speech, and motor behaviors if these are to be investigated as prognostic predictors (arguably, assessment of speech is allowed for initial diagnosis). The reason is that, to determine whether language, speech, and motor behaviors are associated with recovery, these behaviors cannot be used as well to define cases that persist or recover. Otherwise, if speech is used to assess persistence versus recovery and then the speech of these two classes of speakers is examined to establish differences between the groups, the argument is circular. Thus, if you classify a child as persistent when he or she shows prolongations, you cannot then say prolongations predict whether the child will persist or recover. The following sections describe the approaches that have been used by the Illinois and London research groups to classify speakers of different ages (onset–8; 8–teenage) as persistent or recovered (both use longitudinal data).

1.5.1 WAYS IN WHICH PERSISTENCE/RECOVERY HAS BEEN ASSESSED (YAIRI & AMBROSE, 2007)

Yairi and Ambrose (2005) discuss at length the procedures they employ to classify young participants whom they contacted close to onset of stuttering and who they subsequently followed up. The average age of onset is 33 months, so the children cannot read and self-report from the children would not be reliable. Thus, Yairi and Ambrose employed instruments specifically developed for working with children this young that were mainly based on parental or researcher report.

1.5.1.1 Inclusion Criteria (Diagnosis of Stuttering)

For a child to be included in the Yairi and Ambrose (2005) study, he or she had to be diagnosed as stuttering. For this, the child had to meet all the following criteria (p. 29):

1. The child was 6 years of age or younger.

2. Parents reported that they considered their child to stutter. Parent rating of stuttering severity was at least 2 on an 8-point scale (where 0 = normal, 7 = very severe).
3. Yairi and Ambrose both considered that the child was stuttering.
4. A severity rating on the Illinois Clinician Stuttering Severity Scale (ICSSS) greater than 1. (The ICSSS and the way it is scored are described below.)
5. The child had to exhibit at least 3% of stuttering-like disfluencies (SLD). SLD consist of part-word repetitions, monosyllabic whole-word repetitions, and "disrhythmic phonation." The latter includes sound prolongations, blocks (audible or inaudible sound prolongation within words), and word breaks (p. 97). SLD and some limitations are discussed in full in Chapter 3.
6. There was no reported history of neurological disorder.

The ICSSS is shown in Figure 1.1. Yairi and Ambrose (2005, p. 31) state that the ICSSS draws on, among other sources, early work by Riley (1981) that subsequently led to his SSI-3. An important difference is that the ICSSS includes counts of SLD that includes whole-word repetitions as stutters, whereas Riley (1981, 1994) does not. (See Chapter 3 for further consideration of the implications of this difference in assessment method.) Apart from whole-word repetitions, ICSSS assesses most of the same elements discussed in connection with SSI-3 (frequency of stuttering, duration of stuttering, tension of disfluency [which is not scored separately in SSI-3] and physical concomitants, which Yairi and Ambrose, like Wingate, 2002, call accessory characteristics). Scores for frequency, duration, and tension were obtained on the 7-point scale (0–6) on the ICSSS, which is shown in Figure 1.1, where higher scale values reflect more severe problems. These three characteristics were averaged. Secondary characteristics were scored between 0 and 1 (as shown at the bottom of Figure 1.1). The accessory characteristic score was added to the mean score of the other three characteristics to give a score on an 8-point scale (0–7).

1.5.1.2 Statistical Assessment

The ICSSS was assessed for reliability using video recordings of ten participants selected at random who had been rated previously using the ICSSS. Yairi and Ambrose (2005) independently rerated each of the recordings. The mean difference in rating was 0.17 and ratings that differed by more than 0.5 scale points were rare (p. 31).

1.5.1.3 Persistent/Recovered Outcome on Yairi and Ambrose's Longitudinal Samples

A child was designated persistent if he or she met *any* of the following criteria after a minimum period of four years since onset of the disorder (Yairi & Ambrose, 2005, p. 164):

Name _____   Date _____

Session # _____   Rater _____

Instructions

1. On the scale from 0 to 6 as indicated, circle the number of Stuttering-Like Disfluencies (SLD) (part-word repetitions, single-syllable word repetitions, and blocks or prolongations) per 100 syllables.
2. Rate the length of the average of the 5 longest disfluencies in repetition units.
   a. (bu-bu-bu = 2 units, and-and-and-and = 3 units)
3. Rate the tension of disfluencies.
4. Assign points for secondary characteristics.

SLD	Score	Duration or Repetition Units		Score	Tension	Score
0–3	0	None	1	0	None	0
3–5	1	None/fleeting	1+	1	None to slight	1
5–7	2	<0.5 sec	1.5	2	Slight	2
7–10	3	<1 sec	2	3	Slight to moderate	3
10–15	4	<1.5 sec	3	4	Moderate	4
15–20	5	<2 sec	4	5	Moderate to excessive	5
>20	6	>2 sec	>4	6	Excessive	6

Secondary Characteristics

.25 _____ mild, very few, infrequent, minimal; not noticeable unless looking for it

.33 _____ mild, few, and occasional; barely noticeable

.50 _____ moderate, few, and sometimes; noticeable

.66 _____ moderate, some, and/or often; obvious

.75 _____ severe, many, and/or frequent; distracting

1.00 _____ severe, many, and frequent; severe and painful looking

(SLD points + Duration points + Tension points) divided by 3 =   _____

(_____ + _____ + _____) = _____/3 =   _____

Additional points for secondary characteristics: _____

Total Severity Score:

FIGURE 1.1   The Illinois Clinician Stuttering Severity Scale (ICSSS)

1. Parent report of stuttering episodes.
2. Parental rating of higher than 1 (borderline) on the scale used at diagnosis.
3. Investigators' observation of speech characteristics that they judged as stuttering.
4. A severity rating of higher than 1 on the ICSSS.

Four comments about these criteria include: (1) use of low ("borderline") scale points maximizes the chance of locating cases of persistent stuttering and minimizes the chance of misdiagnosing a speaker as recovered; (2) the requirement to meet one criterion alone allows persistence to be based solely on parental report (i.e., a child who only meets criterion 1); (3) SLD is used implicitly in ICSSS, but not explicitly elsewhere (criterion 2 does not specify what characteristics were judged as stuttering); and (4) the four-year follow-up period should have been specified as an inclusion criterion for the initial phase of the study so that attrition rate can be estimated over the onset reassessment period. With the follow-up period specified as a requirement at the time of assessment as persistent or recovered, this means that there is no way of knowing what the attrition rate was from initial inclusion to this assessment, nor whether recovered speakers were selectively lost from the study.

A child was designated recovered if he or she met *all* of the following criteria after a minimum period of four years since onset of the disorder:

1. Parental report that the child did not exhibit stuttering.
2. Parental rating of zero (normally fluent) on the ICSSS.
3. Clinician's general judgment that the child was not stuttering.
4. A severity rating of zero on the ICSSS by a clinician.
5. Fewer than 3% SLD.
6. No remission of stuttering for 12 months after this assessment for persistence/recovery as judged by parent and clinician.

Comments 1 and 4 made in connection with the persistent children are also relevant here. Additionally:

1. Criterion 5 should not be used if speech symptoms are to be used as a risk factor for recovery from stuttering in order to avoid circularity as indicated at the end of section 1.5 (the same may apply with persistent cases, but there is no way of telling based on the way that criterion 2 was described for persistent cases).
2. Criterion 5 is not independent of criterion 4 as SLD are used in ICSSS.
3. Also, as stated earlier, investigations that do not start from stuttering onset cannot produce an absolute estimate of recovery rate. Yairi and Ambrose (2005) do everything they can to get samples as close to onset as possible. However, they are only alerted about children who stutter after the disorder onset. Parents may say that a child suddenly started

stuttering, but the bottom line is that they are parental reports (so they are memory-dependent and reliant on the parent possessing skills they have not been trained in).

4. Recovery is estimated at least four years after onset and the children were followed up for at least another year. Withdrawal from the study will occur at different age for different children. This does not allow recovery rate at particular ages to be estimated very easily as there are possibilities of selective biases (more recovered than persistent children may withdraw after the four-plus-one year period).

5. Most of the children received treatment and the type of treatment varied between children. Consequently, the impact of treatment on recovery cannot be determined.

6. It is not possible to designate a child with a score of 1 as persistent or recovered.

1.5.2 WAYS IN WHICH PERSISTENCE/RECOVERY HAS BEEN ASSESSED (HOWELL, DAVIS, & WILLIAMS, 2008A)

The London group works with older children (8 to the teens), who are able to take more performance tests than younger ones. The methods for establishing persistence and recovery are standardized and published, while presenting the tests here will make them conveniently available for others who may wish to use them. There are few other standardized tests available for stuttering (SSI-3 being a notable exception).

It was determined whether a child was stuttering at age 8. The child was classified as persistent or recovered when reaching the teenage years based on questionnaire information from the child, parent or caregiver, and a researcher (the same one saw all children). The scales used in each of these three assessments have been normed, using results from more than 300 children (see section 1.5.2.2 below).

1.5.2.1 Inclusion Criteria (Diagnosis of Stuttering)

The inclusion criteria were

1. An initial diagnosis made by a trained speech pathologist.
2. The child was referred to a clinic that specialized in childhood stuttering,
3. The specialist clinic confirmed the diagnosis and admitted the child to group (rather than individual) treatment.

Criterion 3 kept treatment and follow-up constant for all participants.

1.5.2.2 Child and Parent Questionnaire: Reliability and Validity

Only the child questionnaire is described (the parent questionnaire being identical except that statements described below were changed from the first to the third person). The questionnaire was based on one published by Boberg and Kully

(1994). Seven items were selected from their 15-item questionnaire (the first seven items listed in Table 1.7). A further item was constructed, which combined three more items from Boberg and Kully's questionnaire (the eighth item listed in Table 1.7). The remaining items on the questionnaire concerned a particular therapy and these were dropped. For each of the eight items, the child or caregiver answered on a 5-point scale. Each item produced a score of 1 to 5, where 1 represented fluent behavior and 5 represented disfluent behavior. The scores across all questions were summed, the maximum score being 40. Scores 21 or lower were considered "recovered" and scores greater than 21 were considered "persistent." The raw scores on these questionnaires were correlated with SSI-3 scores as a criterion for validating the cutoff. Inspection of the SSI-3 scores showed that these cutoffs divided speakers at the low end of the moderate scale from those with more severe problems on the scale (speakers who were on the margin between fluent and moderate were not deemed to have recovered and had to be at least moderate to be designated persistent). The SSI-3 scores were made from digital

---

TABLE 1.7

The Left-Hand Column Gives Eight Questions Which Speakers Who Stutter Used to Rate Their Speech

Question	Scale Endpoints	Boberg & Kully (1994) Question Number
How would you currently rate your speech?	1 = Terrific 5 = Terrible	2
How often are you able to speak fluently without thinking about your speech?	1 = Always 5 = Never	6
How much are you stuttering/stammering now compared to before you first saw your therapist/pathologist?	1 = Much less 5 = Much more	9
How do you feel about your speech now compared to before you first saw your therapist/pathologist?	1 = Much better 5 = Much worse	10
How would you describe your consultation with your therapist/pathologist?	1 = Very helpful 5 = Of no help	11
Overall, how much of a problem to you is your stuttering/stammering now, compared to before you first saw the therapist/pathologist?	1 = Much less 5 = Much more	12
At this time do you consider yourself a person who stutters/stammers?	1 = Definitely not 5 = Definitely yes	14
Do you think you would benefit from seeing the therapist/pathologist again?	1 = Definitely no 5 = Definitely yes	3, 4, and 5

Note: The scale endpoints are given in column two and the question numbers from Boberg and Kully's (1994) questionnaire, from which the questions were derived, are given in the third column. A modified version of these questions was also used by the parents to assess their child's stuttering.

records as described in section 1.3.1.1 and the SSI-3 scores are more sensitive and more reliable than estimates made in real time.

1.5.2.3   Researcher Assessment

The researcher visited each child's home as soon as possible after the child reached age 8 and recorded an interview that lasted approximately 90 minutes. During his visit, the researcher talked with a caregiver and the child about the speech problem and experience in the clinic. He also sought their views about communication style and self-confidence in a range of typical environments. These included home and social gatherings with adults and children in and out of school. Performance and experience in school were assessed in terms of interpersonal relationships with staff and other children (including bullying). General health issues were also examined, including frequent absence from school and childhood illnesses. The researcher reviewed the interview and notes taken at the home visit and assessed: (1) speech fluency, (2) social-conversational skills, and (3) whether the child had a positive self-image/confidence about speech. Each of the three assessments was scored on a scale of 0 (good) to 3 (poor). The scores for the three factors were summed to give one score of between 0 and 9. A score of 5 or above indicated still stuttering. When the distribution of raw scores from the researcher's report form were examined, it was not significantly different from normal.

1.5.2.4   Persistent/Recovered Outcome on
Howell et al.'s Longitudinal Samples

A child was designated persistent if he or she met *all* of the following criteria as soon as the child reached the teenage years:

1. Child indicated on the child report questionnaire that he/she was still stuttering.
2. Caregiver indicated on the parent report questionnaire that the child was still stuttering.
3. Researcher indicated on the researcher assessment form that the child was still stuttering.
4. Neither the child, caregiver, nor researcher reported any recovery for at least a year after reaching his/her teens.

A child was designated recovered if he or she met *all* of the following criteria when becoming a teenager:

1. Child indicated on the child report questionnaire that he/she was not stuttering.
2. Caregiver indicated on the parent report questionnaire that the child was not stuttering.

3. Researcher indicated on the researcher assessment form that the child was not stuttering.
4. Neither the child, caregiver, nor researcher reported any remission for at least a year after reaching his/her teens.

These instruments for designating speakers as persistent or recovered have been used in several studies (Davis et al., 2007; Howell, 2007a; Howell, Davis, & Williams, 2006; Howell et al., 2008a; Howell et al., 2008b). In these studies, all participants have been followed up for a minimum of 12 months and substantially longer in some cases (mean length of follow-up for all speakers is 31.5 months) and, as indicated earlier, all were followed up for a minimum of 12 months after treatment as this has been suggested as the maximum time needed to determine whether a child has responded to treatment (Finn, 1998). A further feature to note is that speech symptoms were not included as inclusion or persistent/recovered criteria, so speech symptoms can be used as a factor for assessing risk of persistence/recovery.

1.5.2.5   Statistical Assessment of the Child, Parent, and Researcher Instruments

Three hundred and eleven children (252 boys and 59 girls) were used to standardize and norm the child report questionnaire. The ages of the children who stuttered ranged from 8 years to 19 years 7 months. Three hundred and two sets of data (246 boys and 56 girls) from parents were used to norm the parent report questionnaire. The children about whom the parents reported were aged between 8 years and 19 years 7 months. The data for both questionnaires were normally distributed (skewness and kurtosis were checked for departures from normal distributions). These data were used for the statistical assessments described below.

1.5.2.6   Construct Reliability

Cronbach's alpha statistic was used as an indication of how well the set of items (or questions) from the questionnaire measured a single unidimensional latent construct (reliability). When the data do not measure a single dimension (they are multidimensional), Cronbach's alpha is low. An alpha value of 0.8 or higher was used here as an indication of whether the psychometric instrument measured a single dimension. The Cronbach alpha coefficients were above 0.8 for both the child and parent report questionnaires. This indicates high internal consistency of the items, so the questionnaires are reliable.

1.5.2.7   Test–Retest Reliability

Test–retest reliability across test occasions was also assessed. For the child questionnaire, the correlation coefficient for the two sets of scores was .74, which indicated acceptable test–retest reliability. The correlation for the parent questionnaire was .85, which indicated even better reliability.

1.4.2.8 Internal (Construct) Validity

Internal (construct) validity was assessed by separate factor analyses for the child and parent questionnaires. There were interesting differences between the results for the children and their parents, which are mentioned in section 1.4.5. First, for the children, the principal factor accounted for 44.9% of variance and all items loaded at .45 or above on this factor. The second factor accounted for a further 13.6% of the variance. The identity of the factors was established by rotating the factors. In this analysis, it was apparent that items 1, 2, 7, and 8 loaded heavily on the first factor (.6 and above) and items 3, 4, 5, and 6 loaded heavily on the second factor (again .6 and above). Examination of the child report questionnaires showed that the items loading on the first factor were all related to how the child currently felt (for example, "How would you currently rate your speech"). The items that loaded on the second factor were all related to comparative assessments (e.g., "How much are you stammering/stuttering now, compared to before you first saw your speech therapist?"). The interpretation of both factors was in terms of judgments either about current stuttering alone or how this related to their stuttering in the past. The questionnaire that measured both factors provided a valid indication of stuttering over time.

For the parent report questionnaire, all questions loaded at .6 or above on one factor. This factor accounted for 54.3% of the variance in the questionnaire. All the items in the parent report questionnaire refer to stuttering (current and past) by the child. As such, the factor provides an integrated impression of stuttering over time. As current and past stuttering weighted on different factors for the children's responses, there are differences in the way parents and children evaluate stuttering, which need to be examined further. The point that needs to be stressed here is that the statistical analysis supports the view that the parent questionnaire provided a valid measure of stuttering across time for their child.

1.5.2.9 External (Criterion) Validity

The child report questionnaire correlated highly with the SSI-3 scores ($r = .66$). A linear regression analysis showed that the raw score from the child report questionnaire was a significant predictor of the child's SSI-3 score. The parent report scores also correlated highly with the SSI-3 score ($r = .65$) and showed that the parent report questionnaire was a significant predictor of the child's SSI-3 score.

1.5.2.10 Researcher Assessment: External Validity

The researcher's report form was designed as a scale to rate observations about the children and, as such, was not a psychometric measure. Consequently, construct reliability, test–retest reliability, and internal validity were not relevant and were not computed. However, external validity was computed on 328 reports. The raw total scores from the researcher's report form correlated highly with the SSI-3 score ($r = .77$).

1.5.2.11   Standardization of Child and Parent Questionnaires and Researcher's Assessment

The total raw scores from the child and parent questionnaires and for the researcher's assessment have been standardized to t scores with a mean of 50 and a standard deviation (sd) of 10. Percentiles for the child report questionnaire raw scores are given in Table 1.8, for the parent report questionnaire in Table 1.9, and for the researcher's assessment in Table 1.10. The reported percentiles were chosen so that they corresponded with the SSI-3 stanines used by Riley (1981, 1994) discussed earlier in this chapter. The class names correspond to those used in SSI-3, and they are arbitrary and problematic if these names are used in diagnosis (section 1.3.1.4).

1.6   ATTRITION

With longitudinal work, some participants are always lost. So, it is necessary to consider when this is a problem that affects the results of studies. For instance, the Andrews and Harris (1964) estimates of incidence and prevalence have been questioned (Ingham, 1976) because there was an attrition rate of 33.2% over the course of the study. Although attrition rate is high, it should be recalled that the Andrews and Harris study was conducted on the same children for a long period of time and the rate might not be considered unreasonable in the light of this.

The attrition issue may apply to other longitudinal studies (see comments about this in the Yairi and Ambrose, 2005, study in section 1.5.1.3) Also, more recent views on whether attrition in a sample is problematic, examine whether there is evidence that the participants that were lost differ in critical respects from those

TABLE 1.8
Raw Child Report Questionnaire Scores and Corresponding Percentiles Based on 311 Questionnaires

Total Raw Score on Child Report Questionnaire	Percentile	SSI-3 Severity Rating for Same Percentiles	Raw SSI-3 Scores
9–10	1–4	Very mild	6–8
11–12	5–11	Very mild	9–10
13–15	12–23	Mild	11–15
16–17	24–40	Mild	16–20
18–21	41–60	Moderate	21–23
22–23	61–77	Moderate	24–27
24–25	78–88	Severe	28–31
26–28	89–95	Severe	32–35
29 and up	96–99	Very Severe	36 and up

Note: SSI-3 taxonomic severity ratings and actual SSI-3 values are given for the same percentiles.

TABLE 1.9

Raw Parent Report Questionnaire Scores and Corresponding Percentiles Based on 302 Questionnaires

Total Raw Score on Parent Report Questionnaire	Percentile	SSI-3 Severity Rating for Same Percentiles	Raw SSI-3 Scores
9–10	1–4	Very mild	6–8
11–14	5–11	Very mild	9–10
14–16	12–23	Mild	11–15
17–19	24–40	Mild	16–20
20–23	41–60	Moderate	21–23
24–27	61–77	Moderate	24–27
27–29	78–88	Severe	28–31
30–32	89–95	Severe	32–35
33 and up	96–99	Very Severe	36 and up

Note: SSI-3 taxonomic severity ratings and actual SSI-3 values are given for the same percentiles.

who remain in the sample. Selective attrition means that participants are not lost at random, but rather the characteristics of those participants who dropped out are not similar to those who remain. When selective attrition occurs, this may result in research findings being compromised, threatening both the internal and external reliability of the research (Flick, 1988).

TABLE 1.10

Raw Researcher's Report Form Scores and Corresponding Percentiles Based on 328 Questionnaires

Total Raw Score on Researcher's Report Questionnaire	Percentile	SSI-3 Severity Rating for Same Percentiles	Raw SSI-3 Scores
0–1	1–4	Very mild	6–8
1	5–11	Very mild	9–10
2	12–23	Mild	11–15
2–3	24–40	Mild	16–20
4–5	41–60	Moderate	21–23
5	61–77	Moderate	24–27
6	78–88	Severe	28–31
6–7	89–95	Severe	32–35
8 and up	96–99	Very Severe	36 and up

Note: SSI-3 taxonomic severity ratings and actual SSI-3 values are given for the same percentiles.

Attrition rate in our longitudinal study was 32.4% over 10 years and 9.0% over the last four years within these 10 years. The attrition pattern in our data does not appear to be selective. For example, 84.6% of the original research sample was male and 85.6% of those lost to attrition was male. Similarly, 19.0% of the original research population came from families where English was not the only language spoken as did 18.9% of the participants lost to attrition.

1.7 SUMMARY

This chapter gave some definitions that highlight the major features of stuttering (DSM and Wingate). It also indicated how severity of the disorder is assessed, and linked this to the two procedures for classifying longitudinal cases as persistent or recovered. The latter schemes are used in the next chapter to classify cases and then examine epidemiology of persistent and recovered cases (everyone does not have an equal chance of being affected). It will be indicated where investigations into epidemiological factors in stuttering are backed up with assessment instruments.

1.8 EXERCISES

The purpose of the study questions that appear at the end of each chapter is to invite readers to consider topics raised in the text. Often a particular interpretation has been given about the topic in the text. However, these are not the final answers. Thus, only certain evidence is discussed in detail and readers may draw on other literature and draw different conclusions. Alternative interpretations about some topics that are backed up by empirical work and logical argument help to pinpoint what additional research needs to be done to advance our understanding. The alternative interpretations are a healthy sign and should be encouraged. The questions can be used for formal assessment of students or they can be considered as invitations to consider a stimulating and, in some cases, controversial topic by professionals.

  1. This chapter discusses the ways different research groups have designated speakers who stutter as persistent or recovered. In both the main surveys discussed, children who were known to stutter were followed up for a period and then stuttering was reassessed. The reassessments used different criteria. Yairi and Ambrose (2005) specified criteria that maximized the chance of a speaker being considered as continuing (persisting) in stuttering and minimized the chance of a speaker being considered as recovered from stuttering. Howell, Davis, and Williams (2009) used three independent assessments and checked whether stuttering still occurred after a period of at least a year. The four criteria had to be in agreement to designate a child as persistent (i.e., all three independent assessments indicated the child was still stuttering and stuttering still occurred at least a year later) or recovered (i.e., all three

independent assessments indicated the child was not stuttering and stuttering did not occur at least a year later). Consider what impact these alternative formulations have when they are used to estimate persistence and recovery of stuttering over development and as a result of treatment.

2. All current studies about the onset of stuttering rely on parental reports that their child stutters. What are the problems in relying on such reports and are there feasible ways that children who stutter could be recorded before onset of the disorder so that criteria could be based on speech analysis?

3. Recovery from developmental stuttering is usually considered to occur at any age up to the teenage years. If surveys stop at ages younger than teenage, how will this affect estimates of persistence and recovery? Restricting the age range of follow-up periods helps keep attrition rates low. However, age ranges need to be specified, otherwise attrition rate cannot be estimated. Explain why this is so and also indicate why and how you would check whether the attrition is selective or not.

2 Epidemiology

This chapter considers studies that use tools like those provided in Chapter 1 to compare the epidemiology of persons who persist or recover in their stuttering.

2.1 INTRODUCTION

Epidemiology is the study of factors affecting the health and illness of populations, and these studies identify risk factors for disease. As was stated at the end of the Chapter 1, the risk of being affected by stuttering varies from person to person. The chances of starting to stutter and recovering from it are dependent on population characteristics. This chapter examines (1) the factors that give one person a higher chance of starting to stutter than another and (2) once stuttering has started, what factors give one person a higher chance of recovering from stuttering than another. To address the first statement, clear and comprehensive inclusion criteria are needed in order to identify speakers who stutter. A number of sources of information obtained on children in a single age group can be used for this purpose. To address the second, information needs to be obtained that will allow a speaker to be classified as persistent or recovered. Ideally, longitudinal data should be available to classify speakers as recovered, as it is necessary to know the speaker was stuttering at a certain age and has now stopped. In order to establish risk factors for persistence, these same data need to be available for it to be known that the speaker was stuttering at an early age and continued to do so at the end of the study. Persistent and recovered cases then can be compared at different developmental ages to identify how and when the two groups of speakers diverged from each other.

The Yairi and Ambrose (2005) and the Howell et al. (2008) work reported in the previous chapter gave inclusion criteria that allow for an initial diagnosis. The information provided shows what criteria Yairi and Ambrose used for the age range from onset to age 6 (their first inclusion criterion required children to be 6 years of age or younger) and what criteria Howell et al. used with children at age 8. Both sets of authors also supply the criteria they used to designate children who stutter as persistent or recovered after a follow-up period. Other studies do not always have such clear-cut criteria. For example, retrospective designs sometimes use self-report of having stuttered, and thus standardized measures about stuttering are not available. Although, in the latter cases, the criteria are more lax than in Yairi and Ambrose's and Howell et al.'s, these studies have provided some useful results. Details about the methods are reported the first time each study is discussed in order to inform the reader of any limitations in the design of these studies and the criteria they employed for diagnosis, persistence, and recovery.

2.2   INCIDENCE AND PREVALENCE

In epidemiology, the prevalence of a disease or condition in a sample is the total number of cases of the disease divided by the total number of individuals. Prevalence is a measurement of all individuals affected by the disease within a particular period of time. Incidence is a measurement of the number of new individuals who contract a disease during a particular period of time. Period prevalence is a measure of the proportion of people in a population who have a disease or condition over a specific period of time, such as from onset of stuttering to age 8.

Incidence and period prevalence were reported by Andrews and Harris (1964), who studied stuttering in 1,142 families in Newcastle-on-Tyne in the United Kingdom with children born between May and June 1947. The children were initially seen by health visitors and any children suspected of having a speech–language disorder were examined by trained speech–language pathologists. Over the course of the study, some children were identified as stuttering. Information was obtained from these children and their families by detailed clinical interview on a range of issues including general health of the child and parent (including birth complications), family and school background, and general development of the child including social and educational adjustment. An equal number of control children who were matched for age and gender was also examined. The data were analyzed to see whether there was any association between each measure and fluency group (children who stuttered or the control group). When the associations were significant, this revealed that there was something different about the two groups of children. Diagnosis of stuttering was based on the clinical interview. The children were subsequently seen at regular periods over the course of the study and speech pathologists determined whether the child was still stuttering or not (this was based on expert judgment because assessment instruments were not available at the time). The study (usually referred to as the 1,000 Family Survey) ended in 1962 when the children were age 15, at which time 750 children were still participating. Period prevalence up to age 15 was about 4.9%. The authors established that, at the end of the study, the incidence of stuttering was about 1%. Bloodstein (1995) estimated the lifetime incidence also to be 1%, which along with Andrews and Harris's report, suggests that incidence remains approximately constant after reaching the teenage years.

Some notable strengths of the 1,000 family survey were (1) that an unbiased sample from the population was used, (2) an extensive age range was examined from birth to 15 years, (3) the sample was reasonably large (just over 1,000), (4) it focused on a range of factors that could be related specifically to language development, and (5) the assessments were thorough, well documented, and reasonably comprehensive.

There were some procedural issues that are inherent to the design. Looking first at diagnosis, the children were seen initially by health visitors. A general problem in studies of incidence and prevalence with disorders that are infrequent (such as stuttering) is that a large sample is needed in order to provide a reasonable-sized (and statistically reliable) subsample with the disorder. Given that experts may have difficulty in assessing stuttering (Kully & Boberg, 1988), the screening by the health visitors is likely to have missed some cases and misdiagnosed others. The misdiagnoses of stuttering would have been picked up when the children were examined by the speech–language pathologists after the initial screening. However, this does not apply to the ones not examined by the speech–language pathologists. The problem of missed cases is compounded because no recordings were taken that would have allowed the child's speech and the interview information to be checked.

One problem that potentially affects diagnosis and outcome is that the criteria used to determine persistence or recovery are not explicit. If the criteria are wrong in any way, this would affect the estimates of both incidence and period prevalence, which also have been questioned (Ingham, 1976) because of the 33.2% attrition rate in the entire sample over the course of the study. (The attrition rate for children who stutter is not stated separately, so it is not clear whether the children who stuttered had a higher chance of remaining in the sample.) Attrition would not be a problem if it is not selective as documented in Chapter 1 with respect to the Howell et al. (2008) study. If the data are still available, it should be easy to check whether factors (e.g., gender, education) were comparable across the subsample of children who continued in the study and those who dropped out. If rates are comparable on all factors, the attrition rate is less likely to be a problem for interpretation of the results.

Given the expense involved in conducting such studies and the increased rate of mobility of families that would further exacerbate maintaining contact (keeping attrition rate low), such investigations are rare. The Andrews and Harris (1964) study has served as the benchmark for incidence and period prevalence. As will be seen, the estimates of these statistics in other studies all fall close to the figures Andrews and Harris reported.

A more limited study in terms of variables investigated and examinations made in the follow-up assessments was reported by Mansson (2000), who studied 1,042 children born on a Danish island over a two-year period; 1,021 of these participated in the study (98% of all the births in this period). Diagnosis was made by the author and a team of four qualified clinicians each with several years' experience. They also met weekly to discuss issues associated with the study, which ensured similar procedures were employed (guaranteeing good practice). When the children were first seen, the team also assessed speech, hearing, and language in face-to-face interviews.

The inclusion criteria were:

1. Assessed as stuttering by the clinical team
2. Parent confirmation of diagnosis of stuttering

The assessments took the form of 1-hour structured interviews with the parent. Play activities took place with the child to assess interaction with the clinician, and the session included tasks aimed at eliciting specific language forms (vocabulary, phonology, receptive language, syntax, grammar, and fluency). No details are given of these tests. For instance, it is not clear how syntax tests differ from grammar tests. Fluency was assessed by the clinicians who indicated the major characteristics of disfluency. Repetitions and prolongations are mentioned as examples of disfluency, but there is no indication what other disfluencies were assessed or whether the repetitions were phrase, word, or part-word repetitions, or some mixture of them. This is critical, as schemes for assessing symptoms put some of these symptoms of repetition in the class considered more usual of stuttering and others in the class considered more usual of the disfluencies seen in typically developing children (see Chapter 3 on symptomatology for coverage of this debate). The assessment of hearing ability was informal; it just established whether the child could hear whispered speech. No recordings were made. Incidence of stuttering at age 3 was 4.99%.

Limitations in terms of the diagnostic criteria are the reliance on subjective reports and detail about how these were administered was sparse. The lack of recordings is also a problem because speech assessment is difficult and permanent records need to be available when, for instance, estimating severity, which requires several passes on the recordings if Riley's (1981, 1994) advice is followed (see Chapter 1).

Some work also has been done on a large longitudinal sample of twins; this is called the Twins Early Development Study, or TEDS (Trouton, Spinath, & Plomin, 2002). The work on TEDS is not solely on language development and, with testing being on a wide range of abilities, time to investigate stuttering is limited. TEDS consists of a database of all twins born between 1994 and 1996 in the United Kingdom and is ongoing ($N = 25,830$).

Diagnosis of stuttering was based on questionnaire data provided by the parents (further details are given below). Information on stuttering is currently available at ages 2, 3, 4, and 7 years (Dworzynski, Remington, Rijksdijk, Howell, & Plomin, 2007) from responses in the Preschool Behavior Questionnaire.

The inclusion criteria were based on one question at age 2 and two questions that appeared at ages 3 and 4. The question at age 2 was the same as one of the questions asked at ages 3 and 4 and it was in the form of a statement, namely: "Has a stutter or stammer." Parents were asked to answer it with the responses: *not true, sometimes true, or certainly true*. The second question was given at all other ages (this was the only question at age 7). This question was in a specific section on language concerns and asked: "Do you have concerns about your child's speech and language? *yes, no*." If a *yes* answer was given, parents were asked to indicate what the concerns were and option 6 was: "She/he stutters."

The inclusion criterion to admit the child into the stuttering group at age 2 was an affirmative answer to question 1 (by answering at least: *sometimes true*).

The specific inclusion criteria to admit the child to the stuttering group at ages 3 and 4 were either:

1. Both of the questions were answered affirmatively (by answering at least *sometimes true* to the first question and *yes*, "she/he stutters" for the second).
2. One answer was missing, but the other was affirmative.

Based on the parents' reports, none of the children who were considered to stutter had indicated concern, but had not indicated stuttering. Using these diagnostic criteria, Dworzynski et al. (2007) reported that the incidence of stuttering ranged between 1 and 3% for the different ages, with most cases reported at age 4: 1.1% (118 children), 2.0% (227 children), 3.5% (493 children), and 1.6% (218 children) at ages 2, 3, 4, and 7, respectively. Period prevalence across all the test ages was 1,812 (7%), with 1,029 boys (4%) and 783 girls (3%), who had been rated as stuttering out of all of the twins in the entire dataset who had been contacted over the seven-year period.

A positive feature of the Dworzynski et al. study is that it involved a large number of twins. TEDS is longitudinal and the study is ongoing and, thus, may provide further information on stuttering. A problem is attrition (although attrition would not be a problem providing it is not selective). Reliance on parental report is another problem and has the same issues discussed in connection with Mansson's (2000) study.

An issue specific to the Dworzynski et al. study is the unevenness of the information available about stuttering across the different ages. This affects the diagnostic criteria and persistence/recovery criteria (the latter are described in the section 2.3). Since children were considered to be stuttering when they were rated as stuttering "only sometimes," this is lax and would tend to overestimate stuttering, perhaps explaining why the period prevalence estimate at 7% is somewhat higher than the generally accepted figure of 5% (Bloodstein, 1995).

Ooki (2005) also reported a study on twins that included data that can be used to estimate stuttering prevalence. Ooki recruited 1,896 pairs of twin children (1,849 males and 1,943 females). The mean age was 11.6 years and age range was from 3 to 15 years. Data were gathered by questionnaire. Mothers indicated the frequency of stuttering behavior using four categories: *often, sometimes, never, don't know*. The prevalence of stuttering was 6.7% in males and 3.6% in females.

A positive feature of the data from this study is that the number of twins tested was large. The study has the same limitations as Dworzynski et al.'s study due to being based on parental report. In addition, no follow-up data have been reported, and persistence and recovery have not been estimated. There is a large age range and, given the large sample size, it would have been of interest to divide the entire group by age. As some of the children were quite old at the time the survey was conducted, this would affect memory of stuttering (as the author notes). The Dworzynski et al. (2007) and Ooki (2005) studies are discussed further in Chapter 4 on genetics.

Reilly et al. (2009) reported a study that investigated stuttering in 1,619 children who had completed a range of language questionnaires at age 2. The parents were asked to report stuttering onset between ages 2 and 3 years (they were quizzed every four months). Parents were given a refrigerator magnet that defined stuttering and illustrated examples. They were contacted by research assistants who were trained speech–language pathologists as soon as possible after the parents reported suspected stuttering. The parents were interviewed about a similar range of issues to those examined by Andrews and Harris and a video recording of a play session with the child and parent was made. The video tapes were reviewed by two experts on stuttering (Onslow and Packman).

The inclusion criteria to admit the child into the stuttering group were:

1. Parents returned language questionnaires when the child was age 2 years.
2. Parent reported stuttering by telephone.
3. Research assistant confirmed stuttering on a visit soon after the telephone call.
4. Two experts gave the child a rating of two or greater on the Lidcombe severity scale (scale point 1 is: *no stuttering*).

It was noted that 8.5% of the children were classified as stutterers up to 3 years of age. It is of note that the most common symptom (reported by 71% of parents) was whole-word repetitions. Detailed speech analysis to confirm this does not appear to have been performed. This is an important issue because there in considerable debate as to whether this feature should be considered a symptom of stuttering or not. (See discussion of Yairi and Ambrose's (2005) work on recovery rates in section 2.3 and further discussion in Chapter 3.) It is also possible that cases were missed as only children whose parents alerted the researchers were examined. The Reilly et al. (2009) study on modeling risk factors for stuttering is discussed further in Chapter 13. In summary, Andrews and Harris (1964) provided estimates of incidence and period prevalence from birth to age 15. Since then, there has not been any large-scale longitudinal studies on children that has used an unselected target sample of fluent speakers and speakers who stutter on which to estimate incidence and prevalence of stuttering that covers this age range. A number of other studies that provide information about incidence and period prevalence were reported. Limitations in all the studies were identified. However, and somewhat surprisingly, incidence and period prevalence in these studies lie close to the 1 and 5% estimates reported by Andrews and Harris, though some estimates are higher (Dworzynski et al., 2007; Reilly et al., 2009).

2.3   RECOVERY RATE

Comparison of incidence and prevalence provides information about recovery rate. The 5% period prevalence and 1% incidence rate reported in Andrews and Harris's (1964) 1,000 Family Survey shows 80% of the respondents recovered from stuttering and only 20% persisted up to age 15.

The Yairi and Ambrose (2005) study provides estimates of the recovery rate using their procedures for both diagnosis and determination of whether a child persisted or recovered, which were detailed in Chapter 1. Yairi and Ambrose found that recovery rates were between 65 and 80%, three to five years after onset.

There is one further potential limitation that might affect the recovery rate estimates in Yairi and Ambrose's study that should be mentioned that was also commented on with respect to the Reilly et al. (2009) study. Wingate (2001) argued that recovery rates are actually lower than those reported because inappropriate ways of counting stuttering symptoms were used. Wingate's main objection was inclusion of whole-word repetitions as symptoms of stuttering. (The exchange between Wingate and Yairi and Ambrose is discussed further in Chapter 3.) For present purposes, the point is that if Wingate is correct, prevalence would be over-estimated because symptoms that are not characteristics of stuttering are counted as stuttering events. Stuttering-like disfluency (SLD) counts, which are one of the diagnostic criteria for inclusion as a stutterer in the Yairi and Ambrose study, would be inflated. In turn, this would tend to categorize cases as stuttering in those who do not stutter. It would also inflate recovery rates, as cases misclassi-fied as stuttering would appear to have regained fluent control when, in fact, they did not stutter in the first instance.

Mansson's (2000) study also reported recovery rates up to age 9 (he examined the children again at age 5 and 9). The examination at age 5 (two years after initial assessment) involved:

1. Reexamination of records on the child.
2. Interviews with parents *of affected children.*
3. Reexamination of the child to see if there was an indication of continu-ing stuttering, although details about how this was done are sparse.

The next round of examinations made another four years later (at about age 9), provided the basis for classifying children as persistent or recovered. Only speech–language pathologists appear to have been involved at this stage (not other healthcare workers). From the description, parents alone appear to have been interviewed about whether their child was still stuttering.

Two further cases were identified at the age 5 or age 9 follow-ups (the author is not specific at which follow-up these were detected and it is not clear how they were identified). Period prevalence was reported to be 5.19%. The recovery rate was 71.6% after two years and 85% after five to six years.

A limitation of the last two assessments is that few details are given of the procedures. Also, as the author recognized, ideally he and his team should have reexamined all 1,021 children. Failing that, they should at least have reexamined all the children who were diagnosed as stuttering (not just those who persisted). Another limitation is the reliance on kindergarten records and interviews with nurses, social workers, and teachers, who alerted the principal investigator about new cases of stuttering (involvement of speech–language therapists was not men-tioned at this stage). This procedure is not satisfactory because cases will have been missed because the healthcare workers lacked formal training.

More specifically with regards to the last session where persistence and recov-ery were determined, limited information is provided about how recovery was assessed. Despite the limitations indicated, the incidence estimates over these periods are close to the estimates reported in Andrews and Harris (1964).

The final limitation to highlight, as it would influence estimates of recovery rate, is the examination (after the initial screening) for outcomes in cases initially categorized as stuttering. Another is the occurrence of new cases in the cohort of 1,021 who might have been overlooked by general healthcare workers.

Recovery rate can be obtained from Dworzynski et al. (2007) as well. At age 7, a question regarding stuttering only appeared in the language concern part of the parent booklet. (This was the same as the question on language concerns at both years 3 and 4, as described above.) The answers to questions at all ages were used to designate whether each child had persisted or recovered from stuttering by age 7. The first step was to exclude individuals whose parents did not provide sufficient data from this part of the study. The exclusion criteria for persistence/recovery classification were:

1. There had to be answers to the questions posed at age 7. Those who had been classified as stuttering at earlier ages, but for whom there was no data at age 7, were excluded from the recovered/persistent part of the analysis, as were those who were recorded as stuttering for the first time at age 7.
2. Only children with more than one year's data were included. Thus, an indication of stuttering only at age 7 did not allow a child to be classified as persistent or recovered.

The designation as persistent was made as follows:

1. Each child was classified as having a reported incidence of stuttering at only one age or at two or more of the ages. A child had to be rated for at least two ages as someone who stutters.
2. The parents had to indicate concern about language and give an affirmative answer that the child was stuttering at age 7.

The designation as recovered was made as follows:

1. A child who had been rated as stuttering at one age was considered recovered.
2. A child who was rated at more than one age as stuttering, but who was rated by the parents as no longer stuttering at age 7, was classified as recovered.

Dworzynski et al. (2007) reported that 7.4% recovered and 1% persisted based on the above criteria. From these figures, the recovery rate is 88%.

A limitation of persistent/recovered outcome estimates is that these are again based on parental report. Also, the age range is limited and at present does not cover the complete age range over which Andrews and Harris (1964) reported recovery would occur. Thus, recovery is not fully resolved, thus, in the Dworzynski et al. work, recovery means recovery up to age 7.

Investigations that do not start from stuttering onset do not produce an absolute estimate of recovery rate (Yairi & Ambrose, 2005). However, they are useful for estimating recovery at other ages and information on complementary sub-ranges, and can be pooled with information about other subage ranges to provide estimates of recovery. Fritzell (1976) examined a group of children whom he followed from ages between 7 and 9 through to the teens. He reported a recovery rate of 47% between 7 years and teens.

Howell et al.'s (2008) study (again discussed at length in Chapter 1) provided estimates of recovery rate. Their study covered the range from 8 years to teenage years (a similar age range to Fritzell's). Recovery rates were around 50% overall, for both genders. The lower recovery rate was as would be expected given that most recovery happened when the children were young (Andrews, et al., 1982).

There was a chance of around 50% of persistence or recovery and this did not depend on gender or on age of attendance at the clinic. Recovery rate was lower in this study than in others with younger children (Andrews & Harris, 1964; Yairi & Ambrose, 2005), which is consistent with the view that most recovery happened when the children were young. It is also of note that, at 53.9%, the estimate of recovery rate was close to the 47% reported by Fritzell (1976) for children with similar ages to those in Howell, Davis, and Williams's (2008) study. Andrews and Harris's data also show that 25% of stuttering onsets occur in the age range covered by Howell, Davis, and Williams's study.

Three smaller scale studies also have reported recovery rates for selected groups of children. Kloth, Kraimaat, Janssen, and Brutten (1999) examined a selected sample, which followed 93 high risk children, which were born into families with a stuttering parent. The children were at high risk because it has been reported that stuttering runs in families (Yairi & Ambrose, 2005). The study started before any stuttering was reported and followed the children for two years to see whether any had started to stutter. Ages were not given, although it was stated that the children were preschoolers.

The inclusion criteria for diagnosing a child as stuttering were:

1. Parental report that a child stuttered.
2. Both parents agreed that the child stuttered.
3. Both parents had to indicate at least one type of disfluency (rapid sound or syllable repetition, tense silent, or oral prolongation) that had frequently or very frequently been evident in the previous two months.
4. Stuttering had to be noted as present in audio samples (true of 21/23 of the children who stuttered).

The children were examined, using the same criteria, two years after the project commenced. At that time, 23 children were reported to stutter. Four years after that, 70% of the children who had stuttered at the start of the project had recovered, by using the same criteria to diagnose stuttering. No information is provided about classifications of recovered cases.

A feature of note is that the types of disfluency considered to be characteristic of stuttering are specified. Also, they are ones that Wingate (2001) would have agreed to be characteristics of stuttering (see no. 3 above) that does not include whole word repetitions. Although criterion 1 for diagnosis is based on self-report, this is not as much of a limitation as in other studies. One limitation of self-report is that respondents are not experienced about stuttering. These families have experience of stuttering as one of them stutters or stuttered. However, it should be cautioned that they still lack formal training on how to diagnose stuttering.

Ryan (2001) followed 22 2- to 3-year-old children for two years and the criteria for inclusion in the study as a stutterer were:

1. Three stuttered words per minute (where stutters were specified as whole-word and part-word repetitions, prolongations, and struggle). At least two investigators assessed independently each child's speech. Agreement for stutters was 91.4% and for syllables 94.6%.
2. English had to be the child's first language.
3. The child had to be perceived by one or both parents to stutter.

For all cases reexamined after two years (whether or not the child subsequently persisted or recovered), he or she had to meet the following criterion:

1. No treatment for two years. Subsequently, all but one had treatment. The author does not mention it explicitly, but presumably only the persistent cases were given treatment.

For persistence, the child had to meet one of two criteria:

1. The child had to be at or greater than 3% stuttered words per minute at the two-year follow-up and the rate had to be constant across ages except that in two cases (out of seven) the rate was allowed to be below 3%, but increased to above this on a test given later.
2. The child could have previously been below 3% stuttered word per minute, but subsequently showed an increased trend in stuttered words per minute. This criterion applied to two of the seven cases classified as persistent.

For recovery, the child had to meet criterion 1 or criterion 2 as well as criterion 3:

1. The child had less than 3% stuttered words per minute at the two-year follow-up and the rate was flat over time.
2. The child was at or above 3% stuttered words per minute initially, but the rate decreased by the two-year follow-up.
3. The child had to be followed-up (this was for an unspecified period) and continue to show less than 3% stuttered words per minute, and testing and the parent had to confirm that the child was not stuttering.

Ryan reported a 68% recovery rate (15/22). Generally speaking, the procedures were well reported and sound. It is of note, however, that whole-word repetitions were counted as stutters, which is controversial as discussed above (Wingate, 2001).

Rommel, Hage, Kalehne, and Johannsen (1999) reported follow-up results for 65 5-year-old children three years into their study and reported a 71% recovery rate. The publication that contains this report is not available because of a mishap during distribution, so the methods have not been scrutinized.

Estimates of recovery rates based on clinical observations have been reported as well. They are somewhat dated and provide values that appear low relative to Andrews and Harris's (1964) survey (e.g., 40% recovery by age 8 reported by Bryngelson, 1938). Major problems are that the methods used are not explicit and there is no way of checking the statements.

There are also studies where adults report retrospectively whether they stuttered or not in earlier life. These studies provide estimates that are close to those of Andrews and Harris (1964). So, for example, Sheehan and Martyn (1966) used self-reports from adults and reported a recovery rate of 80%. Here the main problem is that there is no way of checking whether the report of stuttering was a true case or not. Also, memory about stuttering may be faulty. (See discussion in Chapter 1, section 1.4.5.)

Andrews et al. (1983) carried out a meta-analysis of recovery rates reported in several studies, which is used here to draw together the findings on recovery, as they point to similar conclusions to those based on the studies reviewed. They estimated from this the chance of stuttering for speakers of different ages. They calculated that 75% of those stuttering at age 4 years, 50% of those stuttering at age 6 years, and 25% of those stuttering at age 10 years, recovered by the time they reached 16 years of age. If the problem continued into teenage years, the chance of recovery decreased dramatically. This is specifically supported by the Andrews and Harris's (1964) 1,000 Family Survey where no child who was stuttering after 12 years of age recovered by age 16 years.

2.4   SEX RATIO

Andrews and Harris (1964) showed that more boys than girls stuttered (a ratio of 2.4:1 overall) and that the ratio increased as the children got older, indicating that girls recovered from stuttering at an earlier age than boys.

The predominance of males over females was also confirmed by Yairi and Ambrose (2005), who reported that the sex ratio was 3.75:1 for the persistent group and 2.33:1 for the recovered group. Mansson (2000) found that at age 3 there were 1.65 boys to each girl. Dworzynski et al. (2007) reported that the sex ratio trend increased slightly with age: For each girl who stuttered at ages 2 and 3, there were approximately 1.6 boys, whereas at ages 4 and 7, there were approximately 1.8 boys for every girl who stuttered (the same value for the two ages). Dworzynski et al. also reported that of the 135 children who persisted, 35 (26%) were female and 100 (74%) were male, giving 2.9 boys for every girl who stuttered. Howell et al. (2008a) who worked with older children (8 to teens) found that a higher number of males (64) than females (12) stuttered; a ratio of 5.33 males to each female. This suggests that gender is a major risk factor for persistence (see Chapter 13). The higher sex ratio than reported elsewhere was expected in the Howell et al. (2008a) study, as females tend to recover at a younger age than males (Andrews & Harris, 1964). Consequently, an older sample should consist predominantly of males.

2.5   AGE OF ONSET

The Andrews and Harris (1964) data show that one modal onset age was three years and the other was five years. Although many cases have onsets in early childhood, there are also cases of later onset in children. The 1,000 Family Survey showed that onset can occur up to at least age 11 (Andrews & Harris, 1964).

Yairi and Ambrose (2005) reported that average age of onset in their study was 33 months. Mansson (2000) also reported that mean onset age was 33 months. When broken down by gender, onset age was 34 months for boys and 31 months for girls. Dworzynski et al. (2007) showed an increase in reported cases starting at ages 3 to 4. Age of onset in Howell et al. (2008a) based on 62 participants was 7 years and 7 months overall, and this was the same for both genders as well as for persistent and recovered speakers. Age of onset in these older children was comparable with those reported in other studies, including those with younger children (Andrews & Harris, 1964; Yairi & Ambrose, 2005). Bloodstein and Bernstein Ratner (2007, pp. 82–83) reviewed some of the same studies as examined here as well as other, mainly earlier, ones. The ones that have not been included here are omitted because some details are missing and inclusion criteria are not always rigorously specified, preventing full evaluation. However, one feature they note is that the latest reported ages of stuttering onset across these studies was from 7 to 13 years. This means that studies that do not collect data to the teenage years will underestimate many of the statistics discussed in the chapter (including those in sections 2.6 and 2.7). This will apply, for example, to recovery rate and reported age of onset.

2.6   AGE OF RECOVERY

Age of recovery is less often reported than other statistics that have been considered (e.g., Mansson (2000) does not mention it). Andrews and Harris (1964) showed that recovery can happen at any age up to the teens. Yairi and Ambrose (2005, p. 167) mentioned that most recovery happens three years post onset. Using their age of onset data, this will occur approximately at 6 years of age.

Howell et al. (2008a) reported age of recovery for their older cohort as 13 years 2 months or around five years after attendance at the clinic. Howell et al. also noted that this was statistically the same for both genders and that age of recovery was extremely varied.

2.7 LENGTH OF TIME STUTTERED AND LENGTH OF TIME RECOVERED GROUP FOLLOWED UP POST RECOVERY

It is important to follow up cases who recover for some time after they have recovered in order to ensure that stuttering is not temporarily in remission. Yairi and Ambrose (2005) reported that the highest rate of recovery was three years after onset. They continued to see their recovered children for an average of 40 months.

Howell et al. (2008a) determined the length of time the recovered participants stuttered. The children who recovered had stuttered for nearly nine years, which is appreciably longer than Yairi and Ambrose's younger cohort. No analysis was made across genders as only two females provided data. All of Howell et al.'s children who recovered were followed up for a minimum of two years up to a maximum of 11 years. There was a big range as the children were offered the option of withdrawing after the follow-up period. The average follow-up time was five years ten months.

2.8 SUMMARY

The feature that stands out most from the work discussed in this chapter is that there is good consistency in the estimates. This was so despite the fact that the studies examined used very different methodologies.

2.9 EXERCISES

1. What are the risk factors for onset of stuttering? Please do not restrict your list to those discussed in the chapter.
2. What are the risk factors that determine the course of stuttering into persistence? Again, please do not restrict your list to those discussed in the chapter.
3. Wingate (2001) argued that recovery rate is overestimated when inappropriate symptoms are used to diagnose stuttering. Outline his argument and describe how it applies to studies on persistence and recovery of stuttering. Do you think his reasoning is correct? Justify your argument.
4. Stuttering is comparatively rare (around 1 in 20 people stutter in childhood). Ideally, one would like to record children before they start to stutter. The abruptness of onset, associated language, and motor characteristics, etc., could then be assessed over the period that stuttering begins. Unfortunately, this is not possible given the low incidence of the disorder. Instead, reliance has to be placed on the parental report. Discuss the drawbacks of parental report and explain how a sample with a high risk of stuttering could be used to examine what happened from before stuttering began to after it starts. What are the drawbacks in using a sample at high risk of stuttering and how might this distort epidemiological findings?

3 Symptomatology

This chapter considers work aimed at establishing what are the appropriate speech–language symptoms that characterize stuttering. The later part of this chapter looks at how symptoms have been grouped into those more typical of stuttering, so that distinguishing children who stutter from typically developing children and differentiation of recovered stutterers from persistent stutterers can be improved.

3.1 INTRODUCTION

There was no comprehensive indication about the entire range of speech symptoms that should be used to characterize stuttering in the two definitions given in Chapter 1 (section 1.2). Consequently, issues like whether certain speech symptoms are exclusive to stuttering or shared with typically developing children and whether the symptoms can be used to distinguish persistent and recovered speakers, could not be addressed using these definitions alone.

Some specific symptoms were mentioned. For instance, both definitions noted that prolongation of sounds is one symptom of stuttering. Many questions about this symptom remain that demonstrate that it is not clear how to use prolongations to decide whether or not a speaker stutters. Prolongations in the speech of people who stutter usually occur on initial consonants (Howell, Wingfield, & Johnson, 1988). A typical example involving a prolongation is "this is my ssssister." However, speakers who do not stutter also elongate certain sounds that are, at least superficially, similar to prolongations, for example, when saying the word "well" in a questioning way. However, the latter tends to occur on the vowels in words. So, when diagnosing stuttering, questions arise about whether there is something different about the prolongations that speakers who stutter produce compared to controls: How long does an "s" need to be to be considered a prolongation; should a sound be considered a stuttered prolongation only when it is in initial position in a word; or, even more restrictively, should a sound be judged prolonged when it is on an initial consonant rather than an initial vowel?

This is a brief (and incomplete) consideration of one type of stuttering symptom and related questions could be raised about all other supposed stuttering symptoms. Evaluation of the literature on persistence and recovery from stuttering is not possible without a clear appreciation of the issues associated with specifying what symptoms have been used to characterize stuttering, what alternative ways there are of characterizing symptoms, and what are the pros and cons for using one selection of symptoms rather than another to indicate stuttering.

This chapter addresses issues such as these. It is organized in three sections. The first section presents a widely used and reasonably comprehensive proposal about what symptoms to consider when making judgments about stuttering (Johnson and Associates', 1959, scheme). In the second section, selected symptoms on this list are examined to assess the case for including each of them to help diagnose and to track changes in stuttering over development. In some cases, this necessitates examining what relevant work there is on the occurrence of the symptoms and the role they play, in typically developing speech (for comparison).

The third section looks at methodological issues associated with persistence and recovery. Four main topics covered include:

1. Is there any overlap between the symptoms shown by fluent speakers and speakers who stutter?
2. Does recovery from stuttering occur?
3. When stuttering persists, does it change in its symptom characteristics over the period of time up to the teenage years?
4. Does stuttering have an abrupt or gradual onset in childhood?

All of these questions rely to some extent on which of several methods are used to identify the symptoms that are more typical of stuttering from lists like Johnson's. The correct set of symptoms may improve separation of children who stutter from typically developing children, help distinguish those speakers who recover from those who persist, highlight changes over development, and characterize onset patterns of stuttering. Consequently, space is given under topic one to considering popular perspectives about how to improve on Johnson's list of symptoms to characterize stuttering. Two approaches about how to use the Johnson list when investigating stuttering are examined: (1) to select symptoms that are more typical of stuttering from the list, and (2) to use all (or almost all) of the list of symptoms in assessment, but distinguish the role the different symptoms play.

3.2 JOHNSON'S CHARACTERISTICS

The classic attempt at specifying the symptoms that characterize stuttering was that of Johnson and Associates (1959). They listed eight symptoms that were associated with stuttering. These include:

1. Incomplete phrases (sometimes called abandonments)
2. Revisions
3. Interjections
4. Whole-word repetitions
5. Phrase repetitions
6. Part-word repetitions
7. Prolongations
8. Broken words

TABLE 3.1
Johnson's Symptoms and Illustrative Examples

1	Incomplete phrases	"that ba…, that car"
2	Revisions	"my unc., my mother
3	Interjections	"ng, ng, ng" or filled pauses such as "erm"
4	Whole word repetitions	"and, and, I went"
5	Phrase repetitions	"in the, in the morning"
6	Part-word repetitions	"p-p-pilchards"
7	Prolongations	"sssssister"
8	Broken words	"ca-tastrophe"

These symptoms are listed in Table 3.1 with an illustrative example of each and are referred to in the remainder of the book.

Though the list of symptoms is widely endorsed as a starting point for many proposals, some authors use other terms for the symptoms and others consider that there are omissions from the list. An example of an alternative term that is used is abandonments instead of incomplete phrases (the term abandonment is used in section 3.3.1). Also, while considering terminology, broken word is probably the least well-defined class because it is sometimes used as a residual category that includes symptoms that do not fit into other categories. Examples of additions that have been made to the symptom list are hard contacts (Bloodstein & Bernstein Ratner, 2007, p. 31) and silent pauses (Wingate, 1988, 2002). More is said about silent pauses when interjections are considered later in this chapter.

Symptoms 3 to 8 occur in the following two short stretches of speech produced by two children who stutter (both male). The first one was spoken by a child aged 5: "One thing er I enjoy is to take my my dog for a walk. Near, near my house there is a canal. Me and my dad set off early in the morning an', and walk along the canal with Tommy, my dog. There's a caff near a bridge where we, where we er sometimes have our, our breakfast." This child shows interjections (after "one thing" and after "where we"), single whole-word repetitions ("my, my"; "near, near"; "an', and"), and a phrase repetition ("where we, where we").

The second child was aged 12: "I don't like sssschool. The other kids tease me about my, about my sssstutter. Lessons are OK except when, when I have to speak in class. Th.there are some teachers who p.p.p.pick on me. They make me sp/ eak in class mmmore than my, my m.mates, er just to embarrass me." This child shows an interjection ("er" before "just to embarrass me"), whole-word repetitions ("when, when"; "my, my"), and a phrase repetition ("about my, about my"), symptoms also seen with the first speaker. Here, in addition, there are part-word repetitions ("th.there," "p.p.p.pick," "m.mates"), prolongations ("sssschool," "ssstutter," "mmmore"), and a break in a word ("sp/eak").

3.3   JOHNSON'S LIST: EXAMINATION OF INDIVIDUAL SYMPTOMS

3.3.1   SYMPTOMS 1 AND 2: ABANDONMENTS AND REVISIONS

Abandonments and revisions appear on Johnson's list. Both of these symptoms have been regarded as signs of linguistic formulation or selection problems, as in the influential work of Levelt (1989) that is discussed in Chapter 10. This work inspired Postma and Kolk's (1993) covert repair hypothesis (CRH) that is briefly discussed in this chapter (section 3.4.1.2.1) and considered in full in Chapter 10.

Though the Levelt and CRH perspectives consider abandonments and revisions as disfluent events in fluent speakers' speech, these symptoms are usually excluded when stuttering is assessed. One of the grounds for omitting them from considerations is that these symptoms do not appear to be allowed in another influential definition of stuttering. The definition in question is that provided by the World Health Organization (1992) in its scheme for the International Classification of Diseases (the specific version referred to here is ICD-10). ICD-10 maintains that speakers who stutter know what they wish to say, but are unable to do so. This appears to be true for all of Johnson's symptoms except for abandonments and revisions. In an abandonment, it is clear that the speaker changes from one message to another. Arguably, the message was changed because the speaker started the utterance, but later abandoned it because he/she did not know what to say. Revisions indicate that, according to some interpretations, something went wrong in linguistic formulation and this was changed. If the ICD-10 definition is accepted, these symptoms would not be indicative of stuttering because the speaker did not know what utterance to say (otherwise he/she would have said the right word). Another argument in support of the position to drop abandonments and revisions as symptoms of stuttering, is that they are often not included in other people's discussions about stuttering. For example, Conture (1990, p. 15) does not mention abandonments in his typology of stuttering symptoms. More specifically (though there are exceptions), most discussions play little or no attention to abandonments and revisions as symptoms that could diagnose childhood stuttering or be implicated in progress to recovery or persistence.

3.3.2   SYMPTOM 3: INTERJECTIONS

All speech is interrupted from time to time. One form is speech-like interjections, such as "erm." In the case of speakers who stutter, this can involve speech and nonspeech vocalizations as well. Also in these speakers, even the speech interjections can be impermissible in the language, such as "ng, ng, ng" (this is a sound not used to start syllables in English). There is a long history of regarding interjections as points where upcoming speech is being planned. Pausing silently would also allow time for planning speech in an ongoing utterance. It has already been commented that Johnson and Associates (1959) omitted silent pauses as a symptom of stuttering. The reason Johnson left pauses out of his list of symptoms was a practical one. He argued that it is difficult to determine whether pauses are part of meaningful speech or not. However, there seem to be increasingly strong grounds for including silent pauses in assessments of the speech of children who stutter and those with typically developing speech. They could be incorporated into the class of interjections (reasons supporting this proposal are discussed below). It should be noted that Wingate (2002, p. 211) makes the case for distinguishing different types of pauses, so presumably he would not have agreed with the proposal to collapse sound and silent pauses into the interjection category.

Though Johnson dismissed silent pauses as indications of fluency problems, there was work going on at the time he was writing on fluent speakers, which emphasized the important role pausing plays in speech control (Goldman-Eisler, 1968; Mahl, 1981). A major concern in this early work was whether interjections and pauses appear at the beginning of clauses. For instance, if pauses and interjections occur in the initial clause position, this would be consistent with the view that planning load is high at these points. When applied to stuttering, long pauses or frequent pausing at these locations might be a sign that speakers who stutter have particular problems planning speech. If they occur at the beginning of clausal units, this may implicate syntactic factors in the etiology of stuttering, though other accounts are possible as detailed next.

In contrast to views that maintain interjections and silent pauses interrupt speech so planning can be completed, these symptoms also have been interpreted as an indication that a speaker has made an error and intends to correct the utterance in what are referred to as speech repairs (Levelt, 1983). Kolk and Postma (1997) have adapted the idea that pauses and interjections indicate points of interruption in their examination of stuttered speech that is considered briefly later in this chapter.

Despite the potential importance of pauses and interjections in regulating speech, they have received limited attention in the literature on differentiating people who stutter from controls and less still on distinguishing speakers likely to persist from those who recover. In an early study, Robbins (1935) compared silent pauses in fluent speakers and speakers who stutter and found pauses were about 3.6 times longer in speakers with severe stuttering. Few and Lingwall (1972), Love and Jeffress (1971), Watson and Love (1965), and Zerbin (1973) all reported a high incidence on brief silent pauses (0.1–0.5 sec) in the fluent speech of speakers who stutter indicating that they could be a useful sign for diagnosis of stuttering. As already mentioned, Wingate (2002, p. 312) argued for distinguishing four types of filled pause and, in empirical work, showed that these distinguish the speech of stutterers and normal speakers (Wingate, 1984, 1988). Prosek, Walden, Montgomery, and Schwartz (1979) found reading rate and frequency of pauses related better to judgments of severity than other measures including frequency of stuttering.

At present, there is no work that examines whether pauses occur at prosodic boundaries, which would potentially challenge the notion that stuttering development is inherently linked to syntax learning in childhood (Bernstein Ratner & Wijnen, 2007, discussed in Chapter 10), or on the relation of pausing to utterance planning variables and to the errors made in speech. However, as indicated above, there is evidence that silent pauses distinguish speakers who stutter from controls and these pauses play an important role in various theoretical accounts. These seem to be sufficient grounds for including them as symptoms in their own right or, as an interim solution, including them with interjections in assessment of persistence and recovery in future studies.

3.3.3   SYMPTOMS 4 AND 5: WHOLE-WORD AND PHRASE REPETITIONS

Several authors who have worked with fluent speakers have noted that typically developing children frequently repeat whole words and have proposed that this action serves the role of delaying the time at which the following word is produced (Blackmer & Mitton, 1991; Clark & Clark, 1977; MacWhinney & Osser, 1977; Rispoli, 2003; Rispoli & Hadley, 2001). The role of word repetition in childhood has been interpreted in different ways by these authors. For instance, Clark and Clark (1977) regarded it as reflecting a problem in lexical selection, whereas Rispoli (2003) considered that it reflects maturation of the syntactic system. Each of these views has relevance for stuttering insofar as such processing may pose particular problems for children who stutter.

It also has been found that children who stutter repeat whole words at a high rate (Bloodstein & Grossman, 1981; Kadi-Hanifi & Howell, 1992). This is discussed in full in Chapter 7, section 7.3.3. While high rates of whole-word repetition in itself may not be a symptom sensitive to differentiating the children who stutter from typically developing children, there have been reports that this is an important indication of whether stuttering will persist or recover (Howell, 2007a; Howell, Bailey, & Kothari, 2010). In particular, children who continue to show high rates of whole-word repetition show a reduction in part-word repetitions, prolongations, and blocks and recover (Howell, 2007a; Howell et al., 2010). In contrast, children who reduce their rate of whole-word repetitions show an increase in part-word repetitions, prolongations, and blocks and persist (Howell et al., 2010).

Other authors have proposed that whole-word repetitions have a role in assessing stuttering. For instance, monosyllabic whole-word repetitions appear as stuttering symptoms in the clinical schemes that Conture (1990) and Ambrose and Yairi use in various publications (Paden, Yairi, & Ambrose, 1999; Watkins, Yairi, & Ambrose, 1999; Yairi & Ambrose, 1999). Also Throneburg, Yairi, and Paden (1994) reported that monosyllabic whole-word repetitions of young speakers who stutter differ in internal segment duration to those of children who did not stutter, though the authors did not give details of what the timing differences were. Nevertheless, the findings would support the view that whole-word repetitions distinguish speakers who stutter from controls and, as such, should be included as symptoms of stuttering. The finding of high rates of whole-word repetition on function words in children who stutter (Bloodstein & Grossman, 1981; Kadi-Hanifi & Howell, 1992) contrasts with what has been found in adults who show more stuttering on content words (Brown, 1945;

Howell, Au-Yeung, & Sackin, 1999). One possibility is that such word repetition could be a sign of whether stuttering will develop into its persistent or recovered forms.

The main protagonist of the view that whole-word repetitions should not be considered symptoms of stuttering was Wingate (1988, 2002). Other authors who do not include whole-word repetitions include Riley (1994), discussed in Chapter 1; Kloth, Kraimaat, Janssen, and Brutten (1999), discussed in Chapter 2: Wall, Starkweather, and Harris (1981); Bernstein Ratner and Sih (1987), both of which are discussed in Chapter 10; and Gaines, Runyan, and Meyers (1991); de Joy and Gregory (1985); and Jayaram (1981). Wingate (2002, p. 147) gave three reasons why monosyllabic word repetitions in particular (like those Bloodstein and Grossman examined) should not be considered stuttering symptoms:

1. They occur in the speech of all speakers.
2. They happen naturally in the speech of fluent speakers, so they are not barriers to producing speech fluently.
3. These symptoms occur in the speech of speakers who stutter and there is no compelling evidence that they differ in any way from the same symptoms produced by fluent speakers.

Curiously, Wingate's own standard definition discussed in Chapter 1 appears to include these symptoms under element (b) (repetitions ... of ... words of one syllable). As far as I am aware, he never commented on why he changed his opinion from regarding them as symptoms of stuttering to arguing that they are not.

Unlike the symptoms discussed so far, symptoms 6, 7, and 8, though not exclusive to stuttering, are generally agreed to be more characteristic of stuttering. Next, some general methodological issues raised by debates about these symptoms are considered.

3.4 METHODOLOGICAL ISSUES

Assumptions are made when dealing with any topic scientifically, including stuttering. The assumptions made by one author are often not shared by others in the field. So, an author needs to defend his or her assumptions against the critics. One way this is done is to find indefensible assumptions or methodological faults in the work of the critics. The fierce debates about individual symptoms and other related issues that rage in the field of stuttering research have not been based on empirical work (the arguments usually rely on precedents or informal arguments like those of Wingate, 2002, p.147). The purpose in this section is to describe the alternative positions and evaluate the arguments that have been presented in favor of alternative schemes.

The perspective of the late Marcel Wingate is used as the starting point. He had an internally coherent point of view about stuttering that contrasted with the views of other authorities (but, as seen, not all). His work is selected as the starting point in this section because he took a position on most of the main areas pertinent to recovery from stuttering, and these challenge many conventional perspectives. Consequently, it will serve as a vehicle by which these topics can be raised and considered from opposing points of view: his and the opposing views of other authors.

Wingate (2002) made four points that are relevant here. (I may not be doing him justice as his argument is not laid out as below and I would recommend reading his 1988 and 2002 texts in addition to what is mentioned here.)

1. He maintained that stuttering is inherently different to typically developing speech. Stuttered speech and typically developing speech are categorically distinct.
2. Recovery from stuttering does not occur.
3. Stuttering does not develop. A speaker has it in its full-blown form and, from there on, it does not change. So, children who persist should show the same characteristics at the start as at the end of a developmental period.
4. The onset of stuttering is gradual in terms of frequency of different symptom types.

These are at odds with some of the work reported so far. For instance, Johnson's list of symptoms (as Johnson himself mentioned) shows a lot of overlap with fluent speech, so, if Johnson is right, stuttering cannot be categorically distinct. Also, there are many reports that children recover from stuttering in childhood that seem to contradict Wingate's view that recovery cannot happen. There also seem to be distinct developmental trends shown by children who stutter. (Some recover as was just mentioned and there are the changes in which symptoms children who recover use that contrast with those that children who persist show). Wingate was aware of these issues that challenged each of his views and, characteristically, he buttressed arguments in defense of his assumptions. His defenses for each of the above points (using corresponding numbering) were:

1. Stuttering may look like it is on a continuum with fluent speech (as assumed by people who support the *continuity hypothesis,* but it is not. The continuity hypothesis is associated most often with Wendell Johnson and Oliver Bloodstein (the latter continued to hold this position). Stuttering appears to be continuous with fluent speech because some authors include the wrong symptoms when assessing stuttering. If authors use the wrong symptoms, some typically developing children will be classified as stuttering and some stuttering children will be classified as fluent. The inherent fuzziness in making classifications about speakers using the wrong symptoms leads to an overlap between fluency groups, and this is why stutterers appear to be on a continuum with fluent speakers.

2. Because incorrect methods for diagnosing stuttering are used, some children will be classified as stuttering when they, in fact, do not do so. When their symptoms disappear, this looks like recovery, but it is not. Another factor is that, while Wingate did not allow recovery to occur in cases who definitely were stuttering, he did permit remission of symptoms. Remission in this case means the state of absence of stuttering with the possibility that it will return. If remission occurs, fluency can ebb and flow, thus an individual has more of a problem at one time than another. Misclassification and remission can lead to apparent (not real) recovery.

3. Since studies have not used the correct set of symptoms to characterize stuttering, samples of speakers thought to persist will include "recovered" cases (i.e., speakers who will cease showing symptoms and become fluent). These will drop out of samples of speakers who stutter as age increases leaving the true stutterers. It is possible to maintain that the true stutterers do not change their behavior. The apparent changes over development are due to the recovered cases, who are actually fluent speakers, having distinct speech patterns from the true stutterers. This makes a developmental trend appear to happen as the fluent speakers drop out from samples of stutterers as they get older. Therefore, it has not been satisfactorily demonstrated that stuttering develops (to do this, it would be necessary to show stuttering development specifically in children who persist).

4. Wingate (2002, p. 71) states that stuttering onset is almost always gradual (though he does not give any supporting evidence). There is some parental report evidence that onset is usually abrupt (Reilly et al., 2009, discussed in Chapter 13).

All of these points require accepting Wingate's selection of symptoms from Johnson's list. In the next section, alternative selection schemes are described and evaluated. Then contrasting opinions on each of the above four points that employ the alternative proposals are discussed. The continuity between stuttering and fluent speech, whether over lax criteria, has been used for diagnosing stuttering allowing apparent recovery to occur, whether stuttering develops in cases who persist, and whether stuttering onset is gradual or abrupt.

3.4.1 Proposals for Improving Performance of the Symptom Schemes

Several authors consider that Johnson's list includes some symptoms that do not distinguish children who stutter from typically developing children (and presumably the list of symptoms would not be useful for distinguishing persistent from recovered speakers, either). Two approaches have been taken to improve this situation.

3.4.1.1 Approach One: Select Those Symptoms That Are Most Typical of Stuttering From a Comprehensive List

The first approach identifies those events that are more and those that are less typical of stuttering, and only uses those that are typical as suitable to characterize stuttering. The view is that if the symptom list is fine tuned, speakers who stutter could be better distinguished from those who are fluent (i.e., a diagnostic issue) and, in some cases, to examine the process of recovery (Yairi & Ambrose, 2005).

Practically speaking, authors identify a selection of symptoms from Johnson's (1959) list to drop (i.e., that are not typical of stuttering). Different authors exclude different symptoms. Perhaps not surprisingly, there has been much debate about what is the right set of symptoms to characterize stuttering, but few investigations have supplied empirical evidence as to whether one scheme is preferred over another.

3.4.1.1.1 Conture's Within-Word Category

Conture (1990, p. 15), based on his clinical experience, proposed that stuttering that occur within words is a sign that stuttering is likely to persist and, as such, is more characteristic of stuttering than stuttering that occurs across words (what he called "between-word disfluencies"). Sound/syllable repetitions, sound prolongations, broken words, and monosyllabic whole-word repetitions were placed into the within-word category. The first three are equivalent to Johnson's characteristics 6, 7, and 8 and monosyllabic whole-word repetitions are a subset of his characteristic 4. The between-word category has multisyllabic whole-word repetitions (part of Johnson's characteristic 4), phrase repetitions (characteristic 5), interjections (characteristic 3), and revisions (characteristic 2).

There are three features to note about Conture's (1990) proposal:

1. Though whole-word repetitions of any type do not seem, from a definitional point of view, to be within-word disfluencies, he assigned them to this class. He commented that monosyllabic whole-word repetitions can sometimes be judged stuttered and at other times be judged nonstuttered. Nevertheless, he treated these events as "within-word or stuttered disfluencies." He also commented that "this judgment [whether monosyllabic whole-word repetitions be considered stuttered or not] seems to be dependent on associated physical tension, rate of repetition, and other, as yet unknown, factors."
2. It is not apparent why multisyllabic whole-word repetitions, unlike their monosyllabic counterparts, are treated as between-word, rather than within-word, disfluencies.
3. As discussed when individual symptoms were considered, he does not mention abandonments and pauses (though, as discussed earlier, these could be included under interjections).

Conture's scheme has been used in studies to diagnose cases, though there has been no validation of it in terms of whether it improves diagnosis relative to other schemes or whether it distinguishes persistent and recovered cases. Within-word disfluencies have been used (either alone or in conjunction with ancillary measures) to specify whether children should be considered as stuttering by Conture and Kelly (1991), Curlee (1993), Wolk, Edwards, and Conture (1993), Zebrowski (1991), Zebrowski (1994), and Zebrowski, Conture, and Cudahy (1985).

In terms of development of stuttering, the idea that a change to within-word disfluencies is a characteristic that acts as a danger sign for persistence has been discussed by Conture (1982, 1990). He suggested that disfluencies change from between-word type to within-word type if children persist in the disorder.

Conture's proposal was not evidence-based and the emphasis was on monitoring individual cases, not for establishing general developmental trends shown by speakers who go on to persist or recover from stuttering. Cordes and Ingham (1995) argued against the characterization Conture offered because both within and between-word disfluencies occur in fluent and stuttered speech.

3.4.1.1.2 *Yairi and Ambrose's Stuttering-Like Disfluencies (SLD) Category*

Yairi and Ambrose proposed the category of stuttering-like disfluencies (SLD), mentioned in Chapter 1, to improve diagnosis and in their examination of persistence and recovery of stuttering (see Yairi and Ambrose, 2005, p. 38, for a recent discussion). SLD includes part-word repetitions (equivalent to Conture's sound/syllable repetitions), monosyllabic word repetitions, and disrhythmic phonation. Disrhythmic phonation includes sound prolongations and blocks (audible or inaudible sound prolongation within words) (p. 97). They grouped these events together into the class of events most typical of stuttering that they termed SLD. A fact to note is the similarity between Conture's and Yairi and Ambrose's schemes for those symptoms considered most typical of stuttering.

Yairi and Ambrose group incomplete phrases, revisions, interjections, and multisyllabic word and phrase repetitions into the other disfluency (OD) category, which are equivalent to Johnson's characteristics 1, 2, 3, 4 (the multisyllabic whole-words), and 5, respectively.

Yairi and Ambrose's book includes data, but its orientation is clinical as indicated by the subtitle: By Clinicians, For Clinicians. It seeks to describe differences between children who persist and who recover and how speech events change over development. For the SLD/OD scheme, a frequency of 3% SLD out of all words has been used to differentiate young children who stutter from normally fluent speaking peers for English (Yairi & Ambrose, 2005, p. 29) and Dutch (Boey, Wuyts, Van de Heyning, de Bodt, & Heylen, 2007). What threshold is used will depend on how assessments were used. Thus, as discussed in Chapter 1, digital methods are more sensitive than those involving listening in real time; therefore, a higher percentage SLD threshold would be appropriate when making the assessments with the more sensitive procedure.

In their more recent work, Yairi and Ambrose use the *weighted* SLD classification, which reflects three dimensions of disfluency: frequency, type, and extent. It is calculated "by adding together the frequency of part-word and single-syllable word repetitions per 100 syllables and multiplying that sum by mean number of repetition units, then adding twice the frequency of disrhythmic phonation (blocks and prolongations) per 100 syllables" (pp. 122–123). The reason for the introduction of the weighted SLD was to give more prominence to disrhythmic phonation that, according to the authors, distinguishes more clearly mild stuttering from normal disfluency. The weighted SLD is a relatively recent introduction to the area of stuttering research. It is noteworthy that it uses single syllable whole-word repetitions that Wingate rejects as symptoms of stuttering, but the weighting reduces the importance of them.

3.4.1.1.3 Wingate Scheme

Wingate's view was that people who stutter differ from people who do not stutter in terms of supra classes of symptoms that he refers to as clonic and tonic. Tonic is a perseverative marker of stuttering associated with prolongations and blocks. Clonic is an iterative marker of stuttering associated with elemental repetitions. The elemental repetitions include repetitions of phones and parts of syllables, but not complete words. As the sample from the 5-year-old boy used to illustrate stuttering symptoms at the start of this chapter showed a lot of whole-word repetitions, but few clonic or tonic symptoms, Wingate would have considered that the child did not stutter, based on the sample of speech presented.

The exclusion of whole-word repetitions as a marker of stuttering put Wingate on a collision course with Conture and Yairi and Ambrose, who included them as symptoms of stuttering in their schemes (Wingate, 2001, 2002, pp. 150–151). An additional feature is that Wingate wanted silent pauses to be included as symptoms of stuttering. Studies have used Conture and Yairi and Ambrose schemes, but have not addressed empirically whether or not Wingate was right to exclude whole-word repetitions. The prediction would be that if Wingate was right, diagnosis of stuttering would be better if whole-word repetitions are excluded when attempting to characterize a speaker as a stutterer.

3.4.1.2 Approach Two: Grouping Schemes That Use a Wider Range of Events Than the Grouping Schemes That Discard Less Typical Stuttering Events

The two proposals in this section are based on theories that will be considered fully in Chapter 10 and Chapter 12, respectively. The proposals that characterize this approach consider that a wide range of events from Johnson's list reflect the processes behind stuttering. The symptoms used in these schemes are the major topics discussed below.

The first proposal is Postma and Kolk's (1993) covert repair hypothesis (CRH). CRH considers that each of the symptoms on Johnson's list arises because a speech error was made and each particular symptom reflects: (1) a form of error in the linguistic system or (2) the process by which the speaker attempts to repair that error. The CRH makes a proposal about how stuttering arises, but it does not address how stuttering develops.

The second proposal, called EXPLAN (Howell, 2004a; 2010), considers that language processing operates independent of speech motor organization. Stuttering symptoms occur when the linguistic system does not provide its output to the motor system in time so that transition to the next word can take place. Consequently, the next speech motor action cannot be issued continuously and smoothly. According to this proposal, the different symptoms Johnson described represent ways of dealing with this problem when it occurs. This proposal includes a mechanism explaining how stuttering develops and the alternative pathways it can take (into persistence or recovery). A common feature of these two proposals is that they are motivated by theoretical stances.

3.4.1.2.1 Covert Repair Hypothesis

The CRH is discussed briefly here and sufficient details are given for understanding how this hypothesis views stuttering symptoms. As mentioned previously, full consideration is given in Chapter 10. An example of speech that contains a repair is: "turn left, turn right at the end of the street" ("right" was in error and was changed for "left"). Related constructions like: "turn, turn right at the end of the street," may have contained the same error. In cases such as the latter, CRH imagines that the speaker detected the error internally (i.e., before speech was output) and, subsequently, interrupted and then restarted the speech attempt. The latter type of utterance is called a covert repair because there is no overt sign of an error (Levelt, 1983; Levelt, 1989; Roelofs, 2004). Kolk and Postma (1997) proposed that covert repairs led to hesitation and repetition of sounds, as in the last repair example, that are commonly seen in stuttered speech. Consequently, stuttering was hypothesized to be due to linguistic errors that led to covert repair processes that were manifested as stuttering symptoms. The important point for considerations about symptomatology is that many types of stuttering symptoms can be explained in the CRH framework. Table 3.2 gives the putative type of internal linguistic error that occurred, the ensuing covert repair strategy, and resulting type of symptom. CRH provides all types of stutters on Johnson's list an interpretation (none are excluded). Kolk and Postma's view has not addressed whether and, if so, how stuttering develops, but it has been used in developmental work by Conture and his students (see Chapter 10).

3.4.1.2.2 EXPLAN Scheme

As for CRH, only brief details are given of the EXPLAN theory (full discussion appears in Chapter 12). Earlier it was mentioned that young speakers repeat words to delay attempts at subsequent words so they have more time to prepare the word for production (Blackmer & Mitton, 1991; Clark & Clark, 1977; MacWhinney & Osser, 1977; Rispoli, 2003; Rispoli & Hadley, 2001). Howell's EXPLAN account maintains that word and phrase repetitions, interjections, and silent pauses on or around function words (conjunctions, pronouns, etc.; see Chapter 7) prior to a content word (nouns, verbs, etc.; Chapter 7) are ways of doing this and these are

TABLE 3.2

Specification of Disfluency Types and Their Origins According to the Covert Repair Hypothesis

Internal Error Source	Covert Repair Strategy	Resulting Symptom Type
	Restart Strategies	
Semantic/syntactic	Restart the phrase	Phrase repetition formulation
Lexical retrieval	Restart the previous word	Word repetition
Phonemic encoding error	Restart syllable from beginning	Block detected *before* word execution has begun
Phonemic encoding error	Restart syllable from beginning	Prolongation or detected after initial sound (sub) syllabic repetition has been produced
	Postponement Strategies	
Semantic syntactic or lexical formulation	Hold execution and reformulation	Unfilled pause (>200 ms)
Phonemic encoding error detected after initial sounds have been produced	Prolong current sound until correct continuation sequence retrieved	Prolong noninitial sounds in target syllable (typically vowel prolongation)
	or	
	Hold execution of next sound	Block in midsyllable (broken word)

Adapted from "The Covert Repair Hypothesis: Prearticulatory Repair Processes in Normal and Stuttering Dysfluencies," by A. Postma and H. Kolk, 1993, *Journal of Speech and Hearing Research*, *36*, pp. 472–487. With permission.

called *stallings*. It also proposes that symptoms involving parts of words (part-word repetitions, prolongations, and word breaks) reflect premature attempts at words before the speaker is completely ready (not as a result of error) and these are called *advancings*. Advancings tend to occur on content words that, statistically speaking, are more complex than function words. EXPLAN contrasts with CRH insofar as stuttering originates in timing problems (not errors), it gives different symptoms different roles (stalling or advancing), and the use of these sets of symptoms change dynamically over development in different ways for persistent and recovered speakers. Once persistent stuttering sets in on content words, it is hard to shift.

3.5 SUMMARY

This chapter has considered different ways of characterizing stuttering for diagnosis and for tracking the development of children who persist or recover. The original Johnson scheme is widely considered to include too many stuttering symptoms, some of which are not specific characteristics of stuttering. Each disfluency symptom on Johnson's list was considered with regards to the likelihood that they might be associated with stuttering (using information, *inter alia,* from fluent speakers). Before alternative proposals about how to improve on Johnson's scheme were considered, conceptual issues germane to this issue were considered. Public scrutiny of cases and symptoms would be ideal in the light of Kully and Boberg's (1988) report of differences between clinics in making stuttering judgments. Although there are ethical issues associated with this, they are not insuperable.

In Chapter 7, the way the different symptom schemes have been linked to linguistic structures and disputes about this linking are discussed. If people disagree about what events are appropriate for specifying stuttering, they will interpret the way these are linked to language structures in different ways as well. The premises of the discussion (how the differences between symptom–schemes fuel the debate about different views concerning the influence of language structure on stuttering) have not always been explicitly recognized in the literature to date.

3.6 EXERCISES

1. Should whole-word repetitions be considered symptoms of stuttering?
2. Is there any overlap between the symptoms shown by fluent speakers and speakers who stutter?
3. Does recovery from stuttering occur?
4. When stuttering persists, do symptoms change over the period of time up to the teenage years?
5. Does stuttering have an abrupt or gradual onset in childhood?
6. Read Wingate (1988) and Wingate (2002) as recommended in the text.

Section II

Factors Related to Developmental Stuttering Based on Experimental Studies

4 Genetic Factors and Their Impact on Onset and Recovery of Stuttering

Twin studies consistently show around a 70/30 split between heritable and environmental influences, and Dworzynski, Remington, Rijksdijk, Howell, and Plomin (2007) reported that these did not differ across persistent/recovered cases. Ambrose and coworkers (1993, 1997) have argued that there is a single major gene locus for stuttering at onset and that polygenic influences emerge during the later course of the disorder. Kidd and his group (Kidd, Kidd, & Records, 1978) who had also thought that there was a single major locus in their initial work, abandoned this notion subsequently and were firmly of the opinion that stuttering is polygenic and involves a non-Mendelian, sex-modified mode of transmission. Studies with genetic markers, mainly on adults who have persisted in their stuttering, have shown that a variety of different genes are involved, and a study by Suresh et al. (2006) has reported different genes are involved for persistent and recovered speakers.

4.1 INTRODUCTION

Some basic background to three methods that have been employed with people who stutter (twin studies, family history, and molecular genetics) is presented in separate sections below. Recent work using these methods with people who stutter follow the respective background material. It has been established for a long time that stuttering runs in families, which may suggest there is a genetic basis for the disorder (Bryngelson & Rutherford, 1937). Past work has shown that between 23 and 68% of stutterers have family members who stutter compared with 1.3 to 18.1% of control families (Conture, 2001). Twin studies have shown that about 70% chance of stuttering is heritable. Heritability is the proportion of phenotypic variation in a population that is attributable to genetic variation among individuals. Phenotypic variation among individuals may be due to genetic and/or environmental factors. (See section 4.4 for a definition of genotype and phenotype and further discussion.) Heritability analyses estimate the relative contributions of differences in genetic and non-genetic factors to the total phenotypic variance in a population. Despite this observation, the link between family history and genetic factors in stuttering has been questioned in the past. For example, it was pointed out that political beliefs also run in families, but they are not hereditary. Inheritance patterns of stuttering in families were investigated in early work.

Recent work, however, has analyzed biological samples in order to locate particular genes involved in stuttering. The findings have shifted the viewpoint heavily in favor of the position that genetics play a crucial role in the onset and, possibly, the course of stuttering although there is no consensus at present about what genes are involved.

4.2   HERITABILITY OF STUTTERING IN TWIN STUDIES

The logical first step toward identifying genetic factors in stuttering is to ascertain the extent to which it is heritable. Early work, mentioned in the introduction (section 4.1), did this by examining the pedigrees of people who stutter with respect to whether other members stuttered (Bryngelson & Rutherford, 1937). One problem with this method is that it relies on respondents' memory about family members that they may not know well because of mobility in contemporary society. A second is that, as discussed below in section 4.5.3.3 and more fully in Chapter 13, the same caregivers report fewer family members who stuttered before their child started to stutter than after (Reilly et al., 2009). Twin modeling techniques do not suffer from these problems and have been used to determine the extent to which stuttering is heritable. This section provides a basic introduction to twin modeling techniques (see Rijsdijk & Sham, 2002, for further details) and to review the handful of recent studies that have estimated environmental influences in people who stutter.

A comparison is made between fraternal (dizygotic) and identical (monozygotic) twin pairs and whether one, both, or neither member stutters. These different types of twins provide vital information about heritability of characteristics. Identical, or monozygotic (MZ), twins result from a single ovum and, therefore, have the same genetic material, whereas fraternal or dizygotic (DZ) twins have separate ova and share, on average, 50% of their genes as would two siblings born at different times. DZ twins (and also MZ twins) have similar shared environments, particularly in early life.

Statistics that reflect degrees of overlap in characteristics shown by MZ and DZ twins is an important source of information about heritable and environmental influences. The three main ones encountered are concordance, covariance, and correlation. Concordance, as used in genetics, usually means the presence of the same characteristic (e.g., stutters) in both members of a pair of twins. Twins are concordant when both have or both lack a given characteristic. Technically, concordance is defined as the probability that a pair of individuals will both have a certain characteristic, given that one of the pair has the characteristic. Covariance is a measure of how much two variables change together (variance is a special case of covariance where the two variables are identical). For example, height and weight covary to a degree. Correlation in the area of genetics refers to the proportion of variance that two characteristics share due to genetic causes (hypothetical examples of variables that correlate to different degrees are discussed in section 4.2.1). The genetic correlation indicates how much of the genetic influence on two characteristics is common to both: if it is above zero, this suggests that the two characteristics are influenced by common genes.

4.2.1   THE LOGIC OF THE TWIN METHOD

The twin method compares the similarity of family members who share genes and environment to different extents. If pairs of individuals who share their environment resemble one another more than those who do not, this suggests an influence of shared environment. If pairs of individuals who share more of their genes are more similar to each other than pairs of individuals who share fewer of their genes, this suggests there is a genetic influence on those behaviors. Estimating environmental or genetic influences does not say anything about particular individuals, but it indicates the extent to which these influences apply to a sample. So, if a study was performed on anxiety in twins, the results would not tell a person the extent to which his or her genes/environment affect levels of anxiety; however, they do indicate the extent to which genes/environmental influences account for individual differences in anxiety scores.

The starting point in twin studies is to establish the correlation between pairs of scores for different types of twins (DZ separately from MZ) on the characteristics of interest. The three panels in Figure 4.1 show scatter plots for MZ twin pairs (twin 1 on the horizontal axis and twin 2 on the vertical axis) for three different characteristics that correlate to different degrees in the twins. Thus, each dot represents scores from a pair of twins. The correlations between twin 1 and twin 2 going left to right are 0.9, 0.5, and 0. The characteristics might be, respectively, height, which would be expected to correlate well; anxiety, which would correlate less well; and performance on games of chance that should not correlate at all. The variance of the twin pair scores is least when the scores correlate well and highest when the scores do not correlate.

The variance usually can be split into three parts using methods such as that described in the next section:

1. Additive genetics (A). These are the individual differences caused by genetic factors whose influences add up. This contrasts with nonadditive genetic variance in which the genetic factors interact (polygenic influences).

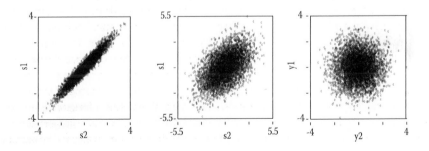

FIGURE 4.1   Shown are scatter plots for three characteristics that correlate 0.9, 0.5, and 0.

2. Common (shared) environment (C). This represents environmental factors responsible for the resemblance between family members (it is assumed that this is the same for the members of both DZ and MZ twin pairs).
3. Environment specific to each twin (nonshared environment, E, which also includes measurement error). E represents environmental influences that contribute to differences between family members.

4.2.2 STRUCTURAL EQUATION MODELS FOR ESTIMATING A, C, AND E

The conventional method for estimating A, C, and E involves structural equation modeling (SEM). SEM is a general technique as indicated by its use in CNS (central nervous system) studies (Chapter 5), in studies on affect (Chapter 9), and for risk modeling (Chapter 13). The basic background for understanding SEM modeling of twin data is described below, but SEM modeling is more complicated than described here. (See Levine, Petrides, Davis, Jackson, and Howell, 2005, for a next step toward an elementary introduction to the topic that uses illustrations from stuttering.)

Differences in genetic relatedness can be used to make predictions about the genetic and environmental factors that lie behind stuttering. Theoretical expectations for correlations of MZ and DZ twins for A, C, and E components are shown in Table 4.1. For A, MZ twins share all genetic material, so the correlation between their scores should be 1. DZ twins share 50% of their genetic material, so the correlations between their scores for A should be 0.5. Both MZ and DZ are exposed to the same common environment (C), so, in both cases, correlations should be 1. Unique environment, E, as its name implies, represents the component that is not shared between twins (either MZ or DZ), so the correlation is expected to be 0.

Figure 4.2 shows a simple path diagram that uses the expected correlations in Table 4.1 to construct an A, C, E model. This then can be used to estimate the contribution of the different components using a SEM. Path diagrams, like the one in Figure 4.2, are pictorial representations of an underlying system of mathematical

TABLE 4.1

Expected Correlations for A, C, and E (Labeled in the Row on the Left) for MZ (First Column) and DZ (Second Column) Twins

Component	Correlation	
	MZ	DZ
A	1	0.50
C	1	1
E	0	0

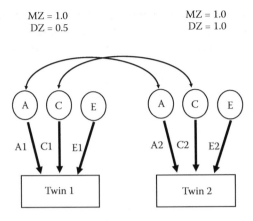

FIGURE 4.2   Path diagram used for modeling A, C, E effects using twin data. (See text for a detailed description of the structure of the model.)

equations. Observed indicators (i.e., the characteristic being studied) are designated by a box. Observations about the first member of each of the pairs of twins are shown by the boxes on the left and observations about the corresponding second member of each of the pairs of twins are shown by the boxes on the right of Figure 4.2. Three circles appear above each box (labeled A, C, and E). The circles indicate that these are latent variables, which means they are not directly observable. Their values are implied by the covariances among the observed indicators and can be obtained after the model has been fitted to obtain A (additive genetics), C (common environment), and E (unique environment). When fitting models, it is not just important to get values for these variables, or parameters, but also to know how well the model fits. The parameter estimates are only sensible if the fit of the model to the data is good.

The latent variables in Figure 4.2 are connected by two curved lines with arrows at each end at the top of the diagram: (1) for A of twin 1 with A of twin 2 and (2) for C of twin 1 with C of twin 2. The arrowheads at both ends indicate that these are nondirectional. The expected correlation structure for both MZ and DZ twin pairs from Table 4.1 for the nondirectional relationship between (1) the As and (2) the Cs are indicated at the left and right, respectively. No relationship is indicated between the Es (as mentioned earlier, unique means not shared, thus correlations would be expected to be zero). These are theoretical expectations and they can be set before model fit and are not adjusted during model fitting. Consequently, they are referred to as fixed parameters. The rest of the parameters are adjusted to fit the model to the data (free parameters) during model fitting.

A second set of connections links the latent variable with the observations. These are the lines from each of the A, C, and E circles with arrows that point to the boxes indicating observations either to twin 1 or to twin 2. Each line signifies that the latent variables directly influence observations on each member of a twin pair. Overall, the structure of the model represents the strength of A, C, and E that then directly influences members of MZ and DZ twin pairs to different extents. Related methods can be used with opposite sex DZ twin pairs, which indicate quantitative and qualitative sex differences in the data, or with different age groups as patterns of heritability estimates can change with age (e.g., IQ becomes more heritable with age).

4.2.2.1   Estimation

Now the model has been specified, estimates of the free parameters can be obtained from the data. To estimate the model based on the data, SEM programs use iterative algorithms that give the best parameter values. This process starts with initial estimates, which are sequentially adjusted until model fit cannot be improved beyond this point.

4.2.2.2   Model Fit

The fit between the data and the proposed model can be reported once the estimation process has been completed. Parameter estimation is done by comparing the actual covariance matrix representing the relationships between variables and the estimated covariance matrices of the best fitting model. Several indices have been developed to evaluate the *goodness of fit* of a model. The most widely reported fit index is the $\chi 2$ statistic. A model that fits the data well will have a close fit between the actual and obtained matrices and the difference will not be significant. Conversely, a model that does not fit the data well will show a significant difference between the actual and obtained matrices (a significant $\chi 2$ value indicates a poor fit of the model to the data). The other main consideration when fitting a model is to select the most parsimonious model, which is one that has the best fit (as before), but, additionally, has fewest free parameters.

4.2.3   Empirical Reports About Heritability of Stuttering Based on Twin Studies

Two early studies used modeling techniques, similar to the A, C, E version discussed above, on adult twin pairs (Andrews, Morris-Yates, Howie, & Martin, 1991; Felsenfeld et al., 2000). At least one member of the pair was affected by stuttering. The two studies produced similar results, both reporting higher concordances for stuttering of MZ as compared to DZ twin pairs.

Andrews et al.'s (1991) investigation was on 135 twin pairs with at least one who stuttered. It found that 20% of the MZ group and 3% of the DZ group were concordant for stuttering (both stuttered). Andrews et al. fitted the following models: (1) only shared environment, (2) additive genetic effects, (3) additive genetic effects with shared environmental effects (AC), and (4) additive genetic effects with unique environmental effects AE. They did not investigate a model with A, C, and E. Models 1 and 3 were rejected based on poor model fit, but 2 and 4 fitted the data well. Model 4 estimated that about 30% of chance of stuttering was due to unique environment and 70% due to additive genetic effects.

Felsenfeld et al. (2000) confirmed Andrews et al.'s estimates of the relative importance of environmental and additive genetic effects. A large population-based twin sample from the Australian Twin Registry (1,567 pairs and 634 singles aged 17–29 years) was screened to identify twin pairs in which one or both members reported themselves to be affected by stuttering. Telephone interview-based diagnoses were obtained for 457 of the self-reported affected single cases, twin pairs, and controls to determine whether the self-report was correct. They reported that 70% of the variance in chance of stuttering was attributable to additive genetic effects, with the remainder due to nonshared environmental effects. Felsenfeld et al. reached virtually the same conclusion as Andrews et al. (1991) using more reliable data (researchers phoned the people involved).

As mentioned, recent work has moved on from solely producing overall heritability estimates and now considers subgroups, such as gender and age (Dworzynski, Remington, Rijksdjik, Howell, & Plomin, 2007; Ooki, 2005). Ooki, as mentioned in Chapter 2, was a study on Japanese twins aged between 3 and 15 years (average age of 11.5 years). Information was obtained by questionnaires. It was reported that heritability was 80% for boys and 85% for girls in this age group.

Dworzynski et al. (2007) assessed the contribution of genetic factors in the persistence of, and early recovery from, stuttering using data from the Twins Early Development Study. As mentioned in Chapter 2, this is a longitudinal study of all the twins born in the United Kingdom between 1994 and 1996 (Trouton, Spinath, & Plomin, 2002). The parental reports regarding stuttering were collected at ages 2, 3, 4, and 7 years, and were used to classify speakers into recovered and persistent groups as described in Chapter 2. Of 12,892 children with ratings at least at two ages, 950 children had recovered and 135 persisted in their stutter. Logistic regressions showed that the rating at age 2 was not predictive of later stuttering. This may reflect the problems in diagnosing stuttering in very young childhood, which was discussed in Chapter 1 of this book (Reilly et al., 2009; Yairi & Ambrose, 2005). Ratings at ages 3 and 4 were predictive of later stuttering. Concordance rates were consistently higher for MZ than for DZ twin pairs (with the exception of girls at age 3).

The study used different analysis methods than those described above, although the essential arguments are the same. Genetic and environmental parameters were estimated from the case-classification data using liability threshold modeling techniques. This method assumes that the risk of being affected by a disorder (in this case, stuttering) has a normally distributed pattern, and that the disorder occurs when a certain threshold, or liability, is exceeded. For liability threshold models, twin resemblance can be summarized using tetrachoric correlations, which are used to describe the relationship between two variables (i.e., one for each twin), each of which is categorized as affected or unaffected. More specifically, tetrachoric correlation takes two normally distributed variables that are both expressed as a dichotomy (MZ/DZ and stutters/does not stutter) and provides a statistical coefficient equivalent to the Pearson's correlation coefficient. The latter is appropriate when two characteristics are continuous measures, such as height and weight.

The model-fitting process then estimates the MZ and DZ correlations for that liability. Variance is decomposed into additive genetic (A), shared environment (C), and nonshared environment (E) components as with continuous data. Nonadditive dominant genetic influences (D) were also included in the model. The best-fitting model for all age groups was one that did not include a shared environment component (i.e., an A, E model). The findings are consistent with Andrews et al. (1991) and Felsenfeld et al. (2000) who also concluded that an A, E model fitted their data.

Dworzynski et al. fitted A, C, E models at different ages separately for persistent and recovered speakers and for the two genders. Also, different liability threshold parameters were estimated for boys and girls because of the different stuttering prevalence rates for males and females. The thresholds obtained for girls were always higher than for boys, which reflected this difference in prevalence rates for different genders (Chapter 2). However, there were no sex differences in the model estimates for A and E.

At 3, 4, and 7 years, the liability for stuttering was moderately to highly heritable (estimates of between 58 and 66%), which also left a significant unique environment (E) influence of between 42 and 34%. Heritability for the recovered and persistent groups was also high (see Dworzynski et al.'s Table 9) and did not differ between the two groups. The authors concluded that stuttering is a disorder that has high heritability and little shared environment, but significant unique environment effects in early childhood and for both recovered and persistent groups of children, up to age 7. Some possible environmental factors that could be involved in the E estimate are discussed in Chapter 9.

4.2.4   LIMITATIONS OF THE TWIN METHOD

Some criticisms have been levelled at the procedure for studying twins. Most question the assumptions about MZ and DZ twins. As indicated, the major premise drawn on in twin work is that MZ twins have identical genetic material, whereas DZ twins only share 50%, which allows comparison between the groups to estimate hereditary influences. The premise also relies on environmental factors being constant across MZ and DZ twins. This premise has been questioned and is relevant insofar as if it is not true, results may not generalize from twins to singleton births. The arguments about differences in environmental influences across MZ and DZ twins are examined below.

MZ twins are more likely to share a chorion (membranous sac enclosing the embryo) which the critics of twin studies assume makes their prenatal environment more similar than that of DZ twins. In fact, the opposite is true, with monochorionic twins more likely to differ in birth weight (as a result of the "transfusion syndrome" whereby twins get disproportionate supplies of blood). To the extent that data are available, chorionicity and its consequences do not seem to threaten the logic of the twin method (Rutter, 2005, p. 42).

Critics of the twin method also have highlighted that there may be important twin–singleton differences that would jeopardize the conclusions from the twin studies. For example, twins are sometimes delayed in language development and twin pregnancies are associated with increased rate of obstetric complications. However, twins with obstetric complications are routinely excluded from twin analyses, and language delay found in twins is very mild, representing variation in the normal range.

Finally, and perhaps most critical, twin pregnancies are often associated with prematurity. This might affect many aspects of behavior including cognitive linguistic performance.

4.3   BACKGROUND TO SINGLE GENE ACCOUNTS OF INHERITED BEHAVIOR (MENDELIAN INHERITANCE)

The twin studies just reviewed indicate that approximately 30% of variance in chance of stuttering is environmentally determined and about 70% is genetic. Methods to establish what features are inherited are covered in the remaining sections of this chapter.

Some basic background to genetics is given. Genetic studies date back to work done by Gregor Mendel in the 19th century. He discovered that by crossing pea plants with white- and purple-colored flowers, the color of the offspring was either purple or white, not intermediate between the two colors (a hybrid). Mendel followed the flowering pattern of several successive generations of his pea plants and recorded the variation in the color of the flowers of the offspring. The novelty of his work was that he expressed the results numerically and he subjected them to statistical analysis. He observed that the purple and white flowers were in the proportions 3 to 1.

To explain this finding, Mendel hypothesized that each parent plant made discrete contributions to the flower color of the offspring (the inherited characteristic). Each parent carries two characteristics and this applies to previous generations, so each parent will also have discrete contributions from its parents and so on back through the generations. During sexual reproduction, the two characteristics that each parent carries split apart. One characteristic from the male plant combines with one characteristic from the female plant according to the statistical rules that govern how independent events combine (with the constraint that one characteristic has to come from each parent). Assuming both the male and female parent each have a characteristic for purple and white flower color to pass on the offspring, the possibilities for the offspring are (1) for a purple characteristic from both its parents, (2) for a white characteristic from both its parents. (3) for a purple characteristic from its male parent and a white characteristic from its female parent, and (4) for a white characteristic from its male parent and a purple characteristic from its female parent.

These four combinations cover all possibilities for combining two characteristics from two parents. There is an equal chance of these four possibilities. Mendel then conceived the idea that one of the characteristics was recessive and the other was dominant. In the case of the color of the flowers of his pea plants, white was recessive and purple was dominant. Whenever the purple color characteristic is inherited from either parent (whether or not it is paired with a purple or a white characteristic inherited from the other parent), it determines the color of the off-spring. Thus, combinations (1), (3), and (4) would result in purple flowers (all have inherited a characteristic for purple from at least one parent) and only (2) would result in a white flower. Because there are three times as many possibilities for obtaining a purple flower as opposed to a white flower, this explains the observed 3:1 proportion.

If the male parent has one characteristic each for purple and white flower color and the female parent has two characteristics for white flower color, there are two possible ways to get purple flowers and two possible ways to get white flowers. Thus, the chances of each color in the offspring is equal so there should be 50% of each flower color. This example is important for understanding sex-linked genetic transmission (see next section).

4.4 TERMS AND CONCEPTS IN GENETICS

There is a lot of specialized terminology in genetics and some of the most impor-tant, as well as particular terms used in this chapter, are explained. The molecule DNA contains the sequence of nucleotides that encodes genetic information and the entire DNA sequence of an organism is called the genome. Together with proteins and other molecules, DNA is tightly packaged into bodies known as chromosomes. A common misunderstanding is that a gene is "for" a particular characteristic. However, it needs to be highlighted that a gene is "a stretch of DNA whose linear sequence of nucleotides encodes the linear sequence of amino acids in a specific protein" (Fisher, 2006). Humans have 23 pairs of chromosomes, which constitute the totality of their genetic material. The sex chromosomes are one of these pairs. Genes appear on chromosomes, and they also come in pairs. One member of each pair of chromosomes is inherited from the female parent and the other member from the male parent and, in this way, genes are passed from each parent to their offspring. More is said about the sex chromosomes at the end of this section after other necessary terms have been introduced (see also Rutter, 2005, for an elementary introduction).

The properties carried on the corresponding pairs of chromosomes are not necessarily identical. The differences occur on the genes and the different forms on two of the genes are called alleles. The set of alleles for a given organism is called its genotype, while the observable characteristics of the organism are called its phenotype. The genotype of an individual is made up of the many alleles it possesses. An individual's physical appearance, or *phenotype*, is determined by its environment as well as by its alleles. Homozygous refers to a genotype consist-ing of two *identical* alleles at a given locus. Heterozygous refers to a genotype consisting of two *different* alleles at a given locus.

When a pair of organisms reproduces sexually, the alleles separate and the offspring randomly inherits one of the two alleles from each parent. A gamete is the cell from one parent that fuses with a gamete from the other parent during fertilization in organisms that reproduce sexually. Gametes carry half the genetic information of an individual, as they consist of one chromosome for each of the 23 chromosome pairs. One pair of chromosomes determines the sex of an individual. The male parent has two types of cells in the sex chromosome (X and Y). These split apart during reproduction as described earlier. The female parent has one type of cell in the sex chromosome (X) of which there are two copies. The two Xs of the female also split apart during reproduction. The X from the male (X^m) can pair with either of the Xs from the female (X^{f1}, X^{f2}) and this presents offspring with two Xs that are male ($X^m X^{f1}$, $X^m X^{f2}$). Likewise, the Y from the male (Y^m) can pair with either of the Xs from the female (X^{f1}, X^{f2}) and this presents offspring with a Y and an X that are male ($Y^m X^{f1}$, $Y^m X^{f2}$).

In like manner, an individual possesses two alleles for all its inherited characteristics: one of which comes from the female parent and the other from the male parent. Thus, when gametes form, the paired alleles separate randomly so that each gamete receives a copy of one of the two alleles. The presence of an allele does not guarantee that the inherited characteristics will be expressed in the individual that possesses it. This is partly due to whether the inherited characteristics is dominant or recessive as discussed in connection with Mendel's work on inheritance of color of flowers. An inherited characteristic (or disease) is referred to as dominant when it only has to occur on one allele to be expressed, and one parent has to have that inherited characteristic. If the other parent does not have the inherited characteristic, it is recessive in that individual. For a disease to be expressed that is recessive, it has to occur on both alleles; this implies both parents had the characteristic. At heterozygous loci, the only allele to be expressed is the dominant one.

It is useful to see how this simple form of inheritance controlled at a single major locus works with the sex-linked genetic disorder hemophilia (although note that most inherited characteristics are polygenic, as indicated in section 4.5 below). This information is drawn on in connection with genetic models that account for the gender effects below. Hemophilia A is a blood-clotting disorder caused by a mutant gene that encodes the clotting factor VIII. This gene is located on the X chromosome. The mutant gene for hemophilia is indicated here by the superscript h (^{h}). Males who inherit the defective gene (always from their mother) are unable to produce factor VIII and suffer from episodes of bleeding that are difficult to control. Heterozygous females will have one mutated (X^h) and one unmutated (X) copy of the gene on the sex chromosome pair. When they reproduce with a male who does not have hemophilia, the offspring produced will have one of the following sex chromosome pairs:

1. XX (X from the father and unmutated X copy from the mother)
2. XX^h (X from the father and mutated X copy from the mother)
3. YX (Y from the father and unmutated X copy from the mother)
4. YX^h (Y from the father and mutated X copy from the mother)

An unaffected female is 1 and an unaffected male is 3; 2 is a heterozygous female, and 4 is an affected male (i.e., will have hemophilia). In case 2, the unmutated copy of the gene provides all the factor VIII the female needs. However, a heterozygous female is a carrier because although she shows no symptoms, she passes the gene on to approximately half her sons who develop the disease, and half her daughters, who also become carriers. This example shows that with sex-linked transmission of characteristics passed on by heterozygous females, half of males are affected and women rarely suffer from characteristics transmitted like this. To do so they would have to inherit a defective gene from their father as well as their mother.

4.4.1   LAW OF SEGREGATION (MENDEL'S FIRST LAW)

The segregation of alleles and discrete inheritance of characteristics are described in Mendel's first law: the law of segregation. The law of segregation states that when an individual produces gametes, the chromosomes separate, and each gamete receives only one member of the individual's chromosome pair. The process whereby alleles are segregated into two different gametes is called meiosis.

4.4.2   LAW OF INDEPENDENT ASSORTMENT (MENDEL'S SECOND LAW)

The law of independent assortment states that alleles assort independently of one another during gamete formation. In this independent assortment, the chromosomes end up in a newly formed gamete that represents a random sorting of maternal and paternal chromosomes. This is essentially what was illustrated in the examples given earlier.

4.5   MENDELIAN CHARACTERISTICS AND SPEECH DISORDER

A disease that is the result of a single gene is called a *Mendelian disorder* in honor of Mendel. A Mendelian characteristic is one that is controlled by a single gene locus and shows a Mendelian inheritance pattern like that described in section 4.3. In such cases, a mutation in a single gene can cause a disease that is inherited according to Mendel's laws. An example is sickle cell anemia, Diseases controlled by a single gene contrast with those that are the effect of problems with many genes (polygenic). An example of a polygenic disease is arthritis, which is affected by several gene loci. It has been reported in different articles that stuttering is either caused by a single gene or that it is polygenic. Before the evidence about this issue is considered, some actual evidence of a clear case of a speech disorder controlled by a single gene is presented (*FOXP2* and the KE family). This is intended to give readers an idea of some of the methods and types of data that are used to deduce details of heritability of stuttering.

4.5.1   *FOXP2* AND THE LANGUAGE OF THE KE FAMILY

All this has got a bit remote from inheritance of speech disorders. To return to these concerns, a classic case of Mendelian inheritance of a language disorder

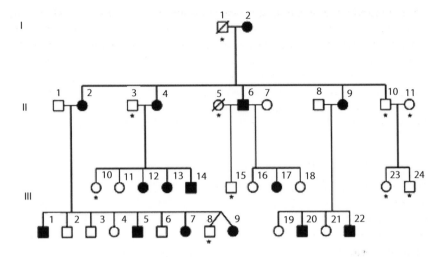

FIGURE 4.3 Inheritance pattern of language disorder in members of the KE family. (See text for details.)

controlled by a single gene is considered. This is the case of the KE family (Hurst, Baraitser, Auger, Graham, & Norell, 1990). The KE family is a three-generation family that consisted of 37 members.

Some members of the family have a severe speech and language disorder involving poor articulatory coordination. This case was interesting because the disorder segregated from generation to generation in a pattern that pointed decisively toward there being just one gene involved. The pedigree of the KE family is shown in Figure 4.3. A slash through a box indicates that the person is deceased.

Of the 37 individuals in the family, 15 are affected by the speech–language disorder (the filled symbols). Thus, about half the family members are affected (as in the pea flower example where the male parent had one characteristic for purple and one for white flower color and the female parent had two characteristics for white flower color). There are 6 out of 20 males who are affected (box symbol) and 9 out of 19 females (circle symbol), so there is about the same chance of males and females being affected. With around 50% of family members affected and roughly the same chance of males and females being affected, the pattern is consistent with the disorder being a simple Mendelian disease that was passed on by one allele from one parent (as with the white/purple flower example described earlier). In subsequent work, Fisher, Vargha-Khadem, Watkins, Monaco, and Pembrey (1998) were able to identify a region on chromosome 7 that was associated with the speech disorder and, subsequently, they were able to identify the gene called *FOXP2*, which was mutant in affected members of this family. It is worth stressing that behaviors that are controlled by a single gene (such as *FOXP2*) are rare.

4.5.2   GENETICS OF STUTTERING

Similar studies to those conducted on the KE family have been done on the families of stutterers to ascertain which members stuttered. Inferences can be drawn about heritability by comparing the frequency and pattern of affected relatives against expectations based on particular genetic models or against the results of a control group.

Much of the early information on the genetics of stuttering comes from the Yale family history study, which looked at over 600 adult stutterers and several thousand first-degree relatives (Kidd, 1984). Kidd also reanalyzed data from the study of Andrews and Harris (1964) and collected additional data to amass the large dataset. Early results indicated that a single-major locus model fitted the data (Kidd, Kidd, & Records, 1978). Subsequently, Ambrose, Yairi, and Cox (1993) also reported statistically significant evidence for a Mendelian single major locus model. Ambrose, Cox, and Yairi (1997) included polygenic components, but still considered that there was also a single major locus.

Viswanath, Lee and Chakraborty (2004) have looked at inheritance patterns in a group of adults with persistent stuttering. They concluded that a dominant major gene effect, influenced by parental stuttering and sex, was an appropriate model. All of these accounts point to one major gene being responsible for stuttering.

4.5.3   POLYGENIC INHERITANCE OF STUTTERING

In contrast, early analyses by Andrews and Harris (1964) of their family history data on children who stutter (see Chapter 2) suggested that a single gene was a highly unlikely explanation of stuttering. They found that the risk of stuttering was highest in the male relatives of female stutterers (not 50/50). Later work by Kidd retracted support for the single major locus model and, instead, reported that a polygenic model was more likely (Kidd et al., 1978). Subsequently, Cox, Cramer, and Kidd (1984) also ruled out a single major locus and they concluded that their data were consistent with a polygenic or polygenic plus major locus model where the major locus was non-Mendelian (i.e., it did not follow the pattern of strict Mendelian transmission). As mentioned, Ambrose et al. (1997) conceded polygenic influences, but they still maintained there is a single major locus that showed Mendelian transmission.

4.5.3.1   Kidd's Analysis of Familial Patterns of Stuttering and the Polygenic Model With Sex-Modified Inheritance to Explain the Gender Effect on Stuttering

Wingate (1964) reported that 67% of female stutterers ($N = 18$) had male relatives who stuttered, whereas 21% of male stutterers ($N = 32$) had male relatives within their immediate family who also stuttered. This is consistent with Andrews and Harris' (1964) observations that ruled a single major locus out as an explanation of stuttering, as mentioned above. Wingate's findings challenge a simple, single, major locus model in two ways: (1) females have more relatives who stutter than expected (there should be an equal chance of inheriting stuttering for both genders) and (2) There is a higher chance that affected relatives are male (although there should be an equal chance for both genders to be affected).

Kidd (1983, 1984) confirmed these findings and calculated how the risk of stuttering for family members depended on the sex of the proband and for different classes of relatives. Six significant differences were found for male and female probands and relatives, which are as follows:

1. Males are more commonly affected than females.
2. Transmission from an affected father is more often to an affected son than a daughter.
3. An affected mother transmits the disorder to more sons than daughters.
4. Affected females have an affected parent more frequently than affected males.
5. Affected males may frequently have both parents unaffected.
6. Even if both parents are affected, some offspring, especially females, may be unaffected.

One possibility that can be ruled out by these data is that stuttering has a sex-linked Mendelian inheritance pattern, as is the case for hemophilia. Instead, based on these results, it appears that males are biologically more susceptible to stuttering, and relatives of a female stutterer are more likely to have stuttered than relatives of a male stutterer (Kidd, 1983, 1984). This suggests that more genetic factors for stuttering are required in order for a female to stutter. Along these lines, Kidd, Heimbuch, and Records (1981) explained the pattern of higher incidence in relatives of females who stutter on the assumption that females have higher thresholds to the disease, therefore, they require more genetic factors to express stuttering. They then have more factors to transmit to males. The six properties indicated above are consistent with stuttering being inherited as a sex-modified characteristic where they are defined as "ordinary genetic transmission, but the genotypes are expressed as different susceptibilities to the disorder depending on sex" (Kidd et al., 1978, pp. 19–20).

MacFarlane, Hanson and Walton (1991) used the related procedure of studying a large family with high incidence of stuttering individuals. The advantage of this method is that it eliminates heterogeneity and makes it possible to demonstrate a clear mode of transmission for the family being considered, as was seen with the KE family shown in Figure 4.3. The drawback is that, by definition, the results obtained only apply to this particular family. MacFarlane and colleagues reported on a 1,200-member, five-generational family that contained a higher number of stutterers than would be predicted by population prevalence estimates. They used these data to examine, and confirm, that stuttering was a sex-modified characteristic in this family.

Ambrose et al.'s (1993) data on children who stutter agreed that more males than females were affected, but they did not agree with the remainder of the statements set out by Kidd for sex-modified characteristics. Of particular note is the fact that they did not find more male relatives of female stutterers stuttered than male relatives of male stutterers. They suggested that the different results may have reflected the fact that different age groups were tested in the two sets of studies. Subsequent replication of Ambrose's study with adult probands (Janssen, Kloth, Kraaimaat, & Brutten, 1996) has also contested Kidd's claims, although this was a small-scale study that might have led to nonsignificant results.

4.5.3.2   Genetic Factors at Onset and in Course to Persistence and Recovery

Yairi and colleagues monitored their young stutterers as they progressed from the ages of onset toward early adolescence (Chapter 1, also see Yairi & Ambrose, 2005). They claimed this provided better information about recovery than studies that used retrospective reports by adults who said that they stuttered in childhood. Although it can be agreed that follow-up data are important, there are other points that should be kept in mind concerning Yairi's study. Chapter 1 already pointed out that the age ranges of the children is too restricted to give a definite statement as to whether the child has recovered or was persisting. It will be shown in Chapter 13 that the sample may be biased toward more middle class families. Also, the thresholds for declaring a person as stuttering (Chapter 1) and the symptoms used to characterize stuttering (Chapter 3) are not necessarily appropriate for classifying children as stuttering (Wingate, 2002). Finally, although the authors refer to "natural" recovery, many of the children had treatment as mentioned in Chapter 1, so the recovery is not entirely natural.

The results of Yairi's group on whether genetics contributes to the onset of stuttering are examined first. Yairi and Ambrose (1999) used data from family histories collected in a series of studies that used between 66 and 147 children. They found that 74% of participants recovered and that a higher percentage of females recovered than males (Yairi & Ambrose, 1999). Yairi and colleagues claimed that both persistence and recovery were transmitted within families and persons who either recovered or persisted over time did not appear to be genetically different from each other (Ambrose et al., 1997). As stated earlier, they concluded in favor of a single major gene involvement in the onset of stuttering and that recovered and persistent forms seem to share the same basic inheritance pattern.

Concerning the later course of stuttering, Ambrose et al. (1993) examined whether genetic transmission is different in persistent and recovered cases. They found that, in addition to the single major locus component discussed earlier, there are polygenic factors that determine the path the disorder will take, as pointed out above that individuals with a family history of persistent stuttering also tended to persist, whereas individuals with a family history of recovered stuttering also tended to recover. Thus, they consider that there are specific predispositions determining the path stuttering will take. This suggests that speakers who will persist have latent polygenic influences, which eventually lead them to diverge from recovered cases.

Janssen, Kraaimaat, and Brutten (1990) found that people who stuttered and have a family history of stuttering differed from those without such a history in frequency with which sound prolongations were used and in their speech motor skills. They suggested that persistent speakers with a family history may have inherited more of a tendency to show sound prolongations and to have motor difficulties than speakers without a family history of stuttering, suggesting why more severe forms emerge in some speakers, but not others.

4.5.3.3 Evaluation

The idea that persistent stuttering runs in some families and recovered stuttering in others is reexamined here using the data in Figure 9.4 in Yairi and Ambrose's book (2005). Looking at the persistent cases first, there seems little reason to doubt Yairi and Ambrose's argument that persistence runs in families. Persistent speakers have a much higher proportion of persistent relatives, which is a different pattern to that shown by recovered speakers and the fluent "population."

However, examination of their data show that the recovered patterns are like those of the fluent sample (fewer persistent relatives than recovered relatives), not like the stutterers who persisted, except that incidence rates are higher in the recovered cases than in fluent speakers. Yairi and Ambrose interpreted the higher incidence rate in those who went on to recover compared to fluent controls as showing that recovered patterns run in families. If this is true, this pattern would differ from what happens in the fluent speakers; rates overall are lower in the fluent sample. However, the higher rate shown by the recovered speakers could be due to the artifacts that Reilly et al. (2009) discussed that are considered in Chapter 13. In particular, before children in the Reilly study started to stutter, family history was reported to be much lower than after these same children were reported to have acquired the disorder. The increase in rates, but with the same relative proportions for the recovered over the fluent children, could be explained by the increased rate of reporting family history of stuttering after onset of the disorder in the recovered sample. The similarity between fluent and recovered samples would be consistent with Wingate's (2002) view that the recovered speakers in the Yairi and Ambrose study were not stuttering.

Yairi and Ambrose (2005, p. 301) also state that recovered stuttering "is less familial than persistent stuttering, and may have a greater environmental component." However, Dworzynski et al.'s (2007) Table 9 showed that it is not true that recovered speakers have greater environmental components. In Dworzynski et al.'s large twin sample, the children designated persistent had higher unique environment scores (E, estimated as described above) than did the recovered speakers. The results were in the opposite direction to what Yairi and Ambrose concluded.

4.6 MOLECULAR MARKERS AND EVIDENCE FOR THE GENE RESPONSIBLE FOR THE LANGUAGE DISORDER IN THE KE FAMILY

Recent advances in the field of genetics have led to introduction of techniques that can be used to identify more precisely the genetic material that may have a role in stuttering. Genetic markers are used to study the relationship between an inherited disease and its genetic cause (e.g., a particular mutation of a gene that results in a defective protein). It is known that pieces of DNA that lie near each other on a chromosome tend to be inherited together. This property enables the use of a marker, which can then be used to determine the precise inheritance pattern of the gene that has not yet been exactly localized.

In practice, this means that when a marker gene is co-inherited with stuttering, the gene is on the same chromosome as the marker gene. These regions can be studied further to locate specific genes involved in stuttering. This is done by first identifying the general location of possible genes using DNA extracted from samples of body tissues. Then, known marker genes are identified for every chromosome (or just those chromosomes that are of interest). When a marker gene form is co-inherited with stuttering (linkage), this indicates that the gene contributing to stuttering is on the same chromosome as the marker gene and, in fact, the gene and the marker are close together on the chromosome. This is the technique used in paternity testing where genetic markers from the child are compared with those of the alleged father. Using such techniques, Fisher et al. (1998) showed that a mutation of the *FOXP2* gene on chromosome 7 was associated with the speech and language difficulties of affected members of the KE family. *FOXP2* codes for a type of regulatory protein, which is called a transcription factor. It comes from a specific subclass of transcription factors known as "forkhead" proteins with a particular structure on which DNA can bind to it, and the protein is designated as FOXP2. When DNA binds to it, a transcription factor modulates the expression of other genes (i.e., switching on or off). There are a number of different forkhead proteins and many of them have important functions in controlling genetic cascades during embryonic development.

The fact that FOXP2 is a transcription factor gives it special interest with respect to speech and stuttering: small changes in a transcription factor influence a wide variety of genes and their functions, and transcription factors have roles both during development and in the mature organism. During development, they set up structures and functions. In the mature organism, they regulate these same structures and functions. This would allow a disorder, such as that experienced by the KE family, to develop and for the role of FOXP2 to change in adulthood. Transcription factors associated with stuttering would potentially be particularly interesting with respect to onset and course of the disorder because of its role in movement coordination, which is a particular problem in people who stutter (see Chapter 6).

Work with animals has helped to identify the brain regions affected by *FOXP2*. *FOXP2* is expressed in similar regions in all vertebrates studied, mainly in the cerebellar and basal ganglia circuits. Chapter 5 shows that these same areas have been implicated in stuttering. Regions include the lateral ganglionic eminence in the developing brain, which gives rise to the striatal medium, spiny projection neurons involved in planning and modulation of movement; the thalamus, in particular the regions that receive input from the basal ganglia; the inferior olives, which are part of the cerebellar motor learning circuitries and function; cerebellar Purkinje cells; and deep cerebellar nuclei as well as sensory auditory midbrain structures. These regions implicate *FOXP2* in the fine sensorimotor coordination/integration that underlies the sequenced behavior and learning processes necessary for speech and language. *FOXP2* is not expressed in the structures that form the trigeminal sensorimotor circuit that controls jaw movements. So *FOXP2* apparently has nothing to do with the activation of the movements of the lower face, but rather with the coordination, planning, and learning of these movements that, as noted above, is a problem in people who stutter. A further factor that is relevant is that *FOXP2* downregulates another protein, CNTNAP2, which is involved in enriching frontal gray matter of the developing cerebral cortex, which, in turn, might cause speech problems in early life.

4.6.1 MOLECULAR GENETICS/GENOME AND STUTTERING

Six genome-wide linkage (see section 4.6) studies have identified several chromosomal regions that appear to be associated with stuttering. In the first study that appeared in a peer-reviewed publication, Shugart et al. (2004) carried out a genome-wide linkage scan for stuttering for samples from North America and Europe. Their preliminary conclusions pointed toward a predisposing locus on chromosome 18.

Riaz et al. (2005), studied Pakistani families and found a strong linkage signal on chromosome 12 pointing to a gene or genes related to stuttering located on this chromosome.

Subsequently, Kang et al. (2010) used DNA sequencing and related technologies to identify the actual genes implicated in the earlier study. Two groups were examined: one consisted of Pakistani families in which stuttering was common and the other was a sample of American and British stutterers. Appropriate control group of nonstuttering Pakistani, and American and British stutterers were employed.

Three mutant genes occurred in the stuttering samples, but only occurred rarely in the nonstuttering control samples. The DNA code of these genes would provide instruction for the cells to produce a protein with a different function to the protein ordinarily produced without the mutation. Mutations in two of these genes are known to be associated with two rare diseases characterized by disorders of the joints, skeletal system, internal organs, and motor development, and by developmental delay.

These three genes provide instructions to cells to build proteins involved in lysosome function. Lysosomes occur in animal cells and their role is to remove damaged molecules and viruses from inside the cell. Without proper lysosome cleaning action, damage builds up inside the cell and interferes with proper cell function. Mutations in the three genes were observed in 25 out of 786 stutterers (3.2%), compared to 4 out of 744 nonstutterers (0.54%). Animal research has shown that two of these genes are expressed in the brain, in regions associated with emotion and motor function, and difficulties in these areas have been reported in speakers who stutter (see Chapters 8 and 9, respectively). Although this discovery is exciting and opens up possibilities for further research into the way the proteins produced by these genes affects speech, not all people with the mutant genes become stutterers, and only a small proportion of stutterers had the gene variants. It is not clear how lysosome enzyme abnormality could lead to a white matter deficit (see Chapter 5, section 5.2.2).

Levis, Ricci, Lukong, and Drayna (2004) performed work on a large Cameroon family. They reported evidence for linkage on chromosomes 1.

Suresh et al. (2006) identified moderate evidence for linkage for the broad category of "ever-stuttered" (including both persistent and recovered stuttering) on chromosome 9, whereas, for persistent stuttering only, it was on chromosome 15. There were sex differences with respect to specific chromosomes, with males showing the strongest linkage signal on chromosome 7 and females showing strongest linkage on chromosome 21.

Two possible genetic routes to stuttering were revealed. First, there was linkage on chromosome 12 for families who had high linkage signal on chromosome 7. The region on chromosome 12 is close to the signal first reported by Riaz et al. (2005) for the Pakistani families. Second, a region on chromosome 2 showed a significant increased linkage signal for families who had a high linkage signal on chromosome 9 or a negative signal on chromosome 7.

Wittke-Thompson et al. (2007) recently reported a worrying finding. They examined DNA markers for stuttering in members of the Hutterite population in North Dakota. Whereas other studies had reported a diversity of genetic loci associated with stuttering, they did not find any significant linkage in the Hutterite sample or in an associated meta-analysis. Finally, it should also be noted that finding linkages is one thing, but work still needs to be done to see what are the transcription factors and how these relate to the specific symptoms seen in stuttering rather than others (e.g., those seen in the KE family).

4.7 SUMMARY

In reviewing research on genetic influences in the origin and course of stuttering, twin work was considered because establishing heritability is a prerequisite to further genetic examination and twin work has given the most consistent results concerning this topic. All the twin studies have reported similar rates, that is, that 15 to 30% of the variance in chance of stuttering is environmentally determined and in most studies the only environmental component is unique rather than shared environment, and 70 to 85% is genetic. No differences have been reported for gender (Ooki, 2005), although Dworzynski et al. (2007) found that threshold estimates that reflect differences in prevalence rates between boys and girls did change in the way expected. There was no evidence that persistent and recovered speakers differed (Dworzynski et al., 2007).

The early family history patterns have left us with the impasse between two theoretical models proposed by the main groups who have worked in the area. Kidd, who worked with samples that consisted mainly of adults, found evidence for non-Mendelian polygenic inheritance with sex-modified inheritance patterns. Yairi and Ambrose concluded in favor of a major gene involvement that follows Mendelian patterns at the onset of stuttering (recovered and persistent forms seem to share the same basic inheritance pattern at this stage). Ambrose et al. (1993) suggest that speakers who will persist have latent polygenic influences that lead them to have a different course from the recovered cases. It is unlikely that this impasse will be resolved in the foreseeable future given that only one group is still active and the fact that modern genetic investigations have moved on from these procedures.

The work with genetic markers so far has failed to find any consistent evidence for a particular gene responsible for the onset and course of stuttering although studies on two independent samples point toward areas on chromosome 12 (Riaz et al., 2005; Suresh et al., 2006). In one case, null results have been reported (Wittke-Thomson et al., 2007).

4.8   EXERCISES

1. Twin studies involve large numbers of respondents and information is obtained mainly by self-referral. Look at the twin studies discussed in this chapter and describe what impact these and other methodological issues may have had on the results.
2. Evaluate the arguments for a single major locus versus polygenic influences for onset and course of stuttering.
3. Yairi and Ambrose (2005) argued that people who recovered from stuttering had a greater environmental and lesser genetic component than those who show persistent stuttering, whereas Dworzynski et al. (2007, Table 9) points to the opposite conclusion. What reasons can you give for these discrepancies?
4. What reasons are there for different genes being reported to be involved in stuttering in different studies?

5 CNS Factors in Investigations Into Persistent and Recovered Stuttering

Scans are not available for young children around the age at which stuttering starts that are required so central nervous system (CNS) influences at onset and early course of stuttering can be studied. However, the age limit at which scans can be made routinely is constantly being lowered and acquiring brain data at the onset of stuttering may be possible in the future (methods using surface electrodes to measure electrical activity in the brain are available and have been used already in a limited number of studies with children who stutter).

At present there are several studies on adults who stutter (i.e., persistent cases). Scans are being made with older children who stutter, who have been followed up, and have been designated as persistent or recovered. Respondents are too limited in number at present to draw firm conclusions about the role of CNS structures over the course of stuttering.

5.1 INTRODUCTION

Jurgens (2002) reviewed the neural pathways that underlie vocal control in normal speech production. A simplified and partial list of the central nervous system (CNS) structures that he proposed were involved in voluntary vocal reactions, as opposed to involuntary ones, as when individuals make shrieks of pain, are listed, and these are indicated in diagrams after a brief description. (1) The pyramidal pathways (primary motor cortex). The pyramidal or corticospinal pathways are a collection of axons that travel between motor cortex and the spinal cord. These pathways are concerned specifically with discrete voluntary skilled movements. (2) The extrapyramidal pathways (parts of the basal ganglia structures). The extrapyrimidal pathways are motor paths that lie outside the pyramidal tract and are not under voluntary control. Their main function is to support voluntary movement and coordination. Nos. 1 and 2 operate together to activate muscles in the face, neck, and torso, which are involved in oral motor functions, including speech. (3) The previous structures need input from the cerebellum, which, according to Jurgens, allows for smooth transitions between speech segments. Other authors emphasize the role of the cerebellum in sensory-motor integration (see Chapters 6 and 11). The primary motor cortex receives additional inputs from (4) the ventral premotor and the prefrontal cortex, including Broca's area, assumed to be associated with motor planning. The primary motor cortex also receives inputs from the two other cortical motor areas usually mentioned in the literature: (5) the premotor area (PMA) and (6) the supplementary motor area (SMA). Nos. 5 and 6 together are assumed to give rise to the motor commands executed by the motor cortex. (7) Somatosensory cortex is the processing center that serves the several sensory modalities. The auditory modality is of particular interest for authors who consider that auditory feedback is important is speech control (see Chapter 8). Most of these structures are bilaterally represented. However, it has been known for several years that the left brain plays a major role in speech control in individuals with no pathology and there has been examination of lateral pathways in people who stutter. The main structures left out of this list that Jurgens included are proprioceptive input from the respiratory, phonatory, and articulatory organs via nucleus ventralis posterior medialis thalami and inferior parietal cortex, all of which supply input to motor cortex.

The three motor cortical areas, primary motor cortex (M1), the premotor area (PMA), and the supplementary motor area (SMA), are partitions that are part of Brodmann area 6. The premotor cortex is part of the motor cortex and lies within the frontal lobe of the brain, near the Sylvian fissure. The supplementary motor area lies just in front of primary motor cortex. Somatosensory cortex lies just behind the primary motor cortex. Somatosensory, premotor, and motor corticess are shown in Figure 5.1.

Other areas that were featured in early work on speech control (and are also mentioned in recent work as well) are Broca's area (Brodmann area 44) and Wernicke's area (Brodmann area 40). These are shown in Figure 5.2.

The remaining structures that are important in connection with stuttering are the basal ganglia and cerebellum, indicated in Figure 5.3.

The idea that there is something wrong in one or more of the CNS structures subserving speech in people who stutter has a long history. Researchers have shown considerable ingenuity in developing methods to investigate these structures indirectly, as direct intervention is not possible for obvious reasons. This led to a number of hypotheses about what damage might have occurred in people who stutter. For instance, the left hemisphere controls speech in most individuals. An undamaged left hemisphere allows unimpaired speech. Several authors have argued that the left hemisphere does not work correctly in people who stutter. This is based on the observation that there is a disproportionate number of left-handed individuals who stutter. The general logic is: (1) The right hand is controlled by the left brain; (2) a switch to left-handedness (controlled by the right brain) might signify that the left hemisphere is not functioning normally; and (3) if handedness is controlled by general motor mechanisms that are also responsible for speech processing, then the damaged left hemisphere might explain why speech is affected too. Consistent with this argument, conventional behavioral measures of lateralized function predominantly show that speakers who stutter tend to have speech lateralized bilaterally or even in the right hemisphere. Some scanning evidence about lateralization in people who stutter is discussed later in this chapter.

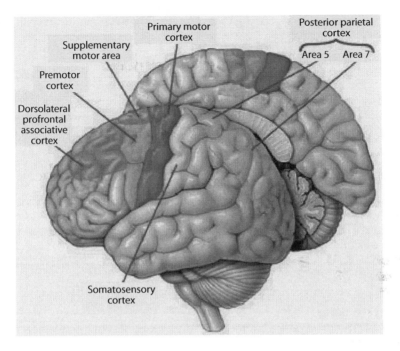

FIGURE 5.1 (See color insert following page 102)   A diagram showing the location of somatosensory cortex, premotor, and motor cortex.

More recently, behavioral evidence where performance is known to be linked to particular CNS structures has suggested which alternative CNS locations are implicated in stuttering. Thus, Howell and his group tested people who stutter on a variety of tests on which people with cerebellar disorders do badly. This is discussed in Chapter 6. The results clearly indicated an association between cerebellar processing and stuttering (Howell et al., 2008). Alm (2004) reported that there was a very high incidence of head injury in his sample of stutterers, and argued that this would lead to damage of the basal ganglia structures. He went on

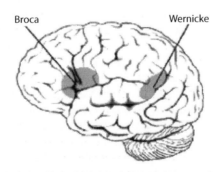

FIGURE 5.2   Shown is the location of Broca's and Wernicke's areas.

Basal Ganglia and Related
Structures of the Brain

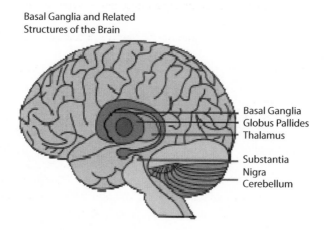

FIGURE 5.3 (See color insert following page 102) Shown is the location of basal ganglia and cerebellum.

to propose a dual-process theory that involved the basal ganglia circuits based on the work of Goldberg (1991). The two processes are organized in a direct and an indirect pathway. These two pathways are assumed to work in synergy to modulate the activity of the frontal cortex. The direct pathway provides focused activation of the desired action and the indirect pathway provides diffuse inhibition of cortical activity. Furthermore, the two pathways are dominated by different types of dopamine receptors, resulting in differential effects of dopamine. The cueing functions of the basal ganglia to the SMA depend on differences between the focal activation and the inhibition of the cortex. The cueing of the basal ganglia can be distorted in different ways. Alm argued that too weak a focal activation by the direct pathway would result in deficient activation of the desired action, for example, difficulties in initiating speech movements. On the other hand, impaired diffuse inhibition of the cortex, provided by the indirect pathway, could result in a combination of release of unintended movements and impaired release of the intended movement. According to Alm, these distortions (motor initiation and impairments in intended movement coupled with release of intended movements) are linked with the symptoms of stuttering.

Significant progress in our ability to examine how CNS structures function in people who stutter, which allow further tests of the above and other ideas, was made toward the end of the 20th century when scanning technology began to be applied to investigate stuttering. Scanning and related technologies are being increasingly used to investigate stuttering and these studies are considered in this chapter, as they are likely to be the dominant techniques for investigating CNS involvement in stuttering for the foreseeable future.

Before such work is reviewed, several points need to be raised about the complications of the scanning literature. First, different scanning technologies have been used, each of which has its advantages and disadvantages. The main procedures are summarized below.

A second potential source of difficulty is that there are a number of structures in the CNS in addition to those involved in speech. Also, more microscopic examinations of parts of the structures mentioned have been made by investigators. Both of these facts can make it difficult to obtain a complete picture of what is going on. This problem is recognized in imaging work in general. Thus, there are various techniques that are used to focus on regions of interest. A study that includes this approach with stuttering is described in section 5.2.1 (Brown, Ingham, Ingham, Laird, & Fox, 2005). Also related to this is the widespread use of meta-analyses (employed in the last cited study), which amalgamate the results across several studies that have used similar methods to identify what common brain areas emerge in some task or patient group, and, equally importantly, rule out areas that are only evident in a minority of studies, which might be spurious.

The third thing that complicates scanning work is that sophisticated analyses are required; very large amounts of data are obtained that can often be analyzed in many ways. In the review, analysis techniques are described when they are first mentioned.

Finally, the designs of studies into stuttering, and into investigating speech production in general, are complicated because of several potential methodological artifacts that need to be avoided. There are two main ones that are relevant to speech production work:

1. Movement artifacts can blur the images and lead to spurious activation patterns. If speakers in one group move more than speakers in another group (as would be the case with stutterers), this can lead to misinterpretation of results. Precautions and checks have to be made to ensure that the results are not affected in this way.

2. When it is necessary for a person to speak in the scanner, the environment could potentially affect results. Thus, although scanners are getting quieter, they are still noisy and noise affects speech control (discussed in Chapter 8). Speakers do not often speak while lying supine and this body position affects how the pulmonary, laryngeal, and articulatory systems operate (Kitamura et al., 2005). Both the noisy environment and atypical body position require a different manner of speech control than normally adopted and might have more effect on speakers who stutter.

For all speakers, the results may not generalize to more natural speaking situations. Research studies have used a variety of ingenious designs to circumvent the aforementioned methodological issues. For instance, control conditions have been used that involve speakers imagining they are stuttering, sparse scanning methods have been employed where speech is collected immediately after the participant has spoken (while the brain is still affected by the speech activity, but the motor effects are absent), and speech has been obtained from people who stutter under fluency-inducing conditions (where it is assumed that speech is closer to fluent speech).

The other major methodological issue is whether the results obtained are due to structural (tissue change) or functional (a reflection of abnormal operation of intact tissue) differences between people who stutter and controls. Structural differences reported in older speakers who stutter might have started as functional problems earlier in life; at present, there are no data at onset ages that would rule one of these alternatives out. This is of particular relevance with respect to developmental stuttering.

It is not possible to deal comprehensively with all these topics in this short chapter. Topics will be selected and arranged in terms of issues they address. Jurgens' model and the behavioral evidence are used as guides to identify general CNS areas involved in voluntary control of vocalization that might be implicated in people who stutter. These areas are compared in people who stutter and controls. This was facilitated by Brown et al.'s (2005) meta-analysis of studies on stuttering. Before the review of studies, a short overview is given about the main scanning methods used in the stuttering literature.

- **Positron emission tomography (PET)** measures emissions from radio-active chemicals that are injected into the bloodstream. These react metabolically with brain structures so that the part of the brain doing most work takes up more of the chemical. The emission data are processed by computer to produce two- or three-dimensional images of the distribution of the chemicals throughout the brain as seen in Figure 5.4. The advantage of PET scanning is that different compounds can show blood flow and oxygen or glucose metabolism in the tissues of the working brain. PET scans were fast relative to other methods that were available at the time they were introduced. The better resolution this entailed

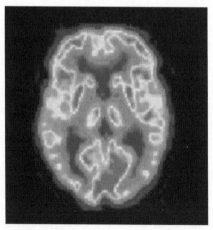

FIGURE 5.4 (See color insert following page 102)   PET scan of a normal 20-year-old brain.

permitted improved study of the areas of the brain activated by a particular task. The main drawback of PET scanning is that the radioactivity decays rapidly, therefore, the technique is limited to investigations into short tasks.

- **Magnetic resonance imaging (MRI)** uses magnetic fields and radio waves to produce high quality two- or three-dimensional images of brain structures, and does not use radioactive tracers as does PET. A circular magnet encircles the participant's head during an MRI. This creates a magnetic field around the head of the participant through which radio waves are sent. Each point in space has a unique radio frequency. Sensors read the frequencies and a computer uses the information to plot an image of the brain. The detection mechanisms are so precise that changes in structures over time can be detected.

  Scientists can create images of both surface and subsurface structures with a high degree of anatomical detail with MRI. MRI scans can produce cross-sectional images in any direction from top to bottom, side to side, or front to back. The problem with the original MRI technology is that while it provides a detailed assessment of the physical appearance, water content, and many kinds of subtle derangements of structure of the brain (such as inflammation or bleeding), it failed to provide information about the metabolism of the brain that PET does (i.e., how actively the brain functioned) at the time of imaging. Whereas MRI provides only structural information on the brain, functional MRI imaging (fMRI) yields both structural and functional data.

- **Functional magnetic resonance imaging** (fMRI) makes use of the hemodynamic properties of the brain. Nerve cells consume oxygen and consumption is increased when neural activity in a region increases and then dissipates. The blood oxygen level dependent (BOLD) response is an index of the oxygen consumption in the brain. After nerves have fired, they require recharging from the blood supply. The BOLD response starts a second or so after firing when extra oxygen is supplied to a region and the BOLD response peaks after about 4 to 5 sec. Local changes in the hemodynamic response indicate the regions where nerve cells have fired recently, and this happens in different regions for different tasks and for different patient groups. fMRI relies on the paramagnetic properties of oxygenated and deoxygenated hemoglobin to see images of changing blood flow in the brain associated with neural activity. This allows images to be generated that reflect which brain structures are activated during performance of different tasks. The resolution of fMRI is about 2 to 3 mm at present, as it is limited by the spatial spread of the hemodynamic response to neural activity. It has largely superseded PET for the study of brain activation patterns. An fMRI image of the brain is shown in Figure 5.5.

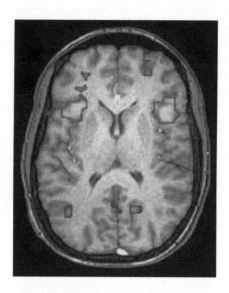

FIGURE 5.5 (See color insert following page 102) Shown is an axial MRI slice at the level of the basal ganglia, revealing fMRI BOLD signal changes overlaid in red (increase) and blue (decrease).

- **Magnetoencephalography (MEG)** is an imaging technique that is used to measure the magnetic fields produced by electrical activity in the brain using superconducting quantum interference devices (SQUIDs). MEG offers a direct measure of neural electrical activity (compared to fMRI, for example) with very high temporal resolution but relatively low spatial resolution. The advantage of measuring the magnetic fields produced by neural activity is that they are not distorted by surrounding tissue.

Section 5.2 reviews studies on brain morphology in people who stutter and controls. There are separate subsections on adults and older children. The subsection on children has some limited comments about scanning studies done in children in the later developmental course of the disorder. Section 5.3 reviews studies that model connectivity. Section 5.4 looks at available work on brain activity and severity of stuttering. Section 5.5 reports on studies that have examined speech in fluency-enhancing and fluency-inducing conditions.

5.2 BRAIN MORPHOLOGY IN PEOPLE WHO STUTTER AND FLUENT CONTROLS

The principal questions to be addressed are whether the brains of persons who stutter are structurally or functionally different to the brains of control speakers. Though gross indications of differences between people who stutter and controls have been reported, these cannot be definitely attributed to structural or functional origins even where there are reasonably clear indications of abnormal tissue somewhere in the brain. This is because scans have not been obtained before onset of stuttering. Reports on adults and children are reported separately to establish whether the effects are progressive over ages (Ackerman & Riecker, 2010; Chang & Ludlow, 2010).

5.2.1   Brain Morphology in Adults: Brown et al.'s (2005) Meta-Analysis and Subsequent Work

Brown et al. (2005) used a specified set of criteria to select studies for inclusion in their meta-analysis. All the studies were performed on adults who stuttered. The studies selected the imaging method used and the task were as follows:

1. Fox et al. (1996) performed a PET study on 10 stutterers and 10 controls (all male). The task was paragraph reading.
2. Braun et al. (1997) reported a PET study on 18 stutterers and 20 controls (mixed gender groups). Two tasks were used: spontaneous narrative and sentence construction. A feature of the analysis was that performance also was correlated with disfluency rate (for this reason, the study is also discussed in section 5.4).
3. Fox et al. (2000) carried out a PET study on 10 stutterers and 10 controls (all male). The task was paragraph reading. Performance was correlated with stuttering rate.
4. De Nil, Knoll, Kapur, and Houle (2000) conducted a PET study with 10 stutterers and 10 controls (all male) and the tasks used were word reading and silent reading. The latter was a control condition that would avoid motor artifacts.
5. De Nil, Kroll, Lafaille, and Houle (2003) ran a PET study with 13 stutterers and 10 controls (all male). The task was word reading.
6. Neumann et al. (2003) was the first of two fMRI studies. Sixteen stutterers and 16 controls (all male) were used. The task was sentence reading.
7. Preibisch et al. (2003) performed the other study that used fMRI. Sixteen stutterers and 16 controls were used, and the task was sentence reading.
8. The last study was by Ingham, Fox, Ingham et al. (2004) and used PET. All participants were female (10 stutterers and 10 controls). The task was paragraph reading. Performance was correlated with stuttering rate, as in Fox et al. (2000).

The authors did separate meta-analyses of the data from the stutterers and from the controls. The meta-analysis of the fluent speakers produced similar results to those reported in other meta-analyses of nonstutterers using single-word reading (Fiez & Petersen, 1998; Indefrey & Levelt, 2004).

The main findings of Brown et al.'s meta-analyses with reference to stuttering were:

1. In the people who stuttered, generally speaking, the same areas were active as seen in fluent speakers, and there was overactivation in the cortical motor areas.
2. There was anomalous right-dominant lateralization in these areas. This is potentially consistent with less left-lateralized activity in people who stutter.
3. Activation in the auditory association cortex and the basal ganglia were absent bilaterally in the stutterers. A difference in basal ganglia activity would have been expected by Alm (2004).
4. Additional motor and nonmotor areas of activation were seen in the stutterers, but not the controls (e.g., frontal operculum and vermis III).

The authors' explanation singled out the underactivity in the auditory area, and the heightened activity in the right frontal regions and the cerebellum. One way that speech motor control may take place is by listening to one's own speech via the auditory system and comparing it with a copy of the intended motor plan (feedforward control, discussed in Chapter 11). Comparison of efferent copy with exteroceptive output is performed in the cerebellum, according to Kawato (Wolpert, Miall, & Kawato, 1998). The lower activation of auditory input and higher cerebellar activation could be a response to a mismatch between intended and consequential action (Howell, 2002). However, two cautions are appropriate. First, higher activation need not necessarily mean higher work rates for that dimension in particular regions. Thus, the area might be an inhibitory area, in which case higher activity means lower work rate. Second, detectability of activation depends on the level of any neural noise that is present. It is possible that people who stutter have higher levels of neural noise in the CNS overall than fluent speakers (Howell, 2007b). The same underlying activation patterns could occur in speakers who stutter and in controls, but the former are less detectable because of the higher background neural noise level. Such an effect might make normal laterality patterns in specific areas difficult to detect, although it would not explain reversed laterality patterns.

The meta-analysis of these studies found evidence that cortical motor activation and cerebellar activity differed between speakers who stutter and controls, but failed to find evidence for basal ganglia involvement in adults. However, studies subsequent to the Brown et al. article have found evidence for the involvement of this structure. For instance, Giraud et al. (2008) performed an fMRI study. They reported a correlation between severity of stuttering and activity in the basal ganglia, and showed that this activity was modified by fluency-shaping therapy that reflected speech production improvement.

Further evidence in support of basal ganglia involvement in stuttering was given by Lu, Peng, Chen et al. (2010). They used structural equation modeling (SEM) and voxel-based morphometry (VBM). A voxel is a three-dimensional pixel. VBM is a neuroimaging analysis technique that allows differences in brain anatomy to be located with good sensitivity. In standard morphometry, the volume of the whole brain or its subparts is measured by specifying regions of interest (ROIs) on images from brain scans and calculating the volume enclosed. However, this only provides measures over large areas so small differences in volume can be overlooked. VBM registers every brain to a template, which gets rid of most of the large differences in brain anatomy among people. Then the brain images are smoothed so that each voxel represents the average of itself and its neighbors. Finally, the image volume is compared across brains at every voxel.

In Lu, Peng, Chen, et al.'s (2010) study, 12 stuttering and 12 fluent controls were scanned while performing a picture-naming task. The results showed significant differences between stuttering and nonstuttering speakers in the basal ganglia-thalamocortical circuit and in the left hemisphere.

Several other studies have looked at lateral patterns of activity. There have been reports of anatomical differences with respect to hemispheric processing as well as the functional imaging work supporting laterality differences that were referred to earlier (e.g., Fox et al., 1996). Foundas, Bollich, Corey, Hurley, and Heilman (2001) showed less asymmetry of the planum temporale. Sommer, Koch, Paulus, Weiller, and Buchel (2002) showed left rolandic operculum white matter disturbance. MEG studies have shown right-sided overactivity of motor and premotor areas (Salmelin, Schnitzler, Schmitz, & Freund, 2000). Overall, these findings suggest that developmental stuttering that persists into adulthood might be associated with a structural lesion in the left hemisphere.

However, Sommer et al. (2009) recently reported a transcranial magnetic stimulation (TMS) study that investigated laterality in people who stuttered. TMS is a noninvasive method that excites neurons in the brain. Weak electric currents are induced in the neural tissue by rapidly changing magnetic fields (electromagnetic induction). In this way, brain activity can be triggered with minimal discomfort, and the functionality of the circuitry and connectivity of the brain can be studied. The interhemispheric inhibition (IHI) studied with transcranial magnetic stimulation is an established measure for examining the interplay between the right and left motor areas. In IHI, a single conditioning TMS pulse is given to one hemisphere and this produces inhibition of the test response evoked from the opposite hemisphere. In the Sommer et al. (2009) study, IHI was examined in 15 young male adults with persistent developmental stuttering and 15 age-matched fluent participants. No significant between-group difference occurred for IHI. It was concluded that the interplay between the primary motor cortices is normal in patients with persistent developmental stuttering. The authors argued that the abnormal right motor and premotor activity observed in functional imaging studies on the persistent developmental stutterers was unlikely to reflect altered primary motor cortex excitability.

Partly answering the questions raised at the start of this section, the brains of adults who stutter appear to be structurally and functionally different from the brains of control speakers: Foundas et al. (2001), Sommer et al. (2002), and

Salmelin et al. (2000) all showed unusual left side anatomy of people who stutter. A caution is that the recent TMS study failed to find hemispheric differences (Sommer et al., 2009). Functional scanning work shows different patterns of activity in motor cortex, insula, cerebellum, and basal ganglia. The structural problems could be a result of different functional use of brain areas by speakers who stutter compared to controls.

5.2.2   BRAIN MORPHOLOGY IN CHILDREN

Watkins, Smith, Davis, and Howell (2008) examined 12 children who stuttered and 12 controls (average age 18 years). Brain structure and function was assessed using functional, and diffusion tensor, imaging (DTI). In DTI, each voxel in an image has an intensity that reflects a single best measurement of the rate of water diffusion at that location. It provides a measure of the extent to which the fiber bundle in a CNS area is oriented in parallel (efficient CNS operation) or not. As in studies on adults, during speech production, the participants who stuttered showed overactivity relative to controls in the anterior insula, cerebellum, and midbrain bilaterally, and underactivity in the ventral premotor, rolandic operculum, and sensorimotor cortex bilaterally, and in Heschl's gyrus on the left. These results are consistent with Brown et al.'s (2005) meta-analysis of functional imaging studies in developmental stuttering in adults. There were two additional findings. First, there was overactivity in the midbrain, which was at the level of the substantia nigra and extended to the pedunculopontine nucleus, red nucleus, and subthalamic nucleus. This overactivity is consistent with suggestions in previous studies of abnormal function of the basal ganglia or excessive dopamine in people who stutter. Second, there was underactivity of the corticomotor and premotor areas associated with articulation and speech production. Analysis of the diffusion data revealed that the integrity of the white matter underlying the underactive areas in ventral premotor cortex was reduced in people who stutter.

Chang, Erickson, Ambrose, Hasegawa-Johnson, and Ludlow (2008) hypothesized that left white matter deficiencies and reversed right–left asymmetries in adults with persistent stuttering compared to fluent controls might be present in children at risk of stuttering and, if so, would indicate brain development differences between speaker groups. They employed eight children with persistent stuttering, seven children recovered from stuttering, and seven fluent peers, all of whom were male and aged between 9 and 12 years. Participants who stuttered were drawn from the Illinois study, which was discussed in Chapters 1 and 3). The authors performed VBM comparisons between gray matter volume (GMV) and diffusion tensor imaging measured fractional anisotropy (FA) in white matter tracts in the three groups. FA is a measure of directional dependency in fiber bundles where it is thought to reflect fiber density, axonal diameter, and myelination in white matter. Both the persistent stuttering and recovered groups had reduced GMV relative to normal speakers in speech-relevant regions: left inferior frontal gyrus and bilateral temporal. Reduced FA was observed in the left white matter tracts underlying the motor regions for face and larynx in the persistent stuttering group. Contrary to previous findings in adults who stutter but consistent with Sommer et al.'s (2009) TMS study on adults, no increases were found in the right hemisphere speech regions in stuttering or recovered children and no differences in right–left asymmetries. Instead, a risk for childhood stuttering was associated with deficiencies in left GMV, while reduced white matter integrity in the left hemisphere speech system was associated with persistent stuttering. They suggested that anatomical increases in right hemisphere structures previously found in adults who stutter may have resulted from a lifetime of stuttering.

Both the studies with children show anatomical and functional effects similar to those in adults, although there is no strong evidence for abnormal lateralization of activity in the children. The studies show, then, that the functional and anatomical differences are evident at young ages (from around 9 years, according to Chang et al. (2008). However, the children who persisted in this study had six or more years' experience stuttering and such effects may or may not occur at onset of the disorder. They are certainly evident at the teenage years when course of stuttering into persistence or recovery is set. Also, some of the children may go on to recover before their teens (Chapter 1).

5.3 MODELING CONNECTIVITY

Three studies from the same laboratory have used SEM to determine connectivity patterns between areas of activation in the brain of adults who stutter and fluent controls (Lu, Chen, Ning et al., 2010; Lu, Peng, Chen, et al., 2009; Lu, Ning, Peng, et al., 2010). When applied to fMRI data, SEM can allow the connections between brain areas to be modeled by relations, interdependencies, and correlations among the various brain areas (de Marco et al., 2009). These analyses implicated the structures suggested by the Brown et al. meta-analysis and work since then (reviewed above in section 5.2.1).

Lu, Peng, Chen et al.'s (2010) study investigated the neural bases of atypical planning and execution processes involved in stuttering in 12 stuttering speakers and 12 controls. Participants were asked to name pictures under different conditions (single syllable, multisyllable, or repeated syllable) in the scanner. Comparison between conditions provided information about planning and execution processes. In an analysis that classified participants as stutterers/nonstutterers, it was shown that, as compared to nonstuttering controls, stuttering speakers' atypical planning of speech was evident in their neural activities in the bilateral inferior frontal gyrus (IFG) and right putamen, and their atypical execution of speech was evident in their activations in the right cerebellum and insula, left premotor area (PMA), and angular gyrus (AG). SEM results further revealed that two parallel neural circuits, the basal ganglia-to-premotor area circuit (Alm, 2004) and the cerebellum-to-premotor area circuit (Howell, 2002) were involved in atypical planning and execution processes of stuttering, respectively. The AG appeared to be involved in the interface between the atypical planning and execution processes in stuttering. This study has particular relevance to the language–speech motor interaction model that will be discussed in Chapter 12.

Lu, Ning, Peng et al. (2009) also used SEM, this time to examine the role of large-scale neural interactions in adults who reported developmental stuttering. Ten stuttering and nine nonstuttering participants performed a covert picture-naming task. Results indicated that the connection patterns were significantly different between stuttering and nonstuttering speakers. Specifically, stuttering speakers showed functional disconnection from the left inferior frontal gyrus to the left motor areas, and altered connectivity in the basal ganglia–thalamic–cortical circuit, and abnormal integration of supramodal information across the cerebellum and several frontal–parietal regions. The authors suggested that the results indicate that the large-scale dysfunctional neural interactions may be involved in stuttering speakers' alleged difficulties in planning, execution, and self-monitoring of speech motor sequences during word production.

5.4   VARIATION WITH SEVERITY

Severity may relate to persistence (as suggested by Howell and Davis's (in press) results that are discussed in full in Chapter 13). Two studies have correlated activation patterns with severity (Giraud et al., 2008; Ingham et al., 2004).

Discussion of Giraud et al. appeared earlier in this chapter (section 5.2.1). In brief, they reported a correlation between severity of stuttering and activity in the basal ganglia, and showed that this activity was modified by fluency-shaping therapy.

Ingham et al. (2004) was a study on females, and the authors compared their results with the Fox et al. (2000) study on males that was discussed above. Both studies used PET to obtain cerebral blood flow and correlated this with speech behavior scores. The total number of voxels per region correlated significantly with speech performance (as in Fox et al., 2000) and also the total numbers of voxels per region were significantly correlated with stuttering rate, but not with syllable rate. Stutter-rate regional correlates were generally right-sided in males, but bilateral in the females. For both sexes, the positive regional correlates for stuttering were in right anterior insula and the negative correlates were in right Brodmann area 21/22 and an area within left inferior frontal gyrus. The female stutterers displayed additional positive correlates in left anterior insula and in basal ganglia (left globus pallidus, right caudate), plus extensive right hemisphere negative correlates in the prefrontal area and the limbic and parietal lobes. The male stuttering speakers were distinguished by positive correlates in left medial occipital lobe and right medial cerebellum. Regions that positively correlated with syllable rate (essentially a stutter-free measure) in stuttering speakers and controls were very similar for both sexes. The findings were interpreted as suggesting that chronic developmental stuttering is functionally related to abnormal speech motor and auditory region interactions. The authors suggested that gender differences may be related to differences between the sexes with respect to susceptibility (males predominate) and recovery from chronic stuttering (females show higher recovery rates during childhood, as seen in Chapter 2). Both studies suggest that severity may be associated with basal ganglia function.

5.5   SPEECH IN FLUENCY-ENHANCING AND FLUENCY-INDUCING CONDITIONS

One important question is whether activation differences compared to fluent speakers remain when speakers who stutter are induced to speak fluently, usually by alterations to auditory feedback (Chapter 8), but sometimes via other known methods (e.g., choral speech, also described in Chapter 8). If the differences remain when fluency is enhanced, it would appear that the results are not due to motor artifacts. Early work using PET scans with people who stutter showed that different areas are active when speaking in their normal manner (i.e., with stuttering) as opposed to when speaking in fluency-enhancing conditions (Ingham et al., 1996; Kroll, De Nil, Kapur, & Houle, 1997; Wu, Riley, Maguire, Najafi, & Tang, 1997). Generally speaking, activity patterns looked more like those of fluent speakers in fluency-enhancing conditions.

To take one early example, Braun et al. (1997) compared scans acquired during fluency- versus disfluency-evoking tasks. They suggested that during the production of stuttered speech, the anterior forebrain regions, which play a role in the regulation of motor function, were disproportionately active in stuttering participants. On the other hand, postrolandic regions, which play a role in perception and decoding of sensory information, were relatively inactive. Comparison of scans, acquired during the same conditions in control participants, provided information about the sensorimotor and cognitive features of the language tasks themselves. These comparisons suggested a mechanism by which fluency-evoking maneuvers might differentially affect activity in these anterior and posterior brain regions, and thus may facilitate fluent speech production in individuals who stutter. Both correlational and contrast analyses suggested that right and left hemispheres played distinct and opposing roles in the generation of stuttering symptoms. The authors argued that activation of left hemispheric regions may relate to the production of stuttered speech, while activation of right hemispheric regions may represent compensatory processes associated with attenuation of stuttering symptoms.

More recently, Stager, Jeffries, and Braun (2003) used PET to characterize the common features of two different fluency-evoking conditions (paced speech and singing). The goal was to identify brain mechanisms that enabled fluent speech in people who stutter. They compared responses under these fluency-inducing conditions with responses in tasks that elicited stuttering. They quantified the degree of stuttering in all conditions and used this as a covariate in analyses. Effectively this removes the effects of a stuttering rate between conditions. The areas that were either uniquely activated during fluency-inducing conditions or in which the magnitude of activation was significantly greater during fluency-inducing than stuttering-evoking tasks included auditory association areas that process speech and voice, and motor regions related to control of the larynx and oral articulators. The authors suggested that a common fluency-inducing mechanism might be related to more effective coupling of auditory and motor systems. While responses seen in both groups were bilateral, the fluency-inducing tasks elicited more robust activation of auditory and motor regions within the left hemisphere of stuttering participants. They suggested that this indicated a role for the left hemisphere in compensatory processes that induce fluency.

One study has examined the effects of fluency-enhancing conditions in older children (the same children as in Watkins et al., 2008). Watkins, Patel, Davis, and Howell (2005) reported significantly greater activation of the right posterior IFG, superior temporal gyrus bilaterally and, extensively along its length, right superior temporal sulcus and the left cerebellar hemisphere (posterior and lateral portions) in a delayed auditory feedback condition relative to a normal hearing condition.

Other methods have been used that rule out motor artifacts. For example, Ingham, Fox, Ingham, and Zamarripa (2000) asked whether overt stuttered speech was a prerequisite for the neural activations associated with chronic developmental stuttering. They used four adult right-handed chronic stutterers and four age-matched controls in a PET study that involved participants' overt and imagined oral reading tasks. During overt stuttering, speech prominent activations occurred in SMA (medial), Brodmann area 46 (right), anterior insula (bilateral), and cerebellum (bilateral) as well as deactivations in Brodmann areas 21/22 (right). These activations and deactivations also occurred when the same stutterers imagined they were stuttering. Some parietal regions were significantly activated during imagined stuttering, but not during overt stuttering. Most regional activations changed in the same direction when overt stuttering ceased (elicited by chorus reading) and when participants imagined that they were not stuttering (also during chorus reading). The control participants displayed fewer similarities between regional activations and deactivations during actual and imagined oral reading. Thus, overt stuttering appears not to be a prerequisite for the prominent regional activations and deactivations associated with stuttering.

De Nil et al. (2008) looked at the converse situation, namely, what happens to activation patterns when stuttering and fluent adults simulated stuttering. They asked, in particular, whether fMRI patterns shown in simulated stuttering were similar to the atypical patterns associated with stuttering. There were 15 stuttering and 15 fluent adult males (mean ages 31 years, 7 months and 33 years, respectively). The critical conditions for the present report involved listening and repeating words in normal and simulated stuttering conditions. Within-group comparisons revealed increased right hemisphere biased activation of speech-related regions during the simulated stuttering task, relative to the habitual speech task, in the stuttering group. No significant activation differences were observed for the fluent participants between these speech conditions. Between-group comparison revealed increased right inferior frontal gyrus activation during simulated stuttering relative to the fluent controls. The observed activation changes were considered to reflect the changed motor behavior regardless of whether or not an increase in speech fluency accompanied this change. Their results suggest, then, functional deficiencies underlying motor planning and execution in people who stutter. This interpretation contrasts with the conventional view that these observed changes result from increased speech fluency under such fluency-enhancing conditions.

5.6   SUMMARY AND CONCLUSIONS

There is evidence for structural and functional differences between adults who stutter and controls in many of the brain regions that Jurgens (2002) indicated are involved in voluntary speech control. However, caution should be expressed about the implications of these findings: The structural differences could be a result of the functional consequences of being a person who stutters. Also, it has not been shown how these CNS differences explain the symptoms of stuttering in a definitive way. The differences are often not found in all individuals in the same way, so many, if not all, of these differences may be neither necessary nor sufficient to explain stuttering. More work is needed with children nearer the onset of stuttering.

Bearing in mind these cautions, some tentative examination can be made of specific sites indicated by behavioral work. Different activity in both the basal ganglia (Alm, 2004) and the cerebellum (Howell, 2002) have been noted between speakers who stutter and fluent controls and, for speakers who stutter, between normal speaking, and fluency-enhancing, conditions. The work by Lu and colleagues (2009, 2010) has identified areas associated with planning, execution, and the language–speech motor interface. The evidence for abnormal laterality patterns was originally supportive of the hypothesis that people who stutter tend to have different hemispheric specialization from fluent speakers. However, recent work has failed to find this in adults (Sommer et al., 2009) or children (Chang et al., 2008).

5.7   EXERCISES

1. Are the activation differences observed between the brains of people who stutter and those of controls a cause or an effect of stuttering?
2. There are methods that involve placing electrodes on the skull (surface electrodes) that can be used to measure brain activity in young children who stutter that are not discussed in this chapter. Investigate these techniques and establish their strengths and weaknesses relative to scanning methods. Describe any results you can find using these techniques with people who stutter.

6 Cognitive Factors

Dual-task experiments have been done exclusively with adults. Though the work has potentially important implications for onset and course of stuttering, the experimental data on children are not available at present. Behavioral evidence suggests that cerebellar mechanisms might be implicated in dual-task performance. The cerebellum also has a role in regulating timing. A proposal is discussed that unifies dual-task deficits, timing control in people who stutter, including the effects of changing timing on fluency and a proposed way in which stuttering persists in some individuals, but recovers in others.

6.1 INTRODUCTION

Stuttering may affect general purpose cognitive mechanisms, not only the ones specifically responsible for processing language and converting language output to speech motor patterns. Results with one well-studied cognitive paradigm, which can be used to examine how nonspeech factors affect language performance in adults who stutter, is described in section 6.2. This is the concurrent or dual-task paradigm where a task, such as speaking, is performed along with a secondary task. Performance in dual-tasks is often linked with cerebellar processes. Some evidence about the role of this structure in dual tasks and a possible link with timing control are given in section 6.3. This section also includes some hypotheses that relate the results to known features of developmental stuttering and the persistent form in particular.

6.2 COGNITION DUAL TASKS

A dual-task paradigm requires an individual to perform two tasks simultaneously. In dual-task procedures, performance is compared between single and dual-task conditions. If two tasks interfere, the performance scores on one and/or both tasks are lower when they are done simultaneously compared to when the tasks are done separately. Interference is usually taken as evidence that both tasks compete for the same type of processing resources in the brain. (See Van Lieshout, 2004, for discussion of issues about such claims.) Evidence is reviewed here from work where comparisons were made between single- and dual-task performance for groups of people who stutter and control groups in studies involving a range of tasks. After the findings have been presented, suggestions about what mechanisms could be involved are listed. Skill learning, which some authors consider to be deficient in people who stutter, follows a process of first acquiring knowledge by fully conscious, focused attention and observation, then by establishing mental connections that make that knowledge automatic (instantly available for a given context). Dual-task paradigms are used to study learning skills as they afford a way of varying task complexity in a systematic and reasonably well understood way. The cerebellum may be particularly important in dual-task performance because it is the mechanism that appears to be involved in automatizing motor skill learning (Fawcett, Nicolson, & Dean, 1996). The cerebellum is also important in timing control, which makes this a structure of interest for stuttering where timing problems may be implicated.

6.2.1   WORD AND NONSENSE SYLLABLE REPETITION AS THE PRIMARY TASK

Bosshardt (1999, 2002) reported two related studies. Both involved word repetition (saying three nouns repeatedly), but differed in the form of the secondary task. Mental addition was used as the secondary task by Bosshardt (1999). He tested nine adults who stuttered (mean age of 37 years, 2 months) and 10 controls (mean age of 23;1). Silent prolongations, prolongations, repetitions of sounds syllables, and one-syllable words were used as symptoms for inclusion of participants in the stuttering group. Stuttering rate, inhalation, and speech timing were measured in single- and dual-task conditions and the tasks were repeated 10 times each. Inhalation rate was the only dependent variable that showed significant interactions between the speaker groups and task factors. Detailed examination of inhalation rate showed that on repetition 4 in the dual task condition, inhalation rate reduced below single task level for people who stuttered, but not for controls. Bosshardt attributed this to speakers who stutter, reducing their speech effort at this point in the sequence, although the three-way interaction between speaker group, task factor, and repetition number was not significant.

Bosshardt (2002) included word repetition as a symptom again, but this time silent reading and memorizing words comprised the secondary task. The words that were repeated were constructed to be similar (initial consonant and vowel of the first syllable of the word was the same) or dissimilar (each syllable occurred only once). Fourteen adults (11 males) who stuttered and 16 controls (13 males) participated and the average age of the groups was 33;9 and 33;3, respectively. Symptoms counted as stutters were prolongations, repetitions of sounds syllables, and single syllable whole words, and observable tension in articulation. Stuttering rate, pause rate, and number of words recalled in the secondary task were examined as dependent variables. Stuttering rate provided some evidence for dual-task interference. Thus, it was found that speakers who stuttered had significantly higher stuttering rates during word repetition when they concurrently read or memorized similar, but not dissimilar, words. No effect was found for controls. These results were taken as an indication that the speech of people who stutter was more sensitive to interference from concurrently performed cognitive processing than was that of controls. There was no significant interaction between speaker group and task condition for stuttering rate or the other dependent variables.

Study 2 in Smits-Bandstra and de Nil (2009) was a dual-task experiment that used a nonsense syllable reading task and a color recognition task. The nonsense syllable reading task involved producing 10 plosive vowel syllables all with the same vowel /a/. The dependent variables for this task were reaction time (time from stimulus onset to onset of first syllable) and error rate (number of voicing errors, incorrect substitutions, extra or missing syllables). For the color recognition distractor task, participants saw a row of four squares. These squares were illuminated in different colors three times before they disappeared from the screen (e.g., red, blue, green, red). Participants were required to indicate whether the same color appeared in two of the squares (they pressed one of two keys to indicate "yes" or "no"). The dependent variable was error rate.

Nine males who stuttered who ranged in age from 23 years to 51 years with mean age 33;7 and eight controls who ranged in age from 26 to 51 years with mean age 33;5 were employed. The participants who stuttered scored in the very mild (4), mild (3), and moderate (2) range on the stuttering severity instrument-3 (SSI-3) (Riley, 1994). The speech sequences of the speakers who stuttered were initiated significantly slower than those of the controls. The only significant speaker group by task condition interaction was for syllable sequencing accuracy. People who stuttered showed more sequencing errors under dual-task than under single-task conditions, whereas controls showed little change. This finding was interpreted as suggesting that controls, but not people who stutter, demonstrated the ability to switch from a single task where little attention was required, to an attention-demanding dual-task condition in a relatively automatic way.

These three studies on dual-task interference to word and nonsense syllable repetition show some evidence in support of the view that people who stutter are more affected. Bosshardt (1999) and Smits-Bandstra and de Nil (2009) reported speaker group by task condition interactions, and Bosshardt (2002) reported dual-task interference for speakers who stutter, but not for controls. No studies have examined children who stutter, either at onset or during the early course of the disorder.

6.2.2 Sentence Generation as the Primary Task

Two further experiments have been conducted where the primary task was sentence generation (de Nil & Bosshardt, 2000; Bosshardt, Ballmer, & de Nil, 2002). In the generation task, participants were required to form sentences using two unrelated nouns. Participants were instructed to generate their sentences silently for 10 sec before they were allowed to produce them orally.

de Nil and Bosshardt's (2000) participants performed the sentence generation task with continuous rhyme and category decisions as secondary tasks. The dependent variables were rhyme accuracy and category decision accuracy. The experiment was run on 12 stuttering and 12 nonstuttering adults (ages and gender not given). An interesting feature of this study was that fMRI scans were obtained during sentence generation and articulation under single- and dual-task conditions. Looking at single-task performance, both groups were equally adept at performing rhyming and category decisions with high accuracy. For both groups, category decision accuracy was reduced significantly during sentence generation. However, accuracy reduced more for the people who stuttered than the controls in dual-task conditions for both the rhyming and category decision tasks. Overall, under dual-task conditions, stuttering participants were less able than nonstuttering participants to maintain a high performance level. The authors' description suggests there are speaker group by task interactions (statistics that support this are not reported), that is, some speakers were more affected by the task than others. The difference between single- and dual-task conditions with speakers who stutter, showing specific deficits in dual-task conditions, is undermined by a ceiling effect. That is, for both decision tasks in single-task conditions, performance of both groups of speakers was near 100%. The ceiling effect in single-task conditions would prevent any difference between speaker groups being observed in this condition. No ceiling effect occurred in dual-task conditions, thus group differences can be observed in this condition. Because the ceiling effect selectively affects single-task conditions, this would prevent any possible difference between speaker groups from being observed in single-task conditions, and this would give rise to an apparent interaction between speaker group and task conditions.

For the fMRI data under dual-task conditions where participants had to plan sentences simultaneously while making rhyming or category decisions, the group of nonstuttering participants showed a similar pattern to that seen in the single-task sentence planning task with the exception that there was higher activation in premotor (in the dual-task rhyming) and anterior cingulate cortices (in the dual-task category condition). Activation maps of the group of speakers who stuttered showed comparatively higher activations in cortical areas related to motor planning and execution (left inferior and middle frontal cortex, premotor cortex, and cerebellum). The authors' interpretation was that the results suggest that people who stutter need more central processing capacity to generate and overtly articulate a sentence than those who do not stutter. This conclusion has to be qualified because of the ceiling effect noted above.

Bosshardt et al. (2002) used continuous rhyme and category decisions as secondary tasks (as above) and sentence generation as the primary task. The experiment was conducted on 14 adults who stuttered (mean age = 35;9) and 14 matched controls (mean age = 33;7). Stuttering symptoms were defined as prolongation and repetition of sounds, syllables, and single-syllable words, and auditorily identifiable indications of tension. Stuttering rates were not significantly affected by speaking conditions (single- versus dual-task and rhyme versus category) nor were there interactions of these factors with participant group.

The two studies on sentence generation provide no compelling evidence that dual-task interference has a disproportionate effect on people who stutter. The interpretation of the de Nil and Bosshardt (2000) study is complicated by the ceiling effect in single-task conditions. This is unfortunate, as the idea of identifying which CNS areas are differentially active across single- and dual-task conditions for different speaker groups is an important one. The Bosshardt et al. (2002) study failed to find the key interaction between speaker group and task condition that would show speakers who stutter have problems in sentence generation when performed concurrent with another task. Once again, there are no studies of children who stutter around onset or at ages where the course of stuttering resolves.

6.2.3 COMPARISON OF PERFORMANCE ACROSS TWO NONSPEECH TASKS

Smits-Bandstra, de Nil, and Rochon (2006) tested 12 right-handed males ranging in age from 21 to 51 years who stuttered (mean 33;8) and a matched group of 12 right-handed control participants who ranged in age from 22 to 51 years. The stuttering participants were assessed on SSI-3 and scored in the very mild (6), mild (4), and moderate (2) range. The tasks performed were finger tapping and the color recognition task (described above). The tasks were performed as single- and as dual-tasks. In the finger tapping sequence task, participants were presented with a 10-number sequence (*3 1 3 2 4 1 4 2 3 1*). They had to use the four fingers of their dominant hand to press four buttons arranged horizontally on a response box according to the sequence of the numbers on the screen. They were instructed to respond rapidly and accurately. The displayed sequences disappeared as soon as the participants completed the sequence.

There was a significant interaction between single-/dual-task conditions and speaker groups for syllable sequencing error. The accuracy of the control participants was better than that of people who stutter under single-task conditions for syllable sequencing, but the errors of the people who stuttered did not differ from controls in dual-task conditions. The authors found that the control participants responded quicker than the people who stuttered in the single-task condition and noted that this showed control participants did not sacrifice accuracy in order to increase speed.

The question that arises about this study is why the differences between speaker groups were found on the simpler single-task condition rather than dual-task conditions. As dual-tasks are more demanding, more interference would be expected for people who stutter in dual-task conditions, as reported in the recent study by Smits-Bandstra and de Nil (2009). What makes Smits-Bandstra et al.'s (2006) experiment of particular interest is that performance in a nonspeech motor performance task was disrupted by a secondary task. It is unfortunate that there is no evidence for this in children who stutter at onset or at ages where the course of stuttering resolves.

6.3 NATURE OF THE MECHANISM AFFECTED IN DUAL TASKS AND EVIDENCE ON PERSISTENCE AND RECOVERY

Bosshardt and de Nil's groups have provided evidence that a variety of tasks interfere with speech and that the interference in certain conditions is greater in people who stutter than in controls. Their contributions have shown ways in which the speech system of people who stutter can be more sensitive to disruption than in control groups. They have begun to assess what central nervous system (CNS) areas are involved when performing dual tasks and what differences there are between speakers who stutter and fluent speakers. At present, they have not related their findings back to behavioral tests that assess the functioning of the CNS areas identified as being involved in dual-task deficits for people who stutter.

This issue has been addressed for another disorder, dyslexia, by Fawcett et al. (1996) and in other publications.

Fawcett et al. proposed that there was a mechanism in the cerebellum that is sensitive to dual-task interference in dyslexic individuals. They reported that children with dyslexia showed deficits on a set of motor tasks that was developed to assess the integrity of cerebellar operation in patients (Dow & Moruzzi, 1958). The battery is divided into three components: tasks involving balance/posture, complex movements, and hypotonia. Balance is highly affected when children with dyslexia perform a secondary task.

Howell, Davis, and Williams (2008) reported differences between persistent and recovered speakers who stutter on the tasks used by Fawcett et al. (1996). In particular, differences were found in balance, posture, and complex movement. This appears to implicate the cerebellum in this disorder. The finding of cerebellar deficits in children who persist raises a similar question to that which Fawcett et al. faced: Why should a speech–language disorder be associated with deficits in a motor-timing mechanism in the cerebellum?

Fawcett et al.'s answer to the former question proposed that writing involves reading and learning input, thus, in some sense, writing could be regarded as a secondary task. A child who has motor problems, such as those they found in cerebellar tasks in these children, will need to devote more resources to these aspects of performance and, conversely, will have less capacity to devote to other concurrent actions. As a consequence, children with dyslexia have problems automatizing skills. This explains why a child referred with a reading problem also may have problems in motor activities. It is possible that a similar explanation could be developed for children who stutter. However, the following sections offer an alternative proposal.

6.3.1 Variability Estimates in Finger Tapping and the Link to Cerebellar Involvement

Cerebellar involvement in stuttering is interesting for other reasons in addition to those associated with dual-task interference. In particular, rapid rates of speech are often thought to exacerbate stuttering (this is discussed in Chapter 8). Some evidence relevant to the role of the cerebellum in timing control is considered below.

The most popular task used to investigate cerebellar timing mechanisms is one introduced by Wing and Kristofferson (1973). Participants in the standard Wing and Kristofferson procedure hear an isochronous rhythm that they tap to. After entrainment (tracking the rhythm accurately), they try to continue tapping exactly at the same rate (the time of the taps is measured). The task has been modified to examine speech where a syllable, such as /bae/, is used instead of a tap. With either form of the task, the timing variability in the sequence of responses is decomposed into variance of motor processes (Mv) and variance of a timekeeper (Cv). The essence of the analysis procedure is that if the motor system leads to a tap being placed at the wrong point in time, it is compensated for in the next interval. Thus, Mv can be estimated from the lag one autocovariance (covariance over time, in the lag one case, this is between adjacent productions). Taking Mv's contribution away from the total variance leaves an estimate of Cv.

Verification that the Wing and Kristofferson (1973) task is associated with cerebellar processing has been obtained using patients who have a lesion in the cerebellum to see whether, and, if so, which, regions of the cerebellum are associated with Mv and which with Cv (Ivry, 1997). Lateral lesions of the cerebellum affect timing control, suggesting that the timekeeper mechanism is located in this part of the CNS (Ivry, 1997). The medial areas of the cerebellum appear to be involved with Mv, as lesions to this part affect this variance component.

Hulstijn, Summers, Van Lieshout, and Peters (1992) used the tapping and speech versions of the Wing–Kristofferson task with 12 adult male stutterers and 12 controls. Participants were classified as stutterers by two certified speech pathologists. Overall, six tasks were performed, three involved repetitive tapping with one or both index fingers, called tapping tasks, and three involved repetitive production of a voiced sound (either /i/ or /pip/), called speaking tasks. In all conditions, a short tone was played that had a stimulus onset asynchrony of 400 ms. The participant tried to synchronize their response with the tone sequence, which was switched off after 13 synchronization responses. The participant continued responding until an additional 31 (tapping) or 21 (speaking) intervals were recorded.

The three tapping conditions involved the dominant hand, the nondominant hand, and both hands simultaneously. The three speaking conditions involved repeating the vowel /i/, repeating the syllable /pip/, and tapping with the dominant hand and repeating the syllable /pip/ (a dual task). Estimates of Cv and Mv were obtained and compared across speaker groups. There were no significant differences across speaker groups for either estimate in any of the six conditions. This study failed to find evidence of differences between speaker groups that would indicate differences in cerebellar involvement in the disorder. A more recent study that also used the Wing–Kristofferson task also failed to find any evidence for cerebellar deficits in adults who stutter in a study conducted with speech, orofacial nonspeech, and finger tapping versions (Max & Yudman, 2003). However, there are data on the speech version of the Wing and Kristofferson task that indicate that children who stutter (9 children aged 9–10) have problems in the Mv component (Howell, Au-Yeung, & Rustin, 1997). Whether the discrepancy is due to using participants of different ages (only Howell et al., 1997, used children) or because children may have more problems in timing control in general (see Smith, Goffman, Zelaznik, Ying, & McGillem's (1995) work on this issue in Chapter 8, section 8.4.1) remains to be established.

Performance in the Wing–Kristofferson task under delayed auditory feedback (DAF) has been used to examine timing control in the cerebellum. This has relevance to stuttering as it is a procedure sometimes used to induce fluency in such speakers. Under DAF, speech takes place in the presence of a delayed version of itself (like an echo). Importantly, it is shown in Chapter 8, section 8.2.4 that delayed nonspeech noise creates similar effects to speech DAF. These results rule out DAF affecting language planning, but do not identify what motor mechanism is involved. Howell and Sackin (2002) used the speech modification of the Wing and Kristofferson (1973) task to see whether DAF selectively affected the time-keeper. They required fluent adult participants to perform the speech version of the Wing–Kristofferson task in conditions where they heard concurrent DAF. DAF led to a marked increase in Cv, the Cv increase being greater for longer DAF delays and more marked when the syllable had to be repeated for longer periods. Mv, on the other hand, stayed roughly constant across the DAF delay and repetition period. The fact that Cv rather than Mv was affected by DAF delay supports the idea that DAF has a direct influence on the timekeeper and has little effect on the motor processes.

6.3.2 Synchronous and Asynchronous Events and the Cerebellum

Using results like Howell and Sackin (2002), Howell (2002) proposed that the cerebellar timing mechanism is sensitive to rhythmic inputs associated with articulation (motor instructions to produce a sound, the intensity structure of the associated speech output, etc.). Timing performance is smooth and speech is fluent when the inputs are synchronized, as happens when output activities are synchronized with speech actions. Timing performance is disrupted when the inputs are out of synchrony. The delayed sound is asynchronous in the DAF procedure, which creates such a situation and timing is modulated by cerebellar processes (Howell & Sackin, 2002). In the case of DAF, the cerebellar timekeeper is affected because of the asynchronous disturbance that takes place concurrent with speech. Thus, the delayed sound under DAF is not used as feedback to determine whether a speech error occurred, but acts as a secondary disruptive rhythm that interferes with (specifically slows down) speech control. Howell (2002) hypothesized that similar asynchronies occur when the motor instructions and speech output are out of synchrony (i.e., when speech is disfluent) and the cerebellar timing mechanisms again adjust timing. These adjustments made in motor processes allow the speakers more time to plan forthcoming language (see Chapter 12). As mentioned, it is known that DAF improves timing control in speakers who stutter. (See Chapter 8 for a full discussion.) This may arise because of the effect of DAF on cerebellar timing mechanisms.

The question that naturally arises is: How does a speaker detect when inputs are asynchronous and that some speech adjustment is required so that fluency can be reestablished, and how does this process fail in speakers who persist in their stuttering? Howell (2002) proposed a simple way in which synchrony could be checked. If two temporal signals with equal amplitude are in synchrony, then subtracting them cancels out both representations. In the case of timing signals associated with speech, this could be done for efferent copies of motor commands and neural representations of speech recovered from vocal output. Similar arguments apply to other timing signals associated with the speech activity. The cancellation of these two signals means there is no net activity in the CNS. Speech proceeds without the need for any adjustment, thus it is effectively under open loop conditions (with no feedback). Subtracting pairs of signals also can be regarded as a simple form of feedforward control (discussed in Chapter 11) insofar as it uses efferent copy.

When an external signal, such as DAF, is presented, its neural representation would not cancel when it is subtracted from the efferent copy signal, simply because speech and the altered signal are asynchronous. The net signal leads to a sequence of *alerts* that indicate to the speaker that speech control needs adjusting. In the case of DAF, this leads to slowing of motor output. With DAF, a slower speech rate alone would not stop the alerts, as they are externally imposed. Nevertheless, the slowed speech rate could have an indirect effect on the fluency of people who stutter; slowed speech motor rate would allow more language planning time.

Howell (2002) hypothesized that when a speaker stutters in normal speaking situations, the speaker starts to execute an incomplete plan. The efferent copy of the plan continues to be upgraded until it is complete. The neural timing signal recovered from auditory output (partial) and the efferent copy (complete) would not be in synchrony; the speaker is not achieving the output pattern that corresponds to the efferent copy. When the two signals are subtracted, alerts would be generated in a similar way to that described for speech under DAF and the alerts signal that the speaker should adjust speech rate. The discrepancies between the efferent copy and the neural representation of the output pattern can be due to language processing not being completed (efferent copy) at the time speech is initiated or motor control problems that arise after language processing is complete (timing disruption in the output pattern). In either case, a slower speech rate would stop the alerts by allowing more time for the respective processes. Slowing allows speech timing to automatically return to a situation where the timing signals associated with the efferent copy and vocal output are in synchrony (i.e., a full plan is issued before motor processing starts or more time is allowed for motor processing). The timings match and they cancel when the two are subtracted. The alerts stop and speech is fluent and returns to open loop control.

Howell, Rosen, Hannigan, and Rustin (2000) proposed why this alerting process ceases to be effective in people who persist in their stuttering. All brain processes show adaptation to events that happen repeatedly. People who respond to the alerts would experience them less and less frequently maintaining their sensitivity to them and recover. People who persist do not respond to the alerts and they would be experienced increasingly often. The persistent speakers would then adapt to the alerts, so speakers who persist in stuttering become less sensitive to them over time, and thus the adjustment necessary to reestablish fluency is less easily made. A further fact to note is that alerts do not arise when whole words are repeated. Speech timing signals associated with efferent copy and auditory output would match. This may be interpreted as showing that word repetition has a different function from forms of stuttering that involve parts of words (see Chapter 3).

6.4   SUMMARY AND CONCLUSIONS ON DUAL TASKS AND CEREBELLAR MECHANISMS

The dual-task studies showed more interference in people who stutter than in controls. This was the case for two of three studies involving word and nonsense syllable repetition as the primary task (Bosshardt, 2002; Smits-Bandstra & de Nil, 2009), but less convincingly for sentence generation (de Nil & Bosshardt, 2000; Bosshardt et al., 2002). The Smits-Bandstra et al. (2006) study showed dual-task interference between two nonspeech tasks: a motor finger-tapping task and a color recognition task.

The speech performance tasks were simple and required little planning in the studies where they were significant. These speech tasks would seem likely to affect motor, rather than language, processes. Evidence for interference between tasks in dual-task performance is more convincing when dissimilar tasks are used. There are many possible reasons why two related tasks could interfere. For the Smits-Bandstra et al. (2006) study, the results provide evidence that dual tasks affect motor processes, as deficits were found in a nonspeech motor task. One possible locus for the motor process was discussed (the cerebellum), which was also one of several motor areas where de Nil and Bosshardt (2000) noted higher activity in people who stutter compared to controls in their dual-task study. All of these studies were conducted on adults. Thus, interesting questions, such as whether children who stutter are more susceptible to secondary task interference at critical stages in development (at the time when the problem starts or at teenage years where it resolves into persistent and recovered forms), need to be addressed.

Behavioral evidence showing that speakers who stutter have deficits in cerebellar processing tasks were reviewed in the chapter. Two ways in which this mechanism could be disrupted by secondary tasks were discussed: resource sharing and performance with synchronous and asynchronous inputs. Some hypotheses about how a mechanism sensitive to synchronization of inputs might apply to stuttering were presented. It was shown how such hypotheses might account for some known features associated with the disorder (e.g., why speakers become fluent under DAF, why recovery can occur in childhood, whereas recovery is rare in adulthood, and why people persist in their stutter).

6.5   EXERCISES

1. Design experiments to test whether a secondary nonspeech task affects speech control in speakers who stutter and whether the effects change over the ages from 2 years to the teens.
2. What could dual-task experiments with children (a) around age of onset of stuttering and (b) at teenage years tell us about the disorder?

7 Language Factors

This chapter looks at how stuttering symptoms relate to language structure. Language factors at onset and over the course of recovery are examined. Cross-sectional and longitudinal data are reviewed. If the same children are tested over development by the same research group, the same methods are used to assess the language characteristics and stuttering symptoms, whereas this is not necessarily the case if comparison is made across different research groups. The way this may affect results is considered.

7.1 INTRODUCTION

This chapter explores how the patterns of stuttering (the symptoms shown at onset when it persists or recovers) are distributed across speech samples with different linguistic properties (i.e., addressing the question of which language structures are prone to different types of stuttering). In formal terms, linguistic processing involves abstract symbolic elements. The output of language processes are then used to generate motor output. Formal language factors are examined at onset and through the course of the disorder. As well as looking at how linguistic processes relate to stuttering, the chapter also considers how usage of different language structures vary, whether usage properties are linked to stuttering symptoms at onset. Presently there is no work on whether usage factors have different impacts depending on whether a speaker recovers or persists in stuttering. This chapter does not treat the translation of the symbolic language form into speech motor output, as this is considered in Chapter 8, which focuses on the motor system.

Language and motor factors can be examined separately because the two systems operate independently and each of them is controlled by different brain mechanisms. One argument that shows that the language and motor systems act independently is that a particular linguistic representation can be output in several different ways: as speech, as written text, as semaphore signals, etc. This suggests that the linguistic representation is available to each of these motor output modes. This observation can be explained if language processing is done by one general purpose linguistic system that can be plugged into separate motor output systems (one per mode). A second observation that supports the idea that the speech motor system is separate from the linguistic system is that speakers can produce nonsense material as if it is speech even though it has no linguistic content. This shows that the speech motor system can operate whether or not it is driven by linguistically meaningful input. Another observation that makes it unlikely that language and motor processing is done by one system is that the motor mechanisms involved in speaking is developed for other purposes (breathing, eating, etc.). Evolutionarily speaking, language processing developed late and used existing motor control mechanisms with little or no modification. Gaining the ability to speak would not be advantageous if it changed the operation of the motor system to an extent that it would affect life-sustaining abilities. The independence of the language and motor systems is also entrenched in approaches to stuttering where many authors take the stance that stuttering is either a linguistic problem (Bernstein Ratner & Wijnen, 2007; Kolk & Postma, 1997) or a motor one (Max & Caruso, 1997; Van Lieshout, 2004). Some of the exercises invite the reader to explore alternatives to the notion that language and motor processes operate independently.

It has been suggested elsewhere that looking at either language or motor levels is misguided when attempting to explain stuttering (Howell, 2010). While it is possible that speakers who stutter have various minor language deficits, other speakers who have the same deficits do not stutter. This suggests language factors *alone* are not causal in determining whether a speaker stutters. Similarly, speakers who stutter have also been reported to have motor deficits, but other speakers with the same deficits do not stutter. This suggests that, on their own, motor factors, too, are not causal in determining whether a speaker stutters. There has to be something additional to these language and motor deficits that makes a person start, and continue, to stutter. One view of what additional factors are operating is considered in Chapter 12.

After some background information has been presented, language influences on stuttering are examined from two perspectives: formal linguistic and usage. The linguistic aspects considered in the first of these sections are syntactic, lexical, phonological (or prosodic) words, phonological structure of syllables, and morphological structure of words. The second section examines how language performance variables (usage factors) affect stuttering. Usage properties are idiosyncratic to some extent and change most during early development. This means that stuttering starts when language use is changing rapidly, and that dynamic changes in language usage continue during the period when recovery can occur. The usage factors examined with respect to stuttering are word frequency, neighborhood density and frequency, and age of acquisition. Several authors have proposed that one or another of these usage factors explains why linguistic factors affect stuttering. Such studies are in their infancy at present and there are methodological issues, particularly with respect to their implication for understanding childhood stuttering. In addition, as already mentioned, studies have not looked at whether usage factors distinguish persistent and recovered speakers.

There is little longitudinal developmental data that links language structure and stuttering. Exceptions are E. P. Paden's investigations on phonological factors with respect to diagnosis and persistent/recovered outcome up to around age 8, R. Watkins' work on language development on the same database of children around onset, and P. Howell's work on changes in word and symptom type mainly in children aged 8 and above. Some cross-sectional work has been done by a few research groups (including some of our own earlier work). It is important to note that cross-sectional work includes speakers who have persisted in their stuttering up to the test age, but that speakers who have recovered before the test age are not available: Using a phrase introduced in Chapter 1, there is selective attrition of recovered cases from the participant samples. Furthermore, the selective attrition depends on the age range of the group; more attrition of recovered cases has occurred for older groups than younger ones. There also are studies on single groups of speakers at particular ages. The methods used in the selected studies (including symptoms) are scrutinized to give readers sufficient information to evaluate and compare findings from different articles.

7.2   BACKGROUND ISSUES

Two questions arise about the distinction between language and motor systems: (1) Where should the dividing line be drawn between language and motor processes and (2) how is information passed from the language to the motor system? Some background information is necessary before an answer to these questions can be offered. This information is sufficient for current concerns, as obviously this book cannot provide a comprehensive précis of the entire field of linguistics.

Many subdisciplines are concerned with aspects of the linguistic process, including pragmatics (the study of how utterances are used when communicating with others), semantics (the study on the meaning of utterances), syntax (the study of how words are combined to form sentences), morphology (the study of the internal structure of words and the way they are modified), phonology (the study of sounds as discrete abstract elements that distinguish meaning), and phonetics (the study of the physical properties of speech sounds). All of these aspects of linguistics, except possibly phonetics, refer to formal proposals about how an individual acquires and uses language. Each discipline specifies the abstract forms it requires and, as the forms are abstract, they could be used in perception and production. This would not be the case if the forms were modality specific (sensory for perception and motor for production). Motor processing starts at or below the phonetic processes. (See Chapter 8 for further details of the motor processes.)

One idea about the representational form that is passed between the linguistic and speech motor processes stems from de Saussure's (1916, 1966) structuralism (Howell, 2010). de Saussure maintained speech is represented as gestures in the linguistic system. For de Saussure, the linguistic representation for continuous speech is a sequence of states with different degrees of aperture of the vocal tract. Seven different apertures were proposed (from 0–minimum aperture as in /p/, through to 6–maximum aperture as in /a/). The end product of linguistic processing could represent language forms as abstract specifications; in simple form, as a sequence of discrete aperture settings of the elements in a sequence. The speech motor processes could convert these to opening and closing gestures (implosions and explosions), which result in realization as syllables. For instance, passing from an implosive to an explosive gesture marks a syllable boundary.

Authors who focus on the motor system also have used the concept of gestures for establishing how speech motor output is organized. This perspective was pioneered by work at the Haskins Laboratories (New Haven, Connecticut), in particular by Browman, Goldstein, Fowler, and Saltzman in work that started in the 1980s and continues to the present. Their approach has been applied to stuttering

(Max & Caruso, 1997). Since gestures could be used by the language and motor systems, they could be the link that serves as an output of the language system that is then used as a source of input to the motor system.

7.2.1 LINKING SYMPTOMS OF STUTTERING TO LANGUAGE STRUCTURE

As discussed in Chapter 3, authors disagree about the symptoms that characterize stuttering. In addition, it will be seen that in some cases the several symptoms of stuttering tend to be associated with particular language structures. Consequently, the important methodological questions to bear in mind when examining studies are what symptoms were considered as stutters, and whether different symptoms occur on different linguistic structures because these may provide evidence about underlying language problems. (Language-based theories that use these findings are discussed in Chapter 10.)

Because people disagree about which symptoms are appropriate for characterizing stuttering, they can express reservations or dismiss research findings when studies do not use the set of symptoms they themselves favor. Paden, in her chapter in Yairi and Ambrose (2005, p. 201), noted that the designs and methodologies (which would include which symptoms are considered to be typical of stuttering) for assessing whether children who stutter have a phonological delay, vary widely. As has been seen, Wingate (1988, 2001, 2002) in his later work was adamant that whole-word repetitions are not stutters, and, consequently, he faulted many studies that considered them to be characteristics of stuttering. As a specific instance, Wingate (1988, p. 119) criticized Bernstein's (1981) study on syntactic factors in the speech of children who stuttered and typically developing children on the grounds that she characterized stuttering incorrectly, by including whole-word repetitions. It was noted in Chapter 3 that Wingate (2002, p. 144) also admonished Conture (1990) for considering whole-word repetitions as stuttering symptoms.

As the specificity of the link between symptoms and language structure has hardly been examined empirically, the critiques are a matter of opinion to some extent, although this does not apply when methods are inadequate, as Paden implies. Instead of taking a partisan approach about what is and what is not stuttering and using this as the basis for promoting one set of studies against another, thereby imposing my own view, I will list what symptoms were counted as stutters in particular studies, where such information is available, so readers can evaluate the work for themselves.

A variety of methods of assessment are employed in research studies. This includes analyses of spontaneous speech, comparison of speech performance of individuals who stutter in tests with published norms and a wide range of experimental tasks. There are advantages and disadvantages to each method. For example, spontaneous speech has the highest external validity and with experiments the least. Conversely, there is least control over spontaneous speech and most when experimental material is employed. Experimental procedures allow specific utterances to be elicited and controlled for different properties, for example, word frequency and word length might be controlled when examining lexical effects. The tight control commends this approach. However, it is not certain whether the controlled language material is at or beyond the level of the child's ability level (spontaneous speech might be better in this respect). Also, control sometimes can lead to contrived material. For example, a study by Dayalu, Kalinowski, Stuart, Holbert, and Rastatter (2002) compared stuttering on function and content words. They controlled for word frequency across the sets of words. Function words are usually high frequency. In order to do the matching, function words, such as "whenas," were used that have low frequency, but that seem atypical of the function word class. Consequently, results that include such material may not be representative. Studies on spontaneous speech are mainly, but not exclusively, assessed in this chapter.

One question that is examined is what symptoms and language forms are being acquired at the time that stuttering starts which may provide information about whether language development triggers stuttering onset. Also, as recovery mainly occurs in childhood, it is necessary to look at whether symptoms and the language forms associated with stuttering change over development, and whether there are different patterns in the separate aspects (symptoms and language) that reveal the way some speakers recover while others persist. As well as reviewing existing work, areas where there are gaps in our knowledge are identified and new research topics are suggested.

7.3   SYNTAX AND THE ONSET AND COURSE OF STUTTERING

Syntax refers to the rules whereby words and other elements of sentence structure combine to form grammatical forms in a particular language. The main topic focused on by authors interested in stuttering is whether syntactic factors predict why some speakers start to stutter (onset). Bloodstein (2006), Bernstein Ratner (1997), and Bloodstein and Bernstein Ratner (2007) have argued strongly for this position. For example, Bloodstein and Bernstein Ratner (2007, p. 51) state that "stuttering originates in a child's uncertain mastery of syntax." The word *originate* suggests that syntax is a precipitating factor.

Elsewhere, Bernstein Ratner (2005) appears to argue that syntax has a role in the later course of stuttering as well as onset when she says:

> A more straightforward explanation for the well-documented shift between stuttering on function words in children and on content words in adults may be the maturation of the syntactic system (Bernstein, 1981), enabling more fluent assembly of sentence constituent structures (Rispoli, 2001 and Rispoli, 2003), especially because the impact of syntax on stuttering frequency across the age span can be independently validated through experimental measures (Bernstein Ratner and Sih, 1987) rather than purely extrapolated from analysis of spontaneous conversational corpora, in which potentially conflated linguistic factors cannot be easily separated from each other.

Thus, the shift from function to content words happens between childhood and adulthood and Bernstein Ratner links this to maturation of the syntactic system. The proposed role that syntax could have in the development of stuttering will be examined as well below.

The structure of this section is as follows. First, a selection of studies exploring a range of syntactic factors on spontaneous speech is examined in detail. The studies look at single age groups around onset of stuttering and across a range of ages that cover the course of stuttering up to teenage years (cross-sectional investigations). Then a set of studies examining specific syntactic factors is considered, more briefly. This is followed by an examination of 12 arguments presented by Bloodstein and Bernstein Ratner (2007) that they present in support of the view that syntax is associated with onset of stuttering.

7.3.1 Empirical Investigations Close to Onset to Establish an Association Between Syntactic Properties and Stuttering

Three studies are examined: Wall, Starkweather, and Cairns (1981); Bernstein (1981); and Bernstein Ratner and Sih (1987). The first two studies address whether:

1. Pausing by children who stutter at grammatical boundaries happens more frequently in children who stutter than controls. If so, this may suggest the following clause/grammatical unit is not prepared, which would be consistent with a syntactic problem associated with stuttering.
2. Children who stutter have more of a problem with complex syntactic constructions than simple ones.

The Bernstein Ratner and Sih (1987) study described below used an imitation task and specifically addressed the second question. These studies all examined the speech of children shortly after stuttering starts.

7.3.1.1 Wall, Starkweather, and Cairns (1981) Study

Wall et al. (1981b) examined stutters that occurred at clause boundary and non-clause-boundary (henceforth referred to as *nonboundary*) locations within simple and complex sentences in the spontaneous speech of nine male children who stuttered, aged 4 to 6 years, 6 months. Criteria outlined in Van Riper (1971) were used "as a guide" to identify the following symptoms of stuttering: sound and syllable repetitions, prolonged sounds, prolonged articulatory postures with or without tension (with respect to this, they say "because auditory cues were available in this study, silent blocks with audible tension were substituted for this category"), and broken words. Though they do not comment on whole-word repetitions in this article, a companion paper using the same data for analyzing whether the voicing feature affected stuttering (Wall et al., 1981a) stated that Van Riper listed the category of whole-word repetitions in addition to the above symptoms, but "because unforced repetition of words is common in young children, this category was omitted." It appears that they were omitted from the syntax study as well.

The study investigated whether the frequency of stuttering was influenced by clause boundaries, clause type, sentence complexity, and the hierarchical structure of the clause. The speech samples were first broken down into sentences; incomplete sentences were excluded from the analyses. The constituent structure of each sentence was then broken down into clauses and phrases. The complexity of each sentence, the individual clause types, and a hierarchy of clause-internal constituents (which were based on Johnson, 1965) were coded.

The key aspects for analysis throughout this paper were boundary and nonboundary locations. Boundary location was regarded as the word occurring at clause onset; the boundary essentially delineated the clause. Stutters at boundary location were those that occurred on this word at clause onset. However, it was noted that many clauses were preceded by an irrelevant filler word (referred to as the word preceding a clause, WPC) that was not syntactically related to the clause. Often these were interjections (e.g., "well") or the conjunction "and." as shown in the example below. Consequently, there was ambiguity as to whether the WPC (e.g., "and") should be regarded as occurring in boundary location, or whether boundary location should still be designated at the syntactic onset of the clause (e.g., on the word "we" in example 1 below), as would be the case if no irrelevant filler word was uttered. For example:

1. "And we | crossed the road."
2. "We | crossed the road."

To overcome this problem, Wall et al. (1981b) opted to use what they term a "broad" count of boundaries. In their broad count, the clause boundary was regarded as the first syntactic word of the clause plus any filler words preceding the clause (interjections/conjunctions). In example 1 given above, the words "and" and "we" would both be considered boundary words. Clauses containing either an interjection (e.g., "well", that is, with WPC), or the conjunction "and" were analyzed separately.

Words occurring at any other position within the clause were regarded as occurring at nonboundary locations, and stutters at nonboundary locations were those that occurred on these words. Note that nonboundary locations do not necessarily indicate no relation at all to syntactic structure because some of the nonboundary locations mark the boundary of prominent syntactic constituents, such as the onset of the predicate that often corresponds to the onset of the verb phrase.

7.3.1.1.1 *Stuttering at All Boundary Locations*

In Wall et al.'s (1981b) analyses, each of the boundary and nonboundary words was regarded as an opportunity to stutter (OTS), and counts of the OTS for each category of interest (i.e., clause boundaries) were tabulated. Each category was then examined to see whether it contained an actual stutter (AS), based on the modified form of Van Riper (1971) indicated above. An AS/OTS proportion was then computed for each category of interest, and this was used as the dependent variable for all analyses. As a hypothetical example, if sentences were the category of interest, and there were 10 sentences and three had stutters, then the AS/OTS proportion would be 3/10 (0.3 or 30%). AS/OTS proportions are useful since (1) they can be computed for any structural unit (not just syntactic units) and (2) importantly, they normalize any differences in incidence rate thereby making possible comparison between common and rare units. (See section 7.3.1.1.2 below for examples of simple and complex sentences.) Normalization also allows comparison of AS/OTS proportions at boundary and nonboundary positions that would not be possible otherwise (because the count of nonboundary positions is greater than the count of boundary positions for multiword clauses).

Any unit that is associated with stutter production ought to have a high AS/OTS proportion. In total, Wall et al. (1981b) found there were 615 AS out of 2,230 OTS at boundary positions (27.6%) and 242 AS out of 6,304 OTS (3.8%) at nonboundary positions. Boundary position clearly exerted a strong effect on the rate of stuttering.

7.3.1.1.2   Stutters at Boundary Locations on Simple and Complex Sentences

As well as delineating the boundaries of each clause, the clauses were classified into the following 10 types. There were three categories pertaining to simple sentences:

1. Simple sentence clause (SSC)
2. Simple sentence clause plus word preceding clause (SSC + WPC)
3. Simple "and" clause (SAC).

A simple sentence was regarded as a single, independent clause (SSC, SSC + WPC, SAC) that expressed complete meaning and contained only one verb. For example, the sentence *"I am five"* is an SSC.

There were seven clause categories pertaining to complex sentences:

1. Main clause (MC). This implies that there is an embedded or conjoined clause.
2. Main clause plus word preceding clause (MC + WPC).
3. Main "and" clause (MAC).
4. Coordinate clause (CO).
5. An "and" coordinate (ACo).
6. Complement clause (Comp).
7. Relative clause (RC).

Complex sentences were composed of more than one clause, typically a main clause (MC, MC + WPC, MAC) plus at least one conjoined (CO, ACo), or embedded (Comp, RC) clause. For example, the complex sentence *"She knows that I am five"* contains a main clause and a complement clause, in which the complement clause *"that I am five"* acts as the object of the verb in the main clause *"she*

TABLE 7.1

Examples of Clause Types Used by Wall et al. (1981b)

Clause Type	Example
Simple clause	"**My name is John.**"
Simple clause + WPC	"**Well, my name is John.**"
Simple and clause	"**And my name is John.**"
Main clause	"**John went shopping** because he needed socks."
Main clause + WPC	"**Well, John went shopping** because he needed socks."
Main and clause	"**And John went shopping** because he needed socks."
Coordinate clause	"John went shopping **so I went too.**"
"And" coordinate	"John went shopping **and so I went too.**"
Complement clause	"John thinks **that the shop sells socks.**"
Relative clause	"The shop **that sells socks** is closed."

Note: Clause type is indicated at the left and an example is given on the right. The three simple sentences consist of a single clause. The complex clauses occur with other clauses to make sentences. The target clause is in bold throughout.

knows." Definitions of all 10 clause types can be found in the appendix of the Wall et al. paper, and examples are given in Table 7.1.

The rate of stuttering at the onset of simple and complex sentences was first compared by combining the frequencies for the three simple clause types (SSC, SSC + WPC, and SAC categories) to create the category of simple sentences, and by combining the frequencies for the three main clause types (MC, MC + WPC, and MAC categories) to create the category of complex sentences. Because only the boundaries of main clauses were examined, Wall et al. assumed that the onset of all complex sentences is a main clause. There was no significant difference between the rate of stuttering at the onsets of simple and complex sentences.

A second analysis examined the boundary positions of all clauses within simple and complex sentences by combining the frequencies for the three simple clause types (SSC, SSC + WPC, and SAC categories) for simple sentences, and by combining the frequencies for all seven complex clause types (MC, MC + WPC, MAC, Co, ACo, RC, and Comp categories) for complex sentences. Once again, there was no significant difference between the rate of stuttering at clause boundaries within simple and complex sentences. Overall, sentence complexity did not appear to affect the rate of stuttering at any boundary position.

Examining all clause types individually, there was a significant difference between stuttering rates (AS/OTS) at boundary positions across clause types in an ANOVA (analysis of variance), from which the authors concluded that clause types affected stuttering rate. The Scheffe test revealed that the difference between the mean stuttering rates of the MAC category (highest AS/OTS proportion) was significantly different from SAC and of Comp categories (the two categories with lowest AS/OTS proportions).

The four clause types that began with an irrelevant filler word (either a WPC or "and") were singled out for closer analysis of the boundary. Stuttering rate on (1) the WPC or "and," and (2) on the first syntactic word of the clause (e.g., "and" and "we," respectively, for examples 1 and 2 given earlier) within SSC + WPC, SAC, MC + WPC, and MAC categories were compared. There were significantly higher rates of stuttering on the WPC and "and" except for the MC + WPC category. Wall et al. point out, however, that the results of this analysis do seem to be largely influenced by two participants. Thus, according to the authors, the presence of an irrelevant filler word at clause onset attracted high rates of stuttering.

Wall et al suggest that "and" is problematic for children who stutter, irrespective of the complexity of the sentence that follows it. Bloodstein (1974, p. 384) noted in case reports that "and" at sentence onset resulted in an unusually high rate of stuttering, and the children who stuttered made no discernable attempt to avoid this highly stuttered word. Wall et al. (1981b) argued that since "and" is the first conjunction acquired by children (Hood, Lahey, Lifter, & Bloom, 1978; Limber, 1973), stutterers may be operating at a lower level of syntactic functioning than their nonstuttering counterparts. They add that the frequent use of "and" may simply be because children who stutter have few alternative options available to them. Although Wall et al. took the high rate of stuttering on "and" as support for syntactic problems affecting stuttering, it also could be the case that the children used the word "and" as a filler with no syntactic role (Kadi-Hanifi & Howell, 1992). It should be possible to distinguish "and" as well when it is used to conjoin two sentences versus when it is used to conjoin a clause to a sentence (see section 7.4.3.4). Kadi-Hanifi and Howell would predict that the former would be frequent in young children's speech and repetition of the whole of "and" in such cases is nonsyntactic, whereas the latter are syntactic. This might clarify the different roles that "and" can have and establish any relationship with syntactic complexity.

To summarize the clause boundary analysis, stuttering occurred with significantly greater frequency on the first uttered word of a clause, whether that word was a WPC or not (except for the MC + WPC category), and the highest rate of stuttering at clause boundaries occurred on the word "and" at the onset of both simple and complex sentences.

7.3.1.1.3   Analysis of Stutters at Nonboundary Positions

The previous analyses only examined the boundaries of sentences and clauses. Wall et al. (1981b) next analyzed the relationship between stuttering and clause type for all words in clauses, regardless of a boundary or nonboundary location, using an ANOVA. A Scheffe test found that the highest rate of overall stuttering was at nonboundary position within the main "and" clause, which, as mentioned above, is the "and" clause at the onset of complex sentences.

The final analysis by Wall et al. separated out nonboundary words for closer analysis. Within each clause, nonboundary words were classified into one of the following four categories in terms of hierarchical significance: (1) subject–predicate split (S-P), (2) verb–X split (V-X), (3) lesser phrase boundary (LPB), and (4) random (R). S-P marked the boundary between the subject and the first word of the predicate (e.g., "the girl I combed her hair"). This category essentially corresponds to the onset of the verb phrase, and, according to Johnson (1965), is assumed to be one of the most important breaks within the clause, along with the V-X category. V-X marked the boundary between the verb and the first word of the structure that occurs in object position (e.g., "the girl combed I her hair"). LPB indicated the onset of any phrase other than the S-P and V-X breaks (e.g., "the girl combed her hair I with a blue brush"). R referred to any other words not accounted for (e.g., "The I girl combed her hair"). According to the authors, assignment of a word to the R category indicated that it had "no demonstrable positional value in the structure of the sentence." In other words, R is the only category that is of little syntactic importance and that does not mark the onset of a syntactic constituent. Analyzing these four nonboundary categories, no location emerged as being stuttered with significantly greater frequency than the other. Wall et al. did not examine the stuttering rate for these nonboundary categories by clause type, so no indication can be formed regarding complexity here.

To summarize, the clause boundary was shown to influence stuttering in young children. The authors highlighted that this may be related to sentential planning in clausal units, though there are alternative accounts of the effects they report. No indication was found that clause-internal units affected stuttering, and interactions between stuttering and complexity were not clear cut. This comprehensive analysis provided limited and equivocal support with respect to whether stuttering in children near the onset of the disorder is associated with syntactic complexity.

7.3.1.2   Bernstein (1981)

Bernstein (1981) examined whether disfluency occurred at boundary or nonboundary positions in eight children who stuttered (mean age 6;3) and eight control children (mean age 6;4) and whether particular syntactic structures attracted more disfluency. *Disfluency* is used to describe this work, as both stuttering and fluent control children were involved. The use of the term *boundary* here refers to the boundary of constituent structures generally at the level of the phrase, but in one case (potentially) refers to an embedded clause (complement). Both participant groups had six males and two females. The children were engaged in a play task involving randomly selected cartoon characters. The sessions were recorded and transcriptions were made of all the children's utterances. Only complete sentences of type noun phrase–auxiliary verb phrase were selected for analysis.

In terms of symptoms examined, Bernstein stated that "hesitations, repetitions, prolongations, and filled pauses" were noted. Though *repetitions* is a vague term, the subsequent analysis of where stuttering was located, makes it clear that whole-word repetitions were considered as stutters. Thus, when discussing the locus of stuttering, she says this was taken as the word that contained a full or part-word repetition. The word that followed the disfluent incident was taken as the locus in the case of hesitations and filled pauses. It is not clear from the report exactly how many categories of stuttering symptoms were analyzed (as just illustrated) and degrees of freedom for the statistical tests, which might have helped establish this, were not given in this article. Another limitation in the report is that neither absolute nor percentage results are presented anywhere in the manuscript making evaluation of the results problematic.

The boundary events examined by Bernstein was the word at the onset of the subject noun phrase, auxiliary, verb phrase, object noun phrase, prepositional phrase, conjunction, and complement. No definitions or examples are offered by Bernstein for these constituent boundaries. However, as noted, it is presumed that while the majority of these refer to phrase level constituents, *complement* might potentially refer to an embedded complement clause within the sentence, thus, these would correspond to Wall et al.'s (1981b), complement clause boundary category. All other words within each constituent were grouped into a single nonboundary category, which is similar to Wall et al.'s "random" category.

Two main findings were reported. First, although both groups had more disfluencies at boundary than nonboundary positions, children who stuttered had more disfluencies at constituent boundaries than fluent children (disfluency rates at nonboundary positions did not differ between the groups). Second, stuttering at the boundary of different constituents was examined to see whether certain types of constituents attracted more disfluency. One difference between children who stuttered and controls was reported: the boundary of verb phrases (VPs). "VP attracted a significantly high degree of disfluency for the young stutterers. Disfluency on this particular constituent was not significantly represented in the speech of the normal children" (p. 345). VP is located in a similar position within the clause to subject–predicate break in Wall et al. (1981b). They did not find evidence of a similar problem at the onset of the predicate. However, Bernstein separated the auxiliary from the remainder of the VP, and, thus, it is possible that if the children used auxiliaries (or indeed other material between the subject and VP) in their spontaneous speech, her VP category and the subject–predicate break in Wall et al. do not correspond exactly, which may account for the different findings in the two studies.

Bernstein suggested that VPs may be troublesome for children who stutter because "even in the simplest utterance, the constraints of number agreement imposed by the preceding noun, the necessity of encoding semantic notions, such as tense, and aspect to be carried by the sentence as a whole. Similarly, choice of verb will constrain the succeeding elements of the utterance, forcing accommodations to notions of transitivity/intransitivity coded within the verb, as well as complement structures accepted or barred given verb selection. Alternatively, the VP may simply represent another stepping stone to planning the completion of the utterance extending far beyond the scope of the verb. The children may simply be taking advantage of midsentential stopping points to contemplate the rest of the utterance as a whole." As noted, Wall et al. did not find a similar effect on their subject–predicate break category, which frequently corresponds to VP onset. Once again, there is little evidence for syntax affecting stuttering around onset and where there is evidence for this (problems at VP onset), discrepant results have been reported (Wall et al., 1981b).

7.3.1.3 Bernstein Ratner and Sih (1987)

Bernstein Ratner and Sih (1987) looked at sentences that varied in syntactic complexity and length based on sentence type and the addition of embedded phrases and clauses. They did not examine boundary and nonboundary events unlike Bernstein (1981) and Wall et al. (1981b). In other words, sentence-internal syntactic constituents were not examined individually. Instead, disfluencies were analyzed for their occurrence within each sentence type, irrespective of sentence position. Eight children who stuttered and eight typically developing children, aged between 3 years, 11 months and 6 years, 4 months, served as participants. They performed an elicited imitation task in which the syntactic complexity and length of the imitated sentences were manipulated, and the effects of these variables on fluency and accuracy of sentence reproduction were investigated. Bernstein Ratner and Sih differentiated between those disfluencies that are specific to stuttering (termed in this description *stutters*), and those disfluencies that are present in the speech of all children. The authors also examined the children's accuracy of imitation.

The audiotapes of the imitated sentences were transcribed and the following categories of events were tallied for both groups of children: whole- and part-word repetition, phrase repetition and false start, filled pause (urr, well, etc.), unfilled pause, prolongation, and dysrhythmic phonation. Counts of all of these categories were obtained for both groups of children (global disfluency incidence). Separate tallies were made for the children who stuttered of the incidence of behaviors that "primarily defined stuttering." These were multiple sound and syllable repetitions. A fact of particular note is that whole-word repetitions were not included as symptoms of stuttering. They do not appear in the list of stutters, but they are listed in the counts of global disfluencies ("full word"). Omitting whole-word repetitions from stuttering symptoms contrasts with Bernstein (1981), but is consistent with Wall et al. (1981b). No comment was made about why the first author changed the way that stuttering events were counted.

The following 10 sentence types were investigated (in order of increased syntactic complexity):

1. Simple active affirmative declarative: The boy found the lady.
2. Negative: The boy didn't find the lady.
3. Question: Did the boy find the lady?
4. Passive: The boy was found by the lady.
5. Dative: The boy found the lady a chair.
6. Prepositional Phrase: The boy is finding the lady with the red hair.
7. Coordinate with forward reduction: The boy is finding the lady or the man.
8. Right-embedded relative clause: We had thought that the boy found the lady.

9. Left-embedded complement clause: That the boy found the lady was a lie.
10. Center-embedded relative clause: The chair that the boy found the lady was broken.

   The predicted order of syntactic complexity (PRED) was obtained by reference to others' findings and the authors' intuitions. Bernstein Ratner and Sih state that "generally speaking, the developmental literature suggests that children first master simple S-V-O (subject–verb–object) structures that they then are able to negate and invert to form interrogatives (Klima & Bellugi, 1966; Menyuk, 1969; Wells, 1985)". Length (LENGTH) was estimated by the number of syllables in all the sentences of each particular type that were then rank ordered (shortest to longest). Length was included as a factor given that more complex sentences are longer because the complexity comes from the addition of syntactic units. Consequently, the authors considered that length, rather than syntax, may pose a problem for children who stutter.

   Scores were obtained for both groups of children (control and stuttering) for the percentage of sentences containing at least one global disfluency (SDYS), the percentage of global disfluent syllables (SYLLDYS), and the percentage of sentences changed during imitation (CHANGED). For the typically developing children, after Bonferroni correction, PRED correlated with SDYS, SYLLDYS, and CHANGED. Similar analyses for the children who stuttered only led to significant correlations between PRED and SDYS, and PRED and CHANGED. Based on these results, there is some indication of a relationship between syntactic complexity and global disfluencies for both groups of speakers.

   None of the correlations were significant when LENGTH was correlated with SDYS, SYLLDYS, and CHANGED for the typically developing children. Only the correlation between LENGTH and CHANGED was significant for the children who stuttered. The authors took these findings to suggest a weaker effect of LENGTH for both groups of speakers in comparison to the predicted relationship with syntactic complexity (PRED) for global disfluencies.

   Of particular interest are the analyses of percent syllables stuttered (SYLLSTUTT) in each sentence type and percentage of sentences containing at least one stutter (SSTUT) that was only done for the children who stutter. Neither PRED nor LENGTH correlated significantly with SYLLSTUTT. The correlation of PRED with SSTUT was significant, but LENGTH did not correlate with SSTUT. The significant correlation with PRED suggested an effect of syntactic complexity, but the absence of correlations with LENGTH suggested no effect of sentence length.

   The authors concluded that their investigation supported the notion that syntactic complexity, as defined by progressive addition of late-acquired sentence constructions in child language, was correlated with children's abilities to fluently imitate sentences. This is the case whether normal or stuttering children's performances was examined. In contrast, length alone did not predict fluency as effectively as did syntactic complexity. Longer sentences were harder to imitate, but had no effect on fluency for the children who stuttered.

Bernstein Ratner and Sih (1987) pointed out that the order of syntactic difficulty they employed (PRED) is similar to what other authors used in developmental work with typical children. For example, they noted that the first four sentence types in their difficulty hierarchy is similar to that used by Pearl and Bernthal (1980) and Gordon, Luper, and Peterson (1986). They also pointed out that the ordering in these studies differs from their own in several ways, though they did not expand on this. It is reasonable to specify which individual syntactic constructions are considered simple and which are considered complex (Bernstein, 1981). However, putting material in rank order that (1) ignores available schemes (i.e., those from the fluent literature) and (2) bases the selected ordering on unspecified and subjective criteria is problematic. The obvious questions are whether orderings based on other authors' work would have resulted in a correlation with syntactic complexity and, if not, whether this ordering was selected by Bernstein Ratner and Sih because it led to a significant correlation. Similar questions arise about the reasons for the change from including Bernstein (1981) to excluding Bernstein Ratner and Sih (1987), whole-word repetitions as symptoms of stuttering. That is, would the same patterns of correlations have been obtained for the participants who stuttered if whole-word repetitions had been counted as stuttering?

A further point about the analysis involving correlation across the 10 syntactic categories is that it is less rigorous than the Scheffe tests that Wall et al. (1981b) conducted. (The latter compared pairs of syntactic categories.) This may explain why Bernstein Ratner and Sih (1987) found an effect of syntactic complexity, whereas Wall et al. (1981a) did not. Finally, as discussed later in this chapter, the lack of an effect of utterances length is at odds with what other authors report (Gaines, Runyan, & Meyers, 1991; Logan & Conture, 1995).

7.3.2   SYNTAX AND COURSE AFTER ONSET

The corresponding questions to those raised about onset are whether speakers past the onset stage of stuttering pause more often at clause boundaries (break between syntactic components) and whether speakers past the onset stage of stuttering have more of a problem with complex syntactic constructions than simple ones. One study (Howell & Au-Yeung, 1995) has used the Wall et al. (1981b) methods to examine these questions using a cross-sectional data set. The study also allowed Wall et al.'s findings about onset to be checked. The last part of this section also includes studies that examine in more detail specific structures that might have an effect on fluency for stutterers in single age groups, mainly in adults who persisted in their stuttering (Hannah & Gardner, 1968; Palen & Peterson, 1982; Ronson, 1976; Wells, 1979). Two of these studies (Palen & Peterson, 1982; Ronson, 1976) used experimental methods rather than analysis of spontaneous speech samples. Experimental material is necessary to investigate complex syntactic structures that are rare even in adult speech, though children and adults understand them. Consequently, spontaneous samples would not result in sufficient examples to examine them. A further fact to note is that Ronson worked with adults, and Palen and Peterson attempted to replicate that work with children aged between 8 and teens.

7.3.2.1   Howell and Au-Yeung (1995)

Howell and Au-Yeung (1995) obtained spontaneous speech from participants and used Wall et al.'s (1981b) analysis procedure on a cross-sectional data set. Children were assigned to one of three age groups, as detailed below, ranging from around onset to ages at which recovery or persistence was likely to be resolved. Use of syntactic categories across age groups was checked to see if there were developmental changes in the syntactic forms used. The effect of syntactic category on stuttering at constituent boundaries and nonboundaries was also examined, therefore, Wall et al.'s (1981b) study was extended to older age groups.

The spontaneous utterances were collected for the age groups 2;7 to 6;0 (six children who stutter and five controls), 6;0 to 9;4 (15 children who stutter and 31 controls), 9;7 to 12;7 (10 children who stutter and 12 controls). Transcriptions were made as in Kadi-Hanifi and Howell (1992). Symptoms counted were segment, part-word, whole-word or phrase repetitions, segmental or syllabic prolongations, and repetitions of sequences of such prolongations. A difference between this study and those of Wall et al. (1981b) and Bernstein Ratner and Sih (1987) was that the latter two excluded whole-word and phrase repetitions from their list of symptoms, whereas Howell and Au-Yeung did not. Syntactic analyses were conducted as described by Wall et al. (see section 7.3.1).

In terms of usage of the various syntactic categories across age groups, a difference was found between fluent speakers and speakers who stutter, where the children who stuttered initially employed more simple structures and fewer complex ones. This difference decreased over age groups; a finding consistent with Wall (1980).

The percentage of stutters (AS/OTS) collapsed over syntactic categories at boundary and nonboundary locations were in close agreement with those of Wall et al. for the youngest age group. However, significantly more stuttering occurred at nonboundary positions as age increased for the children who stuttered (supported by an interaction between boundary/nonboundary stuttering position and age group in an ANOVA).

Next, syntactic categories were examined separately in analyses. For the stuttering participants, the rankings in terms of which syntactic category showed most stuttering were similar for each age group to those of Wall et al. (1981b). An ANOVA with age group and syntactic category (10 levels) and with stuttering rate as the dependent variable showed an interaction between these factors. This revealed that dependence of stuttering on a syntactic category changed with age for the children who stuttered, with syntactic complexity affecting the older speakers more than the younger ones.

When individual syntactic categories were examined to investigate the latter in more detail for WPC and first word of the clause, only MAC (main "and" clauses) at the youngest age was significant. (Wall et al. [1981b] found effects for

SSC + WPC and SAC as well as MAC.) No analysis for simple/complex syntactic categories was reported.

Stuttering was more likely at clause boundary than nonclause boundary positions in the analysis including the 10 syntactic categories, and the effect was dependent upon age. Overall, Howell and Au-Yeung found that syntactic complexity affected fluency in older speakers more so than in younger speakers, which suggested an effect of syntax in the later course of stuttering.

7.3.2.2 Hannah and Gardner (1968)

Hannah and Gardner (1968) examined the location of stutters within spontaneous speech samples from eight participants. Participants ages were not given, though it is clear that they were adult (as indicated by the abstract and reference was made to the group comprising seven *men* and one *woman*). The symptoms examined were sound, word, and phrase repetitions, any prolongations, blocks, and other filled and unfilled pauses unrelated to the normal juncture phenomena. They reported that stuttering was more often associated with syntactic position than syntactic complexity, that is, stuttering occurred more often in postverbal than in preverbal or verbal units within the sentence. No correlation was found between stuttering and subject, verb, and object/complement/optional adjunct. The postverbal unit might contain a noun phrase or an expansion, such as a relative clause. Not all expansions of the postverbal unit correlated significantly with stuttering rate; however, when the expansion was a coordinate or embedded clause, a positive and significant relationship was noted. Conceivably, these structures might be problematic at both onset and the later course of stuttering. However, since embedded structures, from relative clauses to "that" complements, are hardly ever attested until after age 3, they would appear to be more important during later course.

7.3.2.3 Wells (1979)

Wells (1979) compared stuttering rates, which included whole-word repetitions, of 20 male adults (aged 18–45 years) who stuttered on sentences extracted from spontaneous speech samples that had a single embedded clause with sentences that had multiple embedded clauses. She reported significantly more stuttering in sentences with multiple embedded clauses than those with a single embedded clause, and this effect also depended on severity of stuttering. Although not supported by statistical analyses, Wells noted that there was a trend toward more frequent stuttering in utterances that contained a postverbal, as opposed to preverbal, relative clause. Within postverbal relative clauses, the noun phrase (NP) is functioning as both the object of the main clause and the subject of the relative clause. Within preverbal relative clauses, the NP functions as the subject of both the main and relative clause. Here, unlike in Hannah and Gardner's study, there was an effect of syntactic complexity for embedded structures even though both studies examined similar (adult) samples.

7.3.2.4   Ronson (1976)

Ronson (1976) tested 16 adult males who stuttered who were aged between 19 and 29 years. The participants were divided into three severity groups. Each participant read aloud 36 test sentences that were either SAAD (simple, active, affirmative, declarative) (e.g., "The kind gentle teacher helped the seven new children"), negative (e.g., "The kind gentle teacher didn't help the seven new children"), or passive sentence types (e.g., "The seven new children were helped by the kind gentle teacher"). All sentences were constructed with words of three-word frequency classes; no interaction was reported between stuttering on passive sentences and word frequency for any of the three severity groups. An interaction was found for simple active declaratives and negatives for the severest group only; that is, stutters increased as word-frequency level decreased within SAAD and negative sentences. The more severe adult stutterers were found to have problems with certain syntactic constructions that also depended on word frequency.

7.3.2.5   Palen and Peterson (1982)

Palen and Peterson (1982) tested 15 children who stuttered aged 8 to 12 using the same procedures as Ronson (1976). Similar to Ronson, no relationship between stuttering and passive sentences was found. An interaction was found for negatives (for the severest group only), but not for simple active declaratives. Passives are rarely produced at all ages and it is probable that children do not understand them until they are beyond age 3; however, these structures do not appear to be problematic for stutterers at any point in their life. Negatives do apparently cause problems across ages, but only for severe stutterers. Thus, overall, there are selective indications that more complex structures attract stuttering mainly in its later course, with qualified effects about negatives in early life.

7.3.3   ARGUMENTS THAT ONSET OF STUTTERING IS ASSOCIATED WITH ONSET OF SYNTAX

Bloodstein and Bernstein Ratner (2007, pp. 51–52) listed 12 observations that they considered to be consistent with the hypothesis that onset of stuttering is linked to the period when a child first starts to use syntax (see also Bloodstein, 2006). Many of these are polemical arguments, not supported by evidence. The arguments are reconsidered and have been rearranged under the themes *general observations, onset characteristics, evidence that stuttering is linked to syntactic units, dismissal of alternatives to syntax,* and *linking symptoms and language factors (syntax) at onset.* The numbering of the points that Bloodstein and Bernstein Ratner used is retained for easy cross reference.

7.3.3.1   General Observations

Point 10: By age 6, children have mastered syntax and a lot have recovered from stuttering.

Comments: The suggestion here is that the age at which children master syntax coincides with when most children who are going to recover will have done so. However, recovery continues past age 6 and up to the teenage years. Howell et al., 2008, reported that 50% of children stuttering at age 8 have recovered by their teens (see Chapter 2). Also, as should be apparent from Chapters 1 and 3, stuttering in young childhood is difficult to diagnose, and it has been argued that there are many misdiagnosed cases. Such cases would inflate estimates of how many cases recover at young ages (Wingate, 1988, 2002). This would qualify the premise that a lot of children have recovered by age 6. Finally, not all children have mastered syntax by age 6, but, nevertheless, they do not stutter (e.g., children with specific language impairment). As these children have not mastered syntax, why do they not stutter?

Point 12: Stuttering is more prevalent among boys than girls.

Comments: Presumably the authors are thinking that gender links with higher verbal skills in girls than boys, although they do not say so. A prediction is that gender should act as a risk factor for predicting onset of stuttering, but it does not (Reilly et al., 2009). Additionally, gender does not act as a risk factor for predicting whether a child at age 8 will persist or recover in stuttering at teenage (Howell & Davis, in press).

Point 11: Children who stutter have inferior language skills.

Comments: At best, this is an overstatement of the evidence, as they implicitly acknowledge by adding "though there have been conflicting findings." These conflicting findings have often been based on extensive investigations. For instance, Watkins (2005), who works with Yairi and Ambrose's group, has looked at syntactic factors around onset of the disorder. She did not find any notable pattern of language delay in the stuttering children that were followed. Also, a test for the reception of syntax for use with children from age 2 has been developed (Howell, Davis, & Au-Yeung, 2003). They compared the performance of children who stuttered with those who were typically developing on this test. No differences were reported between the two groups of children across the ages of 2 to 10 years.

Point 7: The frequency of stuttering tends to increase with the length and grammatical complexity of utterances.

Comments: As has been seen above, there are many null and conflicting findings about the relationship between syntactic complexity and stuttering, so Bloodstein and Bernstein Ratner's statement about this aspect needs to be qualified. Many authors agree with the view that utterance length is an important determinant of stuttering, although Bernstein Ratner and Sih (1987) found the opposite result. Authors who stress the importance of utterance length include Logan and Conture (1995) and Gaines et al. (1991).

7.3.3.2   Onset Characteristics

The observations collected under this heading concern a link between stuttering and the transition from the one- to the two-word stage

Point 5: Incipient stuttering is almost never observed on one-word utterances.

Comments: No data are available about stuttering on one-word utterances in children. However, this observation should not only apply to incipient stuttering, as presumably one-word utterances are simple for older speakers as well, so they should not pose problems at any age. Assuming that the statement should apply across ages, it is contradicted by empirical evidence from Dayalu, Kalinowski, Stuart, Holbert, and Rastatter (2002) who reported stuttering on one-word utterances in adults who stutter.

Point 8: Stuttering does not happen before children speak multiword utterances (about 18 months).

Comments: As stated, this point is similar to point 5. The question, however, can be asked about whether multiword onset coincides with stuttering onset that appears to be a corollary of this statement. Children start to use multiword utterances at about age 2 (Labelle, 2005). Mean age of stuttering onset is about 3 years (Yairi & Ambrose, 2005). So children start to use multiword utterances well before most stuttering starts. Given this discrepancy, it would appear that stuttering and use of multiword utterances/syntax are not causally linked.

Point 9: The age range in which stuttering starts is 2 to 5 years and this is the interval in which children are mastering syntax.

Comments: The authors have moved from specifying the "trigger" for stuttering onset as the age at which children start to use multiword utterances (see point 5 above) to a range of ages over which syntactic development occurs. Demuth and McCullough (2009), who worked with fluent children, made a point about development of language that is relevant to the idea that stuttering is triggered by syntactic factors. They noted that articles and verbal inflections appear in selected contexts and usage increases slowly. They went on to point out that the graded process of language development is a problem for accounts that maintain such syntactic events act as a triggering event for aspects of language behavior. This criticism would apply to the proposal that onset of syntax triggers stuttering.

Stuttering onset occurs at different ages with different children, so it is necessary to use statistics that relate to the distribution. The simplest of such statistics is the mean, and mean age of stuttering onset is at about age 3 (33 months), according to one authoritative source (Yairi & Ambrose, 2005). Based on this statistic, roughly 50% of onsets will have occurred before, and 50% after, age 3 years.

Age 3 years can be used as a dividing point to see whether syntax could account for why the older half of the cases started to stutter. If syntax is well developed before age 3, it could not account for about half the cases of stuttering onset (i.e., children whose stuttering onsets above age 3). Research findings indicate that there is appreciable development in syntactic abilities before the age of 3. Limber (1973) made this point succinctly. "From many reports on early syntactic development, it would seem that most children display the ability to construct various complex nominal constructions—syntactically generated names—as well as other complex constructions out of simpler components well before their third birthday (3;0)." Thus, it appears that about half the children will have a basic mastery of syntax before they start to stutter, making it unlikely that starting to use syntactically formed utterances leads to stuttering.

7.3.3.3 Evidence That Stuttering Is Linked to Syntactic Units

The following three points are all related and make the case for a relationship between stuttering and syntax. Other units like phonological words (discussed in section 7.5) would fulfill this function equally well.

Point 1: Stuttering occurs on the first word of an utterance. The start of an utterance may be the onset of a syntactic constituent where planning difficulty is high (although they do not say this).

Comments: The start of an utterance is also the start of prosodic and motor structures, thus these too could also explain stuttering in this position.

Point 2: The stuttering on the first word of an utterance often involves whole words that are produced fluently.

Comments: This point sounds contradictory (effectively, it says stutters are produced fluently). It relates to Wingate's (2001, 2002) point about whether whole-word repetitions should be considered to be stutters or not, which was discussed at length in Chapter 3. As noted above, one of the authors at different times has (Bernstein, 1981) and has not (Bernstein Ratner & Sih, 1987) considered whole-word repetitions as instances of stuttering. This observation can only be considered as potentially implicating syntactic factors in the onset of stuttering once the issue about whole-word repetitions and stuttering is resolved.

Point 3: Such repetition involves function words that start syntactic structures.

Comment: There is evidence that function words often occur at the beginning of sentences (in particular, the conjunction "and" and subject pronouns). As discussed when the Wall et al. (1981a) study was discussed, "and" seems to be used as a filler and does not have a grammatical role. Concerning function words in general at the beginning of sentences, there are other explanations for why these simple words are stuttered (see Chapter 12). Therefore, if this observation is true, it does not necessarily require acceptance of their argument.

7.3.3.4 Dismissal of Alternatives to Syntax

Point 6: Early stuttering is not linked to word-related factors, such as word length or grammatical function.

Comments: The logic of the argument here appears to be that by dismissing a link between stuttering and word-based factors (e.g., word length) leaves syntax as the governing factor. Logically, dismissing other factors that could precipitate stuttering is a necessary, but not a sufficient, basis to argue that starting to use syntax leads to stuttering. Empirically, it is known that long words are more likely to be stuttered in adults (Brown, 1945). If their point 2 is accepted, the lack of an effect of word length in children could be because they stutter on function words and function words are short. If point 2 is not accepted (Wingate, 2001, 2002), then the observation that stuttering is not linked to word factors needs reassessing. Once again, the importance of settling the issue whether whole-word repetitions should be considered as stuttered or not has to be raised.

7.3.3.5 Linking Symptoms and Language Factors (Syntax) at Onset

Point 4: Stuttering at the onset age is similar to the normal disfluencies exhibited by typically developing children.

Comments: Wingate (2001, 2002) stated that stuttering looks like typical disfluencies because whole-word repetitions are included and they are not stutters. Because of this, some typically developing children would be classed as stuttering, which erroneously makes the two groups look similar.

7.3.4 SUMMARY OF FINDINGS RELATING SYNTACTIC STRUCTURE AND STUTTERING NEAR ONSET AND OVER COURSE

Wall et al.'s (1981a) analyses showed that the clause boundary influenced stuttering in young children. The authors highlighted that this may be related to sentential planning in clausal units. No indication was found that clause-internal constituents affected stuttering and interactions between stuttering and complexity were not clear cut (VP, in particular).

Bernstein (1981) reported two main findings. First, although both groups of stutterers and controls had more disfluencies at constituent boundary than nonboundary (constituent internal) positions, children who stuttered had more disfluencies at constituent boundaries. Disfluency rates at nonboundary positions did not differ between the groups. Second, disfluency on different constituents was examined to see whether certain types of clause attracted more disfluency. The main difference between children who stutter and controls was on verb phrases (VP). "VP attracted a significantly high degree of disfluency for the young stutterers. Disfluency on this particular constituent was not significantly represented in the speech of the normal children."

Bernstein Ratner and Sih (1987) concluded that their investigation supported the notion that syntactic complexity, as defined by progressive addition of late acquired sentence constructions in child language, was correlated with children's abilities to fluently imitate sentences. This is the case whether normal or stuttering children's performances was examined; the effect was not unique to children who stutter. Conversely, length alone did not predict fluency as effectively as did syntactic complexity. There are many questions that were raised about this study. For example, why an independent measure of complexity was not used, and why the authors did not count whole-word repetitions as stuttering symptoms as Bernstein did in her earlier work?

A syntactic factor found in one study (Bernstein, 1981), was reported to be non-significant in another (Wall et al., 1981b). Comparison across these studies is complicated because Wall et al. excluded whole-word repetitions, whereas Bernstein did not. Both studies argued that boundary locations affected stuttering, although the type of boundaries differed between studies. Syntactic factors have never been compared with other units, such as prosodic words (see below). Prosodic words could also explain high rates of some types of disfluency at boundary locations and relative complexity of the units can be specified so that influences of the complexity of these units can be examined. The study by Bernstein Ratner and Sih (1987) that reported a correlation between syntactic complexity and stuttering has many unanswered questions. Overall, there seems to be little evidence for the assertion that stuttering starts when a child begins to use syntax.

A link between the onset of syntax and the onset of stuttering might be found by examining whether specific syntactic features are problematic for stutterers at onset. For instance, although auxiliaries start to be used between around the ages 2;0 and 2;6, which is before the average stuttering onset, verification of whether or not auxiliaries attract stuttering is necessary. Use of auxiliaries in "wh" questions can be unreliable through the late 2-year stage and subject–auxiliary inversion for "wh" questions is not complete until age 3 years (and for "why" questions in particular, it is even later). All these developments are happening around the age of stuttering onset. Auxiliaries can occur in more complex syntactic structures (e.g., questions, negatives), and given the finding that certain complex structures affect stuttering, it follows that auxiliaries might be problematic. Although Bernstein (1981) found no effect of auxiliaries in spontaneous speech, there are methods to elicit specific auxiliaries in different sentence types developed for typically developing children (Rowland & Theakston, 2009; Theakston & Rowland, 2009) and these may reveal positive findings.

In contrast with what was found at onset of stuttering, there is stronger evidence (though only from one study) that syntax may relate to the later course of stuttering (Howell & Au-Yeung, 1995). In a cross-sectional analysis using Wall et al.'s (1981b) procedures, stuttering related to complexity at older ages. There was, however, a shift of disfluencies away from clause boundary locations; clause boundary positions are less important in attracting stuttering as age increases. While this may suggest that syntax has a more diffuse effect on fluency at later ages (not tied to clause boundaries), it may indicate other influences are at work. The shift could potentially reflect a shift in locus of disfluency type within other segmental units (see section 7.5 below). Embedded clauses were found to be problematic for adult stutterers in one study (Hannah & Gardner, 1968), but not in a second (Wells, 1979). Negatives may cause problems across ages, but only for severe stutterers (Palen & Peterson, 1982; Ronson, 1976).

There are many counterarguments to the 12 points that Bloodstein and Bernstein Ratner (2007) presented in favor of the view that stuttering originates in problems in mastery of syntax. Overall, there seems to be little firm evidence in support of the view that there is a link between onset of stuttering and syntactic development, although syntax may affect the later course of the disorder.

7.4 LEXICAL FACTORS AND THE ONSET AND COURSE OF STUTTERING

The question addressed in this section is whether certain types of word are more likely to be stuttered than others, and whether this changes as a child ages. These issues are examined for children who stutter near onset, in cross-sectional and longitudinal studies, after some background evidence that function and content words are processed differently in the brain and are presented below.

7.4.1 ARE WORD TYPES PROCESSED DIFFERENTLY BY THE BRAIN IN TYPICALLY DEVELOPING AND STUTTERING INDIVIDUALS?

Recent studies on stuttering have examined content and function words classes. These two lexical classes appear to be processed in different parts of the brain in fluent speakers, which would, in principle, allow individuals to have selective problems on the different word types. Thus, Pulvermüller (1999) argued that processing of function words depends on structures in the left hemisphere of the brain while content words seem to be processed in both hemispheres. This conclusion was primarily derived from work with aphasic patients, but the findings have been generalized to typical cases as well as to patients suffering from a range of language disorders (Caramazza & Berndt, 1985; Chiarello & Nuding, 1987). However, as Pulvermüller pointed out, there is an unfortunate lack of data from cases (using event-related potentials, EEG, and fMRI) that have controlled for word frequency and word length of the stimuli used in tests.

Neuroimaging studies have shown that the processing of function and content words just described for fluent adult speakers is not true of people who stutter. Speakers who stutter show a distortion of the normal pattern of left hemispheric dominance (Kroll, de Nil, Kapur, & Houle, 1997). The changed pattern of cerebral dominance could reflect different functional problems for the two word classes because processing them relies on the two hemispheres to different extents. Alternatively, people who stutter may have structural abnormalities in the left cerebral hemisphere that then lead to the problems with both word classes, which both depend on left hemisphere processing according to Pulvermüller. There is no clear cut answer as to whether one of these alternatives applies at present or in what way different hemispheric activity could underpin different roles of function and content words. An account is also needed on how stuttering symptoms somehow migrate across word types (from function to content) over ages (see below in this section for details).

7.4.2 Use of Function and Content Words in Early Stages of Language Development

The transition from the one-word stage (at around 1 year of age) to multiword utterances (at around 2 years of age) was described in the section on syntax (points 5 and 8 in section 7.3.3). It has been observed that different types of words are spoken at these stages. Children mainly use content words at the one-word stage (Bloom, 1970; Brown, 1973; Radford; 2009). When children start to produce two-word utterances, they introduce function words into utterances, and this occurs at about age 2 (Labelle, 2005). It seems unlikely that word form can account for overt stuttering onset, as children will (1) have been using content words before stuttering starts (at the one-word stage) and (2) have been using function words before stuttering starts (using them from age 2, which is about a year before the average child starts to stutter). Function and content words may have roles in other language processes (e.g., at syntactic levels).

7.4.3 Evidence for an Association Between Function/Content Word Types and Stuttering: Over Ages and With Symptomatology

It has been argued that stuttering is linked with different lexical classes and that the lexical class that poses problems changes with the age of a speaker. In particular, near onset, children have been reported to have more stutters on function words, whereas at teenage years, most stutters occur on content words. The situation with adults was demonstrated in early work by Brown (1937). His research examined how much stuttering was associated with 23 different "parts of speech." The list included words from function and content word classes. These were ordered with respect to the percent of stuttering on each word type produced by 32 adults who stuttered. Brown next collapsed the 23 categories into what he called the eight conventional parts of speech. He collapsed aux-iliaries, which are function words, with other verbs, which are content words. These are listed separately in Table 7.2, listing nine categories rather than the eight he used. Note also, that the pronoun category in Table 7.2 includes only personal and possessive forms (not relative forms, such as "who" and "what"). Later commentators have noted that the parts of speech that cause most diffi-culty for adults are content words. The right-hand column in each row indicates whether the word was function (F) or content (C) in type. The entries are ranked from easiest (least stuttering) to most difficult (most stuttering). The function words appear at the top of the table and the content words at the bottom. Thus, content words appear to pose more of a problem for adults. This may happen for various reasons: The content words carry lexical stress, occur infrequently, and are phonologically and motorically complex, all of which could lead to them being difficult to produce.

Bloodstein and Gantwerk (1967) were the first to report higher rates of stut-tering on function than content words in children who stutter. This study did not specify what symptoms were considered stuttered (they were simply referred to

TABLE 7.2
Order of Difficulty of Nine
Classes of Words for Speakers
Who Stutter

Easy (Least Stuttering)

Articles	F
Auxiliary verbs	F
Prepositions	F
Conjunctions	F
Pronouns	F
Main verbs	C
Adverbs	C
Nouns	C
Adjectives	C

Hard (Most Stuttering)

Note: Function (F) and content words (C) are indicated at the right. Adapted from "The Influence of Grammatical Function on the Incidence of Stuttering," by S. F. Brown, 1937, *Journal of Speech Disorders*, 2, pp. 207–215.

as "stutterings"). The study is not considered further, as arguments about whether there is a lot of stuttering on function words depends on what symptoms are considered to be stutters. In a later study, Bloodstein and Grossman (1981) recorded the spontaneous speech (picture descriptions) of five children who stuttered aged between 3;10 and 5;7. Sound or syllable repetition, word repetition, phrase repetition, prolongation of a sound, hard attack on a sound, inappropriate pause, and audible secondary characteristics, such as gasping were counted as stutters. They reported that, for most participants, proportionately more function words than content words were stuttered.

The argument that children show a lot of stuttering on function words only holds if whole-word repetitions are considered as symptoms of stuttering (children often say "and, and, and" or "I, I, I" where both words are function in type). As mentioned, there are protagonists for and against their inclusion of stutterings, and both Wingate (Chapter 1) and Bernstein Ratner (current chapter) have embraced either convention in different aspects of their work. One way the issue of whether whole-word repetitions are stutters could be settled empirically is by seeing whether the imbalance in the type of words that are stuttered still occurs when whole-word repetitions are excluded from analyses.

7.4.3.1 Onset

There are some data from the Illinois study that offer circumstantial support for the view that near onset certain children who stutter do have problems with content words. Thus, Yairi and Ambrose's (2005) observed blocks and prolongations in children around onset, whereas features of repair (interjections, phrase repetitions, etc.) are rare (p. 68). Blocks and prolongations tend to occur on content words, whereas the repair features are observed on function words (Howell, 2007a). This suggests that childhood stuttering may be more like adult forms (i.e., appearing on content words) in some cases. Yairi and Ambrose's data are not available for scrutiny and no case reports have appeared, therefore, these claims cannot be verified.

7.4.3.2 Cross-Sectional Studies

The change from stuttering on function words in children to stuttering on content words has been examined by Howell and collaborators in English and other languages (Au-Yeung, Gomez, & Howell, 2003; Howell, 2004b, for Spanish; and Dworzynski, Howell, Au-Yeung, & Rommel, 2004, for German).

Howell, Au-Yeung, and Sackin (1999) reported cross-sectional data on English-speaking children. They recorded 51 speakers who stuttered and 68 control speakers in conversation with a speech pathologist. The speakers ranged in age from 2;7 to 40 years. The participants were divided into five different age groups: 2 to 6 years (four boys and two girls) called young children, 7 to 9 years (11 boys and four girls) called middle children, 10 to 12 years (eight boys and two girls) called old children, teenagers 13 to 19 years (seven boys and one girl), and adults aged 20 and over (12 males). The 68 control speakers were unpaid volunteers who reported no history of speech or hearing difficulty. They were divided into the same five age groups using the age criteria set out above for speakers who stutter. The young children group had three boys and three girls, the middle children group had 10 boys and 17 girls, the old children group had nine boys and six girls, the teenage group had one male and seven females, and the adult group had 12 male speakers. Episodes that were counted as stuttering were whole-word and part-word repetition and segmental or syllabic prolongations.

Fluent speakers had a higher percentage of disfluency on function words that preceded a content word (initial function words). Whether disfluency occurred predominantly on initial function words or content words changed over age groups for speakers who stutter. For the young children that stutter, there was a higher percentage of disfluencies on initial function words than content words (Figure 7.1). In subsequent age groups, disfluency decreased on function words and increased on content words.

7.4.3.3 Longitudinal

Although the Howell et al. (1999) data showed a change from stuttering on function words to content words as age increased, a limitation is that the data are cross-sectional. Consequently, some of the younger children would have recovered as age increased. It is possible that the children who dropped out were more like typically developing children (selective attrition of recovered cases). The children

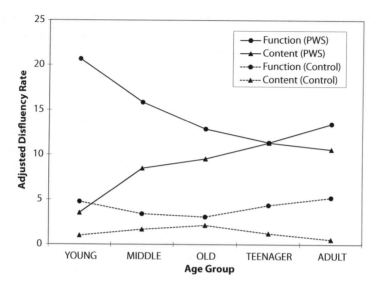

FIGURE 7.1   Illustrated is the stuttering rate on function and content words for speakers in different age groups for people who stutter (PWS) and control (Control).

who recovered may have shown more function word stutters than content word ones; repetition of function words is often seen in typically developing children's speech. The persistent stutterers may always have shown more content word stuttering, and this was gradually revealed across the age groups as they became the majority. This is basically Wingate's (2001) argument that was presented in Chapter 3. Although Howell et al. were careful about their inclusion criteria, it cannot be guaranteed in cross-sectional work that this did not happen.

This possibility was ruled out in longitudinal work reported in Howell (2007a). Seventy-six children were followed up between the ages 8 and 12+. All the children were diagnosed as stuttering at the outset of the study (around age 8). The children were assessed by stuttering severity instrument-3 (SSI-3), by parents, by the children themselves, and by a researcher as persisting in, or recovered from, stuttering at age 12+, at which age stuttering should have recovered if it was going to. Howell, Davis, and Williams, 2006, give full details of how the assessments were made, and these were also described in Chapter 1. Overall, 41 recovered and 35 persisted.

Whole-word and phrase repetitions were grouped together, and were expected to occur predominantly on function words. Part-word repetitions, prolongations, and broken words were grouped together and were expected to occur predominantly on content words.

Children who stuttered at age 12+ change the balance between types of stuttering in different ways depending on whether they persisted or recovered over the test period. The data for the recovered speakers showed that the average number of whole-word and phrase repetitions on function words per 2-min period went down from 3.08 to 1.43 and the number of part-word repetitions, prolongations, and broken stutters on content words went down from 1.17 to 0.44. The reduction of the number of stutters on whole-word and phrase repetitions and of part-word repetitions, prolongations and broken stutters, represented a proportional reduction of both stutter groupings to absolute levels shown by fluent speakers. Recovered speakers converge on fluent speakers.

The data for the persistent speakers showed that the average number of whole-word and phrase repetitions per 2-min period on function words went down from 2.89 to 1.58, but the number of part-word repetitions, prolongations, and broken stutters on content words went up from 1.38 to 1.68. The increase in part-word repetitions, prolongations, and broken stutters on content words, specifically for persistent speakers, shows these speakers diverge from the speakers who recover.

7.4.3.4 Limitations

7.4.3.4.1 Specific Word Types Included Within the Function and Content Word Classes

Bloodstein and Grossman (1981, p. 301) noted that the majority of words stuttered by children were pronouns and conjunctions, which they classed as function words. Wingate (1988, p. 164) commented on the ambiguity of function and content word classes. In the Howell group's work, pronouns and conjunctions were included in the function word class using guidance from two different authorities (Hartmann & Stork, 1972; Quirk, Greenbaum, Leech, & Svartvik, 1985). There are alternative views on what the role of these particular word classes is in stuttering. For instance, as has already been discussed, Wall et al.'s study shows "and" may act as a filler with children and does not have a functional role (e.g., as part of syntactic constructions). There may be differences between conjunctions used to join complete sentences (e.g., "The girl jumped and the boy ran away"), and conjunctions used to join clauses (e.g., "The girl jumped and shouted"). This suggests that these two types of conjunctions should be analyzed separately to see whether they give rise to different patterns of stuttering.

There is also a debate as to whether pronouns are function or content. Some linguists assume pronouns to be determiner phrases. There are related debates about prepositions. It is possible that symptom type could be used as a way of determining the word class to which conjunctions, pronouns, and prepositions belong.

7.4.3.5 Summary on Lexical Factors

Young speakers appear to have more stuttering on function words and older speakers more stuttering on content words, with the proviso that whole-word repetitions are counted as symptoms of stuttering. Use of symptom types change with age and may represent two alternative ways of dealing with stuttering in a (nonsyntactic) contextual unit (see section 7.5).

During the later course of the disorder, children exhibit proportionately more stutters on content words. This remains stable to about the teenage years, which is the age at which stuttering is resolved into persistent or recovered forms.

It was mentioned that function and content words vary on a number of dimensions all of which could contribute toward why the two word classes vary in difficulty.

Function words occur more frequently, do not carry stress, and have simpler phono-logical properties than content words. Any of these properties could account for why words from different classes affect fluency in different ways. Function and content words are useful because they are binary categories, unlike word frequency that is a continuous variable, and because they bring together the several influences that could impact on fluency. Word class can be dismissed if one of the factors associated with word class is shown to be a superior predictor of fluency behavior. Methods that can be used to deconfound the several influences are discussed in section 7.9.

It was also shown that function and content words are associated with different stutter types. The warning to be careful to examine whether whole-word repeti-tions were included as symptoms needs to be repeated. Bloodstein and Grossman (1981) included them and found higher rates of stuttering on function words in young speakers who stutter. Whether they would have found high rates of stutter-ing on function words if they had excluded whole-word repetitions, as Wingate's (2001) work suggests, has not been examined.

It seems likely that the association between word type and stuttering symp-toms is not inherent to word class per se. The reasons for this is that content words can be produced fluently by children who go on to stutter during early develop-ment (section 7.5.1) and only function words in certain positions attract stuttering (as explained in section 7.5.3)

7.5   PHONOLOGICAL OR PROSODIC WORDS

7.5.1   Phonological Words and the Onset and Course of Stuttering

The effects of function and content words on fluency described in the previous section do not reflect a simple word type change over ages. Children start to pro-duce content words fluently, continue to do so to some degree in early childhood (point 5 in section 7.3.3) and only later do problems with content words arise. If the problem was associated with processing particular word types, then it is not clear why late stages of stuttering show problems on words that were, on the whole, produced fluently at younger ages when stuttering was developing.

One class of explanation is that the problem reflects different ways of negotiat-ing suprasegmental units that incorporate function and content words. This could be partly related to the syntactic account of Bloodstein and Bernstein Ratner. However, as stated at the start of section 7.3.3 on evidence that stuttering is linked to syntactic units, a different segmental unit that could also have this role (the prosodic, or phonological, word) is described in this section.

Several authors who have worked on fluent speech have noted contextual effects associated with word type and the form of disfluency. For instance, Maclay and Osgood (1959) noted that 74% of word repetitions preceded a content word, and the repeated word would be a function word. Clark and Clark (1977) and MacWhinney and Osser (1977) noted repetition of conjunctions (a type of function word) was common in young children's speech when they were having difficulty. Gee and Grosjean (1983) made the related argument that pauses were positioned on function words prior to content words. Strenstrom and Svartvik (1994) reported that subject pronouns (again a type of function word), which appear before content words, were produced disfluently more often than object pronouns, which appear after content words.

7.5.2   Usefulness of Phonological or Prosodic Word (PW)

A contextual unit that uses function and content words in their specification is the phonological word (PW), as used by Selkirk (1984), albeit she prefers the term *prosodic word*. She worked with English and the following remarks are specifically about that language. According to Selkirk, content words are the core of a PW. At least one content word has to occur in a PW while the function words are optional and play a subsidiary role. Function words only have weak unstressed forms, in contrast to the strong stressed forms that content words can take.

The close link between a function word and its content words is described by Selkirk as follows: "It is also characteristic of function words that they may exhibit an extremely close phonological connection, or juncture, with an adjacent word—usually to the word that follows, but sometimes to one that precedes" (p. 336). Later in the same text, Selkirk developed the argument with regard to the role of function words further: "We claim that these and other ways in which function words are not treated like 'real' words in the grammar are to be attributed to a single principle, the *principle of the categorical invisibility* (PCI) *of function words*, which says (essentially) that rules making crucial appeal to the syntactic category of the constituent to which they apply are blind to the presence of function word constituents" (p. 337).

Terminologically speaking, a content word is a *host* (also called *head*). Function words belong to the class of *clitics*. For example, the words "will it" and "see you," both of which have content function structure, could be phonologically likened to the single content words "billet" and the name "Mia," respectively. A function word preceding the host is a *proclitic* and a function word positioned after the host is an *enclitic*. Examples of proclitic plus host are "a fence" and "can pile" and an example of host and enclitic is "give it."

The significance of the concept of PW for stuttering arises from the fact that a single constituent (what Levelt, 1989, called a *frame*) can extend beyond one lexical item. This can provide the context in which to understand fluency breakdown. The UCL speech team adopted the interpretation of the PW based on the notion that isolated function words are not PWs (as pointed out by Levelt, 1989; Selkirk, 1984, and others). Instead, function words are viewed as prefixes or suffixes to a neighboring stressed content word (Au-Yeung, Howell, & Pilgrim, 1998; Howell et al., 1999). The UCL group went on to define a PW on lexical criteria as consisting of a single content word (C) plus adjacent function words (F), having the general form $[F_nCF_m]$, where n and m are integers greater than or equal to zero. Consider, for instance, the utterance: "I look after her cats." There are two function words between the two content words "look" and "cats." Au-Yeung et al. (1998) and Howell et al. (1999) developed Selkirk's (1984) semantic sense unit rules to establish which function words were associated with each content word. These are rules, Selkirk had proposed, that defined which words are semantically related in intonational phrases (which are a superordinate prosodic grouping to PW).

Two constituents C_i, C_j form a sense unit if (a) or (b) is true of the semantic interpretation of the sentence:

- C_i modifies C_j (a head).
- C_i is an argument of C_j (a head).

The extensions to the rules by Au-Yeung et al. (1998) were:

- Both C_i and C_j modify C_k (a head).
- Both C_i and C_j are arguments of C_k (a head).

Applying these rules to the "I look after her cats" example, it is necessary to determine whether one or both of the function words that appear after "look" are enclitic to "look" or proclitic to the content word "cats." Applying the rules to the example, "after" is part of the same PW that includes "look," which is a phrasal verb and forms a special meaning with "after." The function word "her" is a prefix of "cats." Thus, the phrase has the following PW form: [I look after] $_{PW}$ [her cats] $_{PW}$.

The interest in PW is that it includes words that vary in difficulty. There is always a content word that is statistically more likely to be more difficult than the function word. There are ways of grading difficulty on content words that will be considered when syllable constituency is examined in section 7.6. Thus, PW can be used to group together words around a content word and the relative difficulty of different content words can be quantified. Syntactic parsing also does both of these things, thus the question is why would anyone want to introduce a new unit to group words together and specify their difficulty if syntax already does this?

Our own view is that PW reveal the important roles different types of symptom have in stuttering. Certain symptoms from Johnson's list can lead to delay (pause, whole-word repetition, and phrase repetition). These occur before the content word in a PW to delay the attempt at its production. To play this role, they have to precede the content word (pausing and repeating enclitics would not serve this role). Of the remaining symptoms in Johnson's list (see Chapter 3, section 3.2), part-word repetitions, prolongations, and word breaks are types that occur on content words (Howell, 2007a) and signify that the person who stutters was not ready to output the word. This presents an alternative perspective to the discussion about selecting symptom types for inclusion or exclusion based on whether they are more or less typical of stuttering. In the current account, all the events mentioned from Johnson's list are deviations from fluency and each event represents one of two different processes (delaying around proclitics called *stalling* or tackling problems on heads that are not ready for output called *advancing*). The notion of dividing symptoms into stallings and advancings was first mentioned briefly in Chapter 3 and is one of the main cornerstones of the language–motor interaction chapter where PW are considered to lie at the interface between the language and motor systems, rather than an aspect of language processing (Chapter 12).

Studies that were interpreted as showing fluency problems occur at the start of syntactic constituents were reviewed above. The PW account just presented suggests that pauses and function word repetition should tend to appear at the start of PW, not syntactic constituents unless the syntactic boundaries happen to correspond with PW boundaries. This can be seen in examples Pinker (1995) used: "[The baby]$_{np}$ [ate [the slug]$_{np}$]$_{vp}$" and "[He]$_{np}$ [ate [the slug]$_{np}$]$_{vp}$." Pinker used these examples to show that pauses do not always occur at syntactic boundaries; it will be argued that they do, nevertheless, occur at PW boundaries. He stated that pausing is allowed after the subject NP "*the baby,*" but not after the subject NP, in the pronominal "*he.*" Note that both these positions involve the same major syntactic boundary, a subject NP, so syntactic factors alone cannot account for this difference in pause occurrence. The PW boundaries in the examples are [The baby] $_{PW}$ [ate]$_{PW}$ [the slug]$_{PW}$ and [He ate]$_{PW}$ [the slug]$_{PW}$, respectively. Assuming pauses are allowed to occur at PW boundaries, pausing between "*baby*" and "*ate*" is allowed in the first sentence (as Pinker observed), as they are in two separate PWs. Pausing should not occur in the second sentence (again as Pinker observed) because there is no PW boundary at the corresponding point. Thus, it seems that PWs are preferred units for specifying boundaries where pauses can occur for this example.

7.5.3   Interpretation of Exchange Findings

The PW unit was developed to account for the reciprocal change from stutters on function to content words with age, shown in Figure 7.1. The function word stuttering rates were calculated just on the proclitics in PW. As Bloodstein and Gantwerk (1967) and Bloodstein and Grossman (1981) had argued, the data showed that young children stuttered more on function words while adult speakers stuttered more on content words. If function words alone are examined, it can be seen that the rate on them is high at younger ages and then drops off with age. If content words alone are examined, it can be seen that they increase with age. Taken together, there is a reciprocal relationship between stuttering rates on function and content words. Thus, young children show a lot of stuttering on proclitic function words, but little on content words, whereas the adults show the reverse. As the function words precede a content word, it is likely that they lead to a pause or are repeated, as observed with fluent speakers (Clark & Clark, 1977; Gee & Grosjean, 1983; Maclay & Osgood, 1959; MacWhinney & Osser, 1977; Strenstrom & Svartvik, 1994).

It should be noted that there is no necessary relationship between stuttering rates on function and content words. Thus, for example, function word rate could have declined while content word rate remained steady. As this is not the case, there seems to be some trading relationship between the two (i.e., if you do one thing, you do not do another). Chapter 12 considers why this might be. Second, the enclitics were dropped because they had negligible stuttering rates. This implies that proclitics have a special role in terms of fluency problems. Again, this will be revisited in Chapter 12. The fact that enclitics show low rates of stuttering for all speakers suggests that function words, per se, do not determine stuttering, only some function words are stalled.

Alternative definitions of heads and clitics (not content and function words) are possible. An alternative definition of head (as content word or as stressed words irrespective of word type) has been compared with content word specification for Spanish and both alternatives result in an exchange function (Howell, 2004b).

7.5.4 SUMMARY AND SUGGESTION FOR FUTURE WORK

The concept of PW reveals particular patterns of stuttering at onset (high rates on function words that precede content words) and the course of stuttering to the teens. PWs are a contextual unit that may be defined in terms of function and content words, but they also suggest that stuttering is only indirectly related to lexical class insofar as they represent parts of speech that are easy and hard to produce respectively. Section 7.6 considers whether sublexical descriptors (syllable constituents) provide an alternative about what components are easy and hard to produce.

Hybrid models that include syntactic and prosodic units to account for pause location have appeared (Gee & Grosjean, 1983; Ferreira, 1993; Watson & Gibson, 2004). These should be compared with the PW account of pause location. These models could also be extended to examine word repetition to test the prediction that whole-word repetition happens on words that start PWs. Together, these would constitute the start of a model of how stuttering symptoms change with age.

7.6 PHONOLOGICAL INFLUENCES

All children have difficulties in handling some phonological structures. These are predictable and present in all typically developing children, so they are not errors in the conventional sense of the word; perhaps "simplification" would be a better word. The predictability for all children makes "simplifications" normal features of developing speech; they are called phonological processes. Typically developing children cease making errors as their phonemic repertoire increases and their phonology becomes more like an adult's.

Other phonological processes are idiosyncratic to particular children and are a sign of disordered phonology. The idiosyncratic processes are often regarded as potential indicators of abnormal phonological development (Small, 2005). (Table A.1 and Table A.2 in the Appendix at the end of this chapter present some common, and idiosyncratic, phonological processes, based on Small.) Neither sort of phonological process has been examined comprehensively in both children who stutter and controls, although some of them are referred to in sections 7.6.2.2 and 7.6.3.2, thus an understanding is necessary to interpret that work. The reasonably comprehensive lists in Table A.1 and Table A.2 are included to motivate further examination of the role of phonological processes in stuttering onset (and possibly course).

It is conceivable that stuttering is associated with phonological problems. One line of evidence for this is that rates of phonological disorder are higher in children who stutter (Nippold, 2002, reports rates of between 30 and 40% in a number of studies) than in children who do not stutter (Shriberg, Tomblin, and MacSweeney, 1999, reported this ranged between 2 and 13%). Although this looks like strong evidence, Nippold (2001) noted that the high rate in children who stutter may be because of differences in the way phonological disorder was defined.

There have been a number of investigations into phonological disorder and stuttering: stuttering and complexity of syllables (syllable constituency), identification of problems in phonological development near onset of stuttering, and identification of problems in phonological development and association with course of stuttering (persistence/recovery). They are discussed below.

7.6.1 STUTTERING AND COMPLEXITY OF SYLLABLES: SYLLABLE CONSTITUENCY

The constituents of a syllable are represented in the tree diagram in Figure 7.2. The two main constituents of a syllable are the onset consonants and the rhyme. The rhyme is further subdivided into the nucleus and coda. The nucleus is a sound peak (usually on a vowel). The coda is the sequence of one or more final consonants. There are phonological rules that apply concerning permissible phoneme sequences within the word, and also rules that apply at the syllable or word level.

A complete list of phonological constraints for each of these elements cannot be given here, but some selected illustrations follow. Up to three consonants can occur in onset position for English. Maximum onsets involve /s/ plus a voiceless plosive (/p/, /t/, or /k/), plus either /r/, /l/, /j/, or /w/. The nucleus can be (1) any vowel or (2) /m/, /n/, and /l/ in certain situations. Any single consonant except /h/,/w/, or /j/ can occur as coda. Usually up to three consonants can occur as coda for English. Codas that have three consonants can have the following structures: (1) lateral approximant plus two consonants: /lpt/, /lfθ/, /lts/, /lst/, /lkt/, /lks/ (e.g., twelfth, waltz); (2) nasal plus homorganic plosive plus plosive or fricative: /mpt/, /mps/, /ndθ/, /ŋkt/, /ŋks/, /ŋkθ/ (e.g., prompt, glimpse); and (3) three obstruents: /ksθ/, /kst/ (e.g., sixth, next).

This breakdown of the constituents of a syllable is important to stuttering. There is general agreement about the importance of syllable, or more specifically, word, onsets as the locus of most stuttering involving breakdown of words

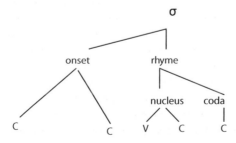

FIGURE 7.2   Tree diagram showing the hierarchical relationship between the constituents of a syllable (σ).

(Wingate, 2002). Thus, prolongations, part-word repetitions, and word breaks tend to occur around syllable onsets. This suggests that syllable onset may have an important role in determining the form of stuttering.

Findings employing two contemporary methods for assessing phonological difficulty of material used with stuttering are discussed below. They are arranged according to whether they examine onset, and course, of stuttering, as previously mentioned. As in earlier sections, attention is given to what symptoms were considered stutters in the studies. Results dependent on syllable position (initial/anywhere in the syllable) are presented where available. Where possible, phonological properties on function and content words are reported separately because these word types attract different stuttering symptoms, which may reflect different underlying processes in stuttering. Stuttering symptoms used in the studies are documented because of the controversy concerning whether whole-word repetitions should be considered as stutters or not.

7.6.2   ONSET

7.6.2.1   Studies Using Spontaneous Speech

Throneburg, Yairi, and Paden (1994)—This group examined whether phonological factors of speech material affected stuttering rate. The participants were 24 preschool children who stuttered (9 girls, 15 boys). The children were aged between 29 and 59 months, with a mean age of 40.5 months.

A spontaneous speech sample was obtained in a play session with the child and a parent. This was approximately 1,000 words long and was obtained over two 20-min recording sessions. The stutters that were counted were:

1. Part-word repetition
2. Single-syllable word repetition
3. Disrhythmic phonation (primarily sound prolongation)
4. Multisyllabic word or phrase repetition
5. Interjection
6. Revision/incomplete phrase

The first three of these occurs in the SLD class described in Chapter 3.

They classified words spoken by the preschool children who stuttered into different categories according to whether they contained: developmentally late emerging consonants (LEC. consonant strings (CS) and multiple-syllables (MS), all of which were considered as potentially making words difficult. The LEC were derived from empirical observations about child language, and consisted of fricatives, affricates, and liquids (Sander, 1972), specifically /r,l,s,z,dʒ,v,tʃ,h,ɵ,ð,ʃ,ʒ/. All possible combinations of the three factors were examined. These were (with examples):

1. Not difficult. Words that contained none of the three factors (e.g., *hot, can*).

2. Words that contained CS, but were simple otherwise (e.g., *twang, bump*).
3. Words that were MS, but were simple otherwise (e.g., *today, summate*).
4. Words that contained LEC, but were simple otherwise (e.g., *chair, ball*).
5. Words that contained CS and were MS (e.g., *dwindle, painting*).
6. Words that contained CS and LEC (e.g., *play, still*).
7. Words that contained LEC and were MS (e.g., *nothing, little*).
8. Words that contained CS and LEC and were MS (e.g., *tractor, elephant*).

The proportion of words with SLDs for each category of phonological difficulty was calculated and the proportion of these that were stuttered was estimated. Similar calculations were made on the word that followed each word with a stuttering-like disfluency (SLD) as control. None of the three factors (LEC, CS, and MS) occurred significantly more often in words with SLDs than in the overall sample. The proportion of words that were SLD and the immediately following words in each of the eight phonological difficulty categories closely resembled the values expected based on chance.

The children were classified into four groups based on stuttering severity (severe/mild) and phonological skill (poor/good). There were no significant differences between the subgroups of stutterers, nor were there any significant differences when the eight categories of phonological difficulty were collapsed to create the three categories:

1. Not phonologically difficult (category 1)
2. Single element of phonological difficulty (categories 3, 4, and 5)
3. Multiple element of phonological difficulty (categories 6, 7, and 8)

They concluded that the phonological difficulty of the SLD word, and the fluent word following it, did not contribute to stuttering.

Further analyses ought to be done to examine different symptom types since SLD includes whole-word repetitions and because their status as stutters has been debated. Also, function and content words ought to be examined separately because they attract different types of stuttering. Finally, the CS and LEC factors ought to be examined in different syllables positions (Wingate, 2002). This is because stuttering occurs in initial position in syllables and CS and LEC factors in these positions might have more influence on whether a word is stuttered or not than ones in final position in syllables. Work on some of these issues is discussed in section 7.6.2.

Weiss and Jakielski (2001)—A different approach to determining which speech sounds children who stutter find difficult was taken by Weiss and Jakielski. This was based on Jakielski's (1998) thesis work, which drew its inspiration from MacNeilage and Davis' (1990) research, suggesting that motor constraints affect early speech development in predictable ways. Jakielski (1998) developed an Index of Phonetic Complexity (IPC) that proposed a relationship between babbling and speech sound development.

Based on observations of babbled speech, Jakielski first identified eight factors that occurred early (easy) or late (difficult) in speech development. The factors that appeared early are listed below. Factors 1, 2, 3, 7, and 8 concern consonant clusters but, as with Throneburg et al., initial and final positions were not distinguished.

1. Young children used dorsal place of articulation less frequently than older children.
2. Nasals, stops, and glides were most common in cluster-token segments.
3. Singleton consonants were reduplicated in the younger age group, whereas variegated consonants emerged increasingly often in the older groups.
4. Nonrhoticized vowels occur most frequently.
5. Final syllables tend to be open.
6. Words are comparatively short.
7. There was a tendency for children to move from producing singleton consonants to clusters as they got older.
8. Clusters progressed from homorganic to heterorganic places with age.

Based on these observations, Jakielski proposed the scheme in Table 7.3 for determining whether each of the eight factors was likely or not to cause difficulty.

To obtain the IPC, each factor was examined on a word and marked as easy or hard based on whether it had an early- or late-acquired property. For example, nonrhoticized vowels were marked easy and rhoticized vowels as hard, or words with open final syllables were marked easy and with closed final syllables as hard. The IPC is the total of how many hard factors a word has. There is some similarity with Throneburg et al.'s (1994) scheme: factor 2 resembles LEC, factor 6 is like MS, and factor 7 is like CS.

TABLE 7.3

Index of Phonetic Complexity Scoring Scheme

Factor	No Score	One Point Each
1. Consonant by place	Labials, coronals, glottals	Dorsals
2. Consonant by manner	Stops, nasals, glides	Fricatives, affricates, liquids
3. Singleton consonants by place	Reduplicated	Variegated
4. Vowel by class	Monophthongs, diphthongs	Rhotics
5. Word shape	Ends with a vowel	Ends with a consonant
6. Word length (syllables)	Monosyllables, disyllables	> = Three syllables
7. Contiguous consonants	No clusters	Consonant clusters
8. Cluster by place	Homorganic	Heterorganic

Weiss and Jakielski (2001) analyzed speech samples from 13 children who stuttered who were aged between 6 and 11 years using this scheme (note that even the youngest child was past onset and the children ranged in age up to 11, close to when recovery is unlikely). The samples were from structured and unstructured conversations. They counted within-word stutters as defined by Conture (2001) and described in Chapter 3, which is appropriate for a word-based analysis. This group includes part- and whole-word repetitions and prolongations as stutters.

Weiss and Jakielski performed word-based analyses. IPC values for all words in 25 sentences were obtained. The IPC values just for those words with a within-word stutter were also obtained. IPC values for the stuttered words would be expected to be higher than all words. Sentence-based IPC scores were also obtained and analyzed in a similar way. None of these analyses showed any relation between the difference in IPC values between all words and stuttered words and age.

7.6.2.2 Identification of Problems in Phonological Development Near Onset of Stuttering Using Methods Other Than Analysis of Spontaneous Speech Samples

Nippold (2002) provided a thorough review of the literature that addressed the question of whether stuttering is linked to phonological development, including some work on phonological processes. The work in this section is on young children and is based on this review. The work examined is about problems in normal phonological development (see Chapter 10, section 10.5.2.2 for studies on phonological disorder).

Louko, Edwards, and Conture (1990) examined 30 children (28 boys, 2 girls) who ranged in age from 2;5 to 6;11 months (mean age was 4;6). They looked for the presence of phonological processes in conversational speech. Nippold gives as examples cluster reduction, stopping, gliding, all of which are typical phonological processes during speech development as indicated by their inclusion in Table A.1 at the end of the chapter. Each child was audio-recorded while playing with his or her mother. A sample of speech about 300 words long was analyzed for phonological processes, using criteria from Edwards and Shriberg (1983), Grunwell (1982), and Stoel-Gammon and Dunn (1985). Correlations were computed between the number of phonological processes that occurred in the speech sample and three different measures of stuttering behavior: frequency, duration, and sound prolongation. None of the correlations for the three measures was statistically significant, so there was no support for a relationship between stuttering and phonology around onset of the disorder.

Ryan (1992) assessed the phonological skills of 20 children (15 boys, 5 girls) by interview. The children ranged in age from 2;10 to 5;9 (mean 4;4) and they were given the Arizona Articulation Proficiency Scale (AAPS) (Barker, 1973). Stutters were struggle, prolongation, part-word repetition, and whole-word repetition. The correlation between the number of stuttered words produced per minute during the interview and raw scores on the AAPS was not significant. Again this suggests that there is no relationship between stuttering and phonology around onset of the disorder.

Anderson and Conture (2000) administered the "Sounds-in-Words" subtest of the Goldman–Fristoe Test of Articulation (GFTA) (Goldman & Fristoe, 1986) to 20 children (16 boys, 4 girls) who ranged in age from 3;0 to 5;10 (mean 3;11). A 300-word sample of conversational speech was elicited from each child during a play session with a clinician and used to obtain an SSI-3 estimate. The speech sample was also used to determine the frequency of Conture's within-word stutters (WWD) and total disfluencies (TD: within- and between-words) per 100 words of speech. Anderson and Conture's analyses showed:

1. The mean percentile rank on the GFTA for all children was 57.25 (range = 23–99)
2. Mean SSI-3 was 21.50 (range = 14–34)
3. Mean percentage WWD was 14.08 (range = 5–33)
4. Mean TD (percent) was 17.54 (range = 10.30–36)

These results indicated that the phonological development of the children was in the normal range, but they showed mild to severe levels of stuttering. Nippold (2002) used data in Anderson and Conture's Table 1 to compute correlation coefficients between the GFTA and each of the fluency measures. None of these was statistically significant, indicating that children who produced more speech sound errors did not necessarily stutter more severely.

All of these studies included whole-word repetitions as symptoms of stuttering. As noted several times already, this symptom occurs predominantly on function words and its inclusion in stuttering counts has been questioned (Wingate, 2002). It would be advisable at some point to reexamine these findings with whole-word repetitions excluded as they may have led to the nonsignificant results. Also, content and function word classes could be examined separately. Finally, examination of phonological processes that affect onsets could be compared with those that affect other parts of words and syllables as it is possible that the former may have more impact on precipitating stuttering, given that stuttering mainly occurs on onsets.

7.6.3 COURSE

7.6.3.1 Studies Using Spontaneous Speech

Both Throneburg et al.'s (1994) scheme and Weiss and Jakielski's (2001) scheme have been used to assess the course of stuttering.

Howell, Au-Yeung, and Sackin (2000)—As mentioned in section 7.6.2, a limitation in the Throneburg et al. (1994) study is that no distinction was made concerning the position where an LEC or CS occurred within a word. Consequently, even for monosyllable words, CS and LEC factors can be distributed over different word positions in several ways: CS can be word initial (e.g., "quick") or noninitial (e.g., "found"), LEC can also be word initial (e.g., "like") or noninitial (e.g., "bale"). A word containing CS and LEC can have both CS and LEC word initial (e.g., "tried" or "school"), both CS and LEC can be noninitial (e.g., "helps") or CS and LEC can be at different positions (e.g., "quiz" has CS initial and LEC noninitial and "lent" has these factors in the reverse positions). There also may be some interaction between CS and LEC such that when they occur in the same word position, this enhances their difficulty. Thus, a word like "school" that has a CS and LEC that occur in word-initial position would be expected to cause more difficulty than "quiz" where the CS occurs before the vocalic segment and the LEC after it.

Consequently, Howell et al. examined CS and LEC dependent on word position in a study that examined different age groups. Howell et al. looked at content words and function words separately. This was because the stutters that occur on function words may delay an attempt at a following content word and, if so, they would not reflect problems in uttering the function word and would not be expected to show effects of phonological difficulty, but stutters on content words would.

Participants were divided into three age groups: group 1 had 21 children with mean age 7;3 years, group 2 consisted of 18 teenagers with a mean age of 13;1 years, and group 3 was 12 adults with a mean age of 28;3 years. Spontaneous speech samples were obtained from all speakers. The same transcription and stuttering assessment procedures were used as in Kadi-Hanifi and Howell (1992) described earlier in section 7.3.1. The stutters in this procedure included whole-word repetitions, as did Throneburg et al. (1994).

No effects of phonological difficulty were reported for function words. For content words, analyses showed that the CS and LEC factors occurred at different rates across the age groups used. A more detailed breakdown of LEC and CS in content words was also reported; all nine combinations of no LEC, word-initial LEC, noninitial LEC with no CS, word-initial CS, and noninitial CS were examined. Usage of certain of these nine categories varied over age groups. In general, simple forms (LEC and/or CS absent) declined with age, whereas forms with these features were used more often. A Friedman statistic on the ratio of stuttering (proportion of stuttered words in a particular word class divided by the proportion of words in that particular word class) showed that the frequency of stuttering on content words remained high for adult speakers when CS and LEC both occurred in a word and when they appeared in word-initial position. As the effect was specific to the adults, the effects of phonological difficulty may have more to say about the later course of stuttering than onset and may represent an acquired effect rather than an innate one.

Howell, Au-Yeung, Yaruss, and Eldridge (2006)—Examination of Weiss and Jakielski's (2001) scheme suggests the same three possible reasons for the lack of a relationship between stuttering rate and IPC, similar to those highlighted in relation to the Throneburg et al. study: (1) no distinction was made between function and content words; (2) only the speech of one age group—young children in this case—was analyzed; this age group would not be expected to show an effect of phonological difficulty based on Howell et al.'s (2000) findings; and (3) the IPC factors do not load specifically on onsets.

Consequently, Howell et al. (2006) replicated the Weiss and Jakielski (2001) study looking at a range of age groups separately for function and content words. The scheme cannot easily be modified to make it sensitive to factors at onset. Howell et al. examined spontaneous speech samples from speakers in the age ranges 6 to 11 (16), 11+ to 18 (16), and 18+ (10). The stuttering symptoms included in the assessments were segment, part-word and word repetitions, segmental and syllabic prolongations, and word breaks.

Stuttering rate on the content words of older speakers (teenagers and adults), but not younger speakers, correlated with the IPC score. In further analyses, the IPC factors that were most likely to lead to stuttering in English, and their order of importance were established. The order found was consonant by manner, consonant by place, word length, and contiguous consonant clusters. (See Table 7.3 for a description of these factors and how they were scored.) As the effects of phonological difficulty were evident in teenage and adulthood again, at least some of the factors may have an acquired influence on stuttering, rather than an innate universal basis, as the theory behind Jakielski's work suggests. Stuttering on function words in early childhood appears to be responsive to factors other than phonological complexity.

The fact that significant effects were only found for the older age groups and that the effect was specific to content words corroborates Howell et al. (2000). Together the Howell et al. (2000) and Howell et al. (2006) studies suggest that phonological difficulty is associated with course of stuttering rather than its onset.

Dworzynski and Howell (2004) have applied the procedure to German, and Howell and Au-Yeung (2007) to Spanish. Howell et al. (2006) also established which IPC factors showed the best relationship with stuttering. Looking across the three languages (English, Spanish, and German) IPC factors 6 and 2 (multisyllable and manner) were significant for all age groups and languages, and factor 7 (contiguous consonants) was significant in four out of six analyses. These factors correspond approximately with Throneburg et al.'s MS, LEC, and CS, respectively.

7.6.3.2   Identification of Problems in Phonological Development and Association With Course of Stuttering (Persistence/Recovery) Using Methods Other Than Analysis of Spontaneous Speech Samples

Paden and Yairi (1996) examined whether the phonological patterns of young children could be a factor that predicts whether stuttering will persist or not. They used 36 children from a pool of stuttering children who were part of their longitudinal project who ranged in age from 2 years, 3 months to 5 years, 5 months when they first participated in the project. The children were followed up for more than 36 months after onset, at which time they were designated as persistent or recovered. The assessment instruments used by the Illinois group were described in Chapter 1 and these were used to classify each child as persistent or recovered. Several of the children who were considered to persist may have gone on to recover subsequently as they would not have reached their teens after 36 months. There were two recovered groups: those who recovered from stuttering 18 to 36 months after onset ("late recovered") and those who recovered from stuttering within 18 months of onset ("early recovered"). Paden and Yairi assigned each stuttering child to one of these three groups and there were 12 members per group. Each child who stuttered was matched by age and gender to a fluent child. All children in the stuttering and control groups had completed the assessment of phonological processes-revised (APP-R) on entry to the study (Hodson, 1986). The conversational speech of all children was analyzed for stuttering using the SLD scheme described in Chapter 3. The samples had not been assessed for phonological development.

The scores on the APP-R by the children who stuttered were compared to those that had been obtained by the matched control children. There were no statistically significant differences between either of the recovered groups and the control group. However, the persistent group made significantly more phonological errors than its control. The researchers noted, however, that there were wide individual differences within each of the stuttering and control groups whereby some of the children in the recovered groups had phonological problems and some of the children in the persistent group did not have these problems.

In ongoing work by the same team, the APP-R was re-administered one year after entry into the study. A subsequent report by Yairi, Ambrose, Paden, and Throneburg (1996) examined these data and reported that the phonological skills of children in all three stuttering groups, including the persistent group, had improved at that time. This suggests that the phonological problems are transient, but if they are measured at the appropriate times, they may help predict risk of persisting in stuttering.

Paden, Yairi, and Ambrose (1999) reported on the phonological skills of a larger group of 84 children (58 boys, 26 girls) who stuttered: 22 whose stuttering persisted for at least 48 months past the point of onset ("persistent group") and 42 whose stuttering would resolve in less than 48 months ("recovered group"). The phonological skills of each child were evaluated at the initial evaluation using the APP-R. At that time, the mean ages of the persistent and recovered groups were 3;8 and 3;3, respectively (range = 2;1–4;11 for both groups).

The scores were age weighted before comparisons were made because the children in the persistent group were, on average, 5 months older than those in the recovered group. The persistent group produced significantly more error scores than the recovered group. Both groups were reported to exhibit normal phonological patterns like those in Table A.1 in the Appendix, but the persistent group developed more slowly than the recovered group. Problems with consonant clusters were reported to be more common in the persistent group. Thus, young children near the onset of stuttering whose stuttering would persist had weaker phonological skills than those whose stuttering would resolve. Similar variability between individuals in the groups was noted as in Paden and Yairi (1996). They concluded that the presence of a phonological delay near the onset of stuttering should be considered a warning sign for persistent stuttering rather than the sole or main predictor.

The Ryan (2001) study that was described in Chapter 2, section 2.2 also examined whether phonological factors could predict persistence/recovery. Like the Illinois group, he included whole-word repetitions as symptoms of stuttering. Also, the 22 children were young (mean age of 4;2, with range 2;4–5;10) and they were followed up for two years. Thus, persistence/recovery would not be fully resolved at the end of the study period (as with the work of the Illinois group). At each of the first four evaluation sessions that were conducted every three to five months, the child was administered the AAPS to monitor phonological development (the same test was administered in the Ryan, 2002, study discussed above). A recording of the child was made and the number of stuttered words per minute (SW/M) were obtained. Using the criteria set out in Chapter 2, at the fourth session 15 children had recovered from their stuttering, whereas seven persisted. The AAPS scores were examined for each child in the recovered and persistent groups for each of the four sessions. Although the scores of both groups on this test improved over time, there were no statistically significant differences between the groups at any of the sessions. Therefore, children whose stuttering persisted were no more likely to have a phonological delay than those whose stuttering stopped.

The three studies by the Illinois group showed that phonological development indicates course of stuttering (persistent or recovered) although Ryan (2001) failed to support these findings. Similar symptoms were counted as stutters and age groups were comparable for the Ryan and Illinois studies, so this would not explain why Ryan found no effect. Different tests were used to assess phonological development (APP-R by the Illinois group and AAPS by Ryan) and this may explain the discrepancy. All that can be concluded is that the majority of studies show that phonological factors may predict course of stuttering.

7.6.3.3 Summary of the Influence of Phonological Factors on Stuttering

Studies where children near to onset of stuttering alone were examined showed no effects of syllable constituency on stuttering (Throneburg et al., 1994; Weiss & Jakielski, 2001). These studies that failed to find an effect of phonological difficulty have not examined function and content words separately and have not investigated whether syllable position where the difficult phonological factor appears has an effect on stuttering (Howell & Au-Yeung, 1995a; Throneburg et al., 1994; Weiss & Jakielski, 2001). Subsequent work by Conture's group that has examined phonology in other ways (not looking for a link between syllable structure and stuttering) also failed to find effects of phonology on stuttering.

Later work that addressed the problem issues indicated in the previous paragraph and examined children across a range of ages found that phonological factors on content words affected stuttering rate (Dworzynski & Howell, 2004; Howell & Au-Yeung, 2007; Howell et al., 2006; Howell et al., 2000) and reported that phonological factors that appear at syllable onsets were particularly influential in determining stuttering (Howell et al., 2000). From this work, there are indications that phonological factors have more of an impact on the later period of development (up to teenage) than at onset using Throneburg and Weiss and Jakielski's methods (Howell et al., 2000; Howell et al., 2006). Alternatively, as the work on later course is cross-sectional, it is possible that older age groups who stutter have better defined cases. Work by the Illinois group (three studies) also found phonological factors were associated with persistent/recovered outcome. However, Ryan (2001) did not find any such effects. It is of particular note that the Illinois studies found phonological factors were associated with persistent/ recovered outcome even though the status of the children as persistent or recovered would not have been fully resolved in all members of their sample at the time of the tests (i.e., they had not reached teenage years).The majority of findings are consistent with the view that there is an association between phonological development and the later course that stuttering takes.

7.7 MORPHOLOGY

A morpheme is the smallest linguistic unit within a language that bears semantic content (adds meaning). There is only one recent report on morphology and stuttering (Marshall, 2005). She reported two studies on word end morphology in English (an analysis of spontaneous speech and an experiment). The spontaneous speech study used 16 male participants who were persistent stutterers aged between 16 and 47 years. Assessment for persistence was made using the UCL procedures described in Chapter 1 and symptom counts were those used in Kadi-Hanifi and Howell (1992) that includes whole-word repetitions. Marshall selected sets of CVC words, which were designated as having simple phonology, and CVCC words, which were designated as having complex phonology. Words from each class were identified that had simple (uninflected) and complex (inflected) morphology. Statistical comparison of stuttering rates in the four categories showed no effect of morphology, nor was stuttering rate associated with phonological complexity.

Two age groups were used in the experiment. The first of these comprised children aged 14 years and younger (12 participants who ranged in age between 8;0–14;5). The second age group was children aged 15 years and older (7 participants who ranged in age between 15;5–21;10). The study examined whether nouns and verbs with inflectional endings attracted more stuttering than noninflected words in spontaneous speech after irregular verbs were excluded. Surprisingly, there was no effect of inflectional ending on stuttering rate. (See discussion of Bernstein's VP effect in section 7.3.1 on syntax.) More information is needed about whether morphology affects stuttering close to onset and whether persistent and recovered speakers differ. Also, given that English has a simple inflectional system relative to many of the other languages of the world, more cross-linguistic work on this feature is warranted.

7.8 OVERALL SUMMARY OF LANGUAGE FACTORS

No definite conclusions can be drawn about the effect of syntax on stuttering at onset. Wall et al. (1981b) did a thorough analysis and found minor effects. The main aspect where syntax was reported to have an effect was the influence of sentences beginning with "and." This word could be used by children as a non-syntactic way of stringing different sentences together. Bernstein Ratner's early work lacks detail about the statistical analysis among other things and Bernstein Ratner and Sih (1987) used different symptom types to that in Bernstein's earlier work and did not relate their results with findings about syntactic complexity in development to research with fluent children. The 12 observations that Bloodstein and Bernstein Ratner (2007) presented do not constitute compelling grounds for accepting that onset of syntax is associated with onset of stuttering. A better case can be made that the later stages of syntactic development may have an influence on the later course of stuttering into persistence and recovery. However, this has to be qualified insofar as all present work is cross-sectional. Consequently, it is possible that the children still stuttering in their teens always had a syntactic problem, but this was disguised by the large proportion of children who recovered who did not have syntactic problems at younger ages.

There is evidence that word type has effects on stuttering type and that this changes over development. It has been shown in several languages that, at onset, children who stutter exhibit problems on function words, whereas speakers who stutter past teenage years have more problems on content words. As is discussed in detail in Chapter 12, the stuttering symptoms that occur on the different word classes differ, thus the word class effect may represent a symptom effect. Some longitudinal data that document symptom class on function and content words have been published (Howell, 2007a). Reasons were given that suggest stuttering is not directly associated with lexical class (e.g., only precontent word function words are repeated). Therefore, prosodic words were used to identify the patterns of stuttering at onset and across development and specify which function words were stuttered.

The influence of phonology on stuttering onset and course has been studied by looking at the relationship between syllable structure and stuttering rate and tests of phonological ability. The latter have usually been used to subdivide children into those with or without phonological delay and see whether stuttering is more severe or more common in groups of children who stutter. These tests have been conducted around onset of stuttering and in children who persist rather than recover over a period of time. Work employing syllabic analysis and tests of phonological ability show that phonological factors have more impact in determining the course of stuttering than at onset. The work-relating syllable structure and stuttering rate has shown consistent findings that phonological factors specifically on content words determine which words are stuttered, though once again, this may be a symptom rather than a word influence. Morphology has hardly been examined and more work on this topic is needed.

7.9   USAGE FACTORS

All parts of speech are not used with the same frequency, and structural properties of speech cause some utterances to have many related utterances (their neighbors), whereas others do not. These (and other) factors derive from the particular experience a speaker has, rather than the formal properties of language discussed earlier and they are referred to as usage properties.

Three aspects of usage are examined. First, word frequency which is the number of times a given word occurs in a language (Kucera & Francis, 1967). Next, neighborhood density, which refers to the number of words that differ in phonetic structure from another word based on a single phoneme that is either substituted, deleted, or added (Luce & Pisoni, 1998). Frequency measures associated with neighborhood density are used as well as scores of number of neighbors. Thus, phonological neighborhood frequency is the mean frequency of occurrence of a target word's neighbors. Anderson (2007) illustrated the latter by noting that the phonological neighbors of the word "dog" (e.g., bog, hog, dig, log, etc.) tended to occur less frequently in language (mean frequency of 11.0 per million) than the phonological neighbors of the word "cat" (e.g., cattle, that, etc.). And, finally, age-of-acquisition where evidence suggest that the age at which words are acquired may affect how well words are represented. Words acquired early may be better learned and less prone to error or disfluency than words acquired late. Gilhooley and Logie (1980) have demonstrated that age-of-acquisition effects continue to occur in adults.

7.9.1   WORD FREQUENCY

7.9.1.1   Word Frequency at Onset

Word frequency is often spoken of as if it is a fixed property associated with a word, but this not the case. Words are added (many terms associated with computing) and dropped from contemporary use (e.g., gasmantle, antimacassar, velocipede). Global changes occur in word frequency over the course of language development. For instance, Wingate (2002, p. 253) stated that 70% of words are content in type in early childhood, but this reduces in later childhood to 50%. There are also idiosyncratic influences on word frequency: Different words may be frequently used by children who have particular hobbies, for example, a favorite football team or TV program.

Putting these issues to one side, some authors argue that the different access to content and function words is largely related to the differences in word frequencies between these two classes, that is, words with high frequencies (function words) are accessed and produced faster than words with low frequencies (content words). For such cases, it is believed that word frequency is a more important factor in lexical access than the distinction between the lexical classes (Gordon & Caramazza, 1985).

7.9.1.1.1   Anderson's Study on Children Who Stuttered Near Onset

Anderson (2007) looked at the effects of word frequency and neighborhood density on stuttering in children. Surprisingly, this is the only study that looked at the effect of word frequency in children who stutter given the earlier observations about how word frequency builds up.

Fifteen children who stuttered (10 males, 5 females) aged between 3 and 5;2 participated. They were recorded in a play task in conversation with a parent, and Yairi and Ambrose's (2005) SLD were determined in initial analyses, and later individual symptoms were examined as described below.

Although Anderson did not select either function or content words for examination, she matched each stimulus and its control for word class. Words containing SLD were randomly paired with the first subsequently produced fluent word that matched it on a predetermined set of dimensions. These dimensions included

1. Grammatical class (content and function words).
2. Number of syllables. This controlled for the possible confound of word length and the neighborhood density effect because shorter words tend to be higher in frequency and have more dense neighborhoods than longer words (Coady & Aslin, 2003; Pisoni, Nusbaum, Luce, & Slowiaczek, 1985).
3. As closely as possible, for number of phonemes. This was a further control for the possible effect of word length.
4. As closely as possible for word familiarity using an online database (Nusbaum, Pisoni, & Davis, 1984). Word familiarity refers to the extent to which a word is considered to be well-known by adult listeners, and while it tends to be correlated with word frequency, this is not always the case (e.g., the frequency of occurrence for the word "acorn" is low, but adults typically rate it as highly familiar; German & Newman, 2004; Nusbaum et al., 1984).

An important feature of Anderson's (2007) study was that she looked at the impact of these variables on individual stuttering symptom types. She reported that words that had a part-word repetition or a sound prolongation disfluency were lower in word frequency and neighborhood frequency than fluent control words, but these frequency variables did not have an effect on single-syllable word repetitions. The symptoms that showed an effect of word frequency were from the advancing category and the symptom that showed no effect was from the stalling category (see section 7.5.2 for a brief description of these categories).

7.9.1.2 Word Frequency and Course of Stuttering

There are no studies that have examined the effects of word frequency across groups of persistent and recovered stutterers. However, it has been reported that older children and adults who persist in their stuttering tend to stutter more on words that occur less frequently in language (Danzger & Halpern, 1973; Hubbard & Prins, 1994; Schlesinger, Forte, Fried, & Melkman, 1965; Soderberg, 1966). The results of these investigations indicated that low frequency words are stuttered more than high frequency words. However, work that would allow a more definitive conclusion would also have controlled for the impact that word type may exert over lexical access. Word frequency needs to be examined in children to assess the impact at onset and during later course of the disorder.

7.9.2 Neighborhood Density (and Frequency) at Onset

Neighborhood density is a currently popular procedure for examining lexical access in perceptual work. It has been used for examining speed of lexical access in people who stutter (Anderson, 2007). If lexical access is slower in people who stutter when neighborhood density is high, this may account for the disorder. The notion is that words with few neighbors have little interference, whereas words with a lot of neighbors have more possibility of interference. To date, neighborhood density has only been examined in speakers who stutter close to onset.

7.9.2.1 Arnold, Conture, and Ohde (2005) and Anderson (2007)

Arnold, Conture, and Ohde (2005) tested nine 3- to 5-year-old children who stuttered in a priming experiment. Priming refers to processing advantages (speed or reduced errors) when participants have had exposure to materials previously. (For further description, see Chapter 12.) Arnold et al. (2007) failed to find effects of neighborhood density, which is what Anderson (2007) reported for the corresponding variable in her study. For the Arnold et al. material, neighborhood density is confounded with some syllable constituent properties. Thus, the dense set has no consonants strings, (gun, key, hat, pig, sock), whereas all the members of the sparse set have consonant strings (heart, tree, start, fork, spoon). It is of note that the material was just content in type and no examination of individual symptom types was performed.

One related variable that ought to be examined is onset density (Vitevitch, 2002). This is important because, as observed earlier, most stuttering occurs on the first parts of syllables and words. Vitevitch's work has shown the importance of onset neighbors. His work is on perception and uses fluent participants, but the procedure could be adapted for analysis of productions to examine stuttered speech.

7.9.3 Age of Acquisition at Onset

It has been proposed that for fluent children, lexical access of a word may be more dependent on the age at which a word is acquired rather than how frequently they have experienced the word (De Moor, Ghyselinck, & Brysbaert, 2001). Research arguing for the importance of age of acquisition considers that children generally learn a small set of content words before they employ function words and this results in faster lexical access for the content words that have been learned early.

De Moor et al. reported that lexical access in children is not predicted better by word frequency than the age at which a word is acquired. They went on to argue that word frequency has less impact on lexical access in children than in adults because young speakers have not yet been biased by frequency effects. This particular factor merits further study with respect to children who stutter.

7.9.3.1 Anderson (2007) Study on Age of Acquisition at Onset of Stuttering

Anderson (2007) reported a priming study on materials with different age of acquisition (AoA) in groups of children who stuttered and controls. There were 22 children in each group aged between 3;1 and 5;7 years. The findings showed that all children's picture-naming latencies and errors were reduced following repetition priming and in response to early AoA words relative to late AoA words. AoA and repetition priming effects were similar for children in both fluency groups, except that children who stuttered benefitted significantly more, in terms of error reduction, than controls from repetition priming for late AoA words.

The words used were content in type and separate symptoms were not examined. Although AoA has received much less attention than word frequency in the literature, it would seem to merit further investigation. Function words are acquired later than some content words. It is possible to match function words to selected content words and establish whether there are lexical effects on AoA.

No studies have compared the size of AoA effects across the lifespan. As many of the factors considered in this chapter have more impact on stuttering during its later course, AoA (and other usage factors) ought to be examined over the course of stuttering. An interesting finding relevant to this was reported by Newman and German (2002). They showed that AoA effects decrease as children mature. Age-of-acquisition may be an important factor in determining which sounds children who stutter find difficult. Newman and German's findings suggest that any effect may be decreased or eliminated with maturation, whereas other language factors that have been examined appear to have more impact as children get older.

7.9.4 Summary of Impact of Usage Factors

Word frequency had an effect on part-word repetition and sound prolongations, but not single-syllable word repetitions. Neighborhood density has not been found to influence stuttering rate, but further examination specifically of onset density is called for based on the occurrence of stuttering mainly on syllable onsets. Age of acquisition appears to affect stuttering rate around the time that the disorder starts.

Examination of the impact usage factors have on stuttering in childhood is in its infancy. It is too early to draw firm conclusions at present. The paucity of studies on older children that might establish the role of these factors on course of stuttering has been noted. Although investigations into usage factors is increasing at present, it should be cautioned that there are as many methodological problems associated with usage factors as there are with formal linguistic factors and many of the problems are shared across these domains, for instance, confounds between factors as indicated in the following section.

7.10   CONFOUNDS AND WAYS OF DEALING WITH THEM

The chapter looked at the following formal and usage language factors: syntax, lexical, phonological, morphological (formal), word frequency, neighborhood density, and age-of-acquisition (usage). Probably all the factors reviewed in this chapter are confounded with each other including formal factors with other formal factors, usage factors with other usage factors, and formal factors with usage factors. This makes it difficult to control for all possible confounds and to do a study that can firmly conclude a particular factor is paramount, as Bernstein Ratner does with respect to syntax.

This final section describes briefly some methods that have been used to control for these confounding influences. One method is to attempt to control for all factors that may affect stuttering rate. An example of this is in the study of Anderson (2007) that was described in section 7.9.1.1. However, as pointed out, it is almost impossible to control for all possible factors. There are several different statistical methods that can be employed after data have been collected. One of these is analysis of covariance (ANCOVA). This technique essentially measures other variables that may affect the results and correct for their influence. An example that used this technique is Howell and Au-Yeung (1995a). They measured the effect of phonological difficulty using Throneburg et al.'s (1994) method and took out the influence of other factors, such as word length, that were reported to affect stuttering in Brown (1945). A second technique that is too complicated to go into here is multiple regression (see Storkel, 2009, for a good description and example of application of this procedure).

7.11   EXERCISES

1. It was argued that one language system serves several separate motor modules. Critically examine each of the arguments and make the case that it is either only necessary to postulate: (1) a language module, (2) a motor module; to explain speech production.
2. Evaluate Bloodstein and Bernstein Ratner's 12 arguments that purport to show that onset of stuttering starts at the time when a child starts to use syntax.
3. Syntactic complexity should be based on externally validated criteria, not intuition. Discuss.
4. Do disfluencies occur at the boundaries of clauses?
5. Why are function and content words *not* associated directly with stuttering, but are, nevertheless, useful for specifying the determinants of stuttering?
6. Discuss the interrelationship between word frequency, neighborhood density, syllable constituents, and phonological disorder.

APPENDIX

TYPICAL AND ATYPICAL PHONOLOGICAL PROCESSES

TABLE A.1
Some Common Typical Phonological Processes

Process	Definition	Example
Weak syllable deletion	The omission of a weak (unstressed) syllable that either comes before or after a stressed syllable	"telephone" pronounced as "tefone"
Final consonant deletion	A child reduces a syllable by omitting the final consonant of that syllable	"cat" pronounced as "ca"
Reduplication	Repetition of part or all of a syllable	"daddy" pronounced as "dada"
Cluster reduction	One consonant is deleted from a consonant cluster or, when there are three adjacent consonants in the same syllable, one or two of the consonants may be deleted	"play" pronounced as "pay"
Stopping	The substitution of a stop for a fricative or an affricate	"zoo" pronounced as "do" (fricative replaces stop); "Jane" pronounced as "dane" (affricate replaces stop)
Fronting	The substitution of velar consonants and palatal consonants with an alveolar place of articulation	"cat" pronounced as "tat" (velar fronting); "get" pronounced as "det" (palatal fronting)
Deaffrication	The substitution of a fricative for an affricate	"chip" pronounced as "ship"
Gliding	Replacing the consonants /l/ and /r/ with the consonants /w/ and /j/	"rabbit" pronounced as "wabbit"
Vocalization (also called vowelization)	Substitution of a vowel for an /l/ or /r/ that follows a vowel; this process is commonly found in words that end in "r" and "el" sounds	"third" pronounced as "thud"
Labial assimilation	The production of a nonlabial phoneme with a labial place of articulation; this happens because there is a labial phoneme elsewhere in the word	"mad" pronounced as "mab"
Velar assimilation	This process occurs when a phoneme is produced with a velar place of articulation due to the presence of a velar phoneme elsewhere in the word	"take" pronounced as "kake"

TABLE A.1 (CONTINUED)
Some Common Typical Phonological Processes

Process	Definition	Example
Alveolar assimilation	This process occurs when a phoneme is produced with an alveolar place of articulation due to the presence of an alveolar phoneme elsewhere in the word	"time" pronounced as "tine"
Prevocalic voicing	When an unvoiced consonant preceding the vowel of a syllable is voiced, it is called prevocalic voicing	"pig" pronounced as "big"
Devoicing	When a syllable-final voiced phoneme that precedes a pause or silence between words is unvoiced, it is called devoicing	"bad" pronounced as "bat"

Note: The usual term for each phonological process is given in the left-hand column (process), a brief definition appears in the second column (definition), and an illustration in the third column (example).

TABLE A.2
Some Common Idiosyncratic Phonological Processes

Process	Definition	Example
Glottal replacement	The substitution of a glottal stop for another consonant	Replacing the "k" sound in the word "pick" with a glottal stop
Backing	The substitution of a glottal stop for another consonant	Replacing the "k" sound in the word "pick" with a glottal stop
Initial consonant deletion	When a single consonant at the beginning of a word is omitted, it is called initial consonant deletion	"cut" pronounced as "ut"
Stops replacing glides	Stop replaces a glide	"yes" pronounced as "des"
Fricative replacing stops	Fricative replaces a stop	"sit" pronounced as "sis"

Note: The table is laid out in the same way as Table A1.

8 Motor Factors

Many different procedures have been used to document motor deficits in people who stutter. For example, reaction times have been reported to differ for nonspeech sounds across groups of people who stutter and controls (Max, Guenther, Gracco, Ghosh, & Wallace, 2004; Peters, Hulstjn, & Van Lieshout, 2000). In this chapter, it has been necessary to be selective about the motor variables examined. For instance, reaction time studies were left out. Likewise, because of the large number of studies, only selected representative ones are examined. The selection of topic areas and studies was partly determined by whether recovery was due to treatment or linked to a positive prognosis (with or without treatment). Broadly speaking, the first two topic areas that are examined relate to treatment (perturbation and speech rate) and the last two are potential prognostic factors (variability and coordination of speech movements).

8.1 INTRODUCTION

It was argued at the beginning of Chapter 7 that language and motor processes are independent. Thus, language or motor factors alone may affect stuttering. When a language factor affects stuttering, speech motor output also will be influenced. This is because if language processing is in error, that error will propagate through to production, although explaining how higher order linguistic errors manifest themselves at the motor level is not a trivial problem. Therefore, to obtain evidence that the motor factors affect stuttering, it is necessary to ensure that the effects are not epiphenomena of a language-processing problem. People who take the view that stuttering is exclusively language-based attribute all observed motor deficits to a passive motor response associated with the language deficit (Levelt, 1989). This view is further evaluated in Chapter 10. The same passivity idea also has been applied in the field of stuttering, as illustrated by Bernstein Ratner and Wijnen (2007). They indicate that the motor processes passively translate linguistic input to speech output when they state in relation to stuttering "what we believe to be a problem in language encoding can lead to apparent motor execution difficulties."

When language factors were considered in Chapter 7, a second point that was made was that language-processing problems are not the sole source leading to stuttering. One reason for this was that the language-processing problems reported in people who stutter are not dramatic and people with language-processing deficits of similar, or greater, magnitude use speech without experiencing fluency problems. This suggests other nonlanguage factors have a role in stuttering, and motor factors are probably the most significant of these. In this chapter, the evidence that supports pure motor problems is reviewed, preceded by a description of procedures that are suitable for identifying pure motor factors. In terms of the goal of this chapter, ideally studies would be available on motor factors conducted near onset and over the subsequent course of development. Unfortunately, there is little motor research that has been conducted with children who stutter near to onset; however, the evidence there is will be reviewed; some important studies have only concerned adults. Children produce speech spontaneously, which make language studies relatively easy, as the speech can be recorded for study, thus obviating the need to develop experimental procedures to work with children this age. In contrast, there are few naturalistic nonspeech motor activities that can be observed in a similar way except, possibly, handedness (Hepper, Wells, & Lynch, 2005). So, predominantly, motor factors that could affect the later course of stuttering are discussed. However, the lack of discussion of studies concerning onset does not mean that motor factors do not precipitate stuttering.

It is also desirable to see whether motor procedures affect the various stuttering symptoms in different ways. For instance, is it easier to reduce incidence of incomplete phrases, revisions, interjections, whole-word repetitions, and phrase repetitions when asked to speed speech up than it is to reduce incidence of other types of disfluency like part-word repetitions, prolongations, and blocks? Such information would be informative with respect to recovery. To give one illustration, several treatments manipulate speech rate directly or indirectly; if this affects particular symptoms, then this would be important for assessing those treatments. However, at present, there is little evidence of whether or not motor procedures affect specific symptoms.

Part of the reason for the dearth of studies on different symptoms is that many procedures used to study motor control have been developed to examine problems in timing control, not type of disfluency. Procedures that examine timing control often exclude trials where there was any type of disfluency, so that one can focus on disfluency-free behavior.

Motor researchers continue to use symptoms to classify participants as stutterers and, as with language studies, the symptoms used as criteria for including a person in a group of stutterers varies across studies. The symptoms used are given where available so that readers can assess for themselves whether the symptoms counted as stutters across studies differed such that they could explain discrepancies in results or call for qualifications about a study.

Theories that account for motor processes are the topic of Chapter 11. However, some theories are mentioned briefly here where they are behind introduction of procedures (i.e., when a procedure was developed as a response to requirements of a theory).

The topic areas covered in this chapter that support pure motor deficits in people who stutter relative to fluent controls are as follows. Section 8.2 considers perturbations to speech. The perturbations include altered feedback procedures that improve fluency, nonspeech rhythmic stimulation, and mechanical loading of the articulators. This section also includes a review of arguments for rejecting a feedback interpretation for the auditory perturbation effects. Section 8.3 considers how variation in speech rate affects stuttering. Some theories consider that rate is modulated at motor levels (as in Guenther's, 2001, DIVA model). However, also rate may be part of language planning. Views in motor control consider that there are two types of timing that correspond to the language planning and motor execution stages (Zelaznik, Spencer, & Ivry, 2002). Although the current author considers that the procedures described in section 8.3 affect motor level timing, this might be disputed (see exercise no. 3 at the end of the chapter). If a compelling case can be made that rate variation occurs at the language level, then this point of view may need to be revised (i.e., studies on rate manipulation may not provide evidence for a pure motor deficit).

Sections 8.4 and 8.5 concern variability and coordination of articulatory movements, respectively. Here, the term variability is used to refer to assessment of the reproducibility of the movements of a single articulator. Coordination measures assess the synchronization of the movements of two or more articulators involved in production of certain speech sounds. Variability and coordination both have been suggested as potentially important for understanding stuttering by people submitting to opposing theoretical positions: generalized motor program versus dynamic systems theories (Van Lieshout, 2004). These two theoretical positions are described briefly as an introduction to these sections and are considered in more detail in Chapter 11. Variability and coordination have each been measured in several ways and most of those have been employed in different studies to investigate people who stutter. These are reviewed.

8.2 EFFECTS OF PERTURBATIONS ON FLUENT SPEAKERS AND SPEAKERS WHO STUTTER

Compensations to the effects of perturbations are an important way of studying the adaptability of the speech motor system. In perturbation studies that investigate speech production, the system is disrupted in different ways and performance is examined to see what disruption occurs and how speakers recover from the perturbations. One commonly used perturbation, important with respect to stuttering, is to change the sound of the speaker's voice in various ways to see whether and how this affects speech control; this is referred to generically as altered auditory feedback. In early work where speech was altered by delaying it, fluent speakers showed an increase in disfluency, and the types of disfluency that were observed were likened to those that occurred in stuttered speech (Lee, 1950). The initial accounts of the effects of why these alterations arose, suggested that the altered sound had been heard by the speaker and interpreted as a speech–language error. The speaker then attempted to correct the error (e.g., repeated the intended sound), which resulted in disfluency patterns similar to those that occurred in stuttering. Several empirical observations that are discussed in this chapter undermined the language feedback interpretation (alternative interpretations are given in Chapter 11). Although some authors still interpret the effects of alterations to auditory feedback as affecting language processing (Kalinowski & Saltuklaroglu, 2006), most contemporary authors interpret the empirical and theoretical work on altered feedback as influences at the motor level.

Alterations to auditory feedback are particularly important in this volume as people who stutter become more fluent when subjected to these alterations, although the extent to which the speech is actually fluent has been debated (Howell, 2002). Because of the fluency-enhancing effects, some of the altered forms of feedback have been produced in miniature digital devices for treating stuttering. The basic background facts about the effects of alterations on fluent speakers and speakers who stutter are presented.

Speech can be perturbed by stimulation other than that derived from manipulations made to the speech itself. Two other important types that have received attention with respect to stuttering are rhythmic stimulation (e.g., flashing lights or metronome pulses) and applying a mechanical load to the articulators while speaking (e.g., when something is held between the teeth). Rhythmic and mechanical perturbations have received less attention than altered auditory feedback, but some discussion is included. Rhythmic stimulation is discussed because it may have parallels to auditory stimulation in inducing fluency (and supports the idea that altering feedback operates at the motor level). Mechanical perturbations are discussed because the evidence they provide has featured in dynamic systems theory, which has been the basis of several studies into stuttering. (This theory is discussed in Chapter 11.)

The topics covered in this section start with a description of the effects of the three main types of alteration to auditory feedback that have been investigated—time, frequency, and loudness—and their effects on fluent speakers and speakers who stutter. After each alteration, the classic feedback interpretation of the results is given. Studies on rhythmic perturbations are then reviewed. (The arguments against the language feedback interpretation are summarized. Chapter 11 has a section that describes alternative theoretical proposals that have been offered that were derived in response to these problems.) Then a brief review of mechanical perturbations follows; there are few studies on the impact these would have on stuttering, although such studies are urgently required. The section ends with a summary of the effects some forms of altered feedback have over the course of the disorder.

8.2.1 Lee's Delayed Auditory Feedback

The most frequently studied type of alteration to speech output is to timing (the speaker hears what was said at a different time to when it was actually spoken, as in a reverberant environment). Timing is almost always changed by delaying when the speaker hears his or her voice, known as delayed auditory feedback (DAF), as mentioned in Chapter 6. In fluent speakers, DAF slows speech mainly by elongating vowels. The speech also has a monotone pitch and high amplitude; both effects being easily discernible on the vowels during DAF speech.

In speakers who stutter, DAF has the effect of reducing the incidence of stuttering events dramatically. It was originally considered that the response to DAF by adults who stutter was opposite to the response of fluent speakers, with fluent speakers stuttering and speakers who stutter becoming fluent. However, a closer look at how DAF affects speech symptoms and how the nature of the symptoms compare with stutters shows that this position is not sustainable. DAF disruption occurs mainly on medial vowels that are prolonged (Howell, Wingfield, & Johnson, 1988), whereas the stuttered prolongations that are lost under DAF occur on initial consonants (Brown, 1945). Thus, although a fluent speaker may prolong certain sounds, and prolongation occurs in speakers who stutter, the two forms of prolongation differ in terms of whether they occur on a consonant or vowel and whether they occur in initial or medial syllable position. Hence, while the prolongations observed in fluent speakers under DAF conditions are superficially similar to the prolonged sounds speakers who stutter produce, this similarity disappears on close inspection. A further fact to note is that speakers who stutter do seem to be affected by DAF the same as fluent speakers after stutters have disappeared. Thus, while speakers who stutter lose consonant prolongations under DAF, they also prolong the vowel sounds as do fluent speakers (Howell et al., 1988).

Lee (1950), Fairbanks (1955), and Levelt (1989), among many others, suggested that one way speakers control speech is that they listen to their speech and do a full linguistic analysis of it. They then use the results of this analysis to determine whether there is a discrepancy between the speech they intended and the form that was output. If there is a discrepancy, they then correct their speech. The way the auditory feedback, or monitoring, process was originally considered to work when speech was delayed was that speakers continued to use the delayed sound for voice control after it was altered. There appeared to be a discrepancy between intention and action because of the alteration. In the case of DAF, speakers responded to the misleading feedback by altering the timing of their speech even though no change was needed. Consequently, this resulted in disruption to speech. Lee (1950), the author who originally described the effect, proposed that speakers monitor all levels of language processing, and DAF can disrupt any of them. Thus, the various forms of disfluency represent disruption at different levels of language processing (e.g., part-word repetitions at the syllable level, whole words at the lexical level).

Although the proposed complementary response of fluent speakers and speakers who stutter under DAF does not seem to be correct, nevertheless the fluency of speakers who stutter clearly changes dramatically under DAF and why this is so needs to be explained. Early explanations of DAF assumed that speakers who stutter have a timing problem in the perceptual system that affects when the sound of the voice is recovered in normal listening situations. This led, in turn, to the speaker getting inaccurate feedback that precipitated stuttering in a similar way to what happens to fluent speakers when sounds are altered. A further feature of these accounts is that the sensory deficit is rectified or made irrelevant by an external DAF delay, which then allows these speakers to regain fluent control (Webster & Dorman, 1970). Two parts of the auditory system that have been proposed that might be a cause of timing disruption in people who stutter that could be corrected by DAF are the middle ear muscle system and the bone-conducted route for auditory feedback. Due to the fluency-enhancing effects of DAF, it has been used as a component in the Ryan's' treatment for stuttering (Ryan & van

Kirk, 1995) and is an option available in some contemporary prosthetic devices (Kalinowski & Saltuklaroglu, 2006).

8.2.1.1   Proposals That People Who Stutter Have a Sensory Deficit

Two specific proposals have been made concerning possible sensory deficits in people who stutter, which could account for the improvement under DAF: (1) people who stutter have problems in dealing with bone-conducted sound (Cherry & Sayers, 1956) and (2) these problems arise because the middle ear structures of speakers who stutter cannot transmit sound in the same way as those of fluent speakers do (Webster & Lubker, 1968b).

Cherry and Sayers showed that delayed sound transmitted through bone is more disruptive to fluent speakers than sound delayed and transmitted through air. Because fluent speakers were supposed to stutter under DAF, they argued that people who stutter have problems in dealing with the more disruptive sound transmitted through bone. Howell and Powell (1984) compared Cherry and Sayers' (1956) bone-conducted sound (created by passing vibration through the skull) with measurements of actual bone-conducted sound obtained while speakers were speaking using transducers attached to the skull and found marked differences between the two. Cherry and Sayers' experimental manipulation created a sound that, although successful at disrupting fluent speech control, was nothing like bone-conducted sound. This result shows that there are no grounds for concluding that speakers who stutter have problems in dealing with sound transmitted through bone.

The proposal that speakers who stutter have problems in transmitting sound through the middle ear system also failed empirical tests. Shearer's (1966) original work included very limited amounts of data. In an extensive study, Howell, Marchbanks, and El-Yaniv (1986) were unable to find differences in middle ear operation between people who stutter and fluent controls (both during listening tests and during vocalization). Abnormal middle ear muscle operation seems, then, an unlikely basis for explaining the disorder. There does not seem to be any compelling evidence that people who stutter have either of the sensory deficits that have been proposed as explanations of why speakers who stutter become fluent when presented with DAF.

8.2.2   HOWELL'S FREQUENCY SHIFTED FEEDBACK/
FREQUENCY ALTERED FEEDBACK

Elman (1981) examined how shifting the speech spectrum up or down (making the voice sound high or low in frequency) affected fluent speakers' speech control. He reported that the speakers shifted vocal pitch down when the speech spectrum was shifted up and up when the speech spectrum was shifted down. This is a compensatory response that could be the result of a feedback mechanism making corrections to achieve an intended pitch target (e.g., if the pitch sounds too high, shift it down to offset this).

Frequency shifted feedback (FSF), such as that used by Elman, has been the subject of intense study in the field of stuttering since Howell, El-Yaniv, and Powell (1987) found that it had dramatic effects in controlling the fluency of people who stutter. Howell et al. (1987) tested six adults (five male, one female) who stuttered. The number of stuttered syllables was counted for each stutterer; counting repeated attempts at a syllable or when a sound was prolonged as one stuttered syllable. Sounds of more than 1s were counted as prolongations. The numbers of stutters in a reading of a set passage (Arthur the rat) were compared in normal listening conditions, DAF, and FSF. The number of stutters was significantly higher in the normal listening condition than the DAF condition, which was, in turn, significantly higher than in the FSF condition. It also was shown that FSF did not slow down overall speech rate. Thus, Howell et al. reported fluency enhancement under FSF occurred even when speakers were asked to speak as rapidly as possible.

Subsequent work has shown that FSF avoids other side effects as well. Thus, there is no increase in the intensity of speech output with FSF as happens when nonspeech noises occur (Howell, 1990). Also, speakers who stutter do not make compensatory shifts in voice fundamental frequency, as did fluent speakers in the study reported by Elman (Natke, Grosser, & Kalveram, 2001).

To summarize the three important features of the Howell et al. (1987) study: (1) FSF induces fluency without any apparent side effects, (2) the fluency-enhancing effect occurs when speakers speak at different rates, and (3) the FSF alteration was made digitally. Making the alterations digitally opened the way for miniaturized prosthetic devices, such as SpeechEasy® (Kalinowski & Saltuklaroglu, 2006). There is a lot of basic research on FSF and work on the SpeechEasy device, which was reviewed recently and, thus is not repeated here (Lincoln, Packman, & Onslow, 2006). However, it should be noted that the fluency improvements with FSF only occur while the alteration is happening; when FSF is switched off, the speaker returns to stuttering. The same applies to the other forms of altered auditory feedback. The temporary nature of the auditory feedback effect contrasts with what is claimed to occur with noninstrumental therapies, which happen more gradually, but the effects can be sustained for long periods of time. The time course over which the two types of fluency treatment operate and the durability of the effects suggest that they affect different processes (see Chapter 15 for further discussion).

8.2.3 CHANGING THE LOUDNESS OF FEEDBACK BY AMPLIFICATION OR NOISE MASKING

The final form of alteration is to change the loudness of speech feedback. This can be done in two ways. First, laboratory studies have shown that when voice level is amplified, speakers reduce voice level and when voice level is reduced, they increase it. This is called the Fletcher effect (Fletcher, Raff, & Parmley, 1918). Second, a high noise level operates like attenuating the voice (i.e., speakers increase loudness when speaking under noise). Thus, speakers increase their voice level when noise level increases and reduce their voice level when noise level is decreased; called the Lombard effect (Lombard, 1911). As with FSF, it is possible that these compensations could be the result of a negative feedback mechanism for regulating voice level. If speakers need to hear the voice to control it but cannot do so, either because noise level is high or voice level is low, they compensate by increasing level. Speakers would compensate in the opposite way if their speech is too loud (low noise level or when the voice is amplified).

All studies except one (Panconcelli-Calizia, 1955) have reported high incidence of the Lombard effect in people who stutter under masking noises. Masking the voice of people who stutter has been studied in empirical investigations. For instance, Cherry and Sayers (1956) reported that a white noise masker improved fluency control in speakers who stutter.

8.2.4 RHYTHMIC NONSPEECH SIGNALS CONCURRENT WITH ARTICULATION

Several studies have shown that rhythmic stimulation induces fluency in situations where a feedback interpretation seems unlikely to apply. One example is choral, or shadowed, speech where another speaker's utterances appear to provide the speaker who stutters with temporal and/or spatial cues regarding their own articulation, which leads to fluency enhancement (Healey & Howe, 1987). As the sound heard with choral speech is not the speaker's own utterance, it does not provide feedback about the speaker's articulation. It does, however, constitute a second rhythmic signal. It has been argued that secondary rhythms affect speech control. Choral speech is one such secondary rhythm. The delayed sound in the DAF procedure also constitutes a secondary rhythm, which is asynchronous with speech in this case. The fluency-enhancing effects of both choral speech and DAF speech might be due to speaking concurrent with a rhythmic stimulus rather than being based on its influence on a language feedback mechanism. Chapter 11 discusses the disruptive rhythm hypothesis (this is also mentioned briefly below), which would offer an explanation for the choral speech effect, DAF effect, and the effects of other rhythmic forms of stimulation (Howell, Powell, & Khan, 1983).

A further type of rhythmic signal that induces fluency is an audible train of clicks. Again, this does not provide feedback on the voice. It has been reported that the fluency of speakers who stutter improves when speech is produced synchronously with an isochronously timed signal produced by a metronome (Fransella & Beech, 1965) or when clicks occur at the onset of each syllable that is spoken (Howell & El-Yaniv, 1987). The click signals have rhythmic structure, but could not provide any linguistic feedback. Once again, they produce signals in synchrony with articulation that may enhance fluency.

There have also been studies that show arrhythmic stimulation has fluency-inducing effects similar to DAF. For example, delayed speech commences after the utterance has started and gating speech (switching the amplitude on and off) creates a similar effect. Gated speech produces similar fluency-enhancement to DAF (Howell, 2007c). Kuniszyk-Jozkowiak, Smolka, and Adamczyk (1996) even reported that a flashing light that was not synchronized to speech and provided no feedback information in people who stutter, induced fluency in a similar way to DAF. All of these findings point to the fact that rhythmic and arrhythmic stimulation induces fluency in people who stutter.

As all the effects described above involve nonspeech sounds, they could not work on language feedback processes. However, all the alterations are forms of rhythmic stimuli that could govern their fluency-enhancing effects. Although these seem to be powerful arguments for a nonlinguistic interpretation of disparate forms of stimuli that produce fluency enhancement, some authors continue to emphasize the importance of linguistic feedback. For example Kalinowski, Stuart, Rastatter, Snyder, and Dayalu (2000) showed that visual gestures of speech, which mimic a situation of choral speaking, induced fluency. The authors interpreted the effects to the speech sound activating the mirror neuron system. (See Chapter 11 for consideration of this account.) Also, Pihan, Altenmuller, Hertrich, and Ackermann (2000) offered an account of the effects of shadowing (similar to choral speech, but where the speaker speaks along with a recorded voice rather than a live speaker) in fluent speakers that supposed that the sound had to be speech in order to facilitate production. They stated that "shadowing studies suggest that perceived speech is rapidly represented by neural networks, which provide an interpretation of the acoustic structure in terms of a motor program" (p. 2348).

8.2.5 ARGUMENTS AGAINST THE LANGUAGE FEEDBACK INTERPRETATION AND FOR THE MOTOR EXPLANATION

So far, the effects of altered feedback have been examined and parallels have been drawn between these procedures and speaking along with nonspeech rhythms. It has been mentioned that there are language feedback accounts. There also has been general concern about the language feedback interpretation of the effects of altered feedback, leaving a motor interpretation as the preferred alternative. Thus, researchers who worked on altered auditory feedback with fluent speakers began to question feedback interpretations in which speech sounds are processed continuously to the level of a full linguistic analysis after each sound has been produced (Borden, 1979; Howell et al., 1983; Lane & Tranel, 1971). There were both conceptual and empirical objections that led to rejection of the view that altered feedback is used as sensory feedback to linguistic planning mechanisms.

Borden (1979) listed several problematic issues for a feedback point of view. One of the issues she raised was how quickly language information can be recovered from the auditory signal so it could be used by the language monitoring system. Auditory processing time is estimated to take around 100 to 200 ms. Auditory output would reach the language feedback mechanism too late to be used for control of its own segment.

A second question she raised was based on the observation that speakers with hearing impairment, who had learned to use language before they sustained the hearing loss, can continue to speak. This suggested that speech control can proceed without the sensory feedback. It seems from this that auditory feedback is not essential for speech production as the monitoring account would maintain.

A further conceptual problem is that the amount of phonetic information a speaker can recover about vocal output is limited because bone-conducted sound masks a speaker's phonetic output. (See the Howell and Powell, 1984, study mentioned above on this issue, and Howell, 2002, for an extended discussion of the problems this raises for feedback accounts.) Degradation to the sound of the voice would limit the usefulness of the linguistic feedback that a speaker can recover by listening to his or her own voice, making it an unreliable source of information for use for feedback control. This is discussed in more detail in Chapter 10, section 10.4.2.1.3.

One question that arises if the sound of the voice does not contain phonetic information is whether the delayed sound during DAF has to be speech to produce the disruptions to fluent speakers' speech. Howell and Archer (1984) addressed this question by transforming speech into a noise that had the same temporal structure as speech, but none of the phonetic content. Then they delayed the noise sound and compared performance of this with performance under standard DAF. The two conditions produced equivalent disruption over a range of delays. This suggested that the DAF signal does not need to be a speech sound to affect control in the same way as observed under DAF, and indicates that speech does not go through the speech comprehension system before it can be used as feedback. The disruption could arise, however, if asynchronous inputs affect operation of lower-level mechanisms involved in motor control. The findings of the experiment by Howell and Sackin (2002), discussed in Chapter 6, suggest that low-level cerebellar timing mechanisms are affected by DAF, rather than cortical structures that would be required if the delayed sound underwent language analysis.

Another argument against DAF supporting feedback control of the voice is based on whether this alteration gives rise to a Lombard, or a Fletcher, effect. As mentioned earlier in this chapter, a Fletcher effect occurs when speech level is altered (the speaker raises voice level when speech level is experimentally decreased and decreases voice level when speech level is experimentally increased). The opposite happens when noise level is changed (Lombard effect), where speakers raise voice level when noise level is increased and decrease voice level when noise level is decreased (Lane & Tranel, 1971). If the delayed speech under DAF is treated like a person's own speech after processing by the speech comprehension system, it should lead to a Fletcher, rather than a Lombard, effect. However, Howell (1990) reported that amplifying the delayed sound during DAF produces a Lombard effect, again suggesting that the delayed sound is treated as a noise rather than speech. Thus, DAF led to speakers responding to the sounds as nonspeech noises, suggesting that speech is not processed through to a full linguistic representation.

Finally, the effects of speaking with a bite block (discussed further below) held between the incisors show that speakers can adapt their articulations so that they produce the desired auditory output before they could perceive any feedback (Fowler & Turvey, 1981).

To summarize, the work reviewed in this section shows that speech can proceed without the person having auditory feedback of the language produced. Chapter 11 considers alternative accounts to the classic feedback proposals of how altered feedback affects fluency.

8.2.6 MECHANICAL PERTURBATIONS

Speech also can be mechanically perturbed, either statically or dynamically. Both types of perturbation have been investigated in people who stutter (Van Lieshout, Hulstijn, and Peters, 2004). One way of making a static perturbation is by immobilizing the jaw using a biteblock (Folkins & Zimmermann, 1981; Fowler & Turvey, 1980). Namasivayam and Van Lieshout (2001) compared the motor patterns of two adults who stuttered and one adult control (all speakers were between the ages 20 and 30 years). The people who stuttered showed more physiological effort in upper and lower lips, compared to a more specific dominant response in the lower lip only for control speakers. They likened the response of the people who stutter to the more primitive movement patterns found in young children for lip closing during early stages of speech motor development. The people who stuttered were rated for severity using SSI-3 (stuttering severity instrument-3), two being rated moderate and the other three rated to be very mild, mild, and severe. Namasivayam, Van Lieshout, and de Nil (2008) extended this report with more participants They used five male adults who stutter, ranging in age from 18 to 41 years (mean age 26;1) and five male controls ranging in age from 22 to 32 years (mean age 25;3).

With dynamic perturbations, a mechanical load is applied temporarily during ongoing movements (e.g., Folkins & Zimmermann, 1981; Kelso, Vatikoiotis-Bateson, Tuller, & Fowler, 1984; Shaiman & Gracco, 2002). Caruso, Chodzko-Zajko, Bidinger, and Sommers (1994) studied the effects of dynamic perturbation in people who stutter and showed that they had longer latencies and reduced upper lip EMG amplitudes compared to matched controls. This suggested a less than adequate compensation (Caruso, Gracco, & Abbs, 1987). However, a more recent study failed to replicate significant group findings in compensation responses to mechanical loads applied to the jaw (Bauer, Jäencke, & Kalveram, 1997). An important development in studying dynamic perturbations in fluent speakers is Tremblay, Shiller, and Ostry's (2003) work, which uses a robot to perturb the jaw. The effect of these perturbations in people who stutter, and potential differences between speakers who stutter and fluent controls, remains to be investigated.

8.2.7 COURSE AND SYMPTOMS

The studies reviewed above use older speakers. They are conducted on speakers who have persisted, so the influence of how perturbations affect onset and course of stuttering are not addressed. There is a little evidence about feedback on the course of stuttering in late childhood. A study by Howell, Sackin, and Williams (1999) compared the effects of FSF between speakers who stuttered who differed in age. They included eight speakers in each group. The ages of the speakers in the youngest group ranged from 9 to 11 years (mean age, 9;11 months), which is less than the age at which recovery from developmental stuttering is resolved. The ages of the speakers in the adult group ranged from 20 to 24 years (mean age, 21;3). They read the well-known "Arthur the rat" passage. The stuttering symptoms that were assessed were segment, part-word, word or phrase repetitions, segmental or syllabic prolongations, and "other" disfluencies (Johnson and Associates, 1959), which were mainly initiators or extraneous sequences (very often glottalic sounds or syllables accompanied by high and/or low pitch and stricture in the glottis). The fluency enhancing effects of FSF were greater for the adult group than for the child group.

Further issues were whether altered feedback affected particular symptoms, and whether studies that use different symptoms to characterize stuttering would lead to different results. There has been one study on adults who stutter that partially addressed the first of these questions for FSF. Stuart, Frazier, Kalinowski, and Vos (2008) recently reported a retrospective analysis of data from 12 adults who stuttered (Armson & Stuart, 1998). The group consisted of 10 males and 2 females with an average age of 35 years. They looked at whether FSF affected incidence of prolongation, part-word repetition, and silent block. They reported that FSF reduced the frequency of all of these symptoms by about 20% (there was no statistically significant difference between symptoms). All of these symptoms are from the class that are usually considered more typical of stuttering (see Chapter 3 for an extended discussion). It would be informative to at least examine whole-word repetition too, since, as has been seen, many authors working with children who stutter include these as a symptom of stuttering. Some other forms of treatment, such as Lidcombe, are arguably more effective when speakers show high incidence of repetitions (Chapter 15). Thus, Onslow, Packman, Stocker, and Siegel (1997) reported on the use of Lidcombe treatment in three children. Two children (DF and JR) showed high rates of repetition and were successfully treated, whereas the third (PB) showed signs of effortful speech, such as prolongation of sounds, tense pauses, and grimacing, and there were no effects on fluency for this child.

In an experiment on the dynamics of interlip coupling in speakers with a repaired cleft lip, Van Lieshout, Rutjens, and Spauwen (2002) argued that the motor system matures over the prepubertal period (Anne Smith has made similar arguments in several of her studies.). This could potentially offer a motor account of stuttering onset and early development rather than linguistic ones discussed in earlier chapters.

8.2.8 SUMMARY

All perturbations (auditory, rhythmic, and mechanical) can be argued to have their effects at the motor level. The response of people who stutter and controls differs for all types of perturbation that have been examined and this suggests some motor involvement in the disorder.

Looking specifically at auditory perturbations, the argument has been made that asynchronous forms of feedback (DAF and gated speech) improve the fluency of people who stutter, but also lead to disruption to timing. Synchronous forms of altered auditory feedback (FSF) also improve the speech control of people who stutter, but timing disruptions are subtle. The next section considers timing control, including some studies using asynchronous and synchronous forms of altered auditory feedback.

A limited amount of work has been done on auditory perturbations over the course of the disorder. The evidence reviewed here suggests that the fluency-enhancing effects of altered auditory feedback are greater for adults than they are for children. All the symptoms associated with persistent forms of stuttering, referred to in Chapter 3 as more typical of stuttering, are reduced by FSF. More needs to be known about whether symptoms seen predominantly in children who stutter (whole-word repetitions) are affected to the same extent by FSF as the more typical symptoms.

8.3   VOLUNTARY RATE CHANGE

There are methodological issues associated with how to measure speech rate (Ryan, 1992). For example, Ingham (1984) instructed a speaker to talk, then started the timing device and ran it for a set period of time regardless of whether the speaker stopped or not. Others, for example, Ryan (1974), have only measured talking time, where if the speaker stops, the timing is stopped until the speaker starts again. Only the speaker's online speaking is timed. Another factor is length of an utterance (Starkweather, 1985). Longer utterances are typically produced more rapidly than short ones.

The main methodological issue concerning speaking rate is whether or not stuttering symptoms should be omitted before speech rate is measured. When symptoms are left in the sample used to measure speech rate, this is referred to as speaking rate and is reported in syllables spoken or read per minute (Ryan, 1974; Ingham, 1984). When symptoms are omitted, the measure is referred to as articulation rate expressed in fluent syllables per sec (Perkins, 1975). The original reasons that articulation rate was suggested was because stuttering symptoms vary in duration within and between symptom classes. For instance, a single repetition of a function word is shorter than a long prolongation. Each of the two stuttering symptoms would count as one event despite the fact that they occupy different amounts of time and, therefore, have different impacts on rate measures. By separating the symptoms out, the impact of variation in duration between symptoms is avoided. For this reason, most authorities on stuttering recommend using articulation rate to avoid this problem (Kelly & Conture, 1992; Kalinowski, Armson, & Stuart, 1995; Logan & Conture, 1995; Yaruss & Conture, 1995; Howell, Au-Yeung, & Pilgrim, 1999). Articulation rate excludes all stuttering episodes and pausing time from the rate calculation.

There are studies that allow estimates of articulation rate for fluent and stuttering children close to the ages where stuttering starts. Meyers and Freeman (1985) reported that the articulation rate of their 12 stuttering preschool children was significantly slower (mean = 3.51 syllables per second) than that of their 12 fluent controls (mean = 4.18 syllables per second). Richardson (1985) reported mean articulation rates for 12 stuttering and 12 fluent preschool children of 4.0 syllables per second and 3.7 syllables per second, respectively. Pindzola, Jenkins, and Lokken (1989) reported speaking rates for 30 fluent children, aged 3 to 5 years, of 3.0 syllables per second. Although there is some variation between these studies (possibly because of differences in methodology), articulation rates of preschool children (fluent and stuttering) are of the order three to four syllables per second. Articulation rate does not seem to vary systematically or dramatically between children who stutter and fluent children.

Speakers can change their mean speech rate, allowing it to go up or down; this is referred to as global rate change. Speakers also can change the rate within an utterance. For example, an utterance can be divided into tone units and the speech rate within the tone units varies (Howell, Au-Yeung, & Pilgrim, 1999). (Tone units are a prosodic unit, which contains one prominent pitch inflection.) The local rate variations may not be evident if mean speech rate measures are used. This is because samples of the same extract of speech recorded in two different conditions can have the same mean but have different spreads of slowed and speeded intervals around that mean. When two conditions have different spreads of intervals, but the same mean, they differ in local speech rate. If intervals extend farther out at the slow end of the range, there also will be intervals that extend farther at the faster end of the range that average out to give the same mean. Local speech rate changes may be sufficient to improve fluency in speakers who stutter if, for example, the speaker makes a strategic reduction in local speech rate at a position where the utterance would otherwise have been stuttered. Speeding up at other points would help achieve the required global speech rate and rapidly produced speech at these points would not matter if there was a reduced risk of disfluency in their vicinity. Before the issue of whether local rate changes have an impact on fluency is considered, the evidence of how global changes affect stuttering is reviewed.

8.3.1 GLOBAL RATE CHANGE

There is considerable experimental evidence that reducing the speech rate of speakers who stutter decreases frequency of fluency failure (Johnson & Rosen, 1937; Perkins, Kent, & Curlee, 1991; Starkweather, 1985; Wingate, 1976). It is also widely reported that rate increase has the opposite effect. Increasing global speech rate increases frequency of fluency failure (Bloodstein, 1987; Johnson & Rosen, 1937).

It was mentioned in an earlier section that FSF improves the fluency of people who stutter when they are asked to speak as fast as possible (i.e., asked to make a change in global speech rate). Although this shows that fluency enhancement under FSF can occur irrespective of global changes, local rate changes may, nevertheless, have occurred.

A study by Kalinowski, Armson and Stuart (1995) looked at global speech rate. They recruited 20 adults who stuttered (17 males and 3 females) aged between 18 and 52 years (mean age was 32 years). Stuttering symptoms were part-word repetitions, prolongations, and inaudible postural fixations. Participants read two different 300-syllable passages at a normal and fast speech rate. Stuttering counts and articulatory rate were determined for each speech sample. No statistically significant difference in stuttering frequency was found between the two speech-rate conditions, although a significant difference was observed for articulatory rate. The finding that stuttering did not increase at fast articulatory rates was considered contrary to the notion that stutterers have reduced capacity for movement coordination and to the explanation of the fluency enhancement effect of slowed speech rate in terms of speech timing.

8.3.1.1 Global Rate and Severity

There appears to be a relationship between speech rate and severity of stuttering. This is important when examining persistence and recovery, as severe cases may be more likely to persist (Howell & Davis, in press). In early work on pauses and severity, for example, the number of brief pauses in a speech sample containing no moments of stuttering was found to be a successful instrumental method for separating stutterers from nonstutterers (Love & Jeffress, 1971). In addition, Prosek, Waldon, Montgomery, and Schwartz (1979) reported that the number of pauses correlated with a perceptual dimension of stuttering severity.

Speech rate could be a feature of stuttering (in which case more severe cases would be expected to have slower speech rates) or a causative factor (severe stutterers may speak too fast, which is why they stutter). The second alternative (rate is a causative factor) appears to be favored in a study by Andrade, Cervone, and Sassi (2003). They showed faster speech rate in speakers with severe stutters. This was recently replicated by Arcuri, Osborn, Schiefer and Chiari (2009) who studied six adults who stuttered (aged 22–35 years). According to SSI-3, two were mild, two were moderate, and two were severe. Material was read, and fluent utterances were selected to measure rate, thus, this corresponds to articulatory rate measures made just on fluent extracts. They showed that people with a more severe stutter as measured by SSI-3 had a significantly higher articulation rate.

8.3.2 Local Rate Change

It was indicated earlier that a local rate change may be sufficient to reduce stuttering if particular stretches are problematic and the speaker can slow rate just in their vicinity so that they can be negotiated without stuttering. In this section, some evidence for local rate changes is presented that would be consistent with this view.

Viswanath (1989) tested four male adults who stuttered (aged 16–43). Each participant read two short stories from a collection of Thurber stories, five times in succession. Repetitions and prolongations of sounds and syllables were counted as stuttering symptoms. Utterances were divided into clauses and the same clauses were compared across speakers who stuttered and the controls. The duration of words in the vicinity of stuttering events showed anticipatory and carryover effects in the immediate vicinity of stuttering events (i.e., durations were affected in positions preceding and following a stuttering event). It was noted that the anticipatory effects were more pronounced than the carryover effects. There also was a significant difference in durations between stutterers and fluent speakers, in particular on the duration of the last word in a clause that immediately preceded another clause that contained a stuttering event. Viswanath interpreted this as an anticipatory effect that occurs across adjacent clauses.

Two studies show that local rate changes occur in the period before recovery and persistence is resolved. Howell, Au-Yeung, and Pilgrim (1999) obtained spontaneous speech data from eight children who stuttered. The children ranged in age from 9 to 11 years and there were seven boys. Assessments obtained of each word were a perceptual rating about how comfortably the word flowed and a categorization of the word as being fluent, a prolongation, a repetition of word or part-word, or whether there was another type of symptom. Howell et al. segmented the spontaneous speech into tone units. The tone units were separated into those that were stuttered and those that were fluent. Syllable rate was measured in the section prior to the stuttering; the whole segment in the case of a fluent tone unit. The tone units were classified into fast, medium, and slow rate categories based on the rate in the fluent section. Howell et al. found that fast tone units (more than five syllables per 10 second) were more likely to be stuttered than medium (between four and five syllables per second) or slow (less than four syllables per second) tone units within the same speech sample. These findings support the idea that fluency problems arise when speech rate is high in the local vicinity of stuttering. McClean and Runyan (2000) also reported results that are consistent with this notion.

Howell and Sackin (2000) reported two experiments, the second of which concerned local rate changes that occurred while participants heard concurrent auditory feedback. Nine children who stuttered participated in this experiment ranging in age from 9;3 to 12 years, of whom eight were male. They investigated timing variability in a simple utterance that was repeated several times by fluent speakers ("Cathy took some cocoa to the teletubbies."). Only fluent productions were used. They asked participants to repeat the phrase under FSF and normal listening conditions, and when speaking and singing. They marked the plosives in the utterance and measured the duration of the intervals between the first and each of the subsequent plosives. The frequency distribution (for each interval type) that a speaker produced was then obtained. Global slowing between speaking conditions would be reflected in a shift in the mean of the overall distribution to longer durations. As explained earlier, local slowing occurs when the distribution of intervals changes, and this can happen when there is no change in the mean (no global slowing between conditions).

Looking at the means of the distributions first to see if there was global slowing, comparisons were made between normal speech in ordinary and FSF listening, sung speech in ordinary and FSF listening, speech versus singing in ordinary listening, and speech versus singing in FSF listening. All revealed significant differences between overall means (global slowing), except speech versus singing in normal listening.

The authors then asked whether, although singing does not induce global slowing in the normal listening condition, it does lead to local slowing (as required if local changes were independent of global changes). To test this, Howell and Sackin estimated the time at the point in the distribution where the 25th percentile occurred, as a measure of whether the fast intervals shifted across the different conditions. When the same comparisons were made as with the means, all conditions showed a significant shift upwards of this percentile. This is not surprising when global shifts occur, as it may simply indicate a shift of the overall distribution. Of particular note, however, is the local slowing that occurred when speaking was compared with singing in normal listening conditions. This indicated significant local slowing where there was no global slowing, supporting the idea that these are two distinct modes of making a rate change. FSF produced local and global slowing (Howell & Sackin, 2000).

8.3.3 SUMMARY

Global speech rates are similar for children who stutter and for controls. Global rate changes correlate with severity and these were interpreted as showing that an over-rapid rate of speech precipitates stuttering. Local rate changes occur and these are linked to stuttering in adults and children. For example, Viswanath (1989) showed durational changes in a clause immediately preceding one with a stutter in adults. Howell, Au-Yeung, and Pilgrim (1999) showed that, with children, local extracts that were spoken rapidly were more likely to be stuttered than those spoken more slowly. Howell and Sackin (2000) showed that when children sang in normal listening conditions, no global slowing occurred, but local slowing did. Singing is one way in which fluency is induced in speakers who stutter and this suggests that local slowing is sufficient for fluency-enhancement to occur.

Three areas need further examination. First, it seems likely that the effects described here are rate effects induced at the motor level. Thus, the experimental paradigms either present utterances to the participants that reduce the need for language planning, or induce rate changes by altered feedback, which do not occur at the language level according to the arguments given in section 8.2.5. Nevertheless, further checks that these rate changes occur at the motor level need to be conducted. Second, more attention needs to be given to rate influences around the age that stuttering starts and over its course into teenage years. Third, further examination of whether there is a link between articulation rate and speech symptoms is required. Taking Viswanath's finding, for example, the question might be asked whether pausing at the end of a clause prior to a clause that contains a stutter depends on the form of the symptom in the next clause. Stutters, like prolongations, might be anticipated across clauses and lead to prior slowing, whereas whole-word repetition might be symptoms that speakers who stutter use as a strategy to slow speech within a clause.

8.4   VARIABILITY

Speakers are able to achieve precise control of the articulators rapidly. They can continue to produce the same speech sound when subjected to changed internal (e.g., anesthetics) and external (e.g., biteblock, Fowler & Turvey, 1981) constraints on speech production. However, the precision is never exact and may be particularly affected in people with speech-motor disorders, such as stuttering. Thus, it might be expected that control would be less precise in these speakers. Various indices have been developed that quantify what amount of variation is natural (i.e., the amount that occurs in fluent adult speakers), and these indices have been used to assess sensitivity to changes in internal and external task demands and across speaker groups. Coordination should not be confused with variability. Variability can be measured on a single articulator and that term is reserved for such cases. Coordination refers to the degree of synchrony between two or more articulators (discussed in detail in the following section).

The high degree of precision (low variability) in speech control is cited in support of two opposed classes of models of speech production. These are generalized motor program (GMP) and dynamic systems theory (DST) (Van Lieshout, 2004). GMP dates back to work by Kozhevnikov and Chistovich (1965), who argued that it is unreasonable to propose different motor programs for producing a particular sequence in different conditions (e.g., at different speech rates). The GMP solution was to include a multiplicative rate parameter that adjusted the execution of a single program. This resulted in a timing pattern whereby intervals within a movement sequence remained proportionally invariant across changes in overall duration of the sequence. Some authors have reported findings that they interpret as consistent with the constant proportionality model (e.g., Viviani & Terzuolo, 1983). Max and Caruso (1997), on the other hand, looked at whether the ratios of acoustically derived temporal intervals at the syllable and/or phrase level remained invariant across different speaking rates. They found several significant changes with rate, which they interpreted as evidence against the proportionality assumption in the GMP model. The idea of an externally applied rate parameter is consistent with a separate timekeeper process. Some evidence that this occurs was presented in Chapter 6 and mentioned again in section 8.2.5 of this chapter. Timekeepers can modulate actions by a constant proportion (i.e., linearly) and are included in GMP models. Feedback and other closed loop processes can operate in the GMP framework.

DSTs maintain that speech timing is inherently nonlinear. In the present context, nonlinear means that the bases on which articulatory events are aligned does not fit with movement kinematics. The emphasis in DST is on invariance of relative timing under varying changes in absolute duration so there is no reason to suppose that durations of elements like pauses, transitions, and steady states in an utterance would scale proportionately as duration changes. However, this is not necessarily inconsistent with external timekeepers. Thus, while DSTs in general assume that movement durations are intrinsic to the gestural specifications, which has no durational parameter as such, recent versions of such theories include proposals to change global speech rate factors. (See the task dynamics model in Goldstein, 2003, and Saltzman, Nam, Goldstein, & Bird, 2006). According to DST, speech is under open loop control, which is why Fowler and Turvey tested whether adaptations to a biteblock required auditory feedback (section 8.2.5). Some specific ways in which variability has been measured and some empirical findings are described next.

8.4.1   SMITH'S SPATIO-TEMPORAL INDEX (STI)

The most popular contemporary technique for estimating variability in performance is Smith's spatio-temporal index (STI) (Smith, Goffman, Zelaznik, Ying, & McGillem, 1995). STI is a statistic that reflects joint temporal and amplitude variation in speech signals. To calculate an STI for lower lip displacement, for example, 10 or more recordings of an utterance that involves lip closures are obtained. The time base of different records is adjusted linearly (proportional stretching or squeezing to give all records a common length). As noted above, the linear scaling in time does not fit with the assumptions behind DST. The individual lip-movement records are then amplitude-normalized using a z transformation. The standard deviation (sd) across all records is then obtained at 2% intervals on the normalized time axis, and the computed quantities are summed to give the single STI score.

Using the STI, people who stutter have been reported not to differ on lip displacement relative to fluent speakers on the "Buy Bobby a puppy" test phrase (Smith & Kleinow, 2000), although they do differ with respect to other lip movement measures (Smith & Goffman, 2004). Howell, Anderson, Bartrip, and Bailey (2009) obtained STI for the lower lip (L-STI) and for speech energy over time (E-STI) in 13 speakers who stuttered (mean age of 14;3) SSI-3, (Riley, 1994), was used to assess stuttering at the time of the test. SSI-3 ranged from very mild to severe. E-STI scores discriminated successfully between fluent speakers and speakers who stutter.

STI has provided extensive data on how speech develops and it affords an index of speech motor disorder (see Smith & Goffman, 2004, and Goffman, 2010, for extensive reviews). A limitation is that the technique is mainly used with single signals (however, see section 8.5.1 below where the single signal represents the difference between upper and lower lip movements). This restricts application to coordination that, according to the earlier definition, involves two or more signals. Other limitations are that STI provides a joint measure of amplitude and timing dimensions. Nonlinear techniques address these issues to some extent (see discussion on Lucero's (2005) work in section 8.4.3 below).

8.4.2   VAN LIESHOUT'S cSTI

Van Lieshout and Moussa (2000) adapted the STI by defining the unit that was repeated in more specific motor terms. They employed individual movement cycles, and termed the measure they derived the cyclic STI (cSTI). It was claimed that the cSTI measure is less susceptible to long-term nonlinear influences relating to local temporal variations in linguistic structures and more indicative of basic motor control stability.

Namasivayam and Van Lieshout (2008) used the cSTI to investigate whether or not people who stutter show effects of motor practice and learning similar to those of people who do not stutter. Five adults who stuttered aged between 18 and 41 (mean age, 26;1 years) and five controls aged between 22 and 32 (mean age, 25;3 years) repeated a set of nonwords at two different rates (normal and fast) across three test sessions. Severity of stuttering was estimated using SSI-3; two of the people who stuttered were rated moderate and the remaining three were rated to be very mild, mild, and severe. The performance measures were obtained from transducer coils that were attached to the midline of the vermilion border of upper and lower lip, the mandible, the tongue blade (1 cm behind the anatomical tongue tip), the tongue body (3 cm behind tongue blade coil), and the tongue dorsum (approximately 2 cm behind tongue body coil).

The results indicated that people who stuttered and controls showed similar performance on a number of variables, such as movement amplitude and duration, but they differed in practice and learning on variables that related to movement stability and coupling strength.

8.4.3   Functional Data Analysis (FDA) Approach (Lucero)

As discussed earlier, speech features may require different amounts of adjustment to bring them into alignment along the time axis, referred to as nonlinear scaling. There are different ways of doing this. The simplest is to mark features manually (Ward & Armfield, 2001). Records are then adjusted linearly (as with STI) between the features that are marked (referred to as piecewise linear). The technique is nonlinear because the amount of adjustment required between the landmark features will typically vary. The disadvantage is that it has to be done manually, making the procedure slow and subjective, and requiring features to be predefined; there may not be enough or too many.

Functional data analysis (FDA) nonlinear technique procedures do the alignment just discussed automatically and it is not necessary to specify the number and nature of the features that are used (Ramsay, Munhall, Gracco, & Ostry, 1996). One advantage of FDA is that it makes it possible to extract information about amplitude (pattern) variability separate from timing variability, which is not possible if an arbitrary linear scaling is done. Thus, pattern and timing variability cannot be separated using the linear STI method.

Because FDA manipulates the time lines of records nonlinearly so as to bring their features into alignment across the set, variation in the degree of adjustment necessary to bring the records into alignment provides an estimate of temporal variability over the course of the records. After the set of records has been aligned, differences on the amplitude axis provide an estimate of amplitude variability over time. This allows separate statistics to be formulated indexing temporal and amplitude variability in an analogous way to that in Smith's STI (Smith et al., 1995). Timing variability can be indexed by estimating the standard deviation (*sd*) in phase (temporal) adjustments over the normalized time axis and averaging across the extract. The *sd* of the amplitudes can be processed in a similar way to index amplitude variability (see also Lucero, 2005).

Howell, Anderson, and Lucero (2010) used FDA to investigate the lip and energy signals associated with STI. They tested 12 participants who stuttered, with a mean age of 14;9, and 12 fluent participants, with a mean age of 16;11. Results were reported for timing deformation for each signal. Both timing signals (lip and energy) differed significantly across the speaker groups, with the group of speakers who stutter showing highest timing variability for each signal. A summary of the work on variability, along with that on coordination, is given below.

8.5   COORDINATIVE BEHAVIOR

Certain gestures need to have their timing precisely linked to each other, such as tongue contact and velar opening for the phoneme /n/. If one gesture is not appropriately timed relative to the others, the speech is not fluent. This idea that movements are not controlled separately, but function as a single unit (coordinative structure), was first derived from DST discussed earlier. Different events that are controlled as a unit would show a high degree of synchronization. Gracco and Lofqvist (1994) embody the idea that speech has to be synchronized and that this does not require programming the individual muscles when they say "rather than explicitly controlling the timing of the different neuromuscular elements involved in the production of a particular sound, the nervous system controls the coordinative requirements of all the active effectors as a unit" (p. 6585). This idea also links with timing deficits in people who stutter, which could arise from poor coordination. Coordination indices are used to provide a measure of how precisely two or more articulators are timed. They make it possible to distinguish between theories and potentially to help identify possible sources of deficit in people who stutter.

In terms of empirical evidence, most of the work is with adults. Van Lieshout and Namasavayam (2010) presented a useful recent review of studies that showed how coordination is affected in people who stutter. One measure used is relative phase; this quantifies the degree of synchronization between events in motor control that is independent of absolute changes in movement duration and amplitude (Van Lieshout, Hulstijn, Alfonso, & Peters, 1997). Ward (1997) compared relative phase differences to other relative timing measures. There were no group differences between people who stutter and controls in articulator sequencing, but they did appear for relative phase (between upper lip and jaw). Thus, people who stuttered showed greater variability in the relative phase measure than controls at fast rates of speech and when altered stress patterns had to be produced. In contrast with these findings, Jäncke, Kaiser, Bauer, and Kalveram (1995) performed a study on 19 adults who stuttered and 12 adult controls using relative phase measures between jaw and lip movements across speaking rates with two different stress patterns. The authors failed to find any group differences in phase angle or phase angle variability. This was also the case in the recent study that examined a biteblock perturbation discussed in section 8.2.6 (Namasivayam, Van Lieshout, & de Nil, 2008). The people who stuttered and controls showed similar intragestural (between upper and lower lip) relative phase variability values at both normal and fast rates of speech.

8.5.1   Smith and Zelaznik (2004): Development of Motor Coordination

There is some limited scope for examining coordination with STI by combining signals from two separate articulators and then conducting STI analyses. Thus, a lip aperture measure can be obtained by combining measures of upper and lower lip. Smith and Zelaznik (2004) tested 180 participants who stuttered aged between 2 years and 22 years. They compared the amount of variability in each single articulator and that in the combined signal. STI measures for the separate articulators were greater than for the aperture measure, which suggests that the upper and lower lips act in coordination. A related study by Van Lieshout et al. (2002) was conducted on nine patients with repaired cleft palate (mean age, 15;8) and four controls (mean age, 17;8) using cSTI. They showed that the upper lip had smaller movement and higher variability than the lower lip, but the patients still seemed able to coordinate the articulators to achieve their goals. They did not compare aperture with separate upper and lower lip measures.

8.5.2   Alfonso and Van Lieshout

Caruso, Abbs, and Gracco (1988) reported a consistent sequencing of lips and jaw for their control participants and much more variability in their group of people who stuttered; this was taken as evidence for an impairment in movement sequencing. Alfonso and Van Lieshout (1997) tested seven people who stuttered and seven controls (ages not given). They tracked tongue, lips, and jaw for the nonsense words pap, tat, and sas. They examined measures of spatial (e.g., displacement and velocity profile) and temporal (e.g., temporal order and inter-articulator relative time) activity. The single measures were not stable across sessions, so were not appropriate to distinguish groups. A coefficient of variation that reflected the variability in the combined movements of lip and jaw was robust for all but one control, but was less robust for people who stutter. This suggests poorer coordination abilities in people who stutter than fluent controls.

8.5.3   Anderson's Coordination Index (Based on FDA)

Recent research has obtained separate spatial and temporal variability of individual articulators. The temporal variability of the signals is then compared to obtain an index of coordination (Howell, Anderson, & Lucero, 2010). Howell et al.'s technique involved obtaining the time deformations for each signal separately. These were then plotted against each other (one on the x axis and one on the y

axis). If the deformations were identical, they would all lie on top of each other (a single line). The extent to which the points are spread about this line can be used as an index of temporal coordination. The amplitudes of the aligned signals then can be processed in a similar way to estimate the amount of pattern variability. An illustrative application of this procedure to patients with Parkinson's disease and Friedreich's ataxia is described in Anderson, Lowit, and Howell (2008).

8.6 SUMMARY OF WORK ON VARIABILITY AND COORDINATION

There is strong evidence that people who stutter are more variable than controls in movement control and a smaller number of studies also show problems in coordinating articulators. It is difficult to see how these aspects of performance could be due to language processing effects. Therefore, these studies offer support for motor processing deficits.

There is some work on variability at onset and over the course of development of stuttering (Smith & Zelaznik, 2004). However, as with the other areas considered, more is needed (work with children is completely absent for most of the paradigms except STI).

This chapter began with the intention of establishing what the motor system does (if anything) and what effect it has on onset and course of the disorder. In this and Chapter 7 on language, it has been suggested that language and motor factors are important separately. However, neither alone seems sufficient to account for the major disruption to speech in cases of severe stuttering. After theories of the motor influences alone have been detailed in Chapter 11, a model of how the two interact is considered that the author believes to provide a better account of stuttering than either factor alone (Chapter 12).

8.7 EXERCISES

1. Make a case for the proposition that altered feedback studies provide evidence either (1) for language monitoring or (2) of disruption to motor processes.
2. Why do speakers who stutter become fluent when they are played DAF while they speak?
3. It is argued in this chapter that global and local changes in speech rate arise at the motor level. Some authors consider that aspects of rate change could occur during language planning stages. Reexamine the evidence presented in this chapter to see whether the case that rate changes occur at the language stage can be sustained.
4. What evidence is there that stuttering is associated with problems in the peripheral auditory system?

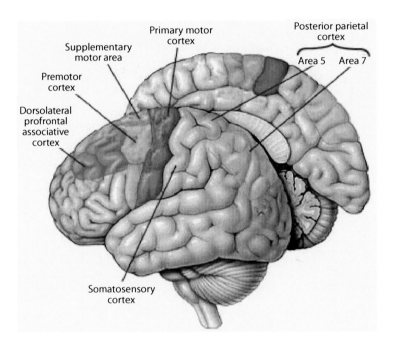

Premotor
cortex

Dorsolateral
profrontal
associative
cortex

Supplementary
motor area

Primary motor
cortex

Posterior parietal
cortex

Area 5   Area 7

Somatosensory
cortex

FIGURE 5.1   A diagram showing the location of somatosensory cortex, premotor, and motor cortex.

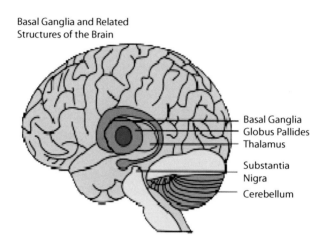

Basal Ganglia and Related
Structures of the Brain

Basal Ganglia
Globus Pallides
Thalamus

Substantia
Nigra
Cerebellum

FIGURE 5.3   Shown is the location of basal ganglia and cerebellum.

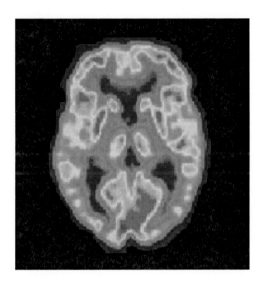

FIGURE 5.4   PET scan of a normal 20-year-old brain.

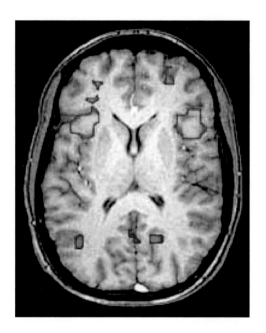

FIGURE 5.5 Shown is an axial MRI slice at the level of the basal ganglia, revealing fMRI BOLD signal changes overlaid in red (increase) and blue (decrease).

9 Environmental, Personality, and Emotional Factors

Stuttering impacts on more than just language, speech, and the other performance-based variables discussed in earlier chapters. In Chapter 4, for instance, analyses of twin data showed that 30% of the chance of stuttering was associated with environmental factors. This chapter reviews environmental, personality, and emotional factors that have been examined to see if they affect stuttering.

9.1 INTRODUCTION

There are several important aspects that have not been addressed so far that are concerned with factors other than genetics and other biological factors, language, motor, and cognitive performance. The main ones are the social and home environment of children and their personality or affectual factors. Stutterers may have different experiences from fluent speakers with respect to these factors, and it is possible that some of them could contribute to why stuttering starts (onset factors) while others may be important with respect to the subsequent course of stuttering (e.g., bullying when the child starts school). The environmental and affectual influences that may operate as risk factors at onset and course into the teenage years and beyond that are examined in this chapter include:

1. Preschool home environment
2. Preschool language environment
3. Intelligence
4. Temperament
5. Anxiety
6. Introversion/extraversion
7. Attitudes to communication
8. Bullying
9. Self esteem and stigma

The first six factors may be relatively more important in early life and the last three factors may be relatively more important in later life. When each factor is reviewed, any evidence that it could have a role at onset and/or during the subsequent course is considered (the emphasis shifts from onset for the first six factors to course for the last three factors).

9.2 ENVIRONMENT

Dworzynski, Remington, Rijksdijk, Howell, and Plomin's (2007) twin study showed that up to 30% of chance of stuttering is environmentally determined. This section and the next consider some factors that could make up the 30% environmental component. The first part of this section looks at whether the home and preschool environments of children who stutter differ from those of typically developing children. The arrangement is to look at whether the preschool environments of children who stutter differs from that of controls and then to examine whether this might exacerbate stuttering (increase the chance of onset and influence subsequent course).

9.2.1 HOME ENVIRONMENT PRESCHOOL AND START OF SCHOOL

Andrews and Harris (1964) documented the influence of several home environment factors that might predispose a child to stutter. This is not the 1,000 family survey discussed in Chapter 2, but another study reported in the same book. The study employed 80 children aged 10 to 11+ who were identified as stutterers by their head teacher. An equal number of fluent controls from the class of each child who stuttered was selected. The children were past the age of stuttering onset, but the home environment probably would not have changed very markedly from when they were young (i.e., at the age at which they started to stutter). The children were close to their teens, so these children were probably likely to persist. Andrews and Harris reported that the children who stuttered came from similar socioeconomic classes as the controls. Related to this, Howell (2007a) reported that there was no association between occupation of the primary wage earner (manual versus nonmanual) and whether children persisted or recovered from stuttering, based on evidence from 76 children who were followed up between the ages of 8 years and teens. Andrews and Harris also reported that the mothers of their 80 children who stuttered had a significantly poorer work and school record than those of the fluent control children. One has to be cautious in accepting these results as evidence for a poor home environment for two important reasons. First, society was very different in the 15 years up to 1964 than today, thus the results may not generalize. Second, a poor work and social record does not necessarily indicate a poor environment. A poor home environment also gains some support from the recent retrospective study by Adjacic-Gross et al. (2009) that is discussed in Chapter 13. They found that stuttering was more likely to occur when the father had a history of alcohol abuse, which probably signifies a poor home environment. In contrast, Reilly et al.'s (2009) study, mentioned in Chapter 2 (see also Chapter 13), found that children were more likely to stutter if their mothers had degrees, which suggests stutterers tend to come from good home environments, although not having a degree does not mean a child has a poor home environment.

9.2.2   MONOLINGUAL LANGUAGE ENVIRONMENT
PRESCHOOL AND START OF SCHOOL

Andrews and Harris (1964) found that the 80 children who stuttered were about four months late in starting to talk compared to the controls. Andrews and Harris's stuttering children also had a significantly higher reported frequency of history of abnormal articulation compared to the controls. Both of these factors may reflect the home language environment, although there are potential biological influences too that may be more significant.

Other research since then has not supported Andrews and Harris's claim of language delay. For instance, only five of the children in Howell et al.'s (2008) sample of 76 children who stuttered (6.6%) were reported to be late talkers (two of whom turned out later to persist and three to recover). In this sample, incidence of late talking does not seem high. Language production difficulties have not usually been reported in young children who stutter. Several years ago, Nippold (1990) reviewed studies of language ability in children who stutter, and noted that there was (1) a high degree of variability among children who stutter, especially in semantic skills; and (2) no tendency for language deficits among children who stutter; their language skills usually did not differ significantly from children who did not stutter. Some of this evidence was discussed in Chapter 7. Contemporary research has confirmed Nippold's observations. Thus, studies have found that expressive language abilities are at or above age-level expectations in preschoolers near the onset of stuttering (Anderson & Conture, 2000; Bonelli, Dixon, & Onslow, 2000; Miles & Bernstein Ratner, 2001; Bernstein Ratner & Silverman, 2000; Reilly et al., 2009; Rommel, Hage, Kalehne, & Johannsen, 1999; Watkins, Yairi, & Ambrose, 1999). However, F. Cook (personal communication, April, 2010) pointed out that the participants in several of these studies are the children of university staff and this may possibly bias the sample toward one with good language skills, although this would not be a problem if a control sample was used that was sampled from the same population.

9.2.3   MULTILINGUAL LANGUAGE ENVIRONMENT
PRESCHOOL AND START OF SCHOOL

Recent work has examined whether exposure to different languages in the home and in society at large has an impact on stuttering. Howell, Davis, and Williams (2009) reported that speaking English and a language other than English in the home in the United Kingdom, increased the chance of starting to stutter and reduced the chances of stuttering recovering relative to children who stuttered and only spoke English in the home before they went to school. Both the effect at onset and subsequent course were significant, although the effects were small. Several studies exclude speakers whose parents do not speak the native language of the country (Reilly et al., 2009) and others exclude them from treatment research (Millard, 2003; Stow & Dodd, 2003). Adjacic-Gross et al. (2009), however, did examine language environment as a factor in their retrospective study on 18- to 20-year-old army conscripts. They found that having a parent from a foreign country was a significant risk factor for stuttering and explained this on the basis of Howell et al.'s (2009) results on an increased risk for persistent stuttering in bilinguals.

9.2.4 SUMMARY

In summary, older work found that children who stutter may come from poorer home environments. This does not seem to apply in later research, although one recent study is suggestive of an association between stuttering and home environment (Adjacic-Gross et al.'s, 2009, report of father's alcoholism and stuttering, although the interpretation is circumstantial). Language environment may have an effect on whether a child stutters when a second language is spoken in the home (Adjacic-Gross et al., 2009) and whether stuttering persists (Howell et al., 2009). None of these effects seem to have major impacts however.

9.3 AFFECT

To get a full understanding of stuttering, it is important to understand all aspects of individual differences. These may have direct effects (e.g., conceivably, temperament may be a causal factor in stuttering onset) or act as moderator variables on stuttering. To illustrate the latter, a personality trait like extroversion might have a moderating effect insofar as it influences the attitude that a person who stutters has toward communication.

Some of the individual features ascribed to people who stutter are that they have been reported to be less intelligent than people who do not stutter (Andrews & Harris, 1964) and they have been stereotyped as being more guarded, nervous, self-conscious, tense, sensitive, hesitant, introverted, and insecure than speakers who do not stutter (Klassen, 2001). This section looks at the evidence concerning some of these factors. It begins with intelligence and then considers work on temperament and personality traits. Temperament differs from personality traits as it is more biologically based (Zuckerman, 2006). Other aspects of affect that are perhaps important after stuttering onset (in school years and later life) are then discussed (attitudes, bullying, and self-esteem). Most of the studies use survey/self-report methods and, consequently, are not described in the same detail as are the studies in other chapters.

9.3.1 INTELLIGENCE

Early work pointed to lower IQ (intelligence quotient) in children who stutter. The Andrews and Harris (1964) study, which compared 80 stuttering and 80 fluent children, showed that the children who stuttered had lower Wechsler IQ scores than controls (in both verbal and nonverbal subtests). Overall, Wechsler score results showed 31/80 stuttering children had IQ scores below 90 compared with 13/80 controls. Other empirical evidence also supports the view that children who stutter score significantly lower on intelligence tests than do fluent controls. Thus, studies with school-age children who stutter have shown deficits in both verbal and nonverbal intelligence tests (Okasha, Bishry, Kamel, & Hassan, 1974; Schindler, 1955). As nonverbal intelligence is affected, it appears unlikely that the IQ deficits could be explained by difficulties in communication because of stuttering.

More recent work has not supported the view that children who stutter have lower IQs than fluent children. Thus, Yairi and Ambrose (2005) reported that the children in their study scored 13 (persistent) to 22 (recovered) IQ points higher than norms on the nonverbal Arthur adaptation of the Leiter scale. Reilly et al. (2009) found higher verbal performance in children who stuttered, although this was not an IQ test. A point to note is that the samples of children used in both of these studies may be biased to the higher end of the social scale for the same reasons as discussed in section 9.2 and this could have affected these results.

It has also been reported that the intelligence and social class of children who stutter and who are receiving treatment are above average (Cox, 1982). This could be because intelligence and social class contribute, in part, to access to health-care. Overall then, although there are some suggestions in the early literature that there is a disproportionate number of children who stutter around one standard deviation below the mean on IQ scores compared to controls (Andrews & Harris, 1964), this finding is contradicted by more recent work and by contemporary work on children in therapy.

9.3.2 TEMPERAMENT

Temperament has been defined as a collection of inherited personality characteristics that "constitute the individuality of the person" (Goldsmith et al., 1987, p. 510). Zuckerman (2006) listed six features that distinguish temperament from classic personality traits. Temperament is:

1. Relatively stable
2. Not expressed in motivational or goal-directed aspects of behavior
3. Present from early childhood (before stuttering starts)
4. Similar to behaviors seen in other species
5. Primarily determined by inborn (genetic) mechanisms
6. Subject to changes caused by maturation and the interaction of the genotype with specific life experiences.

Characteristics 1, 3, and 5 make temperament of particular potential importance with respect to stuttering onset, and characteristic 6 is potentially important with respect to the later course of stuttering.

Some temperament characteristics can be identified as early as the first year of life (e.g., emotional impulse control) and the characteristics are stable, but differ across individuals (Caprara & Cervone, 2000). This leads to the view that temperament "mediates and shapes the influence of the environment on the individual's psychological structure" (Goldsmith et al., 1987, p. 509), and concerns the "formal and stylistic features of behavior, such as the individual's sensitivity and responsivity to environmental demands" (Caprara & Cervone, 2000, p. 87). The standard view is, then, that the way individuals react to and operate in their environments is a function of temperament.

Several authors have expressed the view that temperament may have an influence on stuttering (and indeed other language disorders) at onset and in its subsequent course. For instance, Guitar (2006) hypothesized that a sensitive (i.e., reactive) temperament inclines vulnerable children to develop stuttering (see also Conture, 2001; Zebrowski & Conture, 1998, who express similar views). Guitar suggested that children who stutter tend to be more easily aroused by stimuli, but are inhibited when confronted by unfamiliar people or situations.

Sermas and Cox (1982) considered that a child's temperament is a contributory factor to both the onset and persistence of stuttering. Perkins (1992a, 1992b) also considered that children at risk of persistent forms of stuttering were apt to be those who are more easily intimidated. He proposed that stuttering symptoms were triggered when a child's need to be heard and understood collided with an opposing feeling, usually induced by listener behavior, that such importunate assertions must be kept in check.

Several investigations have been made about temperament in children who stutter. These highlight a number of dimensions where children who stutter differ from children who do not stutter. In general, children who stutter tend to be more responsive or reactive to stimuli in their environment (Wakaba, 1998), and are more sensitive, anxious, withdrawn, and introverted (Fowlie & Cooper, 1978). These findings support Guitar's speculations.

There are four recent studies on temperament, all of which used the children's behavior style questionnaire (BSQ), a parent-report questionnaire (McDevitt & Carey, 1978). Embrechts, Ebben, Franke, and van de Poel (2000) found children who stuttered, who were aged between 3;7 and 7 years old, were judged to have reduced attention span and less success in adapting to new environments relative to controls. Anderson, Pellowski, Conture, and Kelly (2003) found that children who stuttered aged between 3;0 and 5;4 were significantly less likely to adapt to change, were less distractable, and displayed greater irregularity with biological functions than controls. Howell, Davis et al. (2004) found four dimensions differed significantly between children who stuttered and controls for children aged between 3;7 and 7;2. As was the case for both the Anderson et al. and Embrechts et al. studies, children who stuttered were found to be less likely to adapt. In addition, Howell, Davis et al. (2004) found that children who stuttered were significantly more active, more negative in mood, and less persistent (i.e., less likely to stick with their behaviors). Karrass et al. (2006) examined temperament variables in 65 young stuttering children and their controls, aged between 3;0 and 5;11. They found emotional reactivity and emotional regulation differed significantly between groups.

One cause for concern is the lack of consistency in the temperament factors found in the different studies, even though the same instrument was used in all four studies reviewed (BSQ). There is one finding that is consistent over the

Anderson et al. (2003), Embrechts et al. (2000), and Howell, Davis et al. (2004) studies, but not with that of Karrass et al. (2006). All three of the former studies reported that children who stutter were less adaptable to their environment than their controls. However, none of the remaining temperament dimensions matched in significance and direction across the studies. The first two studies found differences between children who stutter and controls in terms of distractability. Here, however, the direction differed between the two studies (Embrechts et al. found children who stuttered were more distractable than the controls, whereas Anderson et al. found the opposite). Howell, Davis et al. (2004) reported that children who stuttered were significantly more active, more negative in mood, and less persistent in their behaviors, but none of these dimensions were found significant in the other studies. A study by Reilly et al. (2009) that used a different form of questionnaire on large samples of 2- to 3-year-old children who stuttered and children who were fluent found no differences in temperament at all. (This study is discussed in detail in Chapter 13.)

A second cause for concern is that temperamental factors do not seem to relate to fluency problems (Howell, Davis et al., 2004). They measured temperament variables from BSQ and correlated them with a number of language measures in a group of fluent 3-year-olds. Temperament measures did not correlate significantly with (1) a measure of vocabulary, the Oxford version of the communication development inventory (Hamilton, Plunkett, & Schafer, 2000); (2) a test that required the child to name pictures of objects they knew and that used number of errors in naming the pictures as the performance measure (based on Gershkoff-Stowe and Smith, 1997); (3) mean length of utterance, which is a standard measure for the development of productive syntax at these ages (Brown, 1973); and (4) a measure of the child's ability to understand syntactic relations, in a perceptual test (the reception of syntax test, Howell, Davis, and Au-Yeung, 2003).

Schwenk, Conture, and Walden (2007) recently reported a study that was based on observations of temperament-related behaviors rather than parental reports. They examined gaze behaviors of preschool children (3–5 years of age), 13 who stuttered and 14 who did not, in response to camera movements. The latency and duration of gazes did not differ between the groups, but the children who stuttered looked at the camera significantly more often than the control children. The authors interpreted these results as showing that children who stutter may be more reactive, and less apt to habituate to environmental changes, compared to children who do not stutter. This is an interesting report and is an advance on previous research insofar as it uses observational, rather then report, techniques. However, it is advisable to await further reports using these methods, given the lack of agreement between studies that all used the BSQ. Moreover, the particular temperament dimensions that were significant in this study were not ones revealed by any of the studies that used BSQ.

Although, intuitively, temperamental variables would appear a promising prospect that could impact on speech–language development and fluency in particular, the evidence at present is not strong. Thus, there is a lack of consistency on which temperamental variables differ between speakers who stutter and controls, and the direction of differences reported across the two groups of speakers do not correspond. Also, the lack of correlation between temperament and language measures suggests that the former is neither influenced by, nor has a direct influence on, language. There is an isolated study that based temperament measures on direct observations of children. The lack of consistency between studies on temperament may be a reflection of the heterogeneity of the disorder. The lack of any correlation with fluency raises the possibility that if treatments were developed that addressed temperament per se, they may not have an impact on fluency.

9.3.3 PERSONALITY

Personality is usually measured by tests of preference (as compared with ability, which is measured by tests involving statistical power). The big five personality dimensions are neuroticism, extroversion, openness, agreeableness, and conscientiousness (Costa & McCrae, 1990). The first two of these have been examined in children who stutter and the work on these is considered in this section.

9.3.3.1 Neurotic, Trait, and State Anxiety

Anxiety is often considered by researchers and clinicians to be a causal factor in stuttering. It also has a role in many theories about the origin of stuttering (Miller & Watson, 1992). Stuttering is often considered to be more acute when a person who stutters speaks to strangers, those felt to be his or her superiors, or when addressing large gatherings. This often leads to a person who stutters avoiding social occasions and public speaking situations or experiencing anxiety when in these situations (Van Riper, 1992).

Two forms of anxiety are distinguished by social psychologists: trait and state. Trait anxiety refers to forms that a person is predisposed to because of his or her biological makeup. This is related to clinical states where it is termed neurotic anxiety. State anxiety refers to forms that arise because of specific situations. To illustrate how these forms are distinguished, a person with low trait anxiety may experience high state anxiety when put in a demanding communication situation.

Trait and state anxiety can be measured by self-report, observational reports by others, or using physiological measures like heart beat, galvanic skin response, etc. In most research, there are surprisingly low correlations between alternative measurement methods. For some authors who have published on stuttering, *subjective* anxiety is crucial, so they advocate self-report. Others prefer physiological measures irrespective of whether speakers who stutter claim to feel stressed or merely aroused.

Findings indicate that there are no differences between school-age children who stutter and fluent controls in neurotic anxiety. Thus, tests using the Sarson general anxiety scale for children and a structured psychiatric interview (Andrews & Harris, 1964), the California test of personality (Prins, 1972), the Minnesota multiphasic personality inventory (Horlick & Miller, 1960; Lanyon, Goldsworthy, & Lanyon, 1978), and the Spielberger anxiety scales (Molt & Guilford, 1979) all showed no difference between participant groups.

Two recent studies have examined state and trait anxiety in children who stutter (Ezrati-Vinacour and Levin, 2004). They used the state-trait anxiety inventory (STAI) (Spielberger, Gorsuch, & Lushene, 1970) for the speech situations described by Brutten (1973), for both a group of people who stutter and a control group. The people who stuttered were divided into severe and mild subgroups based on a median split using SSI severity scores. A task-related anxiety (TRA) scale was also employed, which participants used to evaluate their anxiety level immediately after they had performed two speech and two nonspeech tasks. The three severity groups (severe, mild, and controls) were compared on trait, state, and TRA separately for scores following speech or nonspeech tasks. Trait anxiety was higher for severe and mild people who stutter compared to fluent controls. State scores on the speech situation checklist were higher for those with a severe stutter than for those with a mild stutter or who were fluent. TRA scores were also higher among those with a severe stutter than those with a mild stutter and fluent speakers for the speech, but not the nonspeech task. Ezrati-Vinacour and Levin (2004) interpreted these results as showing that people who stutter have higher trait anxiety than fluent speakers and that state anxiety in social communication was higher among those with a severe stutter as compared to those with a mild stutter or who were fluent. Thus, based on this single study, anxiety may be a personality trait of people who stutter and state anxiety may be related to stuttering severity.

Psychological states may continue after individuals recover from a disorder (as occurs, for instance, in post-traumatic stress disorder), but in other cases the states (anxiety here) disappear once the person has recovered. Clinicians need to know which of these alternatives applies as they would then be able to tell clients whether treating stuttering is likely to remove associated negative psychological states.

To address the question of whether anxiety continues when speakers recover from stuttering, Davis, Shisca, and Howell (2007) used Cattell and Scheier's (1961) state and trait anxiety procedure in children known to have been stuttering as young children and who had either persisted or recovered by adolescence. A group of age- and IQ-matched fluent control children was tested as well. There were no differences between persistent stutterers, recovered stutterers, and the controls with regard to trait anxiety. However, the persistent speakers had higher state anxiety than controls and recovered speakers for three out of the four speaking states examined, while the recovered speakers showed no state differences relative to controls. The findings were interpreted as showing that increased anxiety levels in particular states are a result of the speaking problem. This is consistent with the view that state anxiety is an effect, not a cause, of stuttering.

Further results about the later course of stuttering were obtained by Yairi and Ambrose (2005) using two scales: child anxiety and revised children's manifest anxiety scale. Neither showed differences between persistent and recovered speakers, nor for either of these groups relative to fluent controls.

Although children who stutter do not differ in trait anxiety from controls, trait and state anxiety differences have been found in adulthood when speakers persist in stuttering. Thus, studies using several different methods have shown that anxiety levels of adults who stutter are higher than those of adults who do not stutter. This includes studies that employed the trait anxiety questionnaire (Craig, Hancock, Tran, & Craig, 2003), the inventory of interpersonal situations (Kraaimaat, Vanryckeghem, & Van Dam-Baggen, 2002), the cognitive anxiety scale (DiLollo, Manning, & Neimeyer, 2003), and the Minnesota multiphasic personality inventory (Treon, Dempster, & Blaesing, 2006).

On the other hand, Manning, Dailey, and Wallace (1984) used a bipolar adjective scale (Woods & Williams, 1976) containing pairs, such as *anxious–composed* and *introverted–extroverted.* They found that self-perceived personality characteristics of older people who stutter (29 participants, mean age, 62 years) were not significantly different from those of nonstuttering controls (13 participants, mean age, 65 years). Also, Blood, Blood, Bennett, Simpson, and Susman (1994) found no differences between the anxiety levels of adults who stuttered and those of fluent controls using the state anxiety inventory, trait anxiety inventory, or personal report of communication apprehension. However, they did find that levels of salivary cortisol were significantly higher in the adults who stuttered than in the control group during high stress situations. This indicated higher anxiety levels for the adults who stutter.

An interesting recent direction is in work from Australia. In this work, it is claimed that anxiety can be treated in adults who stutter. This work is discussed in Chapter 15.

9.3.3.2 Extroversion

Work on children who stutter shows they do not have different personality types from control children as measured by Eysenck's Personality Inventory (Hegde, 1972). Also, personality alone does not appear to be a predictor of the developmental pathway of stuttering. Thus, Guitar (1976) showed that neither neuroticism nor extroversion as measured by the Eysenck personality inventory (Eysenck & Eysenck, 1963) were, by themselves, significant predictors of recovery or persistence. However Guitar found that a combination of pretreatment factors (e.g., personality traits, percent stuttered syllables, attitudes) was useful in predicting the outcome of speech therapy. His study showed that a combination of measures on several pretreatment factors taken on 20 adults who stutter was highly correlated with posttreatment speech measures (percent stuttered syllables, percent change in frequency of stuttering). Guitar considered that, of the personality traits, only neuroticism was strongly related to outcome measures. However, in this study, neuroticism was also found to relate significantly to attitude measures, which may be the mediating variable. The important point is that Guitar showed that neither neuroticism nor extroversion, as measured by the Eysenck personality inventory, were predictors of recovery or persistence in stuttering.

9.3.3.3 Attitudes to Communication

It has been proposed that the onset of stuttering is a result of the belief that speech is difficult (Bloodstein, 1987; Brutten & Dunham, 1989). Diametrically opposed to this viewpoint are theories that have proposed that the negative beliefs that people who stutter have about speech are a product, rather than a cause, of their stuttering (Guitar, 1976; Peters & Guitar, 1991). In terms of clinical implications, Erikson (1969) indicated that changes in the self-concept of someone who stutters is an important aspect of success both during and following treatment. Taken together, these observations suggest that an instrument that measures attitude to communication of young children who stutter would be useful for early diagnosis and intervention (Yairi & Ambrose, 1992; Onslow, 1994).

Measuring attitude early in life is important for two further reasons: (1) attitudes have been shown (in particular circumstances) to be causally related to behavior, and (2) stuttering usually starts between 3 and 5 years of age (Yairi & Ambrose, 2005) and attitudes about many things can change in this age range (Perry, Bussey, & Fischer, 1980). Change of attitude is especially likely to occur when a child has a problem that affects overt behavior, such as stuttering. An observation that may be relevant to early recovery is that attitudes are more easily changed during or close to their formation (Niven, 1994).

Communication attitude tests have been developed for work with English children in a version called CAT (Brutten, 1985), and Dutch children, in a version called CAT-D (Vanryckeghem & Brutten, 1992). Both CAT (Boutsen & Brutten, 1989) and CAT-D (de Nil & Brutten, 1991) showed that children who stutter had poorer attitudes to their speech than did children who did not stutter. CAT is limited in that it requires a child to have the ability to read and understand the concepts covered by the test items and, consequently, it is not generally used with children younger than 7 years of age (Vanryckeghem, 1995).

Several studies on adults who stutter have produced evidence that their communication attitudes are more negative than those of adults who do not stutter (Brown & Hull, 1942; Erikson, 1969; Andrews & Cutler, 1974).

9.3.3.4   Bullying

Most bullying starts when children begin school. At this stage, their communication problem is already present. Thus, stuttering is unlikely to be the result of bullying, although the stuttering could be what attracts bullying. So, it could have an impact on the later course of stuttering. Two fundamental questions about the course are (1) whether speakers who stutter are bullied more than fluent children and, if so, (2) whether bullying exacerbates the problem of stuttering. There only appears to be evidence on the former.

Parker and Asher (1987) reviewed work on bullying and concluded that peer rejection and bullying can have severe and long-lasting effects. Low peer acceptance or peer rejection influences later personal adjustment and can result in problems, such as depression and early school dropout. Hodges and Parry (1996) identified three peer-related factors that increased the risk of a child being bullied. These were few friends, low-status friends, and rejection by peers.

The reason for thinking that social acceptance might affect children who stutter is that they are often reluctant or unable to participate verbally in school activities (or social groups, in general). In turn, this may lead to them being seen as shy or withdrawn and, possibly, because of these perceived characteristics, to having difficulties in peer relationships, making them the targets of bullying. There is some previous research investigating sociodynamic factors and their relationship to stuttering, and this is arranged for review under the techniques they have used (retrospective, sociometric). The majority of this research was carried out over 25 years ago and, although useful from a historical perspective, may or may not be relevant to present practice, thus, highlighting the need for work on this topic in current schools.

Studies using retrospective self-ratings by adults who stutter about bullying they experienced in childhood have been reported. Mooney and Smith (1995) used a questionnaire to obtain information from adults who stutter regarding their time at school. They found 11% of adults who stutter said they had been bullied at school and that this had had a negative effect on their fluency. Comparison of the 11% figure with estimates on how many fluent school children are bullied, on the other hand, indicates that children who stutter are no more at risk of being bullying than their peers. Haynie et al. (2001) reported that over 30% of schoolchildren stated that they had been bullied within the last school year; much higher than the 11% of adults who stutter who reported having been bullied in the Mooney and Smith (1995), study.

Hugh-Jones and Smith (1999) studied 276 adults who stuttered. Seventy-four percent of those who took part in the survey reported that they had been bullied during their time at school. Of the 205 respondents who indicated they were bullied at school, 6% reported that the bullying had a long-term effect on their fluency. However, the study lacked a control group who did not stutter to establish whether fluent speakers were bullied less often. The authors also noted other limitations in the project, common to all retrospective studies (e.g., respondents' recollections may be distorted and there is no way of validating the responses). The authors also mentioned that the sample may have been biased since the respondents were volunteers from the British Stammering Association, so the cohort may have been particularly aware of issues associated with disfluency.

Sociometric methods also have been used to assess the dynamics of groups containing children who stutter. Marge (1966) reported a study that used these procedures to assess intellectual and social status, physical ability, and speech skills of children who stuttered. One hundred and ninety-seven third grade (8–9 years) public school students were examined, of whom 36 had been diagnosed with moderate or severe stuttering. Sociograms were obtained on each of the four components that Moreno (1960) investigated. The study required children to rate other children in the class by responding to statements such as: "I would like to work with this child" or "I would like to play with this child." Marge reported that stuttering children held a lower popularity position than fluent ones. Sociograms also were obtained from teachers on the same four components for each child. The data indicated that, with regard to intellectual skills in school and social activity outside school, the child who stuttered held a significantly lower position than that of his or her fluent peers. In the other areas of playground activity and speech skills, no significant differences were found between the groups. The results from the teachers corroborated the findings of the peers. More recently Davis, Howell, and Cook

(2002) used a sociometric scale to assess the peer relationships of 16 children who stuttered and their 403 classmates. They reported that the children who stuttered were rejected significantly more often than their fluent peers, were categorized as less popular, and were less likely to be named as leaders. The children who stuttered were three times more likely to be identified as victims of bullying than their fluent peers and tended to have low social acceptance among peers.

A general problem to note that cuts across assessment methods used in studies of bullying is that the majority of research into the social status of children who stutter uses data from respondents who were in the educational system more than 20 years ago. This was either because the publications are dated or because adult respondents were used, and provided retrospective reports. It is possible that the attitude of children toward their peers with disabilities (including speech disabilities) has changed in the intervening period, although the work by Davis et al. (2002) suggest bullying of children who stutter is still a problem. A second general point is that researchers have advocated using different methodologies to address questions about bullying so that biases associated with each method can be reduced. Finally, it is possible to use other indices to obtain indications about peer relationships. Diaries are one source of information about the social world of a person who stutters.

9.3.3.5   Self-Esteem and Stigma

It is often considered that a person's perception of himself or herself can be affected by speech disorders and can result in low self-esteem (Bajina, 1995; Luper & Mulder, 1964; Shames & Rubin, 1986; Starkweather, Gottwald, & Halfond, 1990; Van Riper, 1982). There is also some evidence that this occurs in early life. Thus, Pukacova (1973) suggested that children who stutter are aware of their speech disorder as being an impediment in their life. She used a projective technique (incomplete sentences) to estimate the self-esteem of 74 children who stuttered; low self-esteem was reported for 94% of the sample.

In contrast, two more recent studies found no evidence for low self-esteem for school-age and adolescent stutterers (Blood, Blood, Tellis, & Gabel, 2003; Yovetich, Leschied, & Flicht, 2000). Yovetich et al. (2000) used Battle's (1992) culture-free, self-esteem inventory. They reported no differences between the mean scores for children who stuttered in comparison to normative data. Eighty percent of the participants (school-age children who stuttered) scored above the standardized mean on the total self-esteem score. Blood et al. (2003) used the Rosenberg (1965) self-esteem scale. They found that 85% of the adolescents who stuttered scored within one standard deviation of the mean.

Three studies have been conducted on the self-esteem of adults who stutter. Bardrick and Sheehan (1965) found a relationship between low self-esteem and high rates of stuttering in adults who stuttered. Bajina (1995) found a trend toward low self-esteem in 28 adults who stuttered. Shames and Rubin (1986) reported that the feelings most commonly expressed by people who stuttered were anxiety, helplessness, victimization, and low self-esteem.

Although there is little evidence from research to warrant clinical intervention to raise self-esteem for people who stutter (Yovetich et al., 2000), self-perception and self-concept have, nevertheless, been a focus for therapists in their treatment of stuttering (Sheehan, 1970; Silverman, 1996; Van Riper, 1982). Sheehan and Martyn (1966) proposed that once individuals have developed a concept of self as a person who stutters, spontaneous recovery becomes less likely. Beach and Fransella (1968), on the other hand, considered that people who stutter respond more positively to therapy if their speech disorder is integrated as part of their self-concept.

Furnham and Davis (2004) pointed out that although self-esteem appears to be easy to research, it is difficult to do well. They gave three reasons for this statement:

1. A satisfactory control group is needed with a large and representative sample of control speakers and speakers who stutter.
2. It is important to measure and analyze *all* the factors that relate to self-esteem. This is because stuttering may be a moderator or mediator variable rather than a variable that affects stuttering directly.
3. It is necessary to do longitudinal research to determine whether self-esteem is a cause or a consequence of stuttering.

9.4   SUMMARY

Older studies consistently reported lower IQs in children who stuttered. Later, studies have not confirmed this (although there is possible bias in the samples used in later studies). Temperament appears to differ between children who stutter and fluent controls, although its subcomponents do not distinguish between the two groups in any consistent way across the different studies. Temperament does not appear to correlate with stuttering. The same may apply to anxiety at these ages, although this is not known at present. State anxiety differs between speakers who persist in their stuttering at teenage years compared with fluent controls. When speakers recover, the state differences disappear. This suggests that treating the stutter is vital, as the associated psychological problems will then diminish. When speakers recover, their anxiety level converges on that of fluent speakers. Most studies in this age range have examined children who persist, and this has provided useful information about how the disorder develops. More needs to be known about how the problem resolves in recovered cases. Introversion and extroversion do not seem to be related to stuttering onset or later course.

Attitude to, and awareness of, stuttering, whether a child is bullied, and self-esteem are problems that arise after the child has experienced the disorder for a while and, at present, the role these variables could have on the subsequent pace at which the disorder progresses is not known. These issues merit future investigation. Based on the research findings reviewed, clinicians should not place exclusive emphasis on environmental factors that may impact stuttering. That said, they should be alert to potential problems caused by a poor home environment, the language community in the child's circle of family and friends, low IQ, and the child's temperament, particularly as regards dealing with communication demands.

9.5 EXERCISES

1. Trait anxiety is usually considered to be a fixed feature of an individual's personality. The work reviewed in this chapter shows that children who stutter do not differ from controls in state anxiety. Adults who stutter (persistent) show trait differences relative to controls. If trait anxiety is observed in adults who stutter, then it also should be present in children who stutter. What reasons can you give that suggest why trait anxiety is observed in adults who stutter but not in children who stutter?

2. Should treatments seek to change state or trait anxiety?

3. Three of the "big five" personality variables (openness, agreeableness, and conscientiousness) have not been examined in people who stutter. Choose one of these, examine the literature on that variable, and design a study to investigate the impact of that variable on stuttering.

4. Why is bullying unlikely to lead to stuttering onset?

Section III

Theoretical Frameworks on Developmental Stuttering

10 Models That Attribute Stuttering to Language Factors Alone

In this chapter, language theories are considered that account for the onset and course of stuttering. The chapter starts by examining a general model of language production that is the basis of the subsequent models for stuttering that are considered (Levelt, 1990). The covert repair hypothesis attempts to account mainly for persistent forms of stuttering. The vicious cycle account is a proposal mainly about what causes stuttering onset. Each of these theories is critically evaluated.

10.1 INTRODUCTION

So far in this book, evidence is kept separate from theory as far as possible (work that tests specific hypotheses derived from theories was presented in earlier chapters and this required some details of the corresponding theory). In Chapter 7, findings were presented that relate to language issues in stuttering. The current chapter is the first of three on theory, and concerns proposals that maintain that language factors are paramount for explaining stuttering. The other two theory chapters cover accounts that maintain that motor factors (Chapter 11), or language and motor factors in interaction with each other (Chapter 12) are needed to account for stuttering.

Research on stuttering in the language and motor areas has developed more or less independently, so it might be expected that theories in these domains would address different issues. However, there is a degree of agreement about issues concerning stuttering that are important for any type of theory to address and these cross language and motor areas to some extent (Bloodstein & Bernstein Ratner, 2007; Howell, 2004a, 2010; Max, Guenther, Gracco, Ghosh, & Wallace, 2004). It should be noted that setting up the requirements that should be met in this way imposes constraints on evaluating the adequacy of theory. An example, outside the area of stuttering, illustrates this. Generative linguistics is a field of enquiry started by Chomsky. He specified what issues are important for a model of language to explain. The requirement he imposed was that a language theory should be able to generate an infinite number of sentences using a limited set of grammatical rules and a finite set of terms. This might be one legitimate goal of language theory, but it is not necessarily the one that all language theorists subscribe to. Thus, setting up criteria can be restrictive with regards to what theories are acceptable; this applies to theories of stuttering just as much as it does to generative theories of language. On the other hand, the agreement about the issues that a theory of stuttering should address is useful, as theories based on language factors, motor factors, or language and motor factors in interaction can be compared in terms of how comprehensive they are. Although the degree of agreement about the issues for stuttering theory has been stressed, there, of course, are some issues that language theorists consider important, but motor theorists do not, and vice versa.

The issues that need to be explained by theories of stuttering were identified mainly from Bloodstein and Bernstein Ratner (2007), Howell (2004), Howell (2010), and Max et al. (2004). Warnings are made about being over-restrictive about each issue. Three language theories are then discussed: Levelt's general account of speech control, Kolk and Postma's covert repair hypothesis, and Bernstein Ratner and Wijnen's vicious cycle account. For each theory, an overview is given, and the theory is evaluated in terms of whether it addresses the issues about stuttering where appropriate (the latter is obviously not applicable to Levelt's theory, which is included because the other two theories are based on this to different extents).

10.2   ISSUES THAT SHOULD BE ADDRESSED BY A LANGUAGE, MOTOR, OR INTERACTIONAL THEORY OF STUTTERING

The fact that people agree that a particular question is important does not imply that there is agreement about how the question should be answered. There is also a tendency in Bloodstein and Bernstein Ratner's (2007) work to phrase the question in a way that only allows particular types of answers to the issues. I have tried to avoid this bias, and, in some cases, to mention the main alternative orientations about the issue. Illustrations of what I interpret as biases are given after the issues have been presented.

1. *Stuttering onset occurs in early childhood*: Authors who have addressed language (Bloodstein & Bernstein Ratner, 2007; Howell, 2010) and motor factors (Howell et al., 2004; Max et al., 2004) all agree that theories should include some account of stuttering onset in early childhood.

2. *Many children recover during childhood*: Only Bloodstein and Bernstein Ratner (2007) and Howell (2004a, 2010), who both work on language, explicitly mention this. Motor theorists have considered how motor factors might change over development (Smith & Goffman, 2004; Van Lieshout, Rutjens, & Spauwen, 2002) that is related to recovery. Although the latter article is not specifically about stuttering, it puts forward the idea of motor maturation that might explain the course of stuttering and why some speakers recover while others persist (Howell & Dworzynski, 2005).

3. *What are the features of persistent stuttering that make it different from early forms?* All the authors mentioned at the start of this section agree about the importance of this issue. Thus, Bloodstein and Bernstein Ratner

emphasized the importance of predicting the "distributional characteristics of stuttering: its pattern near onset *and as it develops*" (p. 40, emphasis added). For Howell, certain language structures that attract different symptoms of stuttering are useful as ways of monitoring the course of stuttering. This allows a language or a motor account of persistence. A motor account is possible because the language structures that are associated with stuttering may be a method that identifies parts of speech that are motorically difficult (Van Lieshout, Hulstijn, & Peters, 2004).

4. *What is the relationship between early childhood stuttering and normal nonfluent speech?* Bloodstein and Bernstein Ratner see distinctive differences between early childhood stuttering and normal nonfluency. Howell allows stuttering to morph into normal nonfluency or vice versa, which suggests the two forms are related. Again, this could be language- or motor-based. Van Lieshout et al.'s (2002) view of motor maturation also suggests a gradual change, in this case, exclusively motor.

5. *Why are certain treatments effective at reducing stuttering symptoms?* Bloodstein and Bernstein Ratner, Howell, and Max et al. (2004) all agree about the importance of this. Thus, for Bloodstein and Bernstein Ratner, it is subsumed under the need to understand the "conditions under which stuttering is exacerbated and ameliorated" (p. 40). Bloodstein and Bernstein Ratner's statement is open-ended and other work has been more precise in considering ameliorating conditions. Thus, Bernstein Ratner and Wijnen (2007) have proposed a language-based theory that specifically includes an explanation of altered feedback, which is one important condition known to ameliorate stuttering. This is discussed in the section on the vicious cycle account below. Howell and Max et al. also consider an account of why altered auditory feedback ameliorates stuttering as well as considering why Lidcombe treatment works. Lidcombe treatment is a learning-based approach and its efficacy has been assessed by Onslow and colleagues (Onslow, 1994; Onslow, Andrews, & Lincoln, 1994; Onslow, Packman, Stocker, & Siegel, 1997). This and other treatments for stuttering, where there is an evidence base, are considered in Chapter 13.

6. *What shapes how stuttering develops over the lifespan?* This is an issue only Bloodstein and Bernstein Ratner raise explicitly, as their handbook is a complete coverage of the field of stuttering. Howell has mainly addressed stuttering up to the teenage years, as forms in later life do not usually have well-documented etiologies of the respondents' stuttering in childhood, and documentation of cases who claim to have stuttered, but that they subsequently recovered, is particularly problematic. Bloodstein and Bernstein Ratner emphasized that learning experience and adaptation to the disorder will shape the speaker, at some age (they use the example of avoidance behaviors), which will happen some time after onset and will probably be progressive into adulthood. While not denying the importance of these aspects for a full understanding of stuttering,

they are probably best studied in established forms of stuttering in adulthood. Therefore, theories are only evaluated on the basis of the first five issues (and issue 5 only with respect to Bernstein Ratner and Wijnen's theory in this chapter).

Bloodstein and Bernstein Ratner have a tendency to add restrictive detail when they discuss an issue. This biases the answer to questions. Thus, statement one as phrased here is: "stuttering onset occurs in early childhood," but they add that this is not when the child first starts using language. The latter is an empirical point to examine, not one to demand that a theory should address. They also emphasize that the speech of children who go on to stutter is fluent and then becomes atypical. Although, in fact, there is no objective evidence for this; the data are based on retrospective reports by parents about their child's stuttering, and such information is not reliable.

Concerning issue 2, why many children recover during childhood, Bloodstein and Bernstein Ratner again include empirical evidence when they state that 80% recover. As seen in Chapter 1, arguably, this is an overestimate, and again reflects a tendency to impose what is an acceptable answer onto an issue. Two sets of authors can agree about the importance of an issue, but there can still be major differences between their positions. Bloodstein and Bernstein Ratner also say children's stuttering "stops spontaneously," as if a child used to stutter and suddenly stopped doing so. In contrast to this, Howell (2004; 2010) and Wingate (2002) maintain that children who recover gradually converge onto fluent speech; the children initially exhibited the same symptoms as fluent children although there were more of them and, as they recovered, they gradually reduced all disfluency symptoms in proportion over the period of recovery (Howell, 2007a). The views of Bloodstein and Bernstein Ratner compared to Howell (2004; in press) and Wingate (2002) are fundamentally different. Bloodstein and Bernstein Ratner's specification of the issue only allows one possibility to be correct (i.e., that stuttering stops spontaneously).

Concerning issue 4, Bloodstein and Bernstein Ratner phrased this in terms of how features of stuttering allow it to be *distinguished* from normal nonfluency. *Distinguished* is not theoretically neutral insofar as it presupposes there is a distinction. It is tied up with the idea that there are more, and less, typical types of stuttering (views about this were discussed in Chapter 3) that offer a better chance of distinguishing speaker groups. Howell (2010) phrased the relationship question less categorically: Why are there different groups of stuttering symptoms that are (1) nonproblematic and (2) problematic?

10.3   APPROACH TO THEORY ASSESSMENT

A language theory that applies to fluent speech may have an explicit position regarding some of the issues raised in section 10.2, but not those specifically concerning stuttering. Comprehensive theories of stuttering would ideally address all of these issues. As mentioned, the three language theories considered in this chapter are Levelt's (1989) blueprint, Kolk and Postma's (1997) covert repair hypothesis (CRH), and Bernstein Ratner and Wijnen's (2007) vicious circle account (VCA). The first of these theories is about fluent speech control, not stuttering. Levelt's model is included because its language feedback monitoring component is included in the two other language-based theories of stuttering in some form. The approach taken is to present Levelt's theory, identify and evaluate the position the theory takes on certain of the issues, and draw some conclusions about the adequacy of the theory as an account of fluent speech. The evaluation of the other two accounts is similar except that the theories are evaluated with respect to the position they take on stuttering issues.

10.4 LEVELT'S BLUEPRINT

10.4.1 OUTLINE OF LEVELT'S MODEL

The Levelt (1989) model is a psycholinguistic theory that continues to receive a lot of attention from many authors. *Note*: The theory is very comprehensive and the only parts of it that are considered here are those that have been incorporated into theories of stuttering.

Figure 10.1 gives a schematic representation of Levelt's model. Production (left) and perception (right) are both involved in speech control. Production starts (top left of the diagram) at conceptualization. The conceptualizer sends information to the formulation stage. Language formulation takes place in a hierarchy of linguistic processing steps, the last of which is to generate a phoneme string. This is input to the speech–motor system, after which speech is output.

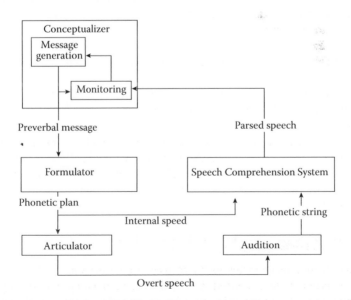

FIGURE 10.1 Levelt's blueprint of speech production and comprehension.

Errors can occur at any point in the language formulation hierarchy. An error occurs in an utterance when at least one phone is wrong relative to the one intended, according to Howell (2004a), thus, saying "hissed" instead of "missed" would have an error in initial position. Levelt's use of the term *error* is consistent with this definition. With respect to the model, the first step that allows errors to be detected occurs because speech production sends information to the perceptual system over two routes (the external and internal loops). The external loop operates when speech is articulated and the perception system can recover this (i.e., the speaker listens to his or her voice). The external loop operates similarly to the processes envisaged in early feedback accounts of speech control that were developed to account for auditory perturbation (see Chapter 8, section 8.2.1). Information about language formulation is also sent directly to the perception system without it being output (i.e., before it is spoken) and this is the internal loop. The speech perception system decodes these two sources of information about what language was formulated. This information is then sent back to a monitor in the conceptualizer. The monitor has a record of what was intended and now knows what was formulated from the information sent via perception (referred to as feedback). Thus, the intended message can be compared with that which perception indicated was actually formulated. If the two correspond, speech was produced as required and output can continue. If there is a discrepancy, an error has occurred, speech is interrupted and the intended message is reinitiated.

If the error was detected by perceptual processing of speech output (external loop), there was an overt error that the monitor detected and then corrected. Information that was sent directly from the formulator (internal loop) can be processed before speech is output. In this case, the correction can occur before the speech that is in error is produced and there is no overt indication of the error. There will be some hesitancy and other features in speech output (details given below) that show an internal processing error occurred, although there is no explicit indication of exactly what error occurred. The hesitancy and other events are taken as signs of covert error repair processes.

An example of an overt speech error and repair that provides support for the *external* loop is "to the left of, no, to the right of the curtain." The speaker has produced the word "left" (the reparandum), which is then substituted by the correct word "right" (called the alteration). The Levelt (1983) account assumes that the speaker heard the error, interrupted speech (signified by the comma), and repeated some components that are not essential ("to the," called a *retrace*) before the correction was made.

As mentioned, Levelt interpreted situations where there were interruptions and whole-word repetitions as evidence for the internal loop. An example, such as "I saw the, the school," has an interruption (indicated by the comma) and a whole-word repetition ("the" is repeated), but no error. This construction could have arisen because the speaker was going to say "house" instead of "school," but corrected him or herself. The error itself never surfaced because it was detected over the internal loop and speech was interrupted before articulation occurred. According to this interpretation, although there is no overt error, there are signs that an error occurred, in the form of hesitation and the retrace, which led to whole-word repetition in this case (symptoms also seen in stuttering).

Levelt did not work further on covert repairs because the source of the error was not known. However, they are important for current concerns as they are the basis for the covert repair account of stuttering discussed later. Levelt proposed a well formedness rule for overt repairs that says repair structures depend on whether parts of speech can be syntactically coordinated. Thus, for example, the repair: "Did you go right, uh go left?" is associated with the syntactically correct coordinated form: "Did you go right and go left?" On the other hand, "Did you go right, uh you go left?" has an incorrect form: "Did you go right and you go left?" Errors of the former, but not of the latter, type were observed in Levelt's corpus of overt errors, which suggests that speakers are constrained by syntax in the way they can make repairs.

Although the Levelt model was established in the late 1980s, updated versions still rely on the two monitoring routes (Roelofs, 2004). As stated earlier, the internal and external loops also are referred to in other literature as feedback routes. It is noteworthy that the loops go from auditory output, or language formulation, right back to the first step in message conceptualization. The feedback provides the latter with a complete analysis of language output. It is worth repeating that the work on errors and their repair that are focused on here is only a small part of Levelt's work and he did not apply it to stuttering.

10.4.2 Assessment of Levelt's Theory

10.4.2.1 Do Fluency Problems Arise Because an Error Is Generated During Language Processing?

According to Levelt, errors occur during speech production and the language system needs a way of dealing with them. The mechanism Levelt proposed was a perceptual monitor. Thus, errors in formulation and the monitoring mechanism used for their correction are inherently linked. The adequacy of these aspects of the model are assessed in detail as they are crucial features for this and the other two models in this chapter; the latter two models also invoke a monitoring mechanism.

10.4.2.1.1   Is Information Supplied by the Production System to the Speech Perception System Sufficient to Allow a Speaker to Detect an Error?

Only around half of overt errors are repaired, according to Nooteboom (2005). In fact, the 50% estimate is probably higher than that which occurs in normal listening conditions, as these data may reflect a collector's bias, given that these estimates were derived from self-reports (Cutler, 1982). Based on low correction rates, it would appear that production either does not transmit information about all errors or that they are not detected or acted on by subsequent processes. Levelt's (1989) answer was that the internal monitor is not always "on duty." This is an ad hoc solution to this problem as it does not explain why it does not operate all the time, which would seem desirable (see also Wingate, 2002, p. 175, for a critique of this assumption).

Errors *are* produced that are not repaired (even when the speaker can detect them). Thus, the output form of children's speech is simpler than that of adults because it is affected by the phonological processes, discussed in Chapter 7, of consonant cluster reduction, homogenization of consonants with respect to place, manner and voicing, etc. These processes would lead children to produce a large number of words that would be characterized as production errors that, perceptually, they are able to detect (Menyuk & Anderson, 1969). It would not make sense for young children to monitor and correct the errors in these productions because children would continue to make the same errors if they are due to cognitive or motor control limitations. This suggests that during phonological development, a child can attempt speech forms and ignore errors that are made. Put another way, there are grounds for supposing that children should suppress perceptual error detection and correction.

10.4.2.1.2   If There Are Errors, Could the Perception System Detect Them So That They Are a Reliable Source on Which the Monitoring System Would Work?

Levelt's monitoring loops use the existing perceptual system. However, the perceptual system makes errors, making it an unreliable source of feedback to the monitor. In addition to speech errors, sometimes listeners misperceive, a phenomenon called *slips of the ear* (Bond, 1999). The perceptual mechanism is reasoned to operate equivalently when used for production or perception (Postma, 2000). Thus, perceptual errors when a speaker processes his or her own voice would signal to the monitor that a correction is required in the same way as a production error, although no production error occurred. Any response the monitor makes on the basis of this incorrect information would create, rather than remove, an error in production (i.e., false alarms that probably surface as repetitions). Thus, the errors made in perception suggest it is *not* a suitable guide for production.

There is other evidence that different speaker groups either cannot or do not use input over the external loop, and this was discussed fully in Chapter 8, section 8.2.5. One of these pieces of evidence is that, although adventitiously deafened speakers could not use the external loop, they do not lose the ability to speak (Borden, 1979). An alternative possibility, rather than losing the ability to control speech, is that loss of the external loop would lead to speech that contains many errors, as the speaker has no way of monitoring whether output is correct or not. However, there is no empirical evidence that supports the view that postlingually deafened speakers produce more errors than hearing controls. On the other hand, perceptual errors, such as those involving judgments of place of articulation, are ubiquitous in profound hearing loss and would occur when listening to self-produced speech. The listening errors would be expected to trigger many false alarms, which would surface as repairs to correct utterances. As these participants do not have high rates of speech errors, the perceptual system does not appear to be implicated in speech control.

10.4.2.1.3   Can the Perceptual System Recover Sufficient Information From the External Loop to Determine Whether an Overt Error Has Occurred?

As mentioned briefly in Chapter 8, section 8.2.5, it is not clear that speakers can recover sufficient sound information from speech output to determine whether a speech error has occurred. The sound of the voice is degraded through internal sources of noise generated during the articulatory processes. The main source of this internal noise is sound generated because bones around the head and chest vibrate during articulation. The bone-conducted sound has a heavily attenuated formant structure that reduces its intelligibility (Howell & Powell, 1984). The formants are the resonant frequencies of the vocal tract and their values depend on where the articulators are positioned. People listening to speech use the formants to infer what sound was articulated. This aspect of speech perception would not be possible if the formant structure is unavailable in the bone-conducted sound. The bone-conducted sound would, instead, mask the air-conducted sound that occurs as speech, making it hard to use for perception of one's own speech, by, for instance, making the formant information harder to perceive. The degraded bone-conducted sound is as loud as the air-conducted sound (von Bekesy, 1960, estimated that bone-conducted sound is at approximately the same level as sound transmitted through air). Thus, there is plenty of energy present to at least partially mask the formants. As said, this is the information that carries details about where the articulators were positioned that indicates what sound was said. These influences lead to the external loop having degraded information about a speaker's speech output, so it would not be able to supply reliable information for the monitor to determine whether an error had been made.

10.4.2.1.4   Examination of the Monitoring Process

So far, it has been argued that the production and perception systems could not provide accurate information to the monitor. Howell (2010) has offered an analysis that maintains that, even if these problems could be circumvented and reliable perceptual information could be extracted from sounds during speech, the way the proposed dual-processing loops would operate poses insurmountable problems for a monitor to deal with. The essence of Howell's argument is that the form of representation available over the internal loop (neural before it has undergone motor processing) and external loop (neural recovered from the motor output representation) have different forms and these representations are available at different times; that from the internal loop is available before that from the external loop. The processing the monitor would need to perform to integrate the two different types of neural information and correct for differences when they are available, is complex and rules out monitoring as a viable concept for speech control. Howell (2004a, 2010) used these arguments as grounds for developing a production theory that accounts for stuttering events that does not incorporate a perceptual monitor, and this is discussed in Chapter 12.

In summary, (1) speakers can tolerate errors they produce, (2) it is not possible to recover accurate information about production by the perception mechanism, and (3) supplying information about articulation from the two proposed loops to the monitor poses a processing task that is ruled out as a candidate for speech control.

10.4.2.1.5 What Is the Fault That Leads to Speech Being Disfluent?

Levelt (1989) gave examples of errors at all points in language formulation (e.g., semantic, syntactic, lexical, and phonological). He considered that these provided evidence of errors that occurred at the respective point in the language formulation hierarchy. The other theories considered below give specific details on which of these processing levels leads to stuttering (CRH at the phonological level and VCA at the syntactic level).

10.4.3 SUMMARY

The assessment of the arguments for a perceptual monitor in the form Levelt describes was critically examined above and rejected on several grounds. If readers submit to this analysis, some other basis for problems in speech control (in fluent speakers and speakers who stutter) needs to be found (the motor and language-motor interaction theory chapters offer other alternatives). The remaining theories considered in this chapter assume that language errors occur, and propose a language monitor to deal with them.

10.5   COVERT REPAIR HYPOTHESIS (CRH)

10.5.1 OVERVIEW AND ASSESSMENT OF THE COVERT REPAIR HYPOTHESIS

Kolk and Postma (1997) proposed a language-based theory called CRH that addresses stuttering. CRH draws its inspiration from Levelt's (1989) hierarchical model of language processing, discussed in the previous section. Kolk and Postma noted that hesitations and whole-word repetitions are common in stuttered speech and also in covert repairs. A covert repair, such as "I hit the, the ball," shows hesitation (signified by the comma) and word repetition ("the" is repeated). Like Levelt, they considered that these were parts of covert repair processes that signified an underlying error detected over the internal loop (e.g., the speaker might have started to say "I hit the bat" and corrected "bat" for "ball" using the internal loop, so no speech was output). If this interpretation applies to similar events that occur in stuttering, it would suggest that word repetition and interruption are the result of covert repairs and would indicate, in turn, that people who stutter are prone to making a lot of errors in language formulation. For the later argument, it is important to note that interruptions (or, to use a neutral term, hesitations) and whole-word repetitions do not appear on the error word per se, but on a word prior to the one which would have been in error if it had been uttered. The covert repair process, hesitation, and whole-word repetition occur on simple words (in the example, the function word "the") as is commonly found.

Kolk and Postma argued that speakers who stutter have high rates of covert repairs of errors relative to fluent speakers because they have slow phonological processing. Their CRH model uses Dell's spreading activation account to illustrate how slow processing leads to word errors. When a speaker makes a lexical selection, several candidate words and other phonologically related words are activated. Activation for all words increases over time, and the activation level for the intended word is greatest when there is sufficient time to reach full activation (at point S in Figure 10.2). There are small-scale random fluctuations, which arise from processing noise in the part up to S. Other words than that intended will have lower activation than this and, consequently, will not be selected for output. When there is time pressure, because the experimenter stresses fast responding or because a speaker has a slow phonological system, decisions are made some time before the word is fully activated (at point S– in Figure 10.2). In this early phase of activation, the word activation patterns are similar. Because of the random noise, on some occasions an intruder word has higher activation than the intended word, as shown at several points prior to S–. If selection was made at any of these points, the wrong word would be activated and produced, and this word would be heard as an error. CRH includes Levelt's concept of an internal monitoring process that allows production of the word to be halted before it was uttered. Pauses and whole-word repetitions (features of covert repairs, but not errors in themselves) are a result of the repair processes and signify that a selection error occurred. Speakers who stutter are more often under time pressure to speak than fluent speakers because of their slow phonological systems (see Chapter 7, section 7.6.3). So, they frequently experience situations where the target word has lower activation than an intruder word. Consequently, they make a lot of covert repairs. This accounts for frequent use of pauses and word repetitions. Postma and Kolk (1993) also offered explanations for how the other stuttering symptoms could arise (as described briefly in Chapter 3).

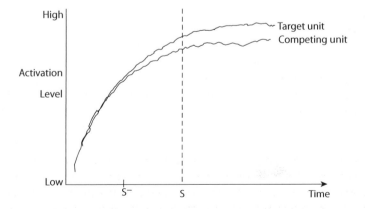

FIGURE 10.2   Activation versus time for target, and competing, word candidates. Two selection points are shown: normal (*S*) and early (*S*–).

Levelt's well formedness rule does not seem to apply to covert repairs. For example, the sentence, "I took the bag," could result in the covert repair, "I took the, the bag," which is not allowed by the rule ("I took and the bag" is an incorrect syntactic form). The example shows that pauses and word repetitions occur at the start of nonsyntactic units. The rule may need to be rejected. although it does seem to describe overt repairs correctly. Another way out of this dilemma is to require that the rule should only apply to overt repairs. This would imply that symptoms, such as whole-word repetitions and pauses are not related to overt repairs (otherwise, they would obey the rule). However, the assumption in the previous sentence appears to undermine the CRH notion that stutters are all a result of underlying phonological processing faults whether they are realized overtly or covertly. Other ways of addressing this problem need to be explored (see section 10.8, Exercise no. 3).

10.5.2   ASSESSMENT OF THE COVERT REPAIR HYPOTHESIS

10.5.2.1   Do Fluency Problems Arise Because an Error Is Generated During Language Processing?

According to CRH, stuttering arises because of an underlying error in phonological processes. According to the definition of error given previously, covert repairs do not contain an error. Levelt (1989) partly acknowledges this for disfluent symptoms seen in covert repairs insofar as he disregards covert repairs in his extended discussion of putative errors in different types of repair. Other authors have noted that errors (consistent with the earlier definition) are infrequent (Garnham, Shillcock, Brown, Mill, & Cutler, 1981) and often go unrepaired (Hartsuiker, Pickering, & de Jong, 2005).

As was seen when Levelt's theory was assessed, the notion that speakers make errors that are corrected by a perceptual monitor has several problems. The CRH suffers from the same problems as does Levelt's model because it also invokes the idea that errors are made and that they are repaired by the internal monitoring process.

10.5.2.2   What Is the Fault That Leads to Speech Being Stuttered?

It could be argued that the CRH should be applied to adult speech and has little to say about the onset or course of stuttering in earlier development. However, Conture and his students have attempted to extend the CRH to developmental stuttering. Their approach has been to identify subgroups of children who stutter who do, and do not, have phonological disorders. The idea behind using groups of children who differ in the number of phonological errors they produce was that children with numerous phonological errors might be more disfluent than those with fewer errors because the presence of those errors might create more opportunities for error detection and self repair. In other words, there should be a lot of covert repairing in these children. Several studies have attempted to determine whether children who stutter have disordered phonology, as opposed to delayed phonological development (these terms were discussed in Chapter 7).

Wolk, Edwards, and Conture (1993) examined the relationship between stuttering and phonology in 21 boys who ranged in age range from 4;2 to 5;11. The children were divided into three groups with seven per group who had (1) stuttering with normal phonology (S + NP), (2) stuttering with disordered phonology (S + DP), and (3) normal fluency with disordered phonology (NF + DP). A conversational speech sample of 300 words was elicited from each child while interacting with his mother in a clinical setting. This was used to obtain an SSI score that is an early version of SSI-3 (Riley, 1980), and to determine the frequency and types of stutters. A picture-naming task also was administered to examine the child's production of English consonants in initial, medial, and final word positions and the presence of phonological processes. Any instances of stuttering that occurred during the picture-naming task were noted as well.

The researchers determined whether stuttering behavior differed in children with normal phonology (Group 1) from that of those with disordered phonology (Group 2). No statistically significant differences were found between the S + DP and S + NP groups in terms of the frequency of stuttering during the conversational speech task or the picture-naming task and total scores on the SSI for those two groups were not significantly different.

The authors also examined whether phonological disorders differed in children who stuttered (Group 2) from those with normal fluency (Group 3). With respect to phonological behavior, the S + DP and NF + DP groups did not differ significantly in the percentage of consonants correct (Shriberg & Kwiatkowski, 1982) on the picture-naming task, and both groups fell into the moderate to severe range of phonological disorder.

These types of phonological processes produced in the speech task were also examined, and the 15 most common processes the children produced were identified. Statistical analyses indicated that the groups did not differ significantly in frequency of occurrence for any of these processes. For both groups, cluster reduction was the most common process. Other processes frequently produced by both groups included vocalization, gliding of liquids, and weak syllable deletion (all of these processes, as well as cluster reduction, appear in Chapter 7, Appendix, Table A.1). Thus, in terms of phonological patterns and behaviors, children who stuttered did not appear to differ from their peers with normal fluency in terms of the phonological processes they used and the types of processes were typical.

For each group, correlation coefficients were calculated between the number of phonological processes (e.g., gliding, vocalization) and the number of within-word disfluencies that occurred during the speech sample. None of the correlations were significant.

The children who stuttered and had a phonological disorder produced a greater percentage of sound prolongations during conversation than those children who stuttered but had no phonological disorder. Although the groups did not show a statistically significant difference on the number of iterations per sound or syllable repetition, the S + NP group produced a significantly greater number of iterations per whole-word repetition than the S + DP group.

The study did not support the hypothesis that children who stutter and have a phonological disorder stutter more frequently than those who stutter but have normal phonology although some differences were found with respect to details of certain symptoms (prolongations and whole-word repetitions).

Yaruss and Conture (1996) tested for a link between difficulty in phonological encoding and stuttering, also using children with and without a phonological disorder. They predicted that the children who stuttered and had a phonological disorder would stutter more frequently than children who stuttered but who had normal phonology. Yaruss and Conture assessed the prediction using two groups of children who stuttered (nine boys in each group, both with mean ages of 5;0). A 30-minute spontaneous conversation between the child and his mother was obtained in a clinic. Seventy-five consecutive utterances from the middle portion of each recording were analyzed for fluency characteristics (e.g., sound–syllable repetitions, sound prolongations, pauses within words) and phonological errors. Nippold (2002) noted that the findings were inconsistent with Wolk et al.'s (1993) earlier report, where there was a significant difference in frequency of prolongations between children who stuttered with disordered phonology and children who stuttered with normal phonology.

Yaruss, LaSalle, and Conture (1998) reviewed the diagnostic data of 99 children aged between 2 and 6 years old (mean age = 4;7). All children had been evaluated at a university speech and language clinic to determine the presence of stuttering and any other speech or language disorders. A phonological disorder was identified if two or more atypical or age-inappropriate processes occurred during a picture-naming task or when a child was talking spontaneously with his or her parent. Yaruss et al. divided the children into two groups to examine whether there was a relationship between stuttering and phonology. The two groups were (1) those who were thought to have a phonological disorder ($n = 37$), and (2) those who were thought to have normal phonological development ($n = 62$). The groups were then compared on measures of stuttering severity, including the stuttering severity instrument (SSI) (Riley, 1980) and the Iowa Scale for Measuring the Severity of Stuttering (Johnson, Darley, & Spriestersbach, 1963). Differences between groups were not significant, indicating that children with phonological disorders did not necessarily stutter more severely than those with normal phonological development.

The remaining two studies looked at only one of the groups of children who stuttered. Logan and Conture (1997) hypothesized that if stuttering is related to impaired phonological encoding, as argued by the CRH, then the frequency and duration of stuttering should increase during the production of words characterized by greater syllabic complexity (e.g., when the syllable contained consonant clusters or multiple phonemes) when a child was engaged in conversational speech. They examined the relationship between stuttering and complexity of syllable structure in a group of 14 boys (mean age, 4;4) who stuttered but who otherwise had normal speech and language development. A conversational speech sample of at least 100 utterances was elicited from each child in interaction with his mother in a clinic. The samples were analyzed for stuttering in relation to syllabic complexity. Correlation coefficients were calculated between syllabic complexity measures (number of filled onsets, filled codas, consonants, and consonant clusters) and measures of stuttering frequency (number of syllables stuttered), and duration (length of stutters in seconds). None of the coefficients were statistically significant. Hence, this study also failed to provide evidence to support the CRH in young children as no interaction was found between stuttering and phonology.

Melnick and Conture (2000) asked whether children who stuttered and had phonological disorder would produce a greater number of phonological process errors, a subset of those in the Appendix, Table A.2, of Chapter 7, during stuttered compared to nonstuttered utterances, particularly when the utterances were long and grammatically complex. Their prediction, based on the CRH, was that "if the frequency of stuttering is greater for longer and more complex utterances, then the reason for this increase may be a greater number of phonological errors, errors that are detected, repaired, and, hence, stuttered on." Melnick and Conture worked with 10 boys who stuttered with a mean age of 4;3. A picture-naming task was administered to each child. This allowed all possible phonological processes the child used to be identified. A conversational speech sample consisting of at least 300 words was also obtained from the child when in interaction with the parent. This was used to obtain 25 stuttered and 25 nonstuttered utterances for each child. These were analyzed for instances of the phonological processes observed in the picture-naming task. The data were pooled over all 10 children to yield 250 stuttered and 250 nonstuttered utterances. A multiple regression analysis was performed to determine if the frequency of phonological processes could be predicted by utterance length (number of syllables), grammatical complexity (number of clauses), and fluency status (stuttered or nonstuttered). The results indicated that none of the factors was a significant predictor of phonological processes in conversational speech. As Nippold (2002, p. 103) stated, "Words produced with phonological processes were not necessarily accompanied by greater amounts of stuttering, and phonological process errors were not necessarily more common in longer and more complex utterances." This study, like the rest of the series, also failed to support the CRH and an interaction between stuttering and phonology except for the features of stuttering symptoms noted in Wolk et al. (1993).

10.5.3 EVALUATION OF THE STUTTERING ISSUES BY THE COVERT REPAIR HYPOTHESIS

1. *Stuttering onset occurs in early childhood*: Kolk and Postma (1997) did not address stuttering in early development themselves, although as seen, this issue was taken up by Conture and his students. Nippold's (2002) review of the evidence that Conture has published that looked for an association between stuttering and phonological disorder showed that there was little support for this hypothesis. Her overall conclusion was that solid evidence for an interaction between phonology and stuttering

remained elusive. Bernstein Ratner and Wijnen (2007) also shared the view that the evidence does not support a link between phonological problems and stuttering. Their main argument was that children who will go on to stutter, appear to be able to use phonology appropriately and only start to stutter later, at what they maintain is the age at which syntactic, rather than phonological, processing starts. The argument that phonological development must be age-appropriate at a young age does not necessarily imply that there is a syntactic processing problem, which is Bernstein Ratner and Wijnen's position (the evidence for a link between stuttering and syntax was discussed in Chapter 7) and does not rule out delayed (but normal) phonological development as a factor.

2. *Many children recover during childhood*: Again, Kolk and Postma do not have anything explicit to say about this point. It might be assumed that since the underlying problem is phonological and phonological disorders can be treated, that this might happen spontaneously, which could lead to recovery. However, the work by Conture that sought to apply the CRH to developmental stuttering failed to find any evidence for a link between phonology and stuttering for children up to the teenage years, so the CRH appears to have little applicability to recovery

3. *What are the features of persistent stuttering that make it different from early forms*? As CRH is not a model of stuttering development, it does not say anything about why some children persist. Two possibilities that would be permitted by CRH are (1) that children have a phonological deficit that might persist (although, as noted, Bernstein Ratner and Wijnen's questioning why this did not show up in early language development would need addressing; this applies to the following possibility, too); (2) Paden (in Yairi & Ambrose, 2005) argues for a slight phonological delay in children who stutter. She stresses, however, that the role of this as a risk factor for persistence should not be overemphasized (see Chapter 7). Again, any explanation based on CRH for a link between phonology and the persistent course has to be qualified based on Conture and his students' work.

4. *What is the relationship between early childhood stuttering and normal nonfluent speech?* CRH takes an explicit position on the relationship of normal nonfluency to stuttering. Repairs are features of speech exhibited by normally fluent speakers (Levelt's original work was based on fluent speakers' speech). Postma and Kolk (1993) showed how all stuttering symptoms also were related to repair structures. As both normally fluent and stuttered speech are, according to this view, directly related to repairs, and repairs are features of fluent speech, there is continuity between the disfluencies in the speech of fluent speakers and speakers who stutter.

According to CRH: (1) errors at the phoneme level result in part-word repetitions or sound prolongations, while (2) lexical errors lead to single-syllable word repetitions. With respect to (2), it was seen, when discussing the application of the well-formedness rule to covert repairs, how word repetition could arise. A problem pointed out was that these events are not predicted by the well-formedness rule. If the rule is correct and applicable to all types of underlying error, then some explanation of word repetition other than the fact that they reflect lexical errors would be needed for whole-word repetitions.

CRH predicts that the phonological processing systems of people who stutter malfunction more often than that of fluent speakers. The symptoms are the same, speakers who stutter just produce more of them (Kolk & Postma, 1997). This predicts that any factor that influences the occurrence of processing errors in fluent speakers also should operate in people who stutter. As Hartsuiker, Kolk, and Lickley (2001) put it, there should be "a parallel between linguistic factors that determine speech errors and factors that determine stuttering" (p. 65). There is support for this prediction for some factors that affect speech errors. Thus, the speech errors of normal speakers tend to be associated with words that are long (Fromkin, 1971) and lower in frequency (Dell, 1990; Dell & Reich, 1981; Stemberger, 1984), and this is also true of words that are stuttered by adults (Wingate, 1988).

However, other factors do not support the prediction that the phonological processing systems of people who stutter malfunctions more often than that of fluent speakers. Thus, speech error research with fluent speakers has revealed that production accuracy is susceptible to influences of phonological neighborhood density (Vitevitch, 1997), whereas Anderson (2007) reported that neighborhood density did not have the same effect in people who stutter. Anderson (2007) also pointed out that the study by Arnold, Conture, and Ohde (2005) on neighborhood density (discussed in Chapter 7) is not consistent with what has been reported with fluent speech (which goes against the CRH assumption that the symptoms of fluent speakers and speakers who stutter are qualitatively similar). Anderson noted that, although the authors indicated that their findings were consistent with those of Newman and German (2002), who reported that school-age children had more difficulty naming words with high neighborhood density than those with low neighborhood density, their findings contradicted those of most other studies in which low density words were reportedly more difficult for children and adults to accurately and rapidly retrieve from the lexicon than high density words (e.g., German & Newman, 2004; Vitevitch, 1997, 2002). This suggests that children who stutter may respond differently to fluent speakers and is against the CRH prediction.

Some authors have noted that the features of repair processes are rare in young children who stutter (Yairi & Ambrose, 2005), and others have pointed out that there are differences between the properties of repairs and stutters (Wingate, 2002). The second of these observations questions the supposed qualitative similarity between repairs in fluent speakers and stuttering. Yairi and Ambrose (2005, p. 68) noted that features of repair, such as interjections and phrase repetitions are rare in early developmental stuttering. Wingate (2002, p. 176) observed that there are several important descriptive differences between stutters and the supposed "repair" of ordinary errors that distinguish between the two phenomena. The difference he emphasized was that the error persists in stuttered speech (there is no correction), whereas this is not the case for repairs made by fluent speakers.

10.5.4 SUMMARY

The CRH relies on a Levelt-style monitoring process, which was critiqued in an earlier in section 10.4.2. A further feature of CRH is the assumption that stuttering is linked to phonological errors. The work of Conture and his students that has tested this hypothesis has failed to find support. CRH does not have anything to say about four of the five issues about stuttering (issues 1–3 and 5). Thus, at best it would have limited scope with respect to this disorder.

10.6 THE VICIOUS CYCLE ACCOUNT

10.6.1 OVERVIEW AND ASSESSMENT OF THE VICIOUS CYCLE ACCOUNT

Bernstein Ratner and Wijnen (2007) hypothesize that "stuttering [is] connected to a maladaptive setting of the monitoring parameters," in particular, children who stutter invest too much time in monitoring their own speech. They also argue that stuttering may occur in "children with weak language and relatively strong self-monitoring, coupled with intolerance for less-than-perfect output" (p. 88). According to the authors, the weak language feature around onset is a syntactic problem (Bernstein Ratner, 1997). Bernstein Ratner and Wijnen (2007) also seem to allow a weak phonological system to occur at later stages in the development of stuttering.

10.6.1.1 Role of the Monitor in Vicious Cycle Account

Bernstein Ratner and Wijnen (2007) hypothesize that monitoring works differently in children who stutter. They suggest that children who stutter have hyperactive monitors that make them sensitive to errors. The specific hypothesis offered is that "stuttering [is] connected to a maladaptive setting of the monitoring parameters."

10.6.1.2 Stuttering as a Syntactic Problem

Bernstein Ratner has argued that the weakness in the language system at the time stuttering starts lies is in syntactic processing (Bernstein Ratner, 1997; Bloodstein & Bernstein Ratner, 2007). Her main evidence is that stuttering does not occur when children produce one-word utterances, but does so when multiword utterances occur that she equates with when a child begins to use syntax (the multiword stage is usually regarded as the stage at which a child starts to produce grammatical utterances). At the multiword stage, function words appear (prior to this, only content words were used).

10.6.2   Assessment of the Vicious Cycle Account

The details of the monitor and the putative language processing problem are considered in turn.

10.6.2.1   Do Fluency Problems Arise Because an Error Is Generated During Language Processing?

Bernstein Ratner and Wijnen (2007) use evidence from delayed auditory feedback (DAF) to support their ideas about the link between monitoring and stuttering. Recall that under DAF, speakers hear their speech shortly after they produce it, and this causes speech control to suffer dramatically. As was seen in Chapter 8, a possible explanation is that the speaker hears his or her speech and this is sent as feedback to the linguistic system where a check is made that the correct sound was uttered (related to what happens with information sent over Levelt's external loop). When a sound is delayed, the language system receives erroneous feedback and acts to correct this, producing an error. However, the view that DAF provides evidence for linguistic monitoring is flawed as discussed in section 8.2.5 (work of Borden (1979) and others).

Bernstein Ratner and Wijnen's argument that children who stutter invest too much time in monitoring is based on a single DAF study (Bernstein Ratner, 1998). An additional problem is that it is not obvious how differences in the amount of time spent monitoring by children who stutter or who are fluent could be assessed. Comparing the size of DAF effects between children who stutter could be misleading. Thus, the effects of DAF have been interpreted in ways that do not require a monitor and would have no relation to different monitoring ability (see Chapter 11). There is literature on different responsiveness of fluent speakers to DAF that suggests differences are strategically related to control of voice level, not to sensitivity to monitoring. This work suggests that the speakers who are most susceptible speak louder than those who are less susceptible (Howell & Archer, 1984).

Although DAF does not provide support for the hypothesis they offer, it might still be tenable if the theory can address the problems associated with child speech and the monitor noted in connection with Levelt's model. The principal problem is that a child's output forms are not the same as the canonical forms that they perceive correctly, due to phonological processes in development. So, what a child hears would often have an error that they can perceive. However, as a child at a particular age has his or her phonological system fixed at a particular level of development, the error would be repeated if they monitored and acted on what they heard, and this process would be repeated indefinitely.

Like Levelt, Bernstein Ratner and Wijnen consider that the motor processes passively translate linguistic input to speech output when they say about stuttering: "What we believe to be a problem in language encoding can lead to apparent motor execution difficulties." In contrast, evidence presented in chapter 8 shows that some problems experienced by people who stutter arise in the motor processes (e.g., coordination between articulators). Thus, the assumptions that invoke monitoring and consider that the motor system responds passively to whatever input it receives are questionable. A model that proposed language and motor interactions, which gets around this problem, is discussed in Chapter 12. This gives the motor system, as well as the language system, an active role in stuttering.

10.6.2.2   What Is the Fault That Leads to Speech Being Disfluent?

Bernstein Ratner and Wijnen's reason for including syntactic and phonological levels is in the pattern of symptoms seen in stuttered speech. Wijnen (2006) argued that whole-word disfluencies reflect syntactic planning, while within-word disfluencies reflect phonological encoding. The quotation from page 88 given in section 10.6.1 may be interpreted as suggesting that there is a shift to phonological processing late in development, confirming the view that children who stutter have weak phonological planning.

With respect to whether stuttering starts at the age at which a child starts to use syntax, a logical flaw in Bernstein Ratner's (1997) coincidence argument is that because things occur at the same time (here stuttering and use of function words), they are not necessarily causally related. Also, the supposition that stuttering starts when speakers first use function words is contradicted by empirical findings that were discussed in Chapter 7. One telling point that was given in that chapter was that the average age that children start to use function words is about 24 months (Labelle, 2005), whereas Yairi and Ambrose (2005, p. 53) report that the average age of stuttering onset is 33 months.

Bernstein Ratner and Wijnen now seem to allow that phonology may be a problem in the later stages of developmental stuttering when they state that children who stutter exhibit more part-word stutters, and ask: "Are they relatively weaker in *phonological* than syntactic planning?" (p. 88, emphasis added). Part-word stutters occur at ages past onset and the change to them appears to be empirical, not theoretical. It is not clear why the authors appear to permit phonology to affect stuttering given their critique of phonological involvement in stuttering discussed in section 10.5 on CRH.

10.6.3   EVALUATION OF THE SPECIFIC ISSUES WITH RESPECT TO THE VICIOUS CYCLE ACCOUNT

1. *Stuttering onset occurs in early childhood*: Bernstein Ratner and Wijnen (2007) emphasize that stuttering starts after a period of perceptually fluent speech in the one-word stage. It may be the case that other output units, such as the phonological words discussed in Chapter 7 that will be discussed further in Chapter 12, allows different patterns to be manifest. Thus, a very young child who is producing isolated content words would not have an opportunity of pausing or repeating function words. It is impossible to tell whether a young child not responding to a prompt does not know a word or cannot output that word. Although

it has been claimed that children who stutter have a syntactic coding problem (Bernstein Ratner, 1997), the evidence reviewed in Chapter 7 on language suggests that this conclusion is tenuous at best.

2. *Many children recover during childhood*: If it is the authors' intention to claim an early syntactic deficit and a phonological one during later course, then it might be the case that syntactic planning problems are not so acute and a child who only has these problems has a better chance of recovery; they do not transmogrify into phonological ones. Although this is a possible hypothesis, it may not be one the authors wish to claim and it is in need of empirical testing. It does seem to be a possibility for the type of question that the authors appear to be interested in when they ask why stutters emerge after syntactic development "is well under way" (Bernstein Ratner and Wijnen, 2007, p. 86). This appears to suggest that there is a second process (possibly the phonological one) that takes over in later childhood.

3. *What are the features of persistent stuttering that make it different from early forms?* The specification of what might lead to recovery implies an answer to why other children persist. The children who persist may be the ones who transmogrify from syntactic problems to phonological ones. This answer raises as many questions as it settles. For instance, what is the relationship, if any, between the supposed syntactic problem and the phonological one?

4. *What is the relationship between early childhood stuttering and normal nonfluent speech?* The relationship between early childhood disfluency and childhood stuttering depends on the severity of the assumed disorders discussed under issue 2 (syntax problems in early development and possibly phonological ones in later development). If problems at one or both of these levels are chronic, this would suggest that stuttering and normal nonfluency are distinct. However, at other points, Bernstein Ratner and Wijnen (2007, p. 86) admit that they do not know whether stutters are normal disfluencies gone amok, which conceivably might have gotten better (which suggests continuity), or are different symptoms. Thus, for them at present, there seems to be no answer about whether the symptoms of normal nonfluency and stuttering are distinct or not. Bernstein Ratner and Wijnen's dominant view seems to be against the idea of continuity between normal nonfluent speech and stuttering as they mention that continuity "may be problematic" (p. 88). They do not offer much in the way of clues about what the distinct problem might be. The literature reviewed in Chapter 7 suggests that syntax problems are mild, if present at all, which suggests that this could not be the basis of a distinction between these speaker groups.

5. *Why are certain treatments effective at reducing stuttering symptoms?* Bernstein Ratner and Wijnen included comments about fluency enhancement in the VCA model (p. 76). They say that DAF acts as a distracter that allows the speakers who stutter to achieve fluency. It is not clear how

the role of DAF as a distracter relates to the other role of DAF that they propose (i.e., to explain differences between fluent and stuttering speaker groups). The authors never comment on whether distraction and language monitoring are compatible. Clarification of this may not be worth the effort if Wingate (2002), who had very strong opinions against the distraction hypothesis, is correct. He said, "'Distraction' is undoubtedly the most ingenuous, superficial, and unreflective of the many indefensible explanations that have been offered in regard to stuttering" (p. 103). His main reason for this attack was as follows: "The crucial, absolute, fault of the distracting account is that the explanation it intends cannot possibly apply! The meaning of 'distraction' is that a person's attention is effectively diverted from that to which he was previously attending. Standard use of the term in relation to stuttering avers, or clearly implies, this meaning. However, in none of the conditions that ameliorate stuttering can the individual be said to no longer have stuttering in mind. In fact, the stutterer himself is well aware that his stuttering has markedly diminished—which means that not only does he have stuttering in mind, but that it is most likely *foremost* in his mind" (p. 103).

Empirically, very little is known about the effects of DAF in children who stutter and whether and how this might be interpreted in terms of monitoring and distraction. Bernstein Ratner and Wijnen cite a small-scale study on DAF in children who stutter by one of the authors (Bernstein Ratner, 1998). This is a conference proceeding and the ages of the children are not given, although the author says that they were tested within three months of onset. In addition, they do not give any criteria for assessing stuttering, nor any indication of what symptoms were considered stuttering. More needs to be learned about the effects of DAF on stuttering in children before an account of supposed fluency-enhancing effects with speakers of this age are incorporated into theoretical accounts.

10.6.4 SUMMARY

VCA is a speculative account and no falsifiable hypotheses have been proposed. The idea that children who stutter are hypersensitive monitors relative to their fluent peers is problematic as children's outputs and their conceptual inputs to the language processes are not equivalent because phonological processes are still in development. Thus, a child may say "guck" for "duck," but know what he or she wanted to say. Full perceptual analysis to send feedback of the language form would constantly lead to an error and the child could never break out of this loop. Problems like this suggest that a child does not rely on feedback from his/her speech to detect and correct errors. Thus, ideas about differences in sensitivity to language monitoring do not seem to be appropriate.

VCA also links stuttering at onset to when a child starts to use syntax. The problems in assuming syntactic production is delayed in children who stutter were reviewed in Chapter 7. One was the lack of empirical support that shows a productive deficit in people who stutter. A second important one was that there is a significant difference between the age of stuttering onset and age at which a child starts to use syntax. Overall there is little to commend the VCA approach as an account of stuttering onset. Furthermore, the possible suggestion of a change to phonological problems at later ages, which would affect the course of the disorder, is not sufficiently well articulated to formulate tests at present.

10.7   OVERALL CONCLUSIONS

The parts of Levelt's model that have been borrowed by theorists interested in stuttering—the language monitoring process, in particular—were reviewed. Problems were identified about the operation of the internal and external loops. It was argued that these loops and the associated monitoring process should be discarded as a possible account of stuttering.

Kolk and Postma's CRH and Bernstein Ratner and Wijnen's VCA use the internal and external loops, respectively. Problems using monitoring in each of these theories were discussed. Also, there are limitations to both of these language models of stuttering in that they do not address recovery. (Bernstein Ratner and Wijnen, 2007, describe characteristics of the speech near onset, and Kolk and Postma, 1997, are concerned with stuttering in adults, although others have applied it to childhood stuttering.) The situation at present is that there is no satisfactory account of how language factors affect stuttering, either at onset or during the course leading to persistence or recovery.

10.8   EXERCISES

1. Discuss the issues a theory of stuttering should explain.
2. Assess critically the analysis that dismisses the two-loop monitoring process.
3. Levelt established a rule that specified whether repairs were well formed. It has been observed here that function word repetitions and pauses are not consistent with this rule. Either (1) the rule needs to be revised or (2) word repetitions and pauses are not parts of repairs. Consider what these two approaches would mean for Kolk and Postma's covert repair hypothesis, which maintains that word repetitions and pauses are surface features that signify an underlying repair.

11 Theories That Explain Why Altered Feedback Improves the Speech Control of Speakers Who Stutter and General Theories of Speech Production That Include Accounts of Stuttering

The various theories that explain why altered feedback improves the speech control of speakers who stutter, presented at the start of this chapter, may point to some of the underlying motor mechanisms necessary for controlling speech fluently. However, it should be noted that other factors are probably implicated in long-term fluency enhancement, as the effects of altered feedback only occur while the alterations are made (see Chapter 15). All three general theories include specific accounts of how stuttering symptoms arise and how they can be ameliorated in different ways.

11.1 INTRODUCTION

Chapter 8 gave evidence, from four areas, that has been interpreted as suggesting that motor factors are operative in stuttering; the motor system does not merely respond passively to linguistic input. The areas included (1) altered auditory feedback, (2) local and global speech rate changes that affect stuttering, (3) articulatory variability, and (4) coordination.

Regarding the first two, it is necessary to investigate the interpretation that they operate at the motor level. Concerning the first area, the early explanations of altered auditory feedback, that were reviewed in Chapter 8 assumed that altering speech in different ways distorted language feedback. According to this interpretation, language, rather than motor, processes could explain this disruption. However, several problems with this account were presented in that chapter. For example, the situation of speaking while delayed auditory feedback (DAF) sounds are heard showed that nonspeech sounds, which occurred in the same particular timing relationships as the delayed speech in the DAF procedure, caused equivalent disruption to speech sounds. (This is discussed in more detail in section 11.2.1.) Consequently, language factors cannot explain disruption under altered auditory feedback of these sounds, since the nonspeech sounds are noises that are devoid of such content. Some of the motor theories outlined in this chapter address how altered auditory feedback effects arise in motor processes.

Concerning the second area, Zelaznik's work suggests that speech rate can be changed at central levels, which could include the language system, or motor levels (Zelaznik, Spencer, & Ivry, 2002). Changes in central language processing would have minor impact on the work considered here. This is because the language used in the research (reviewed in Chapter 7) is simple and given as a script or memorized, thus requires little planning. Hence, it requires little formulation, which suggests motor level adjustments, rather than ones at language levels. Dynamic systems theory, which is one of the theories discussed in section 11.3.2.1, attributes timing control primarily to the motor level, although gross speech rate control is allowed as an external factor (Goldstein & Fowler, 2003). Assuming that the external timekeeper is located at motor levels (Chapter 8), this theory requires that both local and global timing changes occur at the motor level, as assumed here. A further comment about dynamic systems theory is appropriate at this point. Arguments for a distinction between local and global rate change appeared in Chapter 8. Dynamic systems theorists would not necessarily distinguish local and global rate change as separate processes, as they could both reflect the nonlinear way that motor timing changes occur, as assumed by these theorists. Thus, it is possible to adjust the speed of movement of some articulators more easily than others when speech is speeded up. Such adjustment changes the timing relationship of the discrete speech events involved in any articulation in different proportions (nonlinearly).

One issue has dominated research and theory on motor factors and stuttering. This relates to issue 5 mentioned in the previous chapter on language theory: "Why are certain treatments effective at reducing stuttering symptoms?". Motor theorists tend to offer explanations for particular types of ameliorative conditions. The main ones are those involving perturbations (primarily the auditory ones) described in Chapter 8. The theories concerning why alterations to auditory feedback improve speech control are numerous and wide ranging, and a number of the theories only address why altered feedback affects speech control. The work on ameliorations links directly with treatment. Thus, some procedures that were investigated initially as experimental procedures in the laboratory that were found to have positive effects, have been evaluated, and, in some cases, implemented, as treatments.

The other main part of this chapter considers three theoretical approaches (Packman's Vmodel, dynamic systems theory, and Max and colleagues' model).

These can be applied to a wide range of the issues specifically concerning stuttering first discussed in Chapter 10. Several of these have a direct bearing on issues about onset, recovery, and persistence. The other main aspect regarding the way motor factors ameliorate stuttering that has received some attention by theorists is speech rate. Packman's Vmodel, which addresses rate as an ameliorative condition, also has been applied to several of the issues concerning stuttering, first raised in Chapter 10, so it is discussed in section 11.3 of this chapter. The approach taken in evaluating the motor theories is similar to that adopted with the language theories in Chapter 10 (i.e., to see how well each theory addresses the issues concerning stuttering). The complete list of issues covered in Chapter 10 is recapped and extended to include whether they consider the specifically motor issues of variability and coordination.

11.2   THEORIES THAT ADDRESS WHY CERTAIN TREATMENTS ARE EFFECTIVE AT REDUCING STUTTERING SYMPTOMS

Two important ameliorating conditions that are usually considered to operate at the motor level were reviewed in Chapter 8—the effects of perturbations on speakers and voluntary rate control. Explanations that have been offered for these effects are presented below after readers have been reminded about the problems for a language feedback explanation of these effects (see section 8.2.5 of Chapter 8 for a full consideration).

11.2.1   REMINDER OF THE PROBLEMS FOR AN ACCOUNT THAT ALTERED AUDITORY FEEDBACK AFFECTS THE LANGUAGE SYSTEM

Discussed in Chapter 8 were several problems for the interpretation that the sound of a speaker's voice undergoes a full perceptual analysis so linguistic information can be provided in real time for speech control. In brief, these included:

1. Full linguistic analysis would take a long time and slow speech and this is not consistent with the rapid rate with which speech can be produced.
2. People with hearing impairment would have degraded auditory feedback, but speech control is not affected in these individuals.
3. Delayed noises produce similar disruption to delayed speech, so the effects of DAF do not involve language processes (Howell & Archer, 1984).
4. Altered sounds lead to a change in voice level as does noise (Lombard effect), so once again results from studies on altered auditory feedback do not implicate language processes.
5. Compensations to a biteblock can occur before auditory feedback occurred (Fowler & Turvey, 1981).

11.2.1.1 Borden's Account: Use of Feedback in
Circumscribed Circumstances

The bulk of Borden's work prior to her 1979 paper had investigated how alteration to feedback mechanisms affected speech control in fluent speakers and speakers who stuttered. Borden expressed the view that manipulating auditory feedback was important in selected situations. This included when feedback was altered, when language was acquired developmentally, or as a second language, and, of particular interest here, in speakers who stutter. This proposal would not address all the problems noted in section 11.2.1 (points 3, 4, and 5, in particular).

11.2.1.2 Kalveram's Account: Feedback Operates at the Prosodic Level

The problem that perceptual processing of speech segments, such as phonemes or syllables, takes a long time relative to their produced duration would not be as problematic if longer duration segments were involved in feedback control, assuming that perceptual processing time is fixed. In that case, most of the unit that extends back in time would have been processed when the current segment ends. Along these lines, Donath, Natke, and Kalveram (2002), Kalveram (2001), and Kalveram and Jäncke (1989) have argued for an auditory feedback processing mechanism that operates at the prosodic level in stuttering. Prosodic processes operate over longer time periods. Thus, the issue of obtaining auditory feedback early enough would not be as much of a problem if prosodic units are used for feedback control as it is for the view that syllables are the unit that is used. This addresses the processing time limitation, but still needs to be developed to address the other topics about auditory feedback discussed above (section 11.2.1).

11.2.1.3 Howell's Disruptive Rhythm Hypothesis
and Its Application to Stuttering

Howell, Powell, and Khan (1983) developed a nonfeedback account for the effects of DAF based on work with fluent speakers that has wide applicability with respect to ameliorations that affect stuttering. The theory is called the disruptive rhythm hypothesis (DRH).

The theory maintains that speaking is not disrupted when synchronous events are heard, but is disrupted when asynchronous events are listened to. Considering synchronous events first, canon singing that involves some people singing one set of words while others sing a different set of words with the same timing. Canon singing is easy, as shown by the fact that it is one of the first forms of song that children are taught. Canon singing also shows that synchronous activities are easy to produce whether or not those activities contain any information about the speaker's own speech. In this case, two synchronous perceptual events do not interfere with singing.

The improvement in control of speakers who stutter during choral speaking would be attributed to the facilitating effects of synchronous activity. This account could also explain the frequency shifted feedback (FSF) effect, which is also a synchronous form of alteration. Both allow speech to proceed fluently and without any slowing. The hypothesis would even apply to speaking along with pacing signals, such as a metronome (Fransella & Beech, 1965) or a click that occurs at the onset of each syllable that is spoken (Howell & El-Yaniv, 1987), both of which improve the speech control of speakers who stutter. Choral speech and FSF were described in Chapter 8. The lower amounts of disruption with these synchronous events are evident insofar as speakers who stutter can shadow at normal speech rates or speak rapidly under FSF when asked to do so (Howell, El-Yaniv, & Powell, 1987).

There is a form of singing where participants have to perform asynchronously. According to DRH, this should disrupt speech control. The form of song is called hoquetus and is reported to be difficult to perform. Hoquetus involves each singer producing a note synchronized to the offset of another singer's note, making the two versions arrhythmic. The case of hoquetus shows that asynchronous activities (again, whether or not those activities contain any information about the speaker's own speech) are difficult and, by analogy, suggests that this is why DAF causes difficulties in speech control. A further observation concerning the particular timing relationships in hoquetus is that one singer finishes a note as the next singer commences. This would correspond to the DAF situation in which speech is delayed by the length of the note, which would be the length of a syllable for notes in music that are a syllable in length. A delay equal to the length of a syllable is maximally disruptive with DAF. DRH suggests that this delay is most disruptive because of the rhythmic relationship between what is heard and what is spoken, rather than because feedback about the wrong syllable is sent when this delay is used, as in traditional language-based accounts. DAF slows the speech of all speakers. DRH explains the problems in speech control experienced by speakers who stutter in normal listening conditions, by proposing that these speakers are trying to execute speech at too rapid a rate. As rate is slowed under DAF, these procedures allow these speakers more language planning time. Language planning and motor processing happen in independent processes, according to the arguments at the start of Chapter 7. The additional language planning time reduces the likelihood of stuttering, as has been reported to occur (Ryan & van Kirk Ryan, 1995). Thus, arrhythmic stimuli improve fluency in speakers who stutter by slowing speech. The slowing also happens with fluent speakers, but they do not have disfluencies that are necessary to reveal the effect of extra planning time.

According to DRH, the timing disturbance under DAF arises because asynchronous stimulus events disturb low-level motor processes, in particular, timekeeping processes in the cerebellum. Evidence for timekeeping processes in the cerebellum and how they were affected by synchronous and asynchronous stimuli with application to stuttering was discussed in Chapter 6, section 6.3.2. The signals that are asynchronous in the DAF procedure are the direct sound (occurs at the actual time speech is spoken) and delayed sound (occurs a short time after speech has been spoken). The assumption that DAF affects rhythmic mechanisms is consistent with Howell and Archer's (1984) results, discussed in Chapter 8, section 8.2.5, and various procedures that showed arrhythmic stimuli slow speech (section 8.2.4). The Howell and Archer study indicated that the DAF procedures does not disrupt speech because information is sent through the speech perception system to provide information to the language system that the latter uses to reinitiate speech when the language system detects that an error had been made.

11.2.1.4   Models That Include Feedforward Control

Feedforward models get around the problem of feedback being available for control too late by proposing that speakers predict the results of an action in advance of it taking place (Kawato, Furukawa, & Suzuki, 1987). In particular, feedforward models maintain that movement errors are continuously computed and used (when they arise) as correction signals. Such a model has been applied to one of the situations Borden (1979) regarded as reliant on auditory feedback (developmental speech acquisition) by Guenther (2001) in his DIVA model. The DIVA model uses feedforward control in the developmental stages, but becomes less dependent on feedback over time. Max, Guenther, Gracco, Ghosh, and Wallace (2004) also applied the feedforward idea to stuttering. (See the description that appears later in this chapter, as it is a model that addresses several general characteristics of stuttering.) Kawato et al. maintained that feedforward control takes place in the cerebellum.

11.2.1.5   Kalinowski and Saltuklaroglu's Mirror Neuron Account of Short Delay DAF and FSF

DRH explains phenomena, such as choral speech, in terms of a second noise signal (i.e., the second signal is the speech of the person whose voice is being shadowed). The second signal cannot be used as feedback by the person who stutters as it bears no relationship to the speaker's own voice, although it could still serve as a second rhythmic nonspeech signal. I pointed out the idea that second signals affect speech control to Motluk (1997) and this was picked up by Kalinowski and Saltuklaroglu (2006), who developed it in a different way compared to the DRH. Dayalu and Kalinowski (2002) and Guntupali, Kalinowski, Saltuklaroglu, and Nanjundeswaran (2005) considered that the second signal has to be speech and that this reduces stuttering by activating mirror neurons. A mirror neuron is a neuron that fires both when an animal acts or when the animal observes the same action performed by another (Rizzolatti & Craighero, 2004). Early work on mirror neurons suggested that this applies to humans as well. These neurons "mirror" the behavior of the other animal, as though the observer were performing the action. Mirror neurons are of particular interest with respect to speech processing as they may support a link between speech perception and speech production (however, see Lotto, Hickok, & Holt, 2009, for an alterative viewpoint). In terms of stuttering, seeing and/or hearing someone perform an action may facilitate the individual's speech attempt and this could then result in better fluency control. The way the mirror neuron account explains why speakers become more fluent when they are given FSF is that hearing a separate speech sound that is produced by the speaker (created by the altered version of the speaker's speech) activates mirror neurons responsible for speech motor output. This facilitates speech production, and, in the case of people who stutter, induces them to be fluent. This account can be applied to choral speech as well as alterations made to the voice, such as FSF.

Some of the main points that Kalinowski and colleagues have made in support of their theory and some observations include:

1. DAF at short delays and FSF allow speakers who stutter to produce fluent speech (Dayalu & Kalinowski, 2002) and neither form of alteration appears to slow speech. In contrast, other methods of inducing fluency in people who stutter, such as prolonged speech, improve fluency (Costello-Ingham, 1993), but the speech does not sound fluent. This might suggest that short-delay DAF and FSF are different (and superior) to other forms of fluency inducement because they can activate the mirror neuron system that achieves fluency in a different way from other techniques that do not have this possibility.

   There are some problems with this point. The hypothesis that FSF produces entirely fluent speech predicts that there will be no differences between fluent and FSF speech. Statistically speaking, this is a situation where the null hypothesis is predicted, which is against a fundamental principle of statistics. The work of Kalinowski's group actually establishes that FSF leads to high levels of stutter-free speech that, it is claimed, sounds natural. Even though FSF speech is closer to the speech produced by fluent speakers than the end product of prolonged speech regimes, it still may not be fluent and this may be revealed as improved assessment methods become available. For example, FSF produced local and global rate changes in the study by Howell and Sackin (2000) reviewed in Chapter 8.

2. In support of the view that choral speech is fluent, studies have shown that brain image patterns of people who stutter under choral speaking conditions are almost indistinguishable from fluent speakers' patterns. However, the mirror neuron account seems over-restrictive in terms of what second signals are allowed. Thus, the Kalinowski account only allows second *speech* signals. When the DRH was discussed above, ample evidence was provided that shows that nonspeech second signals, such as flashing lights, also affect fluency control. It is not known whether or not these signals also would produce near-normal brain image patterns in people who stutter.

3. Mirror neurons discharge when an action is either performed or is observed (i.e., motor and sensory properties coexist in the same neuron). Mirror neurons could affect fluency, as they are found in Broca's speech motor area (Nishitani & Hari, 2000), so conceivably they might facilitate production. Although this again suggests a speech-specific response, the Howell and Archer (1984) study on fluent speakers indicates the effects of altered feedback arise at a lower level in the central nervous system (CNS) than mechanisms involved in full speech perceptual analysis. This would show that central perceptual processes are not involved in

the case of DAF, assuming Howell and Archer's result applies to people who stutter under DAF as well as to fluent speakers. There is scanning evidence that supports the view that brain areas responsible for timing control are activated when altered feedback is given to people who stutter (Fox et al., 1996, for the cerebellum, and Watkins, Smith, Davis, & Howell, 2008, for the basal ganglia).

4. The mirror neuron system is, according to Kalinowski's group, important in early development (children's imitations). It appears to be used less as speakers become older. However, they argue that the second signal under FSF reactivates the mirror neuron system. This assists production and allows fluency to be regained in speakers who stutter.

To work, the mirror neuron system has to have some input from perception to reflect into production at the time the speech is being produced. Patently, this does not happen with short delay DAF, and commercial devices like the Edinburgh masker has a lag, too. It is, of course, possible to modify the mirror neuron concept. For instance, the mirror neurons could be made more flexible both in terms of (a) how closely timed speech events and the perceptual events they give rise to need to be, and (b) how similar the perceptual events need to be relative to the linguistic events they reflect, which could be related to responses to point 2 (above). Although it is appropriate to postulate some flexibility, neurological data would be needed to support such temporal and linguistic flexibility before they are taken as fact. Also, endowing mirror neurons with too much flexibility seems inadvisable. There needs to be some delimitation of the range of what perceptual events trigger activity in these neurons, otherwise they lose their selectivity in linking speech actions with the perceptual events that gave rise to them.

5. The changes in fluency in people who stutter occur passively when FSF is presented (Saltuklaroglu, Dayalu, & Kalinowski, 2002) and these passive changes occur because the central mirror neuron system is affected directly. This contrasts with the changes that occur with techniques like prolonged speech, which requires the speaker to make an active change to voice control. Such active changes can eventually affect the same system that passive changes influence. This could account for cases where speakers who stutter are successfully treated by techniques like prolonged speech.

Kalinowksi and his co-workers consider that FSF affects the mirror neuron system directly. In contrast, techniques that train speakers to relearn motor patterns, such as prolonged speech, operate at the motor level initially and, only when the patterns have been established, can they be transmitted to the mirror neuron system. Kalinowski's group proposes that these techniques then affect this system in a similar way to FSF. Therefore, FSF and prolonged speech techniques operate initially on different mechanisms. FSF affects speech "passively," bypassing the peripheral level.

11.3   PROPOSED GENERAL MODELS

In this section, attention is shifted to motor theories that have a more general scope. The issues regarding stuttering that were identified in Chapter 10, as drawn from the literature, are recapped:

1. Stuttering onset occurs in early childhood.
2. Many children recover during childhood.
3. The proposed features of persistent stuttering that make stuttering different from early disfluency.
4. The proposed relationship between early childhood stuttering and normal nonfluent speech.
5. Treatments that are effective at reducing stuttering symptoms. Motor theorists have mainly concerned themselves with accounting for the effects of altered auditory feedback and speech rate (although Max et al., 2004, also offer an account of the Lidcombe program).

In addition to these issues, research in the motor area has provided specific evidence that motor timing of people who stutter differs from that of fluent speakers. As a result, two other issues that should be accounted for, which none of the language theories considered in Chapter 10, include:

6. Variability of single articulator movement.
7. Coordination of movement of the articulators.

A theory that can explain all seven points would be preferred to language theories, which can only explain the first five. Two of the motor theories have accounts of stuttering symptoms that they discuss in relation to different issues on this list. Dynamic systems theory mainly considers the perceptually fluent speech of speakers who stutter, although Van Lieshout, 2004, offers a tentative explanation of stutters. The theories considered are Packman's Vmodel, dynamic systems theory, and the model of Max et al. (2004).

11.3.1   OVERVIEW OF PACKMAN, ONSLOW, AND VAN DOORN'S VMODEL

Packman, Onslow, and van Doorn's (1994) Vmodel was developed to explain findings from an acoustic analysis of prolonged speech that is a technique that improves the fluency of people who stutter (a fuller description is given in section 11.3.1.1, issue 5 below). Recordings of acoustic and electroglottographic signals from four participants were analyzed. Changes in the variability of vowel duration occurred in all participants when they used whatever prolonged speech procedures they considered was most effective at reducing their stuttering. Packman and colleagues hypothesized that reducing syllabic stress contrast decreased variation in motor effort between syllables and they suggested that this could be the feature that led to fluency improvement during prolonged speech. Other details of the theory are discussed under the stuttering issues in the following section.

11.3.1.1 Evaluation of the Stuttering Issues

1. *Stuttering onset occurs in early childhood*: Packman and Onslow (1997) proposed that speakers who stutter have an unstable speech system that operates variably. Most of the following comments are based on Packman, Code, and Onslow's et al.'s, 2007, description. They argued that this hypothesis can explain two important features that are associated with the onset of stuttering: (1) onset coincides with children putting words together into short utterances, and (2) syllable repetition is the predominant sign of stuttering at onset. Chapter 7 pointed out that the claim that stuttering starts at the multiword stage is not correct (see the examination of Bloodstein and Bernstein Ratner's, 2007, hypothesis that stuttering is associated with onset of syntax).

   The original Vmodel had proposed that there was an instability of the speech motor system, but did not specify the particulars. By 2007, Packman et al. were confident enough to assert that the proposed instability was caused by difficulty initiating the motor plans for syllables, although they are not specific about the level that this occurs (e.g., at the level of motor program assembly, parameter specification, or initial execution processes). The idea that initiating syllables is the source of difficulty is incorporated in different ways in several other models of stuttering (e.g., the covert repair hypothesis discussed in Chapter 10, and EXPLAN, to be discussed in Chapter 12). What are needed are testable predictions that distinguish between these models.

2. *Many children recover during childhood*:

3. *The proposed features of persistent stuttering that make it different from early forms*:

4. *Proposed relationship between early childhood stuttering and normal nonfluent speech*: The three issues concerning recovery, persistence and how stuttering relates to normal nonfluency are not addressed directly by the authors of the Vmodel. However, some comments are made about how fluency can be enhanced that relate to these issues. The Vmodel attributes syllable-based repetition as a failure to move on to the next syllable, that is, the child repeats the syllable that was just uttered. In their view, repetition is similar to what happens in babbling. They regard stuttering involving whole-word repetition as a retreat to an earlier stage of speech development where less variation in linguistic stress across syllables was required. Consequently, this leads to a reduction in motoric variation, which stabilizes the speech system so that the child can move forward again in speech.

   The model offers, then, a reasonably precise description of what children do to move out of stuttered speech and into fluency. This effectively specifies what a child needs to do to recover and what a child who persists is not doing (i.e., in both cases, to make whole-word repetitions). A stuttering child has done something specifically different from a fluent child that destabilized the speech system, and the Vmodel indicates how the child may recover fluency.

5. *Treatments that are effective at reducing stuttering symptoms*: Packman et al.'s (1994) original work that led to the proposed model concerned rate control in prolonged speech techniques. Prolonged speech is a way of changing global speech rate that ameliorates stuttering. Bothe, Davidow, Bramlett, and Ingham (2006) recently reviewed some of the studies that used prolonged speech procedures in treatment. They located 13 articles that met their criteria for good quality trials and considered that, overall, the studies showed the procedure had positive effects on fluency. They concluded that the techniques gave positive results despite the many differences in the treatment programs categorized as prolonged speech in the studies included in their review. They were complementary about several details of the studies: (1) the selected articles included data from more than 200 speakers; (2) the speakers covered a broad age range (7 years to at least 58 years), although the studies were primarily on adults; (3) most of the reports included speech from extra-clinical contexts, which provided evidence that the reported gains had generalized to multiple settings; and (4) many of these reports included evidence that showed that social, emotional, and cognitive variables were improved or normalized, even though none of these studies included any cognitive, emotional, or other treatments as specific goals to be addressed by the treatment.

Packman et al. also hypothesized that the ameliorative effects of rhythmic speech (a related form of treatment) on stuttering could be due to reduced durational variability of stressed syllables. This prediction was subsequently confirmed, so they concluded that the model generalizes to other treatments. The latter study also showed that the ameliorative effect of rhythmic speech appeared to be independent of reduction in global speech rate, suggesting control of local speech rate is most important with respect to stuttering.

6. *Variability in movement patterns of single articulators*:
7. *Coordination of movement of articulators during speech*: The Vmodel was based on evidence that variability in duration of stressed syllables was affected by prolonged speech procedures. Thus, this cannot be included as a prediction of the theory. The other two theories considered in this section are based on work that used more sophisticated measures that assess variability of individual articulators alone and in coordination with others.

11.3.1.2 Summary

The Vmodel includes an account of stuttering onset. Some suggested ways it could be applied to the course of stuttering and what the model says about the relationship between normal nonfluency and stuttering were considered. The application of the model to various ameliorating conditions was also examined. On the other hand, more empirical investigation of the model is required. Specifically highlighted as a requirement for further examination were (1) more detail about what is meant by difficulty initiating the motor plans for syllables, and (2) more precise specification of the link between stuttering onset and the multiword stage of language development.

11.3.2 OVERVIEW OF NONLINEAR DYNAMIC SYSTEMS (DST) ACCOUNTS (VAN LIESHOUT)

Van Lieshout has endeavored to keep stuttering researchers abreast of contemporary work on motor control, and work on dynamic systems theory in particular. In some ways, DST can be regarded as a proposal of how to deal with problems these theorists see in other models, especially generalized motor programs. It should be stressed, however, that both generalized motor programs and DST refer to the same literature for support, thus the research does not support DST exclusively. The generalized motor program approach, as characterized by Van Lieshout (2004), maintains that behavior is organized by externally imposed memory-based instructions and heuristics that allow that general program to be fitted to particular conditions. In contrast, DST theorists consider that this approach ignores the fact that many actions can evolve spontaneously in the appropriate context without the need or availability, of instructions from a general motor program (Van Lieshout, 2004).

Van Lieshout used the flocking behavior of birds to illustrate some aspects of the DST approach (subsequently, the principles seen at work in this situation are applied to what happens to the articulators during speech production). A flock is comprised of individual birds. Together they are able to adapt their behavior in a flexible manner that is responsive to changing internal and external conditions. The behavior of the flock can be accounted for by three rules: (1) keep separation between members constant to ensure they do not run into each other, (2) do not deviate in flight (keep in alignment), and (3) do not disperse (cohesion). Based on these three principles, the individual birds adopt a flexible coordination pattern without any explicit prescription of this pattern. The birds respond to perturbations (change of wind speed and direction) or activity of individual members of the flock.

Adaptive behavior, that is potentially related to flocking behavior, can be observed when the articulators are perturbed while a person is speaking. That is, they adjust to ensure some intended articulatory activity can be achieved. When perturbations occur, the internal and external conditions are changed and the system response can be examined to see what reorganization took place. When there is adaptation, the articulators act synergistically. Synergy carries the connotation of working together to achieve a goal. In the case of speech, this can take the form of cooperation among muscles and joints that act as a functional unit to accomplish certain task goals (Bernstein 1967; Kugler, Kelso, & Turvey, 1982). If a system responds synergistically, it shows self-organization. This self-organization can be described by task dynamics models (a type of DST) that show how the articulators are coupled.

The dynamic perturbations that were described in Chapter 8 are important ways that allow the motor organization of the speech system to be studied (e.g., to see if it shows the self-organizing behavior that DST predicts). Kelso, Vatikiotis-Bateson, Tuller, and Fowler (1984) did experiments involving motor tasks other than speaking where the system was perturbed. The perturbations were followed by a rapid compensation that preserved the intended task goal that indicated that synergies had occurred. Similar tests were made for speech-related movements in a number of experiments in the early and mid-1980s that confirmed the articulatory system operated synergistically (e.g., Folkins & Zimmermann, 1982; Abbs & Gracco, 1984; Kelso et al., 1984). These were taken as support for DST.

In connection with stuttering, the questions can be raised about whether similar adjustments are made at the motor level in these speakers and why certain of the perturbations impact on fluency. Caruso, Gracco, and Abbs (1987) studied the effects of dynamic perturbation in people who stutter and showed that these speakers had longer latencies and reduced upper lip EMG amplitudes compared to matched controls. This suggested a less than adequate compensation (Caruso et al., 1987) although in a later replication, Bauer, Jäncke, and Kalveram (1997) failed to find any difference between groups.

11.3.2.1   Evaluation of the Stuttering Issues

1. *Stuttering onset occurs in early childhood*: Factors that lead to variability and coordination relate to onset of stuttering within DST. In their proposal about what is the "weak link" in stuttering, Van Lieshout, Hulstijn, and Peters (2004) talked about speakers who stutter having reduced ability to stabilize motor behaviors in tasks, and they followed this by saying that it is necessary to identify what factors (de)stabilize speech motor behaviors. They identified three: speech rate, the interaction between higher order processes and speech motor control, and feedback processes. Speech rate and feedback processes are mentioned under ameliorating conditions (issue 5 below). The suggestion is that certain changes in these conditions can destabilize the coupling between gestures in speakers who stutter and conceivably children are more vulnerable to such influences.

2. *Many children recover during childhood*:

3. *The proposed features of persistent stuttering that make it different from recovered forms*: Van Lieshout has not written anything specifically on how DST affects the later course of stuttering (into recovery and persistence). But an aspect that may be relevant in terms of identifying the weak link in stuttering is Van Lieshout, Rutjens, and Spauwen's (2002) study on patients with repaired cleft palate. This study reported that the upper lip had smaller movement and higher variability than the lower

lip, but the speakers still seemed able to coordinate the articulators to achieve their goals. Of particular relevance to the current issues was that the authors hypothesized that fluency problems are associated with maturation of the motor system (Van Lieshout et al., 2002). In the context of stuttering, a speaker who recovers may show maturation in the processes that lead to coordinated movement, whereas a speaker who persists shows less maturation.

4. *Proposed relationship between early childhood stuttering and normal nonfluent speech*: As work under issue 1 indicates, children who stutter are considered to differ from other typically developing children (they have problems coordinating gestures).

5. *Treatments that are effective at reducing stuttering symptoms*: Perturbations are at the heart of DST. Van Lieshout et al. (2004) commented about altered auditory feedback and rate in general terms, not specifically from a DST perspective.

6. *Variability in movement patterns of single articulators*:

7. *Coordination of movement of articulators during speech*: The accounts of self-organization and recovery from perturbations (not restricted to auditory ones) are central to DST. A lot of attention has been paid to the concern about what is the appropriate way of measuring variability and coordination by DST theorists. For example, Alfonso and Van Lieshout's (1997) work (reported in Chapter 8) showed that single measures of displacement and velocity profiles (spatial measures) and temporal order and interarticulator relative time (temporal measures) were not stable across sessions for controls or stuttering speakers. However, a coefficient of variation that reflected the variability in the combined movements was robust for all but one control speaker. This measure was less robust for people who stutter, which suggested poorer coordination abilities in people who stutter than fluent controls.

Van Lieshout and Namisavayam (2010) provided a comprehensive description of the methods that DST researchers have used to measure variability and coordination, and have reported work on people who stutter, based on the assumption that people with a disorder like stuttering have increased variability. Namasivayam, Van Lieshout, McIlroy, and de Nil (2009) also had interesting findings on the effect of both kinesthetic and auditory feedback manipulations in adults who stutter and matched controls. They showed the role of motor control strategies in stability control and the fact that feedback effects are different at different levels of coordination.

11.3.2.2 Summary

While DST is largely based on fluent work, it has some potentially important implications for understanding stuttering. Van Lieshout et al.'s (2004) final quote indicates what they consider the underlying motor control problem that leads to stuttering to be. "Stuttering is a complex communication problem whose core consists of idiosyncratic limitations in speech motor skill as evidenced in more variable, less effective, and more basic movement patterns in dealing with high demands for movement accuracy and speed required for speech" (p. 341).

11.3.3 MAX ET AL.'S GENERAL MODEL OF MOTOR CONTROL AND APPLICATION TO STUTTERING

The model proposed by Max et al. (2004) is a general model with specific application to stuttering. It is distinct from the well-known "directions into velocities of articulators," or DIVA, model associated with one of the authors (Guenther, 1994). The Max et al. model is shown in Figure 11.1. Speech starts at bottom left with a specification of movement goals and finishes at bottom right where muscle contractions that achieve those goals occur. A feedback and a feedforward controller appear between the start and end points (labeled in the diagram).

The feedback control system is considered first. This receives input from two sources. The first is indicated by the box labeled "afferent signals" on the top left. Afferent refers to sensory signals, which would include, but not be restricted to, auditory feedback of the voice. The second source of feedback is from efferent copy, which is the command instructions prepared for motor output. Feedback from both of these sources is considered crucial by Max et al. (2004), so the problem of feedback arriving too late for use in control can be minimized. The afferent signals suffer from this problem, but the efferent copy does not, so combining them reduces the time lag problem. It does, however, lead to problems in tagging events associated with the same action that arrive at different times (discussed in Chapter 10 in connection with Levelt's model). The feedback controller (top right) that receives these inputs uses them to monitor and correct (if required) ongoing movements.

The feedback controller can do this because it has access to a forward internal model. The forward internal model predicts the sensory consequences of the movements resulting from the efferent copy of the motor commands (forward in this case means it maps efferent input to motor command output). Instead of having to wait for afferent inputs that signal movement errors, which has the undesirable inherent time delay, the efferent copy predicts the sensory consequences in anticipation of the output and uses this and any afferent information available at that time for feedback control.

The feedforward control system has an inverse internal model, which computes the required motor commands from desired movements. Here, inverse means establishing what motor commands are needed to achieve the desired output. Max et al. (2004) included both feedback and feedforward controllers based on other research that supports the role of each of them. For example, they would consider the alterations discussed in the first part of Chapter 8 as support for feedback control. The main justification for a feedforward controller is to get around the problem that feedback would arrive too late to use for controlling speech. Many other models include feedforward control, and they have been successfully tested. Evidence for the involvement of inverse and forward internal models in such a control scheme with both feedforward and feedback controllers has come primarily from two research paradigms: (1) sensory perturbations that show motor systems have considerable adaptability (see Chapter 8), and (2) studies on planning of movements that show that participants adjust muscular force in anticipation of the consequences of a movement (e.g., adjusting grip to hold an object).

11.3.3.1   Evaluation of the Stuttering Issues

1. *Stuttering onset occurs in early childhood*: Max et al. (2004) offered two hypotheses for what the source of stutters in childhood could be. These were that people who stutter could have: (a) unstable or insufficiently activated internal representations of the transformations that occur when central motor commands are converted into speech, and (b) a motor control strategy that relies too much on afferent signals that are associated with considerable time lags. These are considered in turn.

   a. Unstable or insufficiently activated internal representations: Children constantly need to update their internal models because of the rapid neural and craniofacial developmental changes that happen during childhood. If the commands are not updated, it is impossible for the feedforward controller to correctly derive the necessary commands for a desired sensory outcome or for the feedback controller to predict with any great precision. The authors maintain that there are several ways that children who stutter might not be able to acquire stable and correct internal representations. The ones they mention include failure to update these mappings during speech development, and failure to sufficiently activate and successfully use these mappings for efficient sensorimotor control of the speech mechanism.

      Max et al. (2004) discussed how impoverished internal models could give rise to the symptoms of stuttering. Any problems that arise in connection with the inverse models would result in incorrect computations of the feedforward commands in Figure 11.1. If these motor commands were executed, there would be a mismatch between the sensory and desired consequences. In turn, this would result in increased feedback-based corrections, which lead to interruptions, and resets of the feedforward commands that give rise to sound/syllable repetitions and sound prolongations.

      In addition to these possible explanations of symptoms Max et al. (2004) also speculated that it may be more likely that the types of stutters result from problems with forward internal models. Based on the integration of afferent and efferent information in this component of the model, this would result in problematic feedback control. If the consequences of prepared motor commands cannot be accurately predicted based on an efference copy and concurrent afferent inflow, a mismatch may arise between predicted and actual consequences of the executed movements, regardless of whether or not the generated commands were accurate with respect to the

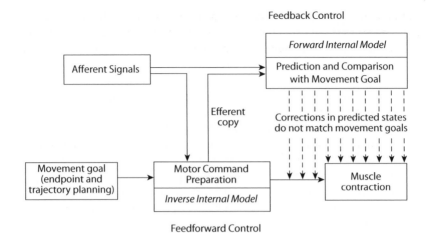

FIGURE 11.1   Schematic representation of a global model of motor control. The model represents a hybrid control scheme consisting of a feedforward controller and a feedback controller that make use of inverse and forward internal models, respectively. Adapted from "Unstable or Insufficiently Activated Internal Models and Feedback-Biased Motor Control as Sources of Dysfluency: A Theoretical Model of Stuttering," by L. Max, F. H. Guenther, V. L. Gracco, S. S. Ghosh, & M. E. Wallace, 2004, *Contemporary Issues in Communication Sciences and Disorders, 31*, pp. 105–122.

desired movement outcome. As a result of such a mismatch, the CNS may respond by reattempting the movement and reissuing the central commands until the sensory consequences are interpreted as matching the desired consequences, sustaining the already ongoing commands until the conflict is resolved or avoided by relying on moment-to-moment afferent feedback, or generating a different set of commands. The authors argue that these types of attempted repairs could result in prolonged or repeated muscle contractions, and, thus, give rise to the sound/syllable repetitions and sound prolongations that are characteristic of stuttering.

b. Weak feedforward control and overreliance on afferent feedback: The second hypothesis does not assume any problems with the internal models or their use by speakers who stutter. Instead, the authors proposed that an overreliance on strictly afferent feedback was not a strategy selected to avoid stuttering, but rather a strategy that actually resulted in stuttering due to instabilities inherent in this type of control. There is always a time lag between a motor command and its auditory and sensory consequences. When movements are primarily under afferent feedback control (i.e., weighted more toward afferent feedback control rather than, as is common for well-practiced tasks, toward feedforward control), the delay in arrival of the sensory signals may render the system unstable. Such instabilities would be expected particularly for fast movements and could lead to effector oscillations and system resets. Resets of the sensorimotor system would result in the observable stutters in a similar way to the proposal discussed above in connection with the first hypothesis.

Max et al. consider that their perspective is consistent with the fact that the onset of stuttering typically occurs during early childhood, and that most stuttering starts between 2 and 5 years of age (Andrews et al., 1983). The first hypothesis suggests that stuttering may develop because of an incorrect learning/updating or insufficient activation of the various inverse and/or forward internal models used for sensorimotor control of speech movements. They consider that such difficulties would be most likely to develop during an early childhood period in which rapid neural and musculoskeletal changes as a result of maturation require continuous updating and refining of the internal models. Their second hypothesis suggests that, since part of the motor learning takes place during speech development, it is during these early childhood years that fluent individuals gradually replace a motor control strategy that is biased more toward afferent feedback control with one that is biased more toward feedforward control. The overreliance on feedback control may lead to the instabilities that they describe when neuromotor limitations (possibly anatomically based) cause a failure to make this transition at the time when articulatory complexity and rate start to increase.

2. *Many children recover during childhood*: Max et al. (2004) offered an explanation for one seeming puzzle that has a potential bearing on recovery from stuttering. They raise the question of why people who stutter continue to use a control strategy that is biased toward afferent feedback control, if that strategy results in system instabilities and stuttering moments (Howell et al., 2000, offered a different account of this, as discussed in Chapter 6, section 6.3.2). According to the authors, fluent individuals do not do this, they replace afferent feedback control with a feedforward strategy after initial practice and learning of speech motor actions early in development. The developmental change in mode of feedback control is part of normal development, but does not occur in people who stutter, which potentially explains why speakers persist. Speakers who stutter who make the change that was reasoned to occur in normal development would recover spontaneously.

One answer Max et al. provide for the conundrum raised at the beginning of the previous paragraph is to propose a form of deficit in people who stutter: They tentatively suggest that people who stutter have weakened feedforward control projections, which lead, in turn, to the need or preference for a speech motor strategy that depends primarily on afferent input. They also note that slower movements (that are found in people who stutter), as compared with faster movements, are less affected by the delays associated with afferent information. This might suggest that slow movements are a way of accommodating to the instabilities that are inherent when high reliance is placed in afferent information. Diffusion tensor imaging findings of Sommer, Koch, Paulus, Weiller, and Buchel (2002), that were discussed in Chapter 5, showed that stuttering adults had abnormalities in the white matter pathways underlying the orofacial area of the left hemisphere primary sensorimotor cortex. Max et al. interpret these findings as possibly showing that damage to these pathways compromises the feedforward command from premotor to primary motor areas that would leave people who stutter more reliant on using afferent feedback.

Recovery from stuttering during childhood may represent either a successful acquisition and updating of the required internal models or a successful transition toward more feedforward-based control as a result of sensorimotor learning in parallel with neuroanatomical/neurochemical maturation (see discussion of this under issue 5 below).

3. *The proposed features of persistent stuttering that make it different from early forms*: Failure to make the transition from reliance on afferent feedback to feedforward control that occurs in normal development, according to the authors, if it continues may explain why speakers persist.

4. *Proposed relationship between early childhood stuttering and normal nonfluent speech*: The Max et al. (2004) model specifies at least one potential difference between typically developing children and those who stutter. The former make the transition to feedforward control, whereas the latter do not. There seem to be, therefore, clear differences between children who stutter and those who are normally fluent, according to this account.

5. *Treatments that are effective at reducing stuttering symptoms*: Max et al. (2004) described how their two original hypotheses (unstable or insufficiently activated internal representations and weak feedforward control, leading to overreliance on afferent feedback) could explain a variety of well-documented conditions that ameliorate stuttering. This included DAF, FSF, masking, and choral reading. The interpretations depend on which of the two hypotheses discussed under issue 1 is adopted. A suggestion that is in line with the first hypothesis, is that all of these effects could be a result not of the modifications per se, but of their common role in providing an external auditory stimulus that facilitates general activation of the auditory cortex. They argued that the auditory stimulation increases activation of the internal models used to monitor efference copies of the motor commands. More specifically, the activation of auditory cortex by external auditory stimuli may improve the efficiency of feedback monitoring by improving the feedback controller's predictions of the auditory consequences of planned movements. Like DRH (section 11.2.1.3), this hypothesis predicts that altered auditory stimuli are not processed linguistically. However, DRH maintains that the effects are due to the rhythmic properties of stimuli, including nonauditory ones.

Their suggestion, based on the second hypothesis, is that alterations effectively switches off the feedback circuit because they provide consistent indications via perception, that the speaker's own actions are inconsistent with intentions. As is implemented in the model, this could be achieved by a normalization process that reduces the output gain of the feedback controller and increases the output gain of the feedforward controller. The increased output gain of the latter would compensate for the problem with the previously weak feedforward signals.

Max et al. (2004) offer some general observations, but not precise details, about their simulation work and how it would impact on the specific stuttering issues. The simulations start with a period where babbled speech is used as input. In the subsequent phases, which correspond with early development, the feedforward commands are inaccurate, and the model depends on feedback control. The projections in the feedback control subsystem constitute *forward models* encoding the expected sensory consequences of the sounds to be produced. The feedback system compares these expectations to the system's current state as signaled by incoming *afferent* information. If the current auditory and somatosensory states are outside the target regions for the produced sound, error signals are generated in higher order sensory areas. The error signals are then transformed into corrective motor commands by *inverse model* projections from the sensory areas to the primary motor cortex. Over time, however, the feedforward command becomes well tuned through monitoring of the movements controlled by the feedback subsystem. Once the feedforward subsystem is accurately tuned, the system can rely almost entirely on feedforward commands because no sensory errors are generated unless external perturbations are applied to the system. These compensatory responses between afference and feedforward control also can occur with altered sounds as discussed in the previous paragraph.

Although, as stated above, they do not report any actual simulation data, Max et al. (2004) discuss how performance of the model is affected by different parameter settings that have some potentially interesting implications for the relationship between normal nonfluency and stuttering, which relates back to issue 2. They assume that children have a high threshold for sensory error-based motor resets early in development. This prevents them from constantly resetting parameters while learning new sounds, which was noted to be a problem for language feedback monitoring in childhood (Chapter 10). This threshold decreases as a function of age (solid line in Figure 11.2). For typically developing children, the size of the error signals during speech decreases due to improved use of feedforward commands (dotted line), but in children who stutter, the weak feedforward system does not sufficiently decrease the magnitude of sensory error signals (dashed line). This leads to the onset of stuttering when the threshold for motor reset dips below the error signal magnitude in these individuals (vertical line). Learning new sounds by listening to

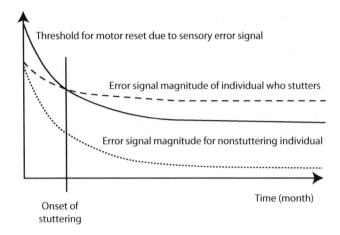

FIGURE 11.2 Hypothesized threshold for motor reset (solid line) as a function of time during the first months of speech, along with a typical sensory error time course for normally developing individuals (dotted line) and individuals who develop stuttering (dashed line; vertical line denotes the onset of stuttering).

self-generated speech is complicated by the presence of nonconducted feedback (as discussed in section 10.4.2.1.3 of Chapter 10).

6. *Variability in movement patterns of single articulators*: Max et al. review pertinent work on speech and nonspeech motor control. They summarize the findings as showing "a general slowness, possibly sensory based, in the speech movements of individuals who stutter rather than a difference specifically in the timing of those movements."

7. *Coordination of movement of articulators during speech*: Max et al. also looked at coordination work on oral and laryngeal movements. They considered that "they are appropriately timed relative to other movements within and across the articulatory, phonatory, and respiratory subsystems," but that speakers who stutter are slower than fluent speakers (i.e., comparatively few coordination problems, but differences in speech rate). They consider that the distinction between slow versus mistimed movements may be crucially important with respect to whether there are differences between stuttering and fluent individuals during perceptually fluent speech, and whether this reflects basic aspects of the mechanisms underlying the disorder or a preferred motor strategy that is used to avoid or minimize stutters.

8. *Neural processing*: As an additional point relative to the other motor theories, Max et al. (2004) also discussed the possible neural structures that could underpin their model. The main goal was to show that the hypotheses that were formulated were consistent with neural data. They note that theoretical and experimental work has suggested that the cerebellum (Blakemore, Frith, & Wolpert, 2001; Imamizu et al., 2000; Miall, Weir, Wopert, & Stein, 1993; Wolpert, Miall, & Kawato, 1998)

and posterior parietal cortex (Desmurget & Grafton, 2000; Wolpert et al., 1998) are possible sites for the formation of internal models.

Data on the basal ganglia dopaminergic system is also consistent with the notions in the model that stuttering may result from problems with movement preparation and sensory monitoring or sensorimotor integration. This neural system is involved in both motor planning/programming (Suri, Bargas, & Arbib, 2001) and sensorimotor integration and learning (Fattapposta et al., 2002). They also note that their perspective is consistent with de Nil et al.'s (2001) interpretation of their cerebellar activation data as indicating an increased need for sensorimotor monitoring in people who stutter. While it is important that behavioral data are consistent with neurophysiological findings, most other motor models implicate these same structures, so the available neural evidence does not help discriminate between approaches.

11.3.3.2 Summary

The Max et al. (2004) article provides a well-argued case and comprehensive coverage of issues to do with stuttering. The model provides an alternative view on auditory alterations, which has similarities to and differences from some of the other models offered (e.g., DRH). The relative importance of slow speech rate compared to the impact of coordination difficulties contrasted with Van Lieshout's DST view about the importance of the latter, although Van Lieshout has also discussed specific motor control strategies that are directly or indirectly related to this (slowing down or increasing movement/gestural amplitude). Like all the models described in this chapter, that of Max et al. needs further empirical test, particularly in terms of ones that can discriminate between this and other formulations. One particularly strong feature of the model is that it is implemented computationally as is the task dynamics model (section 11.3.2.1). Computer implementation allows demonstration that the ideas can lead to the behaviors they purport to predict.

11.4 OVERALL SUMMARY

Probably the main thing that has concerned theorists interested in how motor factors are implicated in stuttering is the ameliorating conditions of altered auditory feedback and, to a lesser extent, rate control. Theorists have shown considerable ingenuity in developing accounts of these. There seems to be some consensus that motor structures in the brain (rather than language ones) lie behind the explanations, and that computational principles need to be developed that can compute the effects of an action in advance of when it takes place (feedforward mechanism) or in real time (Howell, 2002, suggested the simple procedure of subtracting two rhythms that will cancel if they are synchronous, see Chapter 6, section 6.3.2). Feedforward processes are currently being popularized in the Max et al. (2004) model that may account for a range of issues in the area of stuttering. This and the two other general models account for a range of the issues relating to stuttering that language theories can account for and, in some case, other (motor issues) as well. In some respects, these models offer a broader coverage than do language theories. On the other hand, the motor theories do not give detailed explanations about some features that language theories focus on (e.g., the link between stuttering and formal or usage-based properties). The next chapter considers an account that includes both language and motor components that, in principle, should have a broader scope than either language or motor theories alone.

11.5 EXERCISES

1. Four areas that have been interpreted as motor aspects were listed at the beginning of the chapter. However, the interpretations that some of the effects occur at the motor level might be disputed. Present cases for and against the view that data from each of these areas are motor aspects.

2. Argue the pros and cons of whether a distinction should be drawn between local and global rate measures. As part of your answer describe why dynamic systems theory that sees both of these as aspects of the operation of a single system would still support local and global rate analyses.

3. What arguments are there for preferring motor theories over language theories as accounts of stuttering?

4. Design some new ways of creating arrhythmic stimuli that are not delayed forms of speech that should work like DAF according to the disruptive rhythm hypothesis (i.e., improve the speech control of speakers who stutter).

5. Do second signals have to be speech or can they be noise to improve the fluency of speakers who stutter?

6. The Vmodel argues that stuttering starts when children begin to produce multiword utterances. What reformulation would be needed to the theory if stuttering onset does not coincide with the multiword stage and how satisfactory is the revised version of the theory?

7. Design a new form of perturbation that could be applied as a speaker speaks. Describe how it could be accounted for from a general motor perspective and a dynamics systems approach. How would your proposed experiment help to distinguish between these theories? What would you predict the effects would be of this perturbation on a speaker who stutters?

8. Max and colleagues (2004) offered two accounts of why people stutter. These were (1) unstable or insufficiently activated internal representations and (2) weak feedforward control and overreliance on afferent feedback. Suggest designs for experiments that would distinguish between these alternatives.

12 Model That Proposes an Interaction Between Language and Motor Factors

EXPLAN

The EXPLAN theory described in this chapter was specifically developed to account for how forms of stuttering that appear in early development compare to typically developing speech and the course that stuttering takes during later speech development (into persistence or recovery). The essential assumption is that mistiming can occur in the process by which language plans are transferred to motor processes that can lead to stuttering. The theory considers ways in which treatments may work, consistent with the principles behind the theory. Predictions that (1) are falsifiable and (2) discriminate between EXPLAN and other theories have been derived and tested (e.g., priming work and the ways speakers who stutter respond to rhythmic stimuli).

12.1 INTRODUCTION

Previous chapters have considered findings and theories from language and motor approaches. One theory presented in this chapter maintains that both language and motor factors are important and that many observations about stuttering are explicable in terms of the way these two processes interface. The theory stresses timing at the interface between these processes and it does not assume that either of the processes is error-prone in people who stutter. As errors are not responsible for how speech is controlled, a feedback mechanism that passes information about the accuracy of production back to the language process is not required. Such a feedback mechanism appeared in Levelt's theory, discussed in Chapter 10, where the perceptual process was used to make a feedback loop to the conceptualization process.

The first section summarizes the arguments for the view that there are independent language and motor processes, as assumed by the theory. This was also discussed in Chapter 7, but here it is used to identify properties of the interface. This is followed by a section that indicates the main roles performed by the language and motor processes that are pertinent for the theory. The operation of the language–speech interface process is then described in detail. Two formulations of the theory are given. In the next section, some predictions of the theory that have been tested are presented. Some of the theories considered in earlier chapters are compared with the interaction theory. The answers that the interaction theory offers concerning the issues raised when evaluating language and motor theories (Chapters 10 and 11) are then discussed.

12.2   ARGUMENTS FOR THE INTERDEPENDENCY OF THE LANGUAGE AND MOTOR PROCESSES

The name of the theory, EXPLAN, signifies that two processes are implicated in fluent speech control. PLAN generates a symbolic language representation that takes different amounts of time to generate, depending on the complexity of the language processes (these also may be affected by usage properties). EX implements the sections of speech that are passed over from the language planning system and processes them into forms that drive vocal output. EX also takes a variable amount of time, which depends on the motor complexity of the sections of speech that have to be generated. It is assumed that language planning (PLAN) and speech-motor programming and execution (EX) are independent processes; the same assumption is made by Levelt and those that have followed his theoretical approach. The way the independent language and motor processes interface determines whether speech is fluent or not.

The EXPLAN model maintains that to understand the onset and course of stuttering, the language and motor processes each make a separate contribution. (Some of the functions the language and motor processes perform were reviewed in Chapters 7 and 8.) The advantage of EXPLAN is that it not only includes an account of the effects of a wide range of language and motor variables, but it also specifies how the language–motor interface operates, allowing still further tests and findings to be performed. This breadth is not possible when either of the component processes is considered in isolation. The language–motor interface is specified in EXPLAN so that it can generate testable and falsifiable predictions.

Four arguments were presented in Chapter 7 that supported the position that language and motor levels are independent. In brief, these included:

1. There appears to be one language system and several motor modalities. It would be efficient if the linguistic processing was the same for all of these motor output modalities. An independent linguistic representation could then be connected and disconnected to different motor output modules.
2. It is possible to read nonsense material. Assuming the same configuration as described in the previous point, this observation would then allow speakers to disconnect the language process and use the speech motor output process with nonlinguistic input.
3. In terms of evolution, language processing developed late. When humans started to use language, they employed motor control mechanisms that served other primary roles. Thus, the mechanisms used

in speech existed for life-sustaining functions (eating, drinking, and breathing). Consequently, there is little or no scope to modify the way in which these mechanisms operated during speech. The language process does not work under these constraints and thus it is adaptable to the requirements of working with various motor mechanisms (see no. 1 above). Adaptation of the language process so that it can serve different motor modules would be easy to achieve if the two processes were independent.

4. There are theoreticians and practitioners who treat stuttering as exclusively a language or a motor process. Either one group is wrong or both language and motor processes are implicated in stuttering and each group is addressing separate issues about the disorder.

All of these are arguments for the independence of the language and motor processes. These two processes also have to work together (they are interdependent). It was argued in Chapter 7 that gestures could be the element passed from the language system and they could be adapted to serve the different motor modalities. A second argument that interdependency between the language and motor systems is implicated in stuttering is that speakers who stutter have been reported to have various language deficits, but other speakers who have the same deficits do not stutter. This suggests that language factors alone cannot be exclusively responsible for the onset of stuttering. Correspondingly, speakers who stutter have been reported to have motor deficits, but some speakers with the same deficits do not stutter. Either process alone does not seem sufficient to account for why stuttering starts and the way it develops. The two processes either have to have independent effects or the two processes have to work together in some way. Interdependency seems more likely, as adding two small effects (from language and motor processes) would not seem to give enough power to trigger stuttering.

The EXPLAN approach to stuttering has been to include both language and motor processes and it is a type of multifactor model. Adoption of multifactor models should be approached with caution. As Max et al. (2004) noted, support for such multifactor models has usually been based on the inability to attribute stuttering to one single cause rather than on direct evidence for the involvement of multiple factors. This does not apply to EXPLAN, where predictions about involvement of factors at the linguistic and motor levels have been derived from the theory and successful tests have been performed (see section 12.5). More details of the way the language and motor processes operate together appear below before the bases for these predictions are given.

12.3   ROLES PERFORMED BY THE LANGUAGE AND MOTOR PROCESSES

It is not the intention to review again all that was said in the language and motor chapters (7 and 8), but there are a few aspects that are highlighted that feature prominently in EXPLAN. The main thing to emphasize about language processes is that the structures generated at different levels in language processing vary in difficulty because of either their formal or usage properties. The question arises as to what is the best way of representing linguistic processing difficulty. Some authors have emphasized that one type of processing in the language hierarchy is paramount. An example discussed in Chapter 7 is Bernstein Ratner's view that syntactic processing is problematic for people who stutter.

Our work has used function and content words as heuristics to identify sections of speech that are related to several of the formal and usage properties considered in Chapter 7. Here, heuristic means a rule that usually predicts some outcome, but it is not guaranteed to predict the outcome all the time. In the case of function words, it is known that word class does not always predict the likelihood of stuttering, which is why the relationship between word class and stuttering is heuristic (Howell, Au-Young, & Sackin, 1999). To illustrate this, note that function words that appear before content words in Selkirk's phonological words are much more likely to be stuttered than ones that appear after content words. Any rule that relates stuttering and symptom type breaks down for function words that are enclitics (see Chapter 7, Exercise no. 4 that invited readers to explore the ramifications of this).

Any of the properties of content words, in principle, can make language processing difficult and could be implicated in stuttering onset or course. The reason why distinguishing word types is useful when determining relative difficulty of sections of speech is that the separate types are useful for dividing language material into classes that vary in difficulty on a number of dimensions. Some of the properties of content words that tend to make them more difficult than function words for English and many other languages, in addition to word type itself, are as follows:

1. *Word stress*: Content words are much more likely to be stressed than function words.
2. *Phonological properties*: The syllables in content words have more complex phonological properties then those of function words.
3. *Word frequency*: Content words occur less frequently than function words.
4. *Neighborhood density*: As explained in Chapter 7, content words have more neighbors than function words, which could make them difficult to retrieve because of the increased chance of lexical interference (Vitevitch, 2002).

All these properties that make content words linguistically more difficult and function words less difficult are involved when words are split between the two word classes. Of course, this mix of properties makes the task of determining the relative importance of what factor governs operation of the word class effect a complex one to disentangle. While division into function and content words is useful, word class is not the only property that can be used to amalgamate different sources of difficulty. Thus, it would also be possible to develop neighborhood density metrics, possibly in a deductive, rather than heuristic, way, in order to incorporate several influences related to difficulty (e.g., word frequency).

Although the difference in difficulty between word classes is important, there are also variations in difficulty within word classes that will be reflected as differences in planning time between members of each word class. A way these differences can be measured would be to use phonological properties, such as consonant manner (certain manners, such as fricatives, are harder for children than others), word length in syllables (longer words are more difficult), and whether words contain consonant strings or not (Throneburg, Yairi, & Paden, 1994). Most function words only have a single syllable and rarely contain difficult manners and consonant strings. The latter two properties show that the syllables in function words are simpler than the syllables in content words (Howell, Au-Yeung, Yaruss, & Eldridge, 2006). A central assumption of EXPLAN is that the amount of time to plan a language section is directly related to its difficulty. Thus, from what has been said above, function words will usually take less time to plan than content words because they are shorter and have simpler phonological properties.

The amount of time needed to generate the motor output form also is important as discussed in Chapter 8. Speech motor timing is affected in several ways in people who stutter (local and global rate, variability and coordination). As with the language processes, motor processing time will be shorter for function than for content words because, for instance, the motor programs for these words are simpler than those of content words. Thus, motor processing for function words is faster than that of content words.

EXPLAN uses the disruptive rhythm hypothesis (DRH) discussed in Chapter 11 to account for motor timing adjustments and how perturbations affect speech control. Essentially, DRH maintains that, when events occur that are in synchrony with articulation, the motor speech sections (timing, in particular) are not disrupted. The timing signals associated with these sections can be internal (e.g., timing signals associated with efferent copy of motor commands, auditory representation associated with speech, modulations of breath control) or external (the various types of speech-synchronous rhythmic signals that affect speech control in people who stutter). The process by which external asynchronous events could affect speech control (e.g., delayed auditory feedback (DAF)) and how asynchronous events arise when speech has advancings and disappears when speech is fluent was described in Chapter 6 as well as an hypothesis about how the operation of this mechanism could change in speakers who persist in stuttering.

12.3.1 LANGUAGE FORMS AND STUTTERING SYMPTOMS

This section describes the EXPLAN interpretation of stuttering symptoms. There is a heuristic relationship between word type and stuttering symptoms as well as the relationship between word class and stuttering rate being heuristic (section 12.3). Pauses tend to occur around function words that precede content words (Gee & Grosjean, 1983) and these same function words tend to be involved in whole-word or phrase repetition. The heuristic-relating content word class and symptom type is that this word type tends to attract prolongation, broken words, or part-word repetition on the first part of the content words (Howell, 2007a).

Pauses, whole-word, and phrase repetitions that occur before a content word could have the role of delaying the attempt at the content word, possibly because its plan is not complete. Howell (2004a, 2007a, 2007b) grouped these symptoms into the class called stallings. Stallings involve words that are already planned, and the motor processes alone are repeated (Blackmer & Mitton, 1991).

Part-word repetitions, prolongations, and broken words are evidence that the content word is fragmented, which would occur if the speaker attempted to generate the motor output for this word before planning was complete. This is not possible in Levelt's (1989) model because the motor system has to wait for a complete language plan before motor programming can start. These symptoms would occur if the speaker stopped stalling in situations where the plan was not ready. The fragmentary types of symptoms were grouped together into the class of advancings (Howell, 2004a, 2007a, 2007b). Advancings occur when speech is not delayed and planning of the content word is not complete. Further language planning needs to take place for the next word when advancings occur.

To summarize so far, it appears that advancing is related to language problems on content words and stallings are motor strategies initiated on or around function words. According to this account, both language and motor processes are required in order to account for stalling and advancing. The two classes of symptom are distinguished in terms of processing requirements, not with respect to some judgment about what symptoms are stuttering-like and which can be considered other disfluencies, as in Conture's (1990), Wingate's (2002), and Yairi and Ambrose's (2005) schemes (Chapter 3). Giving all symptoms a role in fluency control avoids the controversy surrounding the decision as to which symptoms are stuttering and which are not (also discussed in Chapter 3). Covert repair hypothesis (CRH) also includes an account of how all symptoms arise; in CRH, all symptoms are reflections of planning problems.

Some language planning has to take place before motor processing can start. Consistent with this, the assumption that language and motor processes are independent, recapped in section 12.2, allows language and motor processes to operate on sections that occur at different times in the message. In particular, this assumption allows planning for future sections to continue while the speaker is producing the current one. Fluency problems arise when the plan for the next material is not ready at the time motor processing has completed the previous plan. This can happen in one of two ways: (1) if the speaker utters the prior material quickly and consequently needs the next material early, and (2) if the problem material is particularly difficult to generate/retrieve, its plan may not be ready, irrespective of the rate on the lead-in sequence. Fluency problems are most likely when both influences operate within an extract of speech. The speaker has the two ways of dealing with the problem that the plan of the content word is not ready (stalling and advancing), which was described earlier.

EXPLAN's proposal that the language–speech interface can lead to disfluencies in prescribed circumstances requires two additional issues to be addressed:

1. There has to be a common representation that can be passed from the language system and be used by the motor system to allow the two processes to communicate. Gestures were proposed as a representational form common to the language and motor processes in point 2 of section 7.2 of Chapter 7, as mentioned above.
2. A contextual unit is required that allows elements that can be executed rapidly and elements that take a long time to plan to be identified. EXPLAN considers the phonological word is the appropriate unit to represent this interdependency. Phonological words were mentioned briefly in Chapter 3 and discussed more fully in Chapter 7, but not with respect to language and motor interdependencies. This particular role is considered from a theory perspective in section 12.3.2 and some evidence is given in section 12.5.

12.3.2   SELKIRK'S PHONOLOGICAL WORDS

Selkirk's notion of phonological words was considered at length in Chapter 7. According to the current interpretation, phonological words (PW) are a prosodic unit that show the interdependence between language and motor elements and how they lead to the different classes of stuttering symptoms (stallings and advancings). The structure of the PW units is such that they reveal the neural interdependence between elements that are prepared for motor output rapidly and elements that take a long time to plan linguistically. Recall that Selkirk (1984) defined phonological, or PW, as having a content word nucleus and optional function words preceding or following it (see Chapter 7). The "swing" is a single PW with the content word preceded by one function word. Selkirk considered PW to be units at the lower end of the prosodic hierarchy within the linguistic system. In EXPLAN, the elements in PW represent the language-motor interface. First, each PW has a single locus of language planning difficulty (the content word is the problem) and, second, the difficult word can be preceded by function words, which are simple to execute so the motor approach to the content word is rapid. Consequently, the alternation between easy and difficult materials in PW provides a window on how the linguistic and motor processing interface may work.

The interpretation that motor factors are evident as influences on function words and language planning factors are evident as influences on content words would allow language and motor processes to have additive effects on stuttering. Additional influences are allowed that reflect the joint operation of the language and motor processes (i.e., the interface). The assumptions of language-motor independence and that speech planning has to occur before motor planning in PW units, together allow language and motor factors to interact. One alone can give rise to disfluency, but when both occur together the chance increases disproportionately. When speech is fluent, any function word or words prior to the content word can be executed and the plan for the following content word will be ready for output at this point in time. Disfluency occurs when there is insufficient time to plan the content word, or, more generally, the difficult nucleus in PW. When this happens, motor processing up to the content word has been completed, but the complete plan for the content word is not available; language and motor processing are not synchronized.

Different symptom types—motor stalling on function words prior to the content word or advancing on the content word before the plan is complete—are evident on different word types and position in the PW. These patterns of disfluency would not be predicted if only language or motor processing in PW was considered. It would be necessary to propose why the function word type leads predominantly to stalling and the content word type to advancings at either the language or motor level. A problem that faces any account of stuttering on function words is that some function words have very low rates of stuttering (i.e., those that appear after content words in PW). Consequently, in the single level theories (language or motor), it would be difficult to account for the relationship between word and symptom type. Position-dependency of symptom types is one argument for the interpretation that the point of fluency failure in PW units reflects the language–motor interface.

This interpretation may enhance understanding about the onset and course of stuttering into persistence and recovery. It has been established previously that stallings, which include some symptoms that authors dismiss as normal nonfluencies, are seen in early forms of stuttered speech where recovery is more likely. This form of disfluency is associated with repeating an available motor program. Stallings are like normal nonfluencies. Recall the observation that children stutter more on function words and adults stutter predominantly on content words (Chapter 7). Thus, a lot of whole-word repetitions on function words would be expected in children who will recover, as is observed (Howell et al., 1999). Other researchers have noted that stalling is a common feature in typical children. Clark and others have suggested that this form of disfluency has the role of delaying before they start to produce difficult material. EXPLAN theory adds that the difficult material comprises the content words, due to their several associated properties, and proposes the possibility that different types of disfluency should occur on content words. Advancings are seen in persistent forms of stuttering and they are associated with language difficulty. The change from motor- to language-based disfluencies is reflected in a change from stalling to advancing, shift in word types from function to content and movement from the start of a PW to the content word that appears later in the PW. The observation that adults stutter on content words (Brown, 1945) and symptoms change to part-word repetitions and prolongations (Conture, 1990) suggests they stop stalling and then encounter problems on content words. The shift in location of stuttering, change of word type on which stuttering occurs, and in the type of symptoms of disfluency give a logically coherent description of the process that underlies the move into the persistent form of stuttering. What the shift between disfluency types reflects is a change in the process (stalling to advancing, motor to language). According to

EXPLAN, to permit a change from motor to language processes, both elements have to be represented at the interface. The mechanism also has to operate on a section of speech that includes a single difficult nucleus (content word) with associated simple segments (content word and enclitic and proclitic function words). Selkirk's PW unit meet the latter two requirements.

PWs have the advantage that they can allow formal (e.g., content/function words) or usage (e.g., words with low or high frequency) properties to be used to specify the complexity of the constituent elements in the plan. That is, the difficult locus can be specified in terms of formal properties (prosodic, lexical, phonological, phonetic) or usage properties (neighborhood density, word frequency, etc.). If there was compelling evidence that syntax determines where stuttering is located, then that level ought to be included as well.

It is at this point that it is necessary to emphasize that the function/content word is used for several distinct purposes:

1. Function and content words require different amounts of language processing (content words more than function words).
2. Function and content words also require different amounts of motor processing.
3. Words from these classes are associated with different symptom types.
4. Words from these classes are used to specify the elements in a more extended contextual unit (the prosodic or phonological word).
5. All these elements are used in a combined way to explain the processes behind stuttering and why symptoms fall into two groups, which reflect motor and language operation (called stallings and advancings).

12.4   FORMALIZATIONS OF EXPLAN

The arguments that have been made in the above sections provide the assumptions behind EXPLAN theory. The main points are, in summary:

1. The language and motor processes operate independently.
2. Language structure and usage potentially affect the likelihood of stuttering (Chapter 7).
3. Motor factors affect the likelihood of stuttering (Chapter 8).
4. The theory should not assume that speakers make speech errors (Chapter 10).
5. An auditory feedback mechanism that sends information to reformulate language processes (Chapter 10) should not be required.
6. Synchronizing the timing of language and motor processes determines whether or not speech is fluent.
7. Using either language, or motor, processes to recover fluency results in different classes of symptom types (stalling or advancing).

Two implementations of EXPLAN that embody these assumptions are presented in the following section.

12.4.1 THE ORIGINAL EXPLAN PROPOSAL

Howell and Au-Yeung (2002) represented the EXPLAN proposal about how speech could proceed fluently and how stallings and advancings arose in diagrams. In all sections of Figure 12.1, the top row represents planning (PLAN) and the second row motor programming and execution (EX). Time is along the abscissa, so the length of the line indicates the amount of time involved in planning (top row) or motor processing (bottom row). EXPLAN proposes that planning takes place in

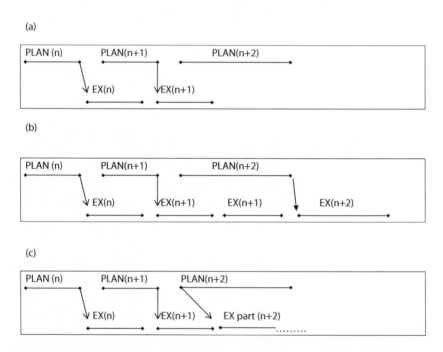

FIGURE 12.1 Diagrammatic representation of the temporal relationship between planning and execution for speech produced fluently (a), with stalling (b), and when a part-word advancing is produced (c). In all three sections, time is along the abscissa. Planning of adjacent words is shown in series for simplicity. The first section (a) shows execution of word "n" commencing after its plan is complete and that there is sufficient time to plan the following word (n+1) while word (n) is being executed. The sections (b) and (c) show situations in which execution of a prior word is complete before the plan for the following word is completed and two ways that speakers can deal with this. Section (b) shows that after word n+1 has been spoken for the first time, it is repeated to allow more time to complete the plan of word n+2. Section c shows that after the first two words (n and n+1) have been completed, even though the plan of the next word is not ready, the speaker commences word n+2 and the plan runs out (indicated by the dots) resulting in part-word advancing.

parallel with execution. Planning starts before execution (the lines on the top row occur to the left of those in the second row). An utterance starts when the speaker begins to plan the first element. When the PLAN is complete, it is input to EX where a motor program is generated and the speech is output. While the first element is being programmed for output, PLAN of the next element occurs. Speech is fluent when the successive plans are sent for motor programming on time, so that the sequence can proceed continuously. Provided that there is enough time during the execution of one word to generate the plan of the next word, the following plan can be picked up when the first word is completed, and speech will be fluent. (The fluent situation is depicted schematically in Figure 12.1a.) The utterance is a PW with three words consisting of two function words and a content word, such as "in the morning." At the time shown, planning for all three words has occurred and the speaker has executed the first two words.

The process at the interface is most likely to fail and speech to be disfluent when a word that is easy to process motorically and execute is followed by a word that is difficult to plan. In these situations, the plan for the next word is not available within the time necessary for executing the previous one and either stalling or advancing occurs. This has happened in Figure 12.1b and c, at the point where execution of word n+1 (the) finishes before the plan of word n+2 (morning) is complete. Stalling deals with this situation by repeating the motor processing of the immediately prior word (or words) again, or by pausing. Word repetition is possible because the language plans of any words that have to be reissued are still available (Blackmer & Mitton, 1991). In the example in Figure 12.1b, word n+1 is reissued. Planning of word n+2 continues and when execution of word n+1 has finished the second time, if the plan of word n+2 is then ready, it will be output, otherwise, word n+1 is repeated again. The output in this example would be "in the the morning." Importantly in stalling types of fluency failure, no word is executed until its plan is complete (either function or content words).

The situation where the plan is not complete also can give rise to advancing fluency failures. In these cases, instead of waiting for the whole plan to be ready, the speaker commences execution of the word with the part of its plan that is available (the choice between the stalling and advancing options is not arbitrary, as described below). Occasionally, advancing will lead to fluent speech when the remaining plan is completed during the time the speaker is outputting its first part. However, in advancing fluency failures, represented schematically in Figure 12.1c, the plan runs out on the first part of the word and fluency fails on those parts of the words.

12.4.2 SPREADING ACTIVATION VERSION OF **EXPLAN**

Subsequently, a revised version of EXPLAN was presented (Howell, 2004a; 2007b; 2010; Howell & Akande, 2005). This used Kolk and Postma's (1997) description of how activation for word candidates builds up (Chapter 10), which was derived from Dell's (1986) spreading activation account. Dell's theory was proposed to explain how speech errors arise in the language system. Kolk and

Postma's CRH described how the activation module supplied information to the monitor over the internal loop (see Chapter 10). In the spreading activation version of EXPLAN, the activation module is used but it is not linked to a monitoring process. Activation of multiple-word candidates is allowed and is used to account for occasional errors that occur (Howell & Akande, 2005). However, to simplify consideration, the situation where the single correct word-candidate is activated is focused on which is the situation that happens most frequently.

Howell (2007b) hypothesized that activation rate varies with the complexity of the material, thus a word like "scramble" that starts with a consonant string is activated more slowly than a word like "ramble," which does not. It was assumed that activation builds up over time (representing planning) and once fully activated, the plan decayed over the time that the word was programmed motorically and executed. The goal was to show how serially organized inputs representing the words in a PW could lead to elements being triggered out of order, which corresponded with stalling and advancing patterns. In addition to the hypothesis about the rate of activation/decay of words in a PW, a criterion was applied to the activation functions that specified which word, or part of a word, would be executed next.

The planning onsets of the successive words are offset so they are in the order they appear in the intended utterance. Activation for function words increases rapidly over a short time (these words are usually monosyllabic and simple phonologically) while content words increases gradually over longer times (these words can be multisyllabic and the syllables are more complex than those in function words). For simplicity, activation is represented as decaying from its maximum as the inverse of the build-up rate. When speech is fluent, the first word reaches full activation, motor processing commences and activation of its plan decays over the time it takes to execute. Planning of the next word in sequence has commenced and it is fully activated after the first word has been output. Consequently, it is selected for execution because it has higher activation than the first word and so the process continues. In other words, when speech is fluent, the words with highest activation are successively the right ones in the sequence. The rise to full activation (representing planning) and decay over the time to execute this word (motor programming and output) is shown for the function word "he" in the PW "he stood" as the inverted tick at the left in Figure 12.2. Activation of the initial function word occurs at a rapid rate. As content words like "stood" are, generally speaking, linguistically more complex and longer than function words, their activation profiles build up more gradually and they have to reach higher levels of activation (shown as the line to the right of the tick in Figure 12.2).

Execution involves all the processes concerned with generating output, using the input supplied from the planning process. As assumed, during time for execution, the activation of a word that has reached its maximum decays. The activation level after it has been uttered depends on how long the word takes to execute and the decay rate of activation. Two key concepts that explain how disfluency arises in the spreading activation version of EXPLAN are (1) the next word has highest, although

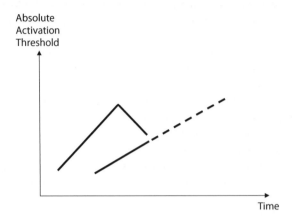

FIGURE 12.2   Activation and decay parameters for the situation leading to stalling for a PW consisting of a function word preceding a content word. The solid lines represent the activation states for the function word (left) and content word (right) at the point where the speaker has just finished uttering the function word. The dotted lines indicate that the activation for the content word still has some way to go before it reaches full activation. Stalling results in this case because the function word has decayed, but its activation is still greater than the activation for the following content word and, consequently, the function word is repeated.

not necessarily full, activation, and (2) the plans of previously produced words or parts of words can be reactivated and reexecuted if their activation is highest.

12.4.2.1   Simulation of Stalling

Selecting words with highest activation can result in the next word produced not being the next one in the planned temporal sequence. In this section, it is shown how the two properties mentioned previously can result in stalling. Stalling can occur after the initial function word in a PW has been produced and some of its activation has decayed. Nevertheless, the activation level of this function word can still be high and may exceed that of the subsequent content word being planned, whose activation is still building up, but has not reached its maximum. This situation arises because the speaker is producing speech at too rapid a rate prior to the content word, so its plan is not ready in time or because planning the word is slow due to its inherent complexity or a retrieval problem on this word. The speaker may deal with the situation where the content word plan is not ready by increasing the time to execute the initial function word in order to obtain more time to complete planning of the content word. Stalling, as described above, is a way of slowing execution rate and should occur when execution rate is high, leading to the content word plan not being ready in time.

The case of single function word repetition is shown in Figure 12.2 for the situation where execution rate is too high for production of the PW "he stood" (FC). The function word has been uttered once. Note that, at this point, activation for the content word is lower than for the function word. Note also that this is so despite the fact that some decay of activation of the function word has occurred.

12.4.2.2 Simulation of Advancing

In this section, it is shown how the content word that follows one or more function words in the planned sequence, can have highest, but not full activation. As the content word has the highest activation level, it will be produced next in order, but as its activation is not full, only the first part of its plan will be available. This situation can lead to the different forms of advancing (prolongations, part-word repetition, word breaks).

If execution rate is matched to the complexity of the constituents in an utterance, the PW will be spoken fluently. If activation rate (reflecting planning) of the content word is slowed slightly or execution time is decreased (speech rate is high), the function word that has just been produced can have a higher activation than the content word that is next in the planned sequence. This leads to function word repetition, as discussed in the preceding section. If activation rate is slowed further or execution time decreased because of the rapid decay on function words, the content word may have higher activation than the function word although activation is not full (as shown in Figure 12.3).

If speakers initiate execution of the content word based on its partial plan (advancing), stuttering involving the first parts of the word ensues. One might ask how the different forms of advancing (e.g., prolongations, part-word repetitions, etc.) arise

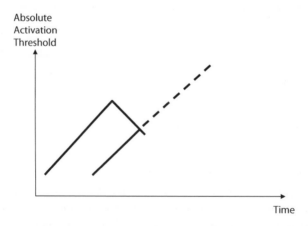

FIGURE 12.3 Activation and decay parameters for the situation leading to advancing for a phonological word (PW) consisting of a function word preceding a content word. The solid lines represent the activation states for the function (left) and content word (right) at the point where the speaker has just finished uttering the function word. The dotted lines indicate that the activation for the content word still has some way to go before it reaches full activation. Advancing results in this case because the function word has decayed below the activation level of the following content word and, consequently, the content word is initiated even though it still has some way to go before it reaches full activation (indicated by the dotted line).

when the plan for the content word is incomplete. The ideas on advancing that were used in earlier parts of the text, when applied to part of a plan, would lead to prolongation and part-word repetition. Prolongation would arise when the onset consonant alone is available, particularly in cases where the consonants are continuants (Howell, Hamilton, & Kyriacopoulos, 1986). Part-word repetitions arise when the plan is complete up to the onset-nucleus boundary. This type of fluency failure tends to occur mainly on interrupted consonants (Howell, Hamilton, et al., 1986). Word breaks occur when the plan is complete to the point between onset plus nucleus, but typically not beyond that point in the syllable (i.e., not to the coda). Speakers would break out of the loop when the subsequent part of the plan is completed.

This version of the model represents how language planning difficulty can lead to stalling and advancing. The activation rates of word classes will need to vary once a measure of difficulty has been developed. Any specific language deficits that are identified in people who stutter (e.g., slow lexical retrieval or phonological processing) also would be represented as variation in activation rate. Motor processing is represented in the assumption that activation decays as the inverse of the buildup rate. Chapter 8 showed that there are influences on motor processing that are independent of language processing. These can be represented by different decay rates. As discussed in the model work in Chapter 6, alerts may be generated when advancings arise and speakers may use this as a signal to slow motor speech rate. Another feature to note is what process changes when a speaker persists in stuttering. Earlier (Chapter 6), this was attributed to adaptation to the alerting sequence leading to lower sensitivity to the alerts. Lowering sensitivity to the alerts would make rate adjustment appropriate to short-term recovery of fluency less likely. In practice, lowered sensitivity to alerts would lead to no alteration to motor timing and an increase in the proportion of advancings. The latter has been noted as a feature of persistent stuttering (Howell, Au-Yeung, & Sackin, 1999).

12.5   PREDICTIONS AND TESTS OF EXPLAN

12.5.1   DO STALLINGS APPEAR AT THE START OF PW OR THE START OF UTTERANCES?

EXPLAN predicts that only function words in PW-initial position can be used to stall speech, whereas function words in PW-final position appear after the problematic content word and could not delay its production. Consistent with this, several analyses have shown that function words that appear at PW-initial position were stuttered more than function words at other positions (Au-Yeung, Howell, & Pilgrim, 1998; Howell, 2004a). However, this does not conclusively demonstrate that this is due to the effect of the function word's PW-initial position. Thus, function words in PW-initial position may also be in initial position in utterances. Au-Yeung et al. (1998) did an analysis to examine whether the PW position effect is the main determinant rather than utterance position. Stuttering rates of function words at the PW-final position of the utterance-initial PW and the stuttering rate of the function words at the first position of the nonutterance-initial PW were compared using a Wilcoxon matched pairs, signed-ranked test. The result showed that stuttering rate of the function words that appeared late in utterance-initial PW had a lower stuttering rate than function words that appeared in initial position in utterance noninitial PW for all the age groups that Au-Yeung et al. tested. That is, given an utterance that contained two function words F1 (final in utterance-initial PW) and F2 (initial in utterance noninitial PW), [....F1].... [F2....]..., F2 is stuttered more than F1 in spite of F1's earlier position in an utterance. This analysis showed that a pure utterance position effect cannot account for the effects of the PW position.

12.5.2 RECIPROCAL RELATIONSHIPS BETWEEN STALLING AND ADVANCING OVER AGES (EXCHANGES)

As seen in 12.4.2.1 and 12.4.2.2, EXPLAN predicts a reciprocal relationship between stalling on function words and advancing on content words. If a speaker stalls, there should be no need to advance and vice versa. Early findings confirmed this relationship as stalling and advancing occurred rarely in the same PW (Howell, Au-Yeung, & Sackin, 1999a).

Also consistent with this view, Howell et al. (1999a) examined the way stuttering rate in PW for different word types varied between age groups. In this study, speakers who stuttered showed more stuttering on function words (stalling) than on content words (advancing) in early development, but the opposite in later development (termed an exchange relation). The authors argued that most of the stuttering on function words would be stalling and most of that on content words would be advancing. If so, the results suggest that older speakers stop stalling and start advancing. Howell et al. (1999a) noted that the exchange to advancing at older ages corresponded with a reduced chance of recovering from stuttering, and suggested that the advancing pattern may be a factor implicated in this change. Similar results have been reported for Spanish (Au-Yeung, Gomez, & Howell, 2003) and German (Dworzynski, Howell, Au-Yeung, & Rommel, 2004).

The studies reviewed above did not look at stalling and advancing directly; they analyzed stuttering rate for function and content word classes and surmised that these reflected stalling and advancing respectively. Consequently, Howell (2007a) examined these stuttering categories directly in a longitudinal study on children who stuttered aged from about 8 up to the teenage years. They were independently assessed at their teens to see whether they were still stuttering (persistent) or not (recovered) using the University College London (UCL) group's methods, outlined in section 1.5.2, Chapter 9. For recovered speakers, the absolute level of disfluencies decreased as they got older, but the ratio of stallings to advancings remained constant. Speakers whose stuttering persisted, on the other hand, showed a reduced rate of stalling and an increased rate of advancing. This is consistent with the EXPLAN predictions about the symptom classes of stalling and advancing.

12.5.3 DIFFICULTY OF THE CONTENT WORDS AFTER A STALLING COMPARED TO AFTER FLUENT FUNCTION WORDS

According to EXPLAN, stalling occurs on function words because the following content word is difficult to plan. Howell (in press) confirmed this prediction when he reported that the word following a stalling was more likely to have consonant strings, more than one syllable, contain consonants that emerge late in development, or any combination of these, than content words where the preceding function words were produced fluently. From this it appears that stalling on the prior word may be in anticipation of the upcoming difficulty (Clark & Clark, 1977; Howell, 2004a). Speakers may pause before or repeat simple words that precede more complex words to stall their attempt at the difficult word.

12.5.4 PRIMING EVIDENCE FOR STALLING ON INITIAL FUNCTION WORDS SUGGESTING PW PROVIDE A BETTER ACCOUNT OF STUTTERING THAN SYNTACTIC UNITS

Recall that priming techniques are a way of manipulating planning time. In the version of the paradigm used with children who stutter, an auditory sentence or syllable was presented (the prime). Participants then described a picture (the probe) and speech initiation time (SIT) was measured. When the auditory prime matched some aspect of the probe, the planning time needed for the production of different elements in the phrase was reduced. Past work has shown that SIT is shorter for children who stutter than children who do not stutter for material that is primed phonologically and syntactically (Anderson & Conture, 2004; Melnick, Conture, & Ohde, 2003), but not lexically (Pellowski & Conture, 2005).

All previous priming investigations looked for effects in formal language processes, whereas EXPLAN stresses the importance of PW units, which reflect operation at the language–motor interface. In a priming study that tested predictions derived from EXPLAN, Savage and Howell (2008) used PW, such as "He is swimming" and "She is running," both of which consist of two function words followed by a content word. On a trial, a child was primed either with function words (e.g., they heard and repeated "he is") or a content word (e.g., they heard and repeated "swimming"). A cartoon (the probe) was then displayed that depicted an action that had to be described, and SIT and stuttering rates were measured. When the auditory prime matched an aspect of the probe (e.g., "he is" was primed and the picture was of a boy, or "swimming" was primed and this was the action), the planning time needed for the production of different elements in the phrase should be reduced.

EXPLAN predicts that priming either the function or the content word (the elements in PW) will have opposite effects (Savage & Howell, 2008). Priming function words should reduce their planning time, allowing them to be produced more rapidly. When rate of production of function words is increased, pressure is placed on having the content word plan ready earlier. If it is not ready, this increases the chance of stalling or advancing. Priming the content word reduces its planning time (as with function words). However, this time, priming should reduce the stuttering rate on function and content words. Priming the content word accelerates planning and decreases the chances of plan unavailability, which should be reflected in a reduction of stalling and/or advancing. In addition to the asymmetric effects of function and content word priming, EXPLAN predicts that there will be bigger effects in participants who stutter than in fluent controls, although both speaker groups should show priming effects.

Savage and Howell (2008) confirmed these predictions in children who stuttered and controls (mean age, 6 years). Priming function words increased advancing on content words, whereas priming content words reduced stalling on function and advancing on content words.

The findings suggest that the same process underpins the production of disfluencies for both children who stutter and controls, and that it takes the form of a timing misalignment between planning and execution. The primed production of a content word immediately before using it in a picture description reduced the time needed to plan the content word online by activating its plan (so that it was available in advance). This reduced the discrepancy between the time needed to plan the content word (relatively long) and the time needed to execute the function words (relatively short), and in turn decreased the likelihood of speaking disfluently.

12.5.5   INFLUENCE OF WORD FREQUENCY, NEIGHBORHOOD DENSITY, AND PHONOLOGICAL NEIGHBORHOOD FREQUENCY: PART-WORD REPETITIONS, PROLONGATIONS, AND SINGLE-SYLLABLE WORD REPETITIONS

Anderson's (2007) study on neighborhood density was described in Chapter 7, section 7.9.1.1. An important feature of this study was that Anderson looked at the impact of these variables on individual stuttering symptom types from both the stalling and advancing categories. Word and neighborhood frequency usage variables were found to be associated with difficult nuclei in utterances. She reported that words that had a part-word repetition or a sound prolongation were lower in word frequency and neighborhood frequency than fluent control words, but these frequency variables did not have a differential effect on single syllable word repetitions compared to their controls.

Stalling occurs to prevent a problem on the following content word, not because of the difficulty of the function word itself. Single-syllable word repetitions are a symptom from the stalling class and repetition of such words should not be a result of difficulty, thus word and neighborhood frequency variables should not affect them. This was what Anderson observed. Advancing is a result of planning difficulty. Part-word repetition and sound prolongation are from the advancing category. They should show an effect of word and neighborhood frequency. Again, this is what Anderson observed.

Thus, her findings about stallings (no effect of difficulty) and advancings (an effect of difficulty) confirm the predictions of EXPLAN. Anderson made a mistake about the predictions based on EXPLAN theory (Howell, in press). Related results about stuttering symptoms on different word types were reported in Howell (2007b). The work on the CS/LEC/MS, and IPC schemes, reviewed in Chapter 7, that showed effects of difficulty on content words but not function words, is also consistent with the view that the type of stuttering that occurs on function words is different to that on content words (Dworzynski & Howell, 2004; Howell & Au-Yeung, 2007; Howell, Au-Yeung, et al. 2006; Howell, Au-Yeung, et al. 2000).

12.5.6   SHOULD ALL OR ONLY SOME SYMPTOMS BE USED TO ASSESS STUTTERING?

The schemes discussed in Chapter 3 either selected the stuttering types that were considered to be more and less typical of stuttering (Conture, 1990; Wingate, 2002; Yairi & Ambrose, 2005) or included a wide range of stutters (Howell, 2004, 2007, in press; Kolk & Postma, 1997). Howell's scheme is unique insofar as it partitions stutters into two groups (stalling and advancing) and gives them a complementary role (if you stall, you do not need to advance and vice versa). Howell has shown the complementarity by the exchange plots, discussed earlier in Chapter 7 (section 7.4.3.2 and section 7.4.3.3), that show stallings reduce as advancings increase over age groups. Accounts such as those of Conture (1990), Wingate (2002), and Yairi and Ambrose (2005) do not predict any relationship between the classes they consider true stuttering and those they discard. Obviously stuttering rate can be calculated for the discarded class and plotted against the rate of supposed true stuttering for these schemes (i.e., a plot equivalent to Howell's exchanges). Howell, Bailey, and Kothari's (in press) work, discussed in Chapter 3, performed these analyses for three schemes (Conture's and Yairi and Ambrose's that are equivalent in Howell et al.'s treatment, Wingate's scheme and Howell's scheme based on EXPLAN theory). All three schemes showed a tradeoff between true, and discarded, stuttering events (advancings and stallings for the EXPLAN scheme). This suggests a functional role for the discarded classes and that a wide range of stuttering types needs to be taken into account when examining stuttering, as predicted by EXPLAN.

12.5.7   COMPATIBILITY BETWEEN THE DISRUPTIVE RHYTHM HYPOTHESIS AND EXPLAN

The predictions given so far have mainly concerned planning processes and symptom types. EXPLAN maintains that motor timing is implicated in several circumstances, whether the speaker stutters or not, when asynchronous sensory stimuli like DAF are presented. These were discussed at length in Chapter 11 (section 11.2.1.3) in connection with the disruptive rhythm hypothesis (DRH). The features of the DRH account that are particularly relevant to EXPLAN (alerts and adaptation) were discussed at the end of the description of the spreading activation version of the model. No further comment about the role of DRH in EXPLAN is given except to flag that the account it offers for the issues Borden (1979) raised about auditory feedback (raised in Chapter 8) is described in section 12.6.1 below.

12.5.8 SCANNING SUPPORT

Two aspects have arisen in scanning studies that are worth noting that confirm predictions of the EXPLAN account, which were described in Chapter 5. First, several studies in that chapter showed cerebellar activation when stutterers spoke. The cerebellum is the structure discussed in Chapter 6 that was expected to be activated when stuttering occurs. Second, Lu, Peng, Chen, et al. (2009) identified specific pathways that they identified as activity at the interface between language and motor processes (see Chapter 5, section 5.3 on connectivity).

12.6 RELATIONSHIP TO OTHER THEORIES

Since EXPLAN can incorporate language and motor findings, potentially it is compatible with a range of theories in each domain. It draws from several recent and past language and motor theories, which gives it some overlap with those as well (e.g., recent work on prosodic phonology and the speech–language interface, and work on the disruptive aspects of rhythmic stimulation. However, a theory that is consistent with every other theory is probably of little value as there would be no test that could discriminate between them. The ways EXPLAN differs from a number of the theories discussed in earlier chapters are examined in this section.

Three topics are considered:

1. It is shown how EXPLAN addresses the problems Borden raised for an auditory feedback account (Chapter 8). These points were selected for discussion because they have driven a lot of theorizing about how to account for the effects of altered auditory feedback.
2. The relationship between EXPLAN and Kalinowski's mirror neuron account is discussed (section 11.2.1.5).
3. Some contrasts between EXPLAN and CRH are then described (see Chapter 10 for details of CRH).

The theories in 2 and 3 were singled out for discussion because they make contrasting assumptions, and generate different predictions, to EXPLAN. The vicious cycle account is left out of this section because it is not precise nor has it been subjected to empirical test. Packman's Vmodel is mainly concerned with treatments rather than accounting for general characteristics of stuttering. Some aspects of Van Lieshout's work (emphasis on motor timing, variability, and coordination) and Max et al.'s (2004) work (motor timing again and a simple feedforward mechanism), are also included in EXPLAN.

12.6.1 Auditory Feedback Models

There are some theories that are not compatible with EXPLAN's assumptions. The EXPLAN account assumes that stuttering is the result of a timing problem in handling incomplete but (mainly) correct language forms, not of errors that arise during linguistic processing. Monitoring is only needed to account for speech control if errors occur frequently in speech and if covert repairs are the result of such errors. This is not to deny that occasional errors occur (Dell, 1986), some of which could be detected by a monitor, such as that described by Levelt (1989). However, the ideas that language is continuously monitored for errors in real time and that speech progresses fluently until one is detected (Levelt, 1989) presents many problems, as was seen in Chapter 10. Since errors do not govern speech control in EXPLAN, perceptual monitoring and feedback sent to the linguistic system are not required.

Thus, EXPLAN avoids the problems in using the type of feedback explanation discussed in earlier chapters. A simple form of feedforward control is included in EXPLAN. This was illustrated in Chapter 6 using the example of the subtraction of timing information in efferent copy and the output signal to determine whether or not there is a discrepancy between timing of the intended and actual motor plans. A requirement that remains is whether this proposal provides an answer to the problems raised by Borden (1979). Borden's first concern was the amount of time involved in processing feedback. She considered that an auditory feedback monitor would not allow speech to progress at the rates observed. Making an efferent copy at time of execution, obtaining basic timing information from a raw auditory signal, and subtracting the two would take little time. Thus, the proposed operations in EXPLAN would not slow speech down to the extent that obtaining and checking a full language representation does. Borden's second point was that auditory feedback is not essential in adults who sustain hearing loss. The absence of auditory input consequent on hearing loss would not stop the mechanism that is responsible for checking whether other timing signals associated with speech outputs are in synchrony or not (e.g., proprioceptive commands for lip, larynx, and other muscles) from operating.

The requirement also was made that the speech control mechanism has to operate without veridical information about speech output. In EXPLAN, the auditory input channel only operates as a serial input for determining timing information; it is not a signal that provides information about how speech is articulated. Since the speaker is not retrieving information about placement of the articulators to produce the sounds, it does not matter whether the auditory version of the speaker's own speech is veridical, only whether its timing pattern is in synchrony with other timing signals associated with the action (although see Houde and Jordan, 1998, for some contrary evidence). If synchronization holds, no modification is made to speech activity.

12.6.2 MIRROR NEURON ACCOUNT

Kalinowski and coworkers' account maintain that altered sound can activate the mirror neuron system. The importance of the mirroring notion is that it allows speech perception and production to be linked and, in principle, for perception to guide action and vice versa. The second signal would need to be speech to activate the mirror neurons (although signals with limited amount of degradation might be sufficiently similar in order to activate them). Three points where EXPLAN contrasts with Kalinowski's account include:

1. According to EXPLAN, FSF does not produce a second speech signal, but acts as a second rhythmic signal while a person is speaking. This second rhythmic signal affects speech-timing control (particularly when it is out of synchrony with the original speech). Howell and Sackin (2002) provided evidence, discussed in section 6.3, that asynchronous stimulation (DAF) affects a timing control mechanism, the site of which is assumed to be in the cerebellum (section 12.5.8). Both the site of the mechanism and the function that it plays rule out the mirror neuron account: Mirror neurons are not found in the cerebellum and the cerebellum does not have a role in speech perception. Thus, DAF affects a mechanism that is not compatible with the notion of mirror neurons.

2. Some of the manipulations discussed in Chapter 11 that are reported to influence fluency are so different from speech that they could not serve as second speech signals that would be able to activate these neurons. Examples include Howell and Archer's (1984) noise stimulus, Howell and El-Yaniv's (1987) metronome signal positioned at syllable onset, and a flashing light and vibrotactile stimulation (Kuniszyk-Jozkowiak, Smolka, & Adamczyk, 1996), see Chapter 8, section 8.2.4. All of these signals could influence the synchrony/asynchrony detector, proposed in DRH that is incorporated in EXPLAN, if they occur while a person is speaking. This same detector would be stimulated by FSF (synchronous) and DAF (asynchronous). Thus, EXPLAN has an account for why a wide variety of rhythmic and arrhythmic stimuli, some of which could not activate the mirror neuron system, affect the fluency of people who stutter.

3. Kalinowski and colleagues' mirror neuron account maintains that FSF does not disrupt timing, whereas motor learning techniques that involve slowed speech rate clearly do influence speech timing. They have only investigated global timing in their work. Special techniques are required to detect the local changes that are induced by some of these manipulations (see Chapter 8). Using such techniques, Howell and Sackin (2000) reported that FSF affects local and global timing. This means that the mirror neuron account assumption that FSF does not affect speech timing at all does not appear to be correct.

12.6.3 COVERT REPAIR HYPOTHESIS

Table 12.1 summarizes the main differences between CRH and EXPLAN. Points where there are differences between the theories are areas where the theories are potentially falsifiable based on empirical tests.

First of all, there are no marked differences between CRH and EXPLAN for the linguistic topics (first two rows of Table 12.1). CRH is rooted in Levelt's theory, which maintains that errors can occur at any level in the linguistic hierarchy (row 1). Although this theory proposes that people who stutter have a specific linguistic processing problem (i.e., generating the phonological form of an utterance, see row 2), it would be possible to modify it to account for other linguistic deficits. Since Levelt has developed his model to account for usage factors, again these could potentially be incorporated into CRH (row 1). Similarly, EXPLAN allows any level in the linguistic hierarchy and any usage factors that affect language planning time to impact on stuttering (row 1). That said, work conducted on EXPLAN has emphasized the importance of prosodic, or phonological words (row 2), and has failed to find evidence for processing problems in people who stutter at other levels in the linguistic hierarchy. The prosodic words can be described in linguistic terms (units with a content word nucleus and function word satellites) or usage terms (units containing elements with different levels of complexity, which arises from their usage properties). The role of syntax needs a specific mention with respect to EXPLAN. It could be incorporated at the language level as a factor that influences planning time. The reason it is discarded at present is that there is no compelling evidence to suggest that syntax should be included in accounts of stuttering (see Chapter 7). Although Bernstein Ratner (1997) supposed that children who stutter have a syntactic deficit around the time the disorder starts,

TABLE 12.1
Main Similarities and Differences Between CRH and EXPLAN

CRH	EXPLAN
Assumes a hierarchy of linguistic processing; usage factors like word frequency can be included	The same as with CRH
Fluency problems can be linked to linguistic forms (e.g., syntactic constituents); phonological processes are problematic and lead to stuttering	Fluency problems are linked to prosodic forms (e.g., phonological words)
Errors are the source of stuttering symptoms	Synchronizing the timing of language and motor processes is the source of fluency problems
Errors are detected by monitoring processes	Errors are different from stutters, thus no monitoring processes are needed for detecting stutters
Passive motor processing	Active motor processing

recent evidence by Reilly and colleagues (discussed in Chapter 13) suggests that children who stutter may have precocious language abilities.

Second, language monitoring is required in CRH because speakers are supposed to make errors during language production. EXPLAN considers that stuttering is a result of the plans for language elements not being ready for motor output on time. There are arguments for and against the view that there are parallels between the speech errors of fluent speakers and stuttering symptoms.

The point was made in Chapter 10 that speech should be considered in error only when the wrong phoneme occurs in the wrong position for the intended word. Such speech errors are so infrequent as to be unlikely as a factor that precipitates stuttering, even if higher rates of speech errors are allowed in people who stutter. If a person stutters on 10% of words, speech errors would need to occur 1,000 times more often than they have been observed to occur in a fluent speaker's speech. Such differences do not fit with the subtle language processing deficits reported in people who stutter.

However, the case for a link between speech errors and stuttering has been made by drawing parallels between variables that affect errors and those that affect stuttering discussed in section 12.5.5. Anderson (2007) noted that speech errors of normal speakers tend to be associated with words that are long (Fromkin, 1971), low in frequency (Dell, 1990; Dell & Reich, 1981; Stemberger, 1984), and susceptible to phonological neighborhood density variables (e.g., Vitevitch, 1997). Some of these have parallels with factors known to affect stuttering (Brown, 1945, for length; Hubbard & Prins, 1994, for word frequency; Anderson, 2007, for word frequency and neighborhood frequency). However, there are some provisos concerning the similarity. First, the effects of word frequency and neighborhood frequency that Anderson (2007) reported only applied to certain stuttering symptoms (prolongations and part-word repetitions, but not whole-word repetitions). Thus, perhaps only prolongations and part-word repetitions act like speech errors. Second, Anderson also reported that neighborhood density did not influence the susceptibility of words to be stuttered for any of the types of disfluency listed above. Errors and stuttered disfluencies differ in this respect.

If stuttering does not arise because speakers make errors during language formulation, a feedback monitor would not be required. The link between speech errors and stuttering that requires a feedback monitor is a major difference between CRH and EXPLAN. The ways that EXPLAN can account for a wide range of features known about stuttering without a feedback monitor have been discussed at length in the earlier part of this chapter and they are not repeated here. However, one comment needs to be made about monitoring. Much of the work that is described as tests of CRH does not examine monitoring. For instance, Conture has described his work that sought to detect phonological problems as a test of CRH (Chapter 10). However, phonological problems alone are not sufficient to distinguish between CRH and EXPLAN.

A final difference concerns the motor processes in the two models. Both CRH and EXPLAN models include a specification for the interface between the language and motor processes. In CRH, this process is passive. Language plans are passed on to motor processes where they are implemented as motor programs for output, and motor processes make no contribution to whether a word is produced fluently or not. In EXPLAN, motor processes can be actively involved in fluency failures. In particular, several factors influence speech timing within the motor processes. If rate is too high prior to a word that is difficult to plan, this increases the likelihood that the plan is not ready in time and fluency will fail.

12.6.4 COMPARISON OF MONITORING IN CRH AND ALERTS IN EXPLAN

At the end of the previous section, it was stressed that there is no feedback monitor in EXPLAN. There is, however, an alerting process in EXPLAN and this is compared briefly with the feedback monitoring process in CRH here (see Chapter 6 for a full consideration). The important differences between error monitoring in CRH and the EXPLAN alert perspective on speech control include:

1. An error monitor obtains information to determine what language process failed. Alerts indicate where failure occurred, not what the failure was.
2. For error monitors to be robust, the monitoring signals should be obtained continuously. With alerts, signals are generated intermittently.
3. After error monitors detect an error, the message is replanned. Alerts cease when a slower speech rate is adopted after advancing has occurred.

With respect to point 1, the error information provided to a monitor is much more detailed than that provided by an alert, as it needs to specify what alterations are needed to correct or retune a speech plan after an error. Full processing of speech to determine the nature of errors is problematic, as Borden pointed out (see the discussion earlier in this section).

Concerning point 3, the two perspectives also differ with respect to the response that is initiated when fluency fails. In an error monitor, speech has to be replanned or tuned to remove the error. In EXPLAN, once a slower rate is adopted, fluency corrects itself, as it is an emergent property of the change to timing. This correction is not based on a reformulation of the message.

12.7 ISSUES TO BE ACCOUNTED FOR BY EXPLAN
AND APPLICATION TO OTHER TOPICS

1. *Stuttering onset occurs in early childhood*: According to EXPLAN, fluency problems arise if there is insufficient time to prepare language forms before the child attempts to output them. As discussed further under issue 4, young children who stutter appear to have qualitatively the same disfluencies in their speech as fluent children, but show a higher

quantity of stallings. EXPLAN accounts for the qualitative similarity between stuttering at onset and fluent speech, but the quantitative difference (much higher rate of stalling in children who stutter than fluent controls) could be a result of factors that predispose some children to start stuttering. If so, the factors that lead to high rates of stalling could indicate why some children start to stutter.

One possible reason for the high rate of stalling is that there could be a genetic difference between children who start to stutter and other children. Evidence that stuttering runs in families, thus supporting a genetic predisposition at stuttering onset, was discussed in Chapter 4 including Drayna's recent work. Evidence for a genetic predisposition would need further work to explain the mechanisms behind why some children produce a lot of stalling.

A second possibility is that the brains of children who stutter are different from fluent children. The differences could either be structural (the children are born with brains that are wired in different ways from those of fluent children) or functional (the brains of children who stutter become different because they are "misused" when stuttering occurs). The structural account might explain why stuttering starts in some individuals; it is a result of brain morphology. The functional account would need some other factor (possibly genetics) that inclines children with a propensity to stutter to actually do so. Once started, the functional differences could take over. At present there is no evidence about children near onset that would distinguish between these alternatives. Available evidence on brain imaging in older speakers was discussed in Chapter 5 where it was noted that young children who stutter close to onset have not been scanned

Chapter 7 considered views that language planning problems account for why stuttering starts. For instance, phonological problems in children who stutter (delay or deficit) might account for high absolute rates of stuttering. Usage factors also might account for onset if it could be demonstrated that the limited period of linguistic development between language and stuttering onset is sufficient to establish differences in usage properties. Both formal- and usage-based accounts would need to account for why the rate of stalling is high.

. Motor factors also have been proposed as factors at onset. Thus, in Chapter 11, it was seen that Van Lieshout suggested that children who stutter have a weakness in motor processing ability, and Max et al. (2004) suggested that these children are slow at motor processing.

As was pointed out earlier in this chapter, EXPLAN allows both speech and motor processes to lead to stuttering symptoms. Consequently, it can incorporate some of the aspects language and motor theorists have proposed as factors that lead to stuttering onset and, in particular, high rates of stalling. A child could be having planning difficulty or motor difficulty or both. A situation where both occur is when speech rate is high around material that is difficult to plan. The factors would interact in the way described earlier and would offer a specific account as to why stalling was so much higher in children who stutter (i.e., they are affected by both language and motor factors). This account specifically maintains that the children use stalling as they are the default for fluent speakers. The changes to advancing that speakers who persist in stuttering make are aberrant (see issue 3).

Finally, Conture has proposed that temperament is established in early childhood and that a poor temperament could lead to stuttering. The evidence for this was reviewed in Chapter 9. There does not seem to be any explanation about why stalling occurs rather than other types of stuttering in this account unless children who stutter are more anxious and, therefore, more inclined to anticipate problems and respond to them by stalling. Overall there are several possibilities why stuttering could start according to EXPLAN. The preferred type of theory at present is one in which language and motor factors in interaction with some possible genetic basis; the evidence for CNS factors is not available to judge the impact of these at present.

2. *Many children recover during childhood*: According to EXPLAN, stallings are the appropriate way of dealing with fluency problems when the plan for a content word is not available. This is supported by the observations that the same relative imbalance between stalling and advancing also was observed in fluent speakers (Howell et al., 2009), and they do not acquire fluency problems. If stalling is a feature of fluent speech at this age, the young speakers who stutter were doing the appropriate thing around the time of onset of the disorder. This would explain why many children recover during childhood. Further support is also offered from Howell's (2007) observation that recovered cases decrease the absolute rate of all types of stuttering, but at the same time they retain the same proportion of stalling to advancing. The fact that high rates of stalling occurs throughout the recovery stage is consistent with the view that stalling plays an important role in recovery.

3. *The proposed features of persistent stuttering that make it different from early forms*: Advancing is a barrier to recovery according to EXPLAN and leads speakers to persist in their stuttering. One piece of evidence in support of this is the increased rate of advancing as speakers persist with age. This change to advancing involves a complex mixture of other associated influences, as well, which have been noted separately by other authors. The main one is the shift to content words. EXPLAN offers an account for this based on the motor/language interface. An experiment by Howell and Sackin (2001) supported this. They used a task where speech motor rate was high and the language task was difficult (commentary on a film), which induced advancing.

What changes occur that could lead to speakers shifting to advancing despite the fact that this decreases their chance of recovery? Howell et al.'s (2000) adaptation account, discussed in Chapter 6, attributes this to reduced sensitivity to alert signals that tell the speaker to reduce speech rate by stalling. The reduced sensitivity, which would occur specifically in speakers who stutter, makes speech reversibility less tractable. Some circumstantial support for this is that some clinicians do not treat clients for childhood stuttering when they pass the age of 12, and the fact that chances of recovery from developmental stuttering is rare from teenage years and beyond.

4. *Proposed relationship between early childhood stuttering and normal nonfluent speech*: Stalling occurs in the speech of fluent children and children who stutter. This suggests some continuity between the types of speaker. On the other hand, the rate of stalling is much higher in the children who stutter than fluent children, which suggests that the two groups differ quantitatively (though possibly not qualitatively). EXPLAN leans toward the view that there is continuity between stuttering at onset and fluent control insofar as symptoms are concerned, while allowing that there may be differences both in symptom rates (high rates of stalling in children who stutter) and other aspects (genetics, brain irregularities, etc.). One fact in support of this is that there is a high rate of recovery in early development because these speakers predominantly stall. The stalling type of symptoms permit development into fluent control.

Some similarities have been noted between fluent speech and stuttering that would favor some continuity. Thus, only the function words before the content word are involved in stuttering (Au-Yeung et al., 2003, for Spanish; Dworzynsk et al., 2004, for German; and Howell et al., 1999, for English). The same has been reported for selected constructs for fluent English speakers (Strenstrom & Svartvik, 1994). Also in support of some similarity is the fact that several people working with fluent speakers have proposed that whole-word repetition serves the role of delaying the time at which the following word is produced (e.g., Blackmer & Mitton, 1991; Clark & Clark, 1977; Maclay & Osgood, 1959; MacWhinney & Osser, 1977). These accounts have not linked stalling to function words nor examined how word repetition depends on the position they occupy in PW contexts, as does EXPLAN.

On the other hand, the high overall rate of stallings may suggest differences between fluent children and children who stutter. As noted elsewhere in this volume, Yairi and Ambrose (2005) submit to this view and state that stuttering starts in full-fledged form in some cases. This suggests that there is a difference in the symptoms of stuttering for some children right from the start of the disorder. Yairi and Ambrose have not presented data for scrutiny to date.

Stuttering at onset and childhood nonfluency may or may not be continuous. Basically, this depends on whether the initial higher rates of stalling distinguish the speaker groups or not. This is an issue that needs further work before a definitive statement can be made. However, there do seem some grounds for considering that the disorder has some continuities with fluent speech.

5. *Treatments that are effective at reducing stuttering symptoms*: According to Howell (2004), fluency problems resulted from mistiming between linguistic and motor planning processes, which either led to stalling or advancing. According to this view, speech is stuttered if linguistically difficult material is being produced and the speech motor output is set at too high a rate. When this situation arises, speakers need to adjust speech rate before they reach the difficult word.

   The EXPLAN account allows fluency-enhancing techniques to operate at either the language and/or the motor levels. Aspects of the EXPLAN account of altered auditory feedback (DAF, in particular) was considered at length in Chapter 6 (alerts) and Chapter 8 (the disruptive rhythm hypothesis [DRH]). Basically, DAF creates a situation where a secondary nonspeech signal slows down the motor processes. This would have the effect of avoiding problems at the language level.

   EXPLAN offers an account of why Lidcombe treatment improves the control of speakers who stutter. Lidcombe is a learning technique for which there is some evidence that it treats stuttering in some cases, and that contrasts in certain respects with altered feedback techniques. Thus, Lidcombe takes a relatively long time to work, but once the improvements occur, they are maintained for some time. This contrasts with altered auditory feedback that has immediate effects that are restricted to the time the alteration is delivered. These differences could arise if Lidcombe and altered feedback operate on different levels. Thus, if altered feedback operates at the motor level, Lidcombe might operate at the language level (Howell, 2002). Thus, EXPLAN has an account of different types of treatment (some occur because they affect the language planning stages while others affect the motor stage). A particular prediction of EXPLAN that has not been tested is that persistent speakers have switched from their stuttering being under motor to language planning control.

6. *Variability in movement patterns of single articulators*: The two important aspects of motor variability that EXPLAN stresses are the effects of synchronous and asynchronous activity that occur while speaking (described under issue no. 5) and local disruptions to timing that are reflected in variance statistics. Variability is likely to lead to some parts of individual movement records being slow and others fast because of the nonlinear nature of speech. Some preliminary work has been done on this (local and global rate change), but more evidence is needed (Howell & Sackin, 2000, 2001; McClean & Runyan, 2000; Viswanath, 1989).

7. *Coordination of movement of articulators during speech*: Coordination of the movement of the articulators has been emphasized by EXPLAN (some of the evidence for this was reviewed in Chapter 11). The main features about variability and coordination have in EXPLAN is to demonstrate activity specifically at the motor level. This point is amplified in section 12.8 below.

12.8   NEW THINGS THAT NEED TO BE EXPLORED

What does the speech motor process do that is not linguistic-symbolic? Most of the work reviewed in this chapter has been concerned with the language level. However, the assumption that the language process is independent from the motor process needs to be demonstrated further, as does the distinctive processing by the motor processes. Our recent work has used Smith's spatio-temporal index (STI) to this end (see Smith & Goffman, 2004, and Goffman, 2010, for reviews). STI was described in Chapter 8, section 8.6.1. The availability of two signals in our work allowed us to show that intercoordination between lips and energy was worse in speakers who stutter than controls (Howell, Anderson, & Lucero, 2010; section 8.5.3) using newly developed metrics related to STI. Articulatory intercoordination is likely to take place in the motor system, at least according to task dynamic theory (Chapter 11).

Second, more work is needed to determine whether the changes that occur in the speech of children who stutter over time are due to development of the language (Bernstein Ratner & Wijnen, 2007) or motor process (Van Lieshout & Namasivayam, 2010) or are due to some different aspect of behavior entirely (e.g., anxiety changes with age). Finally, space has not permitted discussion of the relation of stuttering to other developmental speech disorders (Howell, 2007b). This issue also deserves further attention.

Further specification is needed about what is meant by a "part-plan." Is it incomplete in extent, that is, properly coarticulated to a particular point (Howell & Dworzynski, 2005), but then stops abruptly? Alternatively, are some features absent at the point where speech halts (consistent with the view that coarticulated features of the same utterance are propagated at different rates, as in accounts that allow the mass and inertia of different articulators to determine coarticulation extent)? Howell and Huckvale (2004) presented some examples where speech was interrupted, but coarticulation for the following vowel was appropriate (e.g., the prolonged /s/ in a word subsequently realized as "CD" was appropriate for /i/). This offers slight support for the first proposal about part-plans, but more is needed and there are alternative accounts (e.g., the plan is complete, but the motor system is unable to execute it). Other procedures that may be used to obtain evidence for part-plans is the tip-of-the-tongue phenomenon, which Howell and Sackin (2001) proposed may be related to stuttering.

12.9   SUMMARY AND ALTERNATIVE ACCOUNTS TO EXPLAN

It was mentioned earlier that some authors consider that stuttering has features like part-word repetitions and prolongations and these would occur on content words at the onset of stuttering (Yairi & Ambrose, 2005). However, there have not been any case reports or (better still) examples posted on websites.

Dayalu et al. (2002) argued that word frequency is the important factor that determines whether words are stuttered or not. This seems something of a red herring as EXPLAN could work with usage factors. Also, their study concerned stuttering on isolated words, which is allowed according to EXPLAN; you can have problems matching planning time and motor time of an isolated content word. As the authors themselves state, the proposal that word frequency is the operative factor is not based on evidence, but "conjecture."

12.10   EXERCISES

1. In the section that argues that language and motor processes act independently, one argument presented was that this allowed a single language representation to supply input to several different forms of motor output. You may not agree with this. If so, can you propose an alternative way to account for how one language maps on to different motor processes?
2. Consider alternative ways than presented in this chapter, in which the language and motor processes interface and lead to stuttering?
3. It was proposed in earlier chapters that gestures could be a representation that bridges the language–motor interface. Develop this or another argument about the representation that serves as language output and as motor input.

Section IV

Practical Issues in Developmental Stuttering

13 Early Diagnosis of Stuttering and Its Prognosis to Teenage Years and Beyond

The issues of diagnosis and prognosis relate directly to the process of recovery/persistence. The aim of this chapter is to provide the reader with skills that are essential to understanding the statistical results that are published and some methodological pitfalls that may affect interpretation of the results.

13.1 INTRODUCTION

There are some authors who think that risk factors for onset and later course of stuttering are the same. For instance, this appears to be Bernstein Ratner's position (see Chapter 7 where some of her comments appear to suggest that syntax is important both for onset and later course of stuttering are discussed). It is also possible that risk factors for onset of stuttering (initial diagnosis) are not the same as risk factors for its later course (prognosis). Two separate sections below report on studies that look at onset, and course through to teenage years, and permit some evaluation of this question. Both of these sections start with a review of studies that have reported on individual risk factors. At the end of each of the sections, a single study that has assessed how well these factors predict risk for onset (section 13.2) or risk for course into recovery or persistence (section 13.3) is described in detail. Both studies used prospective designs to predict risk of onset in a sample before any of the children have started to stutter, or chance that children attending a clinic at age 8 will recover or persist at teenage years.

A study appeared recently that used a retrospective design to assess risk of stuttering in a large unselected sample of adults (army conscripts aged 18–20 years). This study is reviewed in section 13.4. Throughout this chapter, some basic statistical background is given to aid interpretation of the studies: logistic regression and path analysis.

The prospective study on the clinical sample of children aged 8 to teens was successful at predicting outcome at teenage years (recover or persist) from information obtained at age 8. Section 13.5 discusses future applications of this work. This section also discusses the ethics of providing this information to children, parents, and pathologists. The importance of obtaining this information has been stressed by some of the main research groups, but the ethical implications have not received much discussion.

13.2 ONSET

13.2.1 Using Logistic Regression for Estimating Risk Factors

Logistic regression is a statistical method used for predicting the probability of occurrence of an event by fitting data to a logistic function. Several predictor variables can be used that may be either continuous or categorical.

The logistic function is:

$$f(z) = 1/(1 + e^{-z})$$

The logistic function is graphed in Figure 13.1. The "input" is z (plotted on the horizontal axis) and the "output" is $f(z)$ (plotted on the vertical axis). An important property of the logistic function is that it can take as an input any value between +/– infinity, and the output is a value between 0 and 1. The variable z represents the exposure to some set of risk factors, while $f(z)$ represents the probability of a particular outcome, given that someone has that set of risk factors. The variable z is a measure of the total contribution of all the risk factors that were included.

z, that is a measure of all risk factors, is defined as:

$$z = \beta_0 + \beta_1 x_1 + \beta_2 x_2 + \beta_3 x_3 + \dots + \beta_k x_k$$

where β_0 is called the "intercept" and $\beta_1, \beta_2, \beta_3, \dots \beta_k$ are the regression coefficients of $x_1, x_2, x_3 \dots x_k$, respectively. The intercept, β_0, is the value of z when the value of all risk factors is zero (i.e., the value of z for someone who has no risk factors for the condition). The regression coefficients indicate the size of the contribution of the respective risk factor. A positive regression coefficient means that the

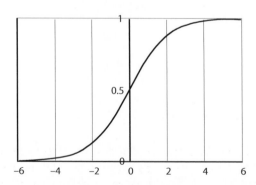

FIGURE 13.1   Shown is the logistic function, with z on the horizontal axis and $f(z)$ on the vertical axis.

risk factor increased the probability of the outcome, while a negative regression coefficient means that risk factor decreased the probability of that outcome. Put in another way, a large regression coefficient means that the risk factor strongly influenced the probability of that outcome, while a near-zero regression coefficient means that the risk factor had little influence on the probability of that outcome.

Logistic regression is a useful way of describing the relationship between one or more risk factors (e.g., age, sex, etc.) and an outcome, such as stuttering or not, that only has two possible values. It also can be used to estimate which risk factors are important in predicting outcomes.

A fictitious example follows that illustrates the application of logistic regression. Children often first attend a clinic for stuttering at around age 8 in the United Kingdom. A decision has to be made about whether the child is stuttering or not (what is the risk that the child is stuttering). Stuttering/not stuttering is a dichotomous dependent variable (0 or 1), which cannot be used in a standard regression. Three risk factors may be considered important: (1) severity using the SSI-3 measure, (2) gender, and (3) percentage of family members who stuttered in the past. Past information about these three risk factors, which were obtained from existing records, would first be used to estimate the regression coefficients of a model that predicts whether the child is stuttering or not. This step might result in the following coefficients for the three variables (x_1, x_2, x_3).

$\beta_0 = -5.0$ (the intercept)
$\beta_1 = +2.0$
$\beta_2 = -1.0$
$\beta_3 = +1.2$
$x_1 = $ raw SSI-3 severity score -10
$x_2 = $ gender, where 0 is male and 1 is female
$x_3 = $ percentage of family members who stuttered

The logistic regression predicts that:

$$\text{Risk of stuttering} = 1/(1 + e^{-z})$$

where, in this case:

$$z = -5.0 + 2.0 \, x_1 - 1.0 \, x_2 + 1.2 \, x_3$$

What the coefficients mean in the model for risk of stuttering is explained next: For factor (1), z goes up by 2.0 for every point increase in SSI-3 above 10. 10 was subtracted from the variable on the assumption that low SSI-3 scores could be obtained even if the child was fluent (i.e., a child could score up to 10 on SSI-3 and be considered fluent). For factor (2), z goes down by 1.0 if the client is female. For factor (3), z goes up by 1.2 for every 1% increase in family members who stuttered.

If a child has a stutter severity instrument-3 (SSI-3) score of 10, is male and has 2.0% of his family members who stutter, z is:

$$z = -5.0 + 2.0 . (10-10) -1.0 . 0 + 1.2 . 2$$

Substituting z into $1/(1 + e^{-z})$ shows the child's chance of stuttering is 0.07 (or 7%).

13.2.2 REILLY ET AL.: STUDY ON ESTIMATING RISK FACTORS FOR ONSET OF STUTTERING

Reilly et al. (2009) studied a large cohort of children to estimate the impact of reported risk factors on the onset of stuttering. They described the work as prospective as information was obtained before any of the children started to stutter, and this was true of much, but not all, of the information obtained. They identified two previous prospective studies. These were the Andrews and Harris' (1964) 1,000-family study conducted in Newcastle-Upon-Tyne in England, and Mansson's (2000) study, which was conducted on the Danish island of Bornholm. Both of these were reviewed in detail in Chapter 2, with several limitations noted (Reilly et al. note similar limitations).

The Reilly et al. study on stuttering is part of a wider ongoing investigation that started to examine a cohort of children at age 8 months with the intention of testing the children again at each subsequent birthday. The test sample consisted of infants born in Melbourne between September 2003 and April 2004. Eighty percent of all the infants were contacted and assessed at 8 months. Children were excluded if they had a congenital (e.g., Down syndrome) or developmental (e.g., cerebral palsy) problem or other intellectual or physical disability that had been diagnosed by 8 months of age. Participants also were excluded if their parents did not speak and understand English, as this prevented them from completing the questionnaires. The final sample consisted of 1,911 children. Participants for the stuttering study were eligible for inclusion once they had returned their 2-year-old child's questionnaires. Fifty-seven children were unavailable at age 2 years and 235 parents opted out of the study, leaving 1,619 participants.

Parents were sent information about the study, including a refrigerator magnet that defined stuttering. The magnet stated that stuttering occurs when children (1) repeat words or syllables, (2) make long, prolonged sounds (illustrated with the example "caaaaaaaaaaaaaaan I go"), and (3) have speech "stoppages or blocks" where no sounds come out.

13.2.2.1 Reports of Stuttering, Its Assessment and Descriptive Statistics

Parents telephoned the researchers if they suspected that their child was stuttering. Parents informed the researchers 1.9 months on average after the actual onset of stuttering. There was then an average of 1.4 months to telephone contact. The research assistants (RAs), who were qualified speech pathologists, called the parents who had reported that their child was stuttering and verified that the speech characteristics reported resembled stuttering. If this was so, or if the RA was unsure, a 45-minute home visit was arranged as soon as possible. The delay between reported onset and home visit was 2.1 months. Overall, on average four months passed between reported onset and the home visit.

At the home visit, the parents were interviewed to provide details about the child at stuttering onset, which included the characteristics of stuttering, and so that a detailed family history of stuttering could be obtained. After the interview, parents were videoed in a 25-minute session while they played with their child as they normally would. They were requested to avoid asking questions, and not to use many one-word utterances. The main outcome measure was the presence of RA-confirmed stuttering by 3 years of age. The paper describes how uncertainties were resolved that involved two experts who were part of the team.

Results indicated that the cumulative incidence of stuttering from onset up to 3 years of age was 8.5%. There were 137 cases confirmed to be stuttering by a trained RA during the initial home visit, and a further 21 "borderline" children in whom stuttering reports were ambiguous. A plot of the proportion from the cohort who had stuttered at any age up to 3 years of age had a constant slope from 25 months, which showed that stuttering had an equal chance of commencing at any age past this. Eleven parents reported that their children started to stutter before 2 years of age (i.e., before the stuttering study started).

With an 8.5% stuttering incidence, it is almost twice the percentage reported in previous studies (see Chapter 2). Previous studies usually examine wider age ranges and report substantial numbers of onset after age 3 (the upper age in Reilly et al.'s study). Thus, it is expected that the 8.5% stuttering incidence will increase even further and the disparity between Reilly et al.'s result and that in other work will be even more marked. Whether all of these cases are stuttering will be debated. The authors stated that the high incidence was plausible and noted that stuttering may have been missed in previous studies, either because it was mild or because it was short-lived. For example, in the Newcastle-Upon-Tyne study, stuttering sometimes seemed to last only a few months. Reilly et al. acknowledged that the cumulative incidence estimate may be inflated because disadvantaged families were underrepresented in this cohort based on the observation that children of highly educated mothers were both more likely to stutter and to be included in the study.

Median age of onset was reported to be 29.9 months. Although this is lower than the 33 months Yairi and Ambrose (2005) give, it should be noted that this estimate is likely to be low as no onsets after age 3 were allowed in Reilly et al.'s study to date. Stuttering was reported to have commenced in one day by 51 parents (37.2%), and over two to three days by 17 parents (12.4%). Thus, nearly half of cases of stuttering (49.6%) occurred suddenly over one to three days. Stuttering was reported to emerge more slowly in some children. In 37 children (27.0%), this was over one to two weeks; in 19 children (13.9%), this was over three to four weeks; in eight children, it was over a period of five weeks (5.8%). Four parents (2.9%) were unsure about the time it took for stuttering to emerge. The datum was missing for one child.

Most parents (133 of 137, or 97.1%) reported that they first noticed stuttering when the child was stringing three or more words together. Note that this does not necessarily mean that stuttering is associated with when a child starts using syntax, as there are other possible explanations as to why stuttering may be observed at this stage of language development. An additional point to note is that the children who stutter do not have a language deficit because other data presented by Reilly et al. (2009) show that, as a group, the children who stutter have precocious language development relative to the rest of the cohort.

The majority of parents (125 of 137, or 91.2%) described the nature of their child's stuttering as episodic rather than continuous. The most commonly reported stuttering behavior was whole-word repetition (97 of the 137 parents, or 71%, noted this). As observed above and in Chapter 3, this symptom is not universally considered to be stuttering. Its inclusion as a symptom of stuttering and its high reported incidence by parents may partly explain why the stuttering rate was higher in this study than in prior ones (Andrews & Harris, 1964; Mansson, 2000), both of which did not provide complete details of symptoms.

13.2.2.2   Differences Between Children Who Stutter and Children Who Were Fluent

Comparison of children who stuttered and children who were fluent showed that for children up to 3 years of age, the stuttering group had higher proportions of children who were male, twins, and had parents who had a degree or higher qualification. The stuttering group had a lower proportion of late-talkers, and higher total scores at two years on two communication measures, than children who did not stutter. The communication measures were Macarthur–Bates Communicative Development Inventories (CDI) and the Communication and Symbolic Behavior Scales (CSBS), both of which are discussed further below. Reilly et al. (2009) noted that mean shyness (measured as described below), birth weight, and maternal mental health scores of children who stuttered were similar to those of children who were fluent.

13.2.3   PREDICTOR MEASURES (RISK FACTORS) FOR THE LOGISTIC REGRESSION

Reilly et al. (2009) used logistic regression to see whether the probability that a person will start to stutter can be predicted from the following risk factors:

1. Male gender
2. Premature birth
3. Twin birth
4. Birth weight
5. Presence of older siblings
6 Family history
   a. No problem
   b. Speech/language/reading problems only
   c. Stuttering problem

7. Social disadvantage score
8. Mother's education level
   a. Did not complete year 12
   b. Completed year 12
   c. Degree/postgraduate
9. Maternal mental health score
10. Temperament score of child at 2 years
11. CSBS total score at 2 years (per 15-unit increase)
12. CDI raw vocabulary score at 2 years (per 100-unit increase)

The following measures were collected before the children reached two years of age, which was usually before stuttering onset. The parent-reported predictor variables were gender, premature birth, twin birth, birth weight, existence of an older sibling, family history of speech, language, reading, and stuttering problems, and mother's education level. Maternal mental health was measured using the Nonspecific Psychological Distress Scale (Kessler-6, or K-6, Kessler & Mroczek, 1994) where low scores (around zero) indicate no distress. The indicator of socioeconomic status (SES) was obtained from the SEIFA Index of Relative Disadvantage. This used participants' postcode to represent SES and low scores represented greater disadvantage (Australian Bureau of Statistics, 2001).

Continuous measures of the child's temperament and language development were obtained before stuttering onset. Temperament was indicated by parents using the five-item Approach/Withdrawal scale that makes up the Australian Temperament Project Short Form and is suitable for toddlers aged 1 to 3 years (Prior, Sanson, & Oberklaid, 1989). Shy/withdrawn children have higher scores.

The development of communicative behaviors up to 24 months of age was indicated by the CSBS Infant–Toddler Checklist (Wetherby & Prizant, 2002); raw vocabulary scores were calculated from the CDI, and children below the 10th percentile for vocabulary production were identified as late talkers (Fenson, Dale, & Reznick, 1993; Fenson et al., 2000).

Family histories of speech–language disorder were obtained from all the children. A more detailed family history of stuttering and related communication problems was elicited after onset from the families of children who stuttered, which revealed a specific family history of stuttering in 71 (51.8%) parents of children who started to stutter. Between 20 and 30% reported family histories of other related conditions including speech problems, problems at school, difficulty with math, and difficulty with reading and/or writing. Less than 20% reported problems in domains, such as epilepsy, intellectual impairment, other language problems, motor difficulties, and attention and concentration problems. The authors noted that the reliability of this information was suspect (and would be in other studies) because reports of family history of stuttering varied according to when the information was obtained. Before stuttering onset, 12 (8.8%) of 137 families with stuttering children reported a family history of stuttering. After stuttering onset, many more of these families recalled a family history (71 of 137 or 51.8%). The authors noted that similar findings have been reported in studies involving screening for hearing impairment (Russ et al., 2002). Also, family history was assessed in different ways for children who stuttered (at the outset of the study and after stuttering was reported) and children who were fluent (only at the outset of the study), so they cannot be compared statistically (group designation is confounded with different data collection procedures). These observations raise serious concern about using their family history data to assess what impact this has on risk of stuttering onset; they found no significant effect of family history.

13.2.3.1   Results of the Logistic Regression

Four factors were significant associates of stuttering onset. These were male gender, twin birth status, higher vocabulary scores at 2 years of age, and high maternal education. Further details of these findings and their interpretation are listed below:

1. Gender is the most widely recognized risk factor in the literature. In the Reilly et al. study, as reported in all other work, boys were more likely to stutter than girls (see Chapter 2). This finding confirmed previous reports about the role of this factor in early stuttering.
2. Although twinning was associated with increased risk of starting to stutter, the authors flagged that the result should be interpreted cautiously because the number of twins who started to stutter was small.
3. The children of mothers with a degree or postgraduate qualification were more likely to have stuttered by age 3 years. This finding was considered surprising, and they argued that it should be interpreted with caution. They noted, on the one hand, that the finding could be due to well-educated mothers being more likely to be aware of (and, therefore, to report) stuttering onset. On the other hand, they noted that it was also possible that the association with maternal education could be an artifact where stuttering onset typically occurred with the development of three-word combinations, and such combinations may simply occur earlier in children of more highly educated mothers.
4. Vocabulary scores at 2 years of age of children who stutter were higher (measured by CDI raw scores) than of the children who did not stutter. An increase of 100 words on the vocabulary score corresponded to an increase of 17% in the odds of beginning to stutter. Although vocabulary scores at 2 years were significantly associated with onset of stuttering, Reilly et al. (2007) noted that these vocabulary scores were not associated with maternal education. It seems that language problems are not associated with stuttering onset because the communication skills and vocabulary were more highly developed in children who start to stutter by 3 years than in the fluent children. This contradicts Bernstein Ratner's (1997) argument that stuttering occurs because they have a syntactic processing deficit.

Although there were some significant effects, the overall point that the authors stress is that the logistic regression had low power for predicting stuttering onset;

they state that only 3.7% of the total variation in stuttering onset was accounted for by their logistic regression. This statement is based on goodness of fit statistics, which should not be used for estimating the proportion of variance. Nevertheless, it is clear that the logistic regression had low predictive power for stuttering onset.

Another factor of note is that children who stuttered were not more shy or withdrawn. Early onset was not associated with language delay, social and environmental factors, nor pre-onset shyness/withdrawal. There was a nonsignificant trend for children with a family history of stuttering to be more likely to develop stuttering in comparison to those with no problems or those with only a history of general language/speech/reading problems. The direction is consistent with Ambrose, Yairi, and Cox's (1993) observations, although they would probably have expected this to play a more important role as a risk factor. Some problems with the family history measure were noted above that might partly explain the minor effect of this factor in Reilly et al.'s study.

13.2.3.2   Evaluation of Risk Factors for Onset of Stuttering

The Reilly et al. (2009) study presents some findings that question statements in the literature, for example, the lack of effects of family history and temperament, both of which have been considered important by some research groups. One of the significant results was expected and is always found: males are more at risk of stuttering than females. Another factor, vocabulary scores, was significant, but went in the opposite direction from that reported in other studies. It should be noted, however, that the reported association between stuttering onset and growth in language development also has the limitation that it is based on the parental report. The effects of twinning and a mother's education could possibly be misleading due to low numbers and selective attrition respectively.

The result that comes over strongly is that only a small amount of variance could be accounted for by the long list of risk factors that were included even though the sample was commendably large. One reason for the low predictive power may be in the inherent way that binary classifiers (like logistic regression) are affected when there are large imbalances in the incidence of the two classes (fluency is much more likely in the cohort than stuttering). With a 90/10% split, a classifier can be 90% correct by classifying all cases as fluent.

Speech characteristics were not examined as prospective factors for risk of stuttering (Reilly et al. made no recordings before stuttering onset). Information about speech forms at stuttering onset was provided by parental report. It would be useful to analyze the recordings from the session *after* stuttering onset, as verification of the parents' reports. For example, were the children having problems on utterances of three or more words, but not on utterances with fewer words?

Although parents were instructed on what features to look out for in order to detect stuttering, the criteria supplied by the authors about onset of stuttering are not unanimously agreed. The list included whole-word repetitions, which Conture (1990) considered ambiguous as symptoms, and Wingate rejected as diagnostic features of stuttering (Chapter 3). Howell (2009) noted that it would be valuable to analyze all symptoms on the recorded session made shortly after stuttering onset for the children reported to be stuttering in order to verify the parental reports. The authors responded by pointing out that the eminent Illinois group used whole-word repetitions and that they followed that lead (Reilly et al., 2009). However, Anderson's (2007) and Howell's (2007a) data, discussed in Chapters 7 and 12, show that whole-word repetitions act differently from other stuttering symptoms that are not disputed as being stutters (part-word repetitions and prolongations). Thus, in Anderson's study, for instance, whole-word repetitions were not affected by certain language factors that did affect part-word repetitions and prolongations. This suggests that whole-word repetitions are either not stutters (Wingate, 2002) or perhaps play a role in maintaining fluency in childhood (Chapter 12). According to both these views, whole-word repetitions are associated with fluent control of speech in all children and this conclusion is backed up by empirical work. Although whole-word repetitions may play a role in maintaining fluency in children who stutter, their role in distinguishing these children from fluent children is not straightforward.

An additional issue concerns the example of a prolongation that was given to parents as an instance of stuttering and that was presumably also used as a symptom by the RAs and the experts in the Reilly et al. (2009) study to classify children as stuttering. The example given was: "caaaaaaaaaaaaaan." This is not a typical prolongation as it occurs on a medial vowel, whereas most stuttered prolongations occur on initial consonants (Howell, Hamilton, & Kyriacopoulos, 1986; Wingate, 2002). Medial vowel lengthening occurs naturally in speech where it is used for emphasis (e.g., "weeell, that was exciting"). Thus, this example of a prolongation is not typical of stuttering; it differs from stuttered prolongations in two ways, and could arguably be a feature of a fluent utterance. Use of this example may have impacted on whether children were correctly classified as stutterers or not.

Sixteen hundred and nineteen participants were included in the study, from a cohort of 1,911 who were sent the original questionnaires. The data showed selective attrition between the cohort and test samples insofar as children with certain risk factor were more likely to have been excluded from the study than others. As Reilly et al. noted, more of the mothers had degrees in the stuttering group than the nonstuttering group, and there was a significant association between mother's education level and whether the sample was from the stuttering or nonstuttering group (Howell, 2009). This further qualifies Reilly et al.'s finding that high maternal education was a risk factor for stuttering onset.

13.3 COURSE INTO PERSISTENCE/RECOVERY: TEENAGERS

13.3.1 HOWELL AND DAVIS STUDY ON ESTIMATING RISK FACTORS FOR PERSISTENCE AND RECOVERY

Howell and Davis (in press) conducted a study on children referred to stuttering clinics who had first been seen when they were aged around 8. Measurements on a range of risk factors were obtained when the children were teenagers. The inclusion criteria (at age 8) and classification as recovered or persistent (teenagers), given in Chapter 1, were applied. Sixty-nine of the group of 132 participants (52.3%) were classified as recovered. The main reason for examining children up to their teens was because of the focus on recovery, which is not fully resolved at ages before teens. The main reasons for using the range eight to teenager was that large numbers of children attend clinics at these ages and recovery rate is around 50%. Consequently, the data are suitable for classificatory analyses as there are roughly equal numbers of persistent and recovered cases.

Recent work on speakers in this age range and older was used to select the risk factors that were associated with persistence of stuttering. Six binary factors were included:

1. *Head injury*: It has been reported that a high proportion of speakers who stutter had head injuries that resulted in loss of consciousness in the period before stuttering started (Alm & Risberg, 2007). Parents/caregivers were asked if their child had sustained a head injury that resulted in loss of consciousness and/or hospitalization. When a positive response was given, they were asked at what age the incident occurred.

2. *Onset age (above/below mean)*: The chances of recovery are best shortly after the condition starts. Thus, the odds for recovery decline the longer the child stutters (Mansson, 2000). Parents/caregivers were asked at what age their child first started stuttering. Semistructured prompts were used to aid recall, e.g., before or after starting school, or when onset occurred relative to the birth of a sibling.

3. *Family history*: Almost half of all children who stutter have a family member who stutters (Yairi & Ambrose, 2005). Parents/caregivers were interviewed about whether any blood relatives of their child had ever (or still) stuttered. For positive responses semistructured prompts were used to establish the degree of relationship and whether the relative concerned recovered or persisted in their stutter. With the benefit of hindsight, this factor might have been left out (based on Reilly et al.'s 2009 observations).

4. *Handedness*: The proportion of left-handed children who stutter is significantly higher (Brosch, Haege, Kalehne, & Johannsen, 1999; Howell et al., 2008), than the 10% in the population at large (McManus, 2002). Parents/caregivers were asked which hand their child used for the majority of everyday tasks, including handwriting, using a computer mouse, cleaning their teeth, etc.

5. *Speaking a second language in the home*: Speaking two languages in the preschool years increases the chances of children starting to stutter and decreases the likelihood of recovery from stuttering, relative to learning English when starting school (Howell, Davis, & Williams, 2009). Parents/caregivers were asked what languages were spoken in the home. If more than one, they also were asked which language was spoken most and to give an approximate ratio (e.g., 70% Wolof/30% English).

6. *Gender*: More boys than girls were found to stutter in the age range onset to teenage (Andrews & Harris, 1964). The ratio increased as the children got older, which indicated that girls recovered from stuttering at an earlier age than boys.
7. *Severity of speech symptoms obtained when the child was first seen*: The seventh risk factor was a continuous measure. The standard instrument for severity is SSI-3 (Riley, 1994). SSI-3 was eight points higher at age 8 for children who persisted than for children who recovered (Howell et al., 2008).

A total of 222 children from 35 primary healthcare trusts, who were referred to specialist clinics and confirmed as stuttering, were seen. The initial logistic regression was based on information from 132 children who stuttered who were assessed at teenage years to see whether they had persisted or recovered (detailed below). Seventy-four cases were used for validation. For these children one or more of the predictor variables other than SSI-3 was missing and unobtainable (e.g., onset age could not be remembered, family history was unknown because the child was adopted, etc.). All of these cases had persistence/recovery outcome assessed in the same way as the other 132 children.

A benchmark model applied a constant category to all cases. All cases were designated recovered, and these made up 52.3% of all cases in the actual sample. Sensitivity of the model (percentage of the group that had the persistent characteristic in this case) was 0% and specificity (the percentage of the group that had the recovered characteristic) was 100%. The –2 log likelihood (–2LL) statistic was 182.718. Subsequent models that have better predictive power should lead to significant reductions in –2LL.

The predictor variables were then entered using the backward stepwise method. The method started with all the variables included in the model and then tested whether any of these predictors could be removed without significantly affecting the model fit. The statistical criterion to establish whether a predictor should be retained is whether the –2LL decreased significantly after its removal relative to the model with only the constant (assessed using the x^2 statistic). Thus, if a predictor was removed and –2LL was significantly reduced, then it should be kept. One nonsignificant predictor was removed per step starting with the one that had the least impact on how well the model fitted the data (selected automatically). It was apparent that all predictor variables except SSI-3 could be removed without affecting the fit of the model. Thus, SSI-3 was a significant predictor and no other predictor added significantly to the fit of the model.

The correct predicted outcome for scores of less than 0.5 was recovered and for scores greater than 0.5 was persistent. Misclassifications for predicted probabilities less than 0.5 were cases with low predicted probability of persisting, who nevertheless went on to persist. Misclassifications for predicted probabilities greater than 0.5 were cases with high predicted probability of persisting, who nevertheless went on to recover. Together there were 25 misclassified cases, which gave an overall correct classification figure of 81.1%. The sensitivity of the model to persistent cases was 53/63 (84.1%). Sensitivity is the percentage of the group that had the persistent characteristic in this case. Specificity with respect to recovered cases was 54/69 (78.3%). Specificity is the percentage of the group that had the recovered characteristic. The model predicted that 68 cases would be persistent, and 53 of these were true positives giving a positive predictive value (PPV) of 77.9%. The model predicted that 64 cases would recover; 54 of these were true negatives giving a negative predictive value (NPV) of 84.4%.

As validation, the performance of the model that included SSI-3 only was explored using the 74 participants who had missing data on some of the categorical variables. They had been characterized as persistent or recovered in the same way as the original 132 participants. The benchmark model placed all cases in the persistent class (there were 51.4% of these, which was the overall percentage the model predicted correctly). The log likelihood statistic (–2LL) with only the constant included for this model was 102.532.

The classification table showed that sensitivity was 76.3% and specificity was 72.2% and that overall percentage of cases predicted correctly was 74.3%. The model predicted that 39 cases would be persistent; 29 of these were true positives, giving a PPV of 74.4%. The model predicted that 35 cases would recover; 26 of these were true negatives, giving an NPV of 74.3%.

Only symptom severity, measured by SSI-3, was a significant predictor for risk of persistence. In the age range 8 to teenagers, approximately 50% of children recover from stuttering (Fritzell, 1976; Howell et al., 2008). The logistic regression model, that included SSI-3 was able to correctly predict 80% of the outcomes at the teens with equivalent specificity and sensitivity. The findings were replicated on a separate group of 74 children in the same age range whose persistence or recovery was determined in the same way as for the main group.

Note that the SSI-3 score was not a criterion for recovery in the teens so as to avoid circularity (i.e., using SSI-3 to determine persistence or recovery and then to use it as a predictor of persistence or recovery). It also may be important that the speech recordings were transferred to computer for analysis because this procedure is more sensitive than listening straight from recording hardware. The first SSI-3 estimates were obtained before treatment so that they were not affected by intervention. All participants then received treatment so there was no "no treatment" condition that would have allowed the effect of receiving/not receiving treatment to be determined.

Outcome at teenage years is not perfectly predicted, so misclassification of individual cases is possible. Use of these results with particular cases needs to reflect this fact. In stuttering, the cost, both physical and financial, of treatment is comparatively low compared to other medical conditions, so it could be argued that erring on the side of intervention is advisable. Clinicians and clients who want to use the information in this report, but who prefer to be cautious might use more conservative cutoffs. Consultation needs to take place with clinicians and clients to establish the best way of using this information (see 13.5.2 below).

13.4 RETROSPECTIVE ANALYSIS OF AN ADULT SAMPLE TO IDENTIFY WHICH FACTORS PREDICT RISK OF STUTTERING

Ajdacic-Gross et al. (2009) used logistic regression and path analysis in a study intended to establish what factors predicted risk of stuttering in a cohort of adult army conscripts. The former technique has been covered. Some basic information about the second technique follows.

13.4.1 BASIC PRINCIPLES OF PATH ANALYSIS

The aim of this section is to provide the reader with details of how path analyses are conducted and how to interpret those that appear in papers. There is insufficient information to allow readers to perform their own analyses. The aim of path analysis is to provide estimates of the magnitude and significance of hypothesized causal connections between sets of variables. The first step is to construct a path diagram. To do this, the names of the variables are written down and arrows drawn from each variable to any other variable that it is hypothesized to affect. Figure 13.2 shows an input path diagram. It is a hypothetical example that models one possible view about how psychological factors might enhance the chances of recovery for a child who is in treatment.

In the model, a child comes to treatment with opinions about whether a treatment will be successful or not. This should correlate positively with his or her involvement in therapy. Involvement in therapy will require much verbal expression, which could make the child anxious (involvement and anxiety correlate positively). Involvement in therapy itself will increase the chances of recovery (involvement and recovery correlate positively). However, the increased anxiety that was a by-product of involvement in therapy may decrease the chances of recovery (anxiety and recovery correlate negatively).

The four variables—opinion, involvement, anxiety, and recovery—are next used to generate three equations. Involvement and anxiety have direct effects on recovery; opinion does not, there is no direct line going from opinion to recovery. Anxiety is directly affected by involvement, which is directly affected by opinion. These are specified formally as structural equations, which are needed so the correlation coefficients for the paths shown in Figure 13.2 can be obtained. They include:

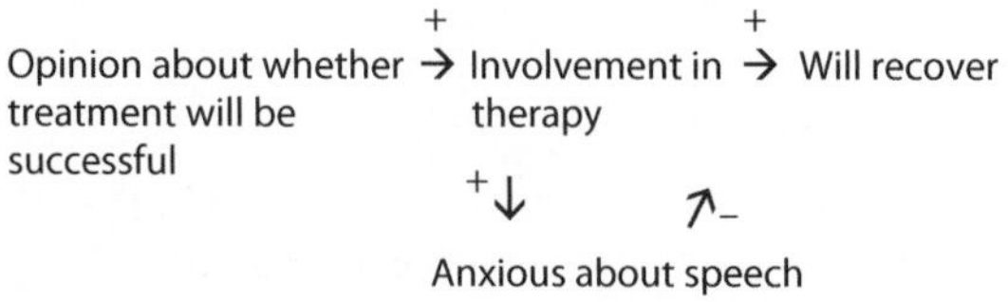

FIGURE 13.2 Idealized input path diagram for a model relating opinion about treatment, involvement in therapy, anxiety, and chance of recovery is illustrated.

Recovery = β_{11} involvement + β_{12} anxiety + e_1
Anxiety = βb_{21} involvement + e_2
Involvement = β_{31} opinion + e_3

The notation indicates that, for instance, β_{11} in the first equation is different from β_{21} in the second and the terms e_1, e_2, and e_3 are the error or unexplained variance. Next, three regression analyses are run to obtain the correlation coefficients for each path (one each for when recovery, anxiety, and involvement is the dependent variable, using the independent variables specified in the right-hand side of the corresponding equations above). The regression analysis supplies the coefficients, which may be $\beta_{11} = 0.30$, $\beta_{12} = -0.44$, $\beta_{21} = 0.15$, and $\beta_{31} = 0.31$. The βs are taken from the output and then inserted into the output path diagram. In fact, Ajdacic-Gross et al. (2009) used the odds ratio rather than correlation coefficients. Odds ratio is a measure of the strength of association between two binary data values and behaves something like a correlation coefficient. The description with correlation coefficients has been included to keep things simple on the assumption that the reader has some familiarity with simple linear regression. The complete output path diagram is given in Figure 13.3.

Within a given path diagram, path analysis can indicate which are the more important (and significant) paths, and this may have implications for the plausibility of prespecified causal hypotheses. Path analysis cannot indicate which of two distinct path diagrams is preferred, nor can it show whether the correlation between A and B represents a causal effect of A on B, a causal effect of B on A, mutual dependence on other variables C, D, etc, or some combination of these.

13.4.2 RISK FACTORS FOR STUTTERING IN A LARGE DATABASE OF ADULT ARMY CONSCRIPTS

Ajdacic-Gross et al. (2009) reported a post-hoc analysis of risk factors for stuttering on a database collected for other purposes, but which had information about whether the respondents stuttered or not. There were 14,157 conscripts aged 18 to 20 who underwent psychiatric screening. Individuals who had incomplete or erroneous records were excluded, leaving 11,905 cases. Cases with high psychiatric scores were excluded (it is stated that these were mainly malingerers) leaving 9,814 records. Responses were obtained from psychiatric interviews and

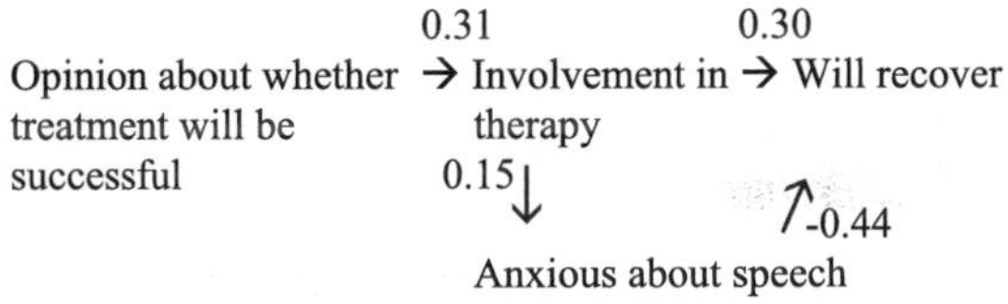

FIGURE 13.3 Idealized output path diagram for a model relating opinion about treatment, involvement in therapy anxiety, and chance that a child will recover.

questionnaires performed and administered by trained personnel. Stuttering was self-reported and recovered cases, who were not stuttering at the time of the interview, and persistent cases were not distinguished. Four hundred and eight men (4.2% of the 9,814) reported having stuttered in childhood. This is comparable with other estimates for incidence discussed in Chapter 2.

Preliminary bivariate analyses (people who stuttered were compared with people who did not stutter) were conducted for 29 variables. The complete list is shown in Table 13.1. Seventeen of these variables were designated as risk factor for stuttering, five as concomitant childhood factors, and seven as risk or concomitant factors. The authors noted, like Reilly et al. (2009), that only small proportions of people who stuttered were influenced by each putative risk factor. The main analyses looked at the 17 variables identified as risk factors, plus the risk or concomitant factor of "frequently beaten by parents or educators." The rest of the review of this paper focuses on the logistic regression and path analyses that were reported on these variables. The 18 variables were entered into a logistic regression. Again there was no overwhelmingly strong risk factor; all odds ratios are about 2 or below. Six variables that were significant predictors after adjustments were used (presumably using a method, such as the backward stepwise method that was used in Howell and Davis' work and which was described above). These were (1) incubator; (2) restless and fidgety in school, which they suggested may reflect ADHD; (3) alcohol abuse of mother; (4) alcohol abuse of father; (5) obsessive-compulsive disorder (OCD) in family members; and (6) having a parent from a foreign country.

The authors' path diagram, shown in Figure 13.4, has 14 risk factors on the left. The six significant predictors and their connectivity with other variables is as follows: Obsessive-compulsive disorder in family members (factor 5) maps directly onto stuttering output (shown on the right). Mother alcoholic (3), father alcoholic (4), and foreign parent (6) map directly onto stuttering output and indirectly onto other predictors that act indirectly on stuttering output. The two remaining significant variables act as indirect factors (incubator, factor 1, and restless and fidgety in school (factor 2). Two other nonsignificant factors operate indirectly: trouble at birth and frequently beaten. All the other insignificant predictors on the left map onto the four indirect factors and, in some cases, directly to stuttering output, too.

13.4.2.1   Interpretation of the Results

The wide spectrum of etiological mechanisms and related disturbances was attributed to the fact that stuttering is a heterogeneous disorder. The points they made about each of the significant risk factors are summarized below.

Predictor 2—They suggested that "restless and fidgety in school" was an expected risk factor for stuttering. Their argument was that it relates to attention deficit hyperactivity disorder (ADHD), which has been reported as a risk factor in other studies (Alm & Risberg, 2007; Blood, Ridenour, Qualls, & Hammer, 2003).

TABLE 13.1
Risk and Concomitant Factors for Stuttering Examined in Swiss Male Army Conscripts

Putative Risk Factors

Troubles at birth
Incubator
Restless and fidgety in school
Mother alcoholic
Father alcoholic
Mother with other addiction
Father with other addiction
Anxiety in family members/relatives
Compulsion in family members/relatives
Depression in family members/relatives
Schizophrenia in family members/relatives
Family member was psychiatric inpatient
Mother is disabled
Father is disabled
Mother had a serious physical disease
Father had a serious physical disease
Parent from a foreign country

Risk or Concomitant Childhood Factors

Sibling is disabled
Sibling had a serious physical disease
Frequently beaten by parents or educators
Not grown up with both parents
Raised (at least for a while) in an asylum
Raised (at least for a while) with grandparents
Hospitalized because of head injury

Concomitant Childhood Factors

Came late to school (8 years or older)
Examined by school psychologist
Troubles with reading and writing
Teased for deformity or did not come to terms with deformity
Had psychological counseling and/or therapy

Predictor 6—They also suggested that having a parent from a foreign country might point to problems in language development in bilingual or multilingual families. They noted that this could relate to Howell et al.'s (2009) study, which reported that bilingual children had a higher risk for stuttering than monolingual children or children speaking an alternative language exclusively.

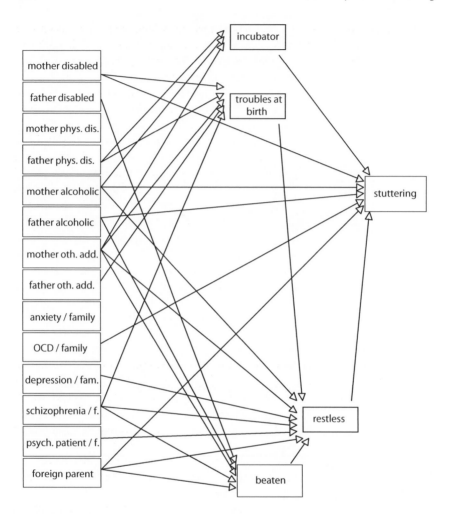

FIGURE 13.4   Ajdacic-Gross et al.'s (2009) path diagram

Predictor 5—Obsessive–compulsive disorder (OCD) in family members and relatives and other parental psychological influences was the only psychiatric disorder of parents in the database to act as a risk factor. They speculated that some pathways in OCD and in stuttering share a genetic and biological background. For example, basal ganglia circuits have been suggested as a possible link between stuttering and OCD (Alm, 2004), and may also be involved in ADHD (Schneider, Retz, Coogan, Thome, & Rosler, 2006). Along with predictors 2 and 3, then, this might have been expected.

Predictors 3 and 4—Alcohol abuse of the parents also needs further examination. Alcohol abuse has rarely been documented as a risk factor in stuttering (Löser, 1995). Their study showed that alcohol, but not other substances, led to increased risk of stuttering. They noted that the selective effect of alcohol as opposed to other substances indicated that the association was unlikely to be the result of adverse social environments, and suggested instead that this was related to fetal alcohol spectrum disorders (FASD). They assumed that alcohol abuse began before pregnancy with the child and pointed out that alcohol misuse by pregnant mothers has serious effects on prenatal brain development, leading to FASD (Spohr, Willms, & Steinhausen, 2007; Steinhausen & Spohr, 1998). However, this would not account for why alcoholism of the father acts as a risk factor which, they suggested, may have acted as a proxy for the alcohol misuse of the mother at lower exposure levels. They also noted that impulsiveness and aggressive behavior by the alcoholic father might reflect adverse environments but this seemed unlikely because other variables indicating adverse social environment were not relevant with regards to stuttering (e.g., "frequently beaten").

Predictor 1—Incubator (premature birth) could not be examined in detail because there was little information available about events that had taken place 18 or more years earlier. However, the authors did note that premature birth has been mentioned as a risk factor for stuttering in other studies (Alm & Risberg, 2007; Jennische & Sedin, 1999; Largo, Molinari, Kundu, Lipp, & Duc, 1990).

13.4.2.2 Methodological Considerations

The authors noted several limitations. First, the exclusion of cases with high psychiatric symptoms may have led to a biased sample. Second, all information was self-reported and details may have been forgotten or not known. Reliance on self-report of stuttering in cases where speakers had recovered is problematic (diagnosing stuttering is difficult as shown by the fact that experts do not agree). More information would be helpful (e.g., whether the parents or teachers sought treatment). Third, the screening data were not specifically designed for the analysis of speech problems. Thus, potentially interesting variables were missing in their data, such as information about persistent and recovered forms of stuttering just discussed.

Although these limitations were acknowledged, the authors also pointed out that a strength of large databases is that they may potentially reveal some less obvious and less frequent risk factors for heterogeneous disorders like stuttering. The ones they mention that they found in their study were premature birth, alcohol abuse of the parents, and having a parent from a foreign country.

13.5 APPLICATIONS

The Howell and Davis work shows that chances of recovery from or persistence in stuttering at teenage years can be predicted for children aged 8 before they have treatment with 80% sensitivity and specificity using only SSI-3 scores. This is the first successful predictive instrument (Yairi and Ambrose's group have not attempted this and Reilly et al. emphasized that the logistic regression for risk of onset had low predictive strength for predicting stuttering/not stuttering which they reported only accounted for 3.7% of the total variation in stuttering).

Nevertheless, both the latter groups have stressed the importance of such attempts. Yairi and Ambrose in earlier work stated:

> The ability to make accurate predictions could have a revolutionary impact on the long-term objective of cost-effective selective treatment for stuttering children. It is not practical, possible, or necessary to put every child who stutters into therapy. Economic conditions and emerging health policies, in fact, may make this option more difficult. For any child who appears likely to continue to stutter, treatment should not be delayed. But it may be advantageous to defer treatment for children with few or no risk factors and/or mild stuttering that does not cause concern for either child or parents (Yairi, Ambrose, Paden, & Throneburg, 1996, p. 74).

Reilly et al. in their paper say:

> Particularly pressing is the need to identify children in whom stuttering is and is not likely to persist, so that differing advice (watchful waiting versus recommending treatment) can be correctly targeted (Reilly et al., 2009, p. 271).

13.5.1 AUTOMATIC STUTTERING FREQUENCY COUNTS AND TELEHEALTH SERVICE

In this section, some ways in which the Howell and Davis result could be employed by practitioners are discussed briefly. Howell and Davis produced a model that predicts persistence and recovery of teens from data before treatment started at age 8 with around 80% sensitivity and specificity. This model could be used with new children attending a clinic to predict their chance of persistence or recovery.

The model was developed over the age range 8 to teenage years because the chance of recovery is approximately 50%. This allows classifiers like logistic regression to work well. Conversely, if samples are dominated by one class (e.g., many more cases who recover than persist), classifiers are unlikely to be successful. Classifiers can obtain high accuracy by putting all cases in the most frequent category. Thus, in Yairi and Ambrose's (2005) report (see Chapter 2), recovery rates were reported to be up to 80% three to five years after onset. Thus, their samples had four times as many recovered cases as persistent ones. This also explains why Reilly et al. (2009) and Ajdacic-Gross et al. (2009) found their logistic regression models showed low predictive power despite the fact that they identified risk factors.

The Howell and Davis model, after replication, could be used by clinicians to estimate prognosis of similar clients to those that Howell and Davis examined. Advances in speech processing should soon allow speech analysis to be automated (Howell, Sackin, & Glenn, 1997a, 1997b; Noth et al., 2000; Ravikumar, Rajagopal, & Nagaraj, 2009; Szczurowska, Kuniszyk-Józkowiak, & Smołka, 2009), and for these to be used as part of a telehealth (health-related services and information via telecommunications technologies) service so clinicians could obtain results quickly and in a standard format. It is also possible that automatic recognition could be made available over the Internet. Next, ethical issues associated with provision of such a service are discussed.

13.5.2   ETHICS AND TELEHEALTH SERVICE PROVISION

Four ethical issues associated with telehealth service delivery are discussed:

1. Do clients have a right, and do they want to know their chance of recovery?
2. Do speech pathologists want to know the chance of recovery and does this pose a dilemma for them?
3. Do health service providers want services that could provide an indication of chance of recovery to be available?
4. Are any of the above likely to differ across countries?

The prognostic indicators are not 100% accurate in issue 1. This means that there can be no guarantee that a child who is classified as going to persist, in fact, will do so or that a child classified as going to recover, in fact, will be so. The results are like actuarial data that is the basis on which insurance companies decide on charges they will make to clients. When they write you a policy, they do not know whether or not you will have an accident, but they do know what chances large groups of people like you have of being involved in an accident.

This situation could lead to positive indications that a child will persist, but in fact does not (a false alarm), and indications that a child will not persist but, in fact, does (a miss). False alarms may cause anxiety or distress and misses may cause problems because such cases would be admitted to treatment late (if they are treated at all). Missed cases may terminate treatment as they may think that because they have a high chance of recovery, there is little reason to attend. True cases of persistence, may lead to cessation of treatment because the client judges that there is not much point in continuing treatment.

This is the first time this issue has been raised in connection with stuttering and underlines the importance of getting the message over to clients; the idea that the findings are actuarial and misclassification can occur in individual cases. It is not appropriate to just ignore this information, as the World Health Organization noted in 1997 when it stressed that everyone is entitled to know any information collected about his or her health.

There are, however, some grounds for considering that occasionally and particularly in the case of life threatening diseases, such as genetic disorder and cancer, patients may not want to know the prognosis (Gordon & Daugherty, 2003). On the other hand, prognostic information has been noted to reduce distress in some cancer patients (Lamont & Christakis, 2001). Stuttering and speech–language disorders in general are not acute and these points may not apply (doctors in the United Kingdom give information on risk of heart attack). The recommended way of dealing with client issues is to discuss and establish the child and parent's view before assessment takes place and respect the wishes they express.

In issue 2, the dilemmas raised by having good prognostic information for speech pathologists is that it can bias patient selection in different ways. For instance, if a client looks likely to recover, they may choose not to treat him or her (resulting in no treatment for recovered cases). Alternatively, if a client has a poor chance of recovery, the pathologist may decide not to treat (resulting in no treatment for persistent cases)

In the case of false alarms, pathologists may be giving treatment to clients who do not need it. The logistic regression model should reduce the chance of such problems, and, as such, ought to be welcomed. Also, in the future when such findings are replicated across different labs and settings, Howell and Davis' system may help reduce misses and prevent pathologists from refusing treatment to clients who need it.

The ethical issues raised by the Howell and Davis' results are ones that have always been faced by speech pathologists. This is indicated in the quote from Yairi et al. (1996) given in section 13.5 when they state, "It is not practical, possible, or necessary to put every child who stutters into therapy." And in the quote from Reilly et al. (2009). In fact, Howell and Davis' results potentially aid pathologists by reducing the chance of false alarms and misses by using objective evidence.

A set of guidelines has been drawn up and it has been discussed with parents, children who stutter, self-help groups, and pathologists. The guidelines are given below, and further consultation should take place before they are implemented in a telehealth service; however, they provide a starting point for discussion.

13.5.2.1 General

1. Disclose as much as possible to therapists, children, and parents of children who stutter.
2. Inform therapists, children, and parents of children who stutter about these issues.
3. Point out that treatment can have positive effects over and above language changes (the result discussed here are only for speech–language performance). Point out that the screening is not 100% accurate.

13.5.2.2 Specific

1. Inform interested parties about classification to minimize the possibility of it affecting search for treatment (client) and delivery of that treatment (pathologist).
2. Inform clients and pathologists about the type of errors that can ensue and attendant dangers.
3. Speech pathologists can use the Howell and Davis' results either to minimize selection bias or to match admission to treatment over those with good and poor prognosis. In support of this, there are some people who think everyone should be given an equal chance to enter treatment (Harris, 1970).

Several research questions could be addressed if admissions were matched over prognosis:

> Do recovered speakers, who have not been treated, have adjustment problems over and above language?
>
> Are there positive or negative effects on recovered speakers who are treated (on communication and other behavior)?
>
> If persistent speakers are not treated, do they show progressive problems (communication and in other realms of behavior) in their subsequent development (i.e., is withholding treatment doing them harm)?
>
> Do persistent speakers who are treated show adjustment problems in realms other than language (e.g., self confidence)? Does giving treatment to persistent speakers benefit them in realms other than language?

4. Pathologists should find out before treatment the clients' views concerning disclosure and check if this has altered when parents become better informed.
5. Involve parents and children (and self-help groups) in consultations about these issues.

Concerning issue 3 in section 13.5.2, health service funders and fundees want patients to be prioritized. Statements from the WHO shows that this is true in the case of funders. The basic premise/ethical issue behind all screening is that the benefits should outweigh the harm. The Yairi et al. (1996) and Reilly et al. (2009) quotes given above indicate the position of funded research groups on this matter.

There are large differences in legal standards for what should be disclosed to patients, as pointed out in issue 4. For instance, United Kingdom and German law take as a standard "what a reasonable doctor would disclose." There also are differences in the views of these two countries. In Germany, it is thought that personal risk information should not be disclosed unless some treatment or prevention is available because the negative impact of distress may be greater than the value of having that knowledge (German National Ethics Council, 2004). Both the United States and The Netherlands (Medical Treatment Agreement Act [*Wet op de geneeskundige behandelingovereenkomst*]) describe the doctor's duty to inform in terms of what Beauchamp and Childress call a "reasonable patient" standard: what a reasonable patient would need or want to know in order to be able to give informed consent. When the complication risk is high and consequences may be severe, it is obvious that doctors have to inform their patients, but in cases of low or negligible risk, doctors have doubts about disclosing information because it is not clear what a reasonable patient would need or want to know. There also may be a danger of information overload, threatening instead of strengthening patient autonomy. The ethical question here is that of what doctors should do when it is unclear whether a reasonable patient would want to have particular risk information.

13.6   CONCLUSIONS

There have been a lot of studies that establish whether particular factors increase the risk of stuttering. A good example is family history, which was covered in Chapter 4 on genetics. The studies typically show that there is likely to be more stuttering in families with a history of stuttering; it is one of the risk factors emphasized by the Illinois group. Showing that family history is more likely to be associated with stuttering does not establish whether this along with other factors can predict whether or not a child in that family will start to stutter. Neither does it predict for a child who already stutters and who attends a clinic, what are the chances of the child recovering from or persisting in stuttering.

This chapter essentially discussed three studies, all of which included logistic regression modeling (the Ajdacic-Gross paper also included path analysis). Two of the studies failed to find much evidence for risk factors previously thought to predict stuttering (Reilly et al., 2009, on 2- and 3-year-olds and Ajdacic-Gross et al., who studied 18- to 20-year-old adults). The reason given in this chapter for the lack of findings in both of these studies was that classifiers do not work well when there are big imbalances in the proportions of the classes. Thus, in the Reilly et al. (2009) study, most children are fluent and, in the Ajdacic-Gross (2009) study, most of the conscripts were fluent.

Howell and Davis' study was successful at predicting whether children would persist or recover based on information obtained before they started treatment (at age 8), due partly to the fact that the likelihood of recovery is roughly 50% for children in this age range. The other main factor was that speech severity was assessed (SSI-3). The potentials that these results offer clinically were discussed as well as ethical issues concerning the use of this to decide who to treat; the ethical issues apply whether or not this technology is introduced (see Chapter 14 for further discussion).

In Reilly et al.'s study, four factors were significant risk factors at stuttering onset. These were male gender, twin birth status, higher vocabulary scores at 2 years of age, and high maternal education. Gender makes sense in terms of previous literature, twin status was problematic because of the small number in the sample, higher vocabulary scores was in the opposite direction relative to other data (Andrews & Harris, 1964), and hypotheses that some authors are pursuing (Bernstein Ratner, 1997), and high maternal education showed selective attrition in the sample (conceivably, this might affect language development, although the authors dismiss this).

Adjacic-Gross et al. found (1) incubator; (2) restless and fidgety in school, which they suggested may reflect ADHD; (3) alcohol abuse of mother; (4) alcohol abuse of father; (5) obsessive–compulsive (OCD) disorder in family members; and (6) having a parent from a foreign country were significant risk factors for stuttering. They considered that OCD, restless and fidgety, having a parent with a foreign language, and alcohol abuse by the mother were all consistent with previous literature on risk factors. Why having a father who abused alcohol caused problems was equivocal and there was insufficient information about incubator/premature birth. Gender could not be included as only male conscripts were selected for examination.

Howell and Davis were the only authors who obtained speech samples before the start of their study and their model predicted recovery or persistence. Reilly et al. have recordings from close after onset, which may be analyzed in the future. Having the pretreatment recordings was fortunate as SSI-3 scores proved the only significant predictor (even though gender and second language in the home were included, as those were significant factors in Reilly et al. and Ajdacic-Gross, respectively). Howell and Davis is the only study to date that has reported any success in predicting either onset or recovery.

13.7 EXERCISES

1. Although the likelihood of recovery or persistence can be estimated using known risk factors on a group of participants, this does not predict any individual child's outcome. Explain why this is so and consider the implications for how a speech pathologist should communicate risk of persisting in stuttering to the parent of a child who stutters.

2. Reported risk factors for persistence between age 8 years and the teens include head injury, onset age, family history, handedness, whether a second language was spoken in the home, gender, and stuttering severity instrument, version 3 (SSI-3) scores. In a study that employed all of these factors, Howell and Davis found that SSI-3 was the only factor that predicted risk of persisting in stuttering reliably. What reasons can you give for why there was a disparity between the number of reported risk factors for persistence and why only one of them predicted persistence?

3. Write a letter to a parent of a child who stutters explaining what the following statistics mean: "positive predictive value (PPV) was 77.9% and negative predictive value (NPV) was 84.4%. For the validation data PPV was 74.4% and NPV was 74.3%." Use this information to help the parent interpret the statistics about their child's chance of persisting or recovering.

4. Why is it difficult to estimate risk of starting to stutter in a sample when only 1 in 20 members are expected to stutter ever in their life?

5. Can Yairi and Ambrose's (2005) data be used to predict chance of persistence and recovery from stuttering?

6. It was pointed out in Chapter 3 that there is disagreement about whether whole-word repetitions should be considered as symptoms of stuttering or not. Reilly et al.'s (2009) study that looked at risk factors for onset of stuttering included whole-word repetitions in the assessment of whether or not a child stuttered. How would the findings of the study be affected if children with a predominance of whole-word repetitions were *not* considered to be stuttering?

7. Reilly et al. (2009) indicated that male gender, twin birth status, high vocabulary scores at 2 years of age, and high maternal education were associated with stuttering onset. Draw a path diagram to indicate what you consider to be a reasonable causal sequence to interpret these findings and indicate which coefficients would be expected to be positive and which negative based on previous literature. Which of Reilly et al.'s risk factors gave an unexpected correlation coefficient based on prior work and why might this be so?

8. All the participants in Howell and Davis' study went on to receive treatment. Consequently, it is possible that SSI-3 might predict responsiveness to treatment, not whether a child has a propensity to recover or persist. How would you test between these alternatives?

9. Construct path diagrams that represent different models for the relationship between the affectual factors anxiety, IQ, bullying and stuttering severity (see Levine, Petrides, Davis, Jackson, and Howell, 2005, for some ideas that may help you get started).

14 Subtyping

This chapter considers how groups of speakers who stutter and have heterogeneous forms of the disorder have been subdivided in various ways and studied to see whether the resulting subtypes are more alike than those who are not part of the selected subtype. Subtyping is intended to be a way of increasing the contrast between subgroups of speakers who stutter. This approach contrasts with that of modeling risk for starting to stutter or persisting in stuttering, which often considers variables used to subtype stutterers as risk factors. Thus, for example, gender has been used as a subtyping factor (Yairi, 2007) and as a risk factor for estimating predictability of stuttering onset (Reilly et al., 2009) and persistence (Howell & Davis, in press). Subtypes factors may operate at onset and (more probably) into later course to teenagers and through to adulthood. Latent variable and network approaches have recently been discussed in the literature on subtypes. Their application to stuttering is examined briefly.

14.1 INTRODUCTION

An approach that has been taken to improve information about stuttering is to distinguish different groups within an overall sample of speakers who stutter and examine them separately. This is called *subtyping*. Affectual factors have often been used to specify subtypes (e.g., neurotic versus psychotic). This approach would be commended if the resulting information provided guidance that allowed diagnosis, prognosis, and treatment of that particular subtype to be improved. To give a hypothetical example, if a heterogeneous group of children who stutter contained some who had difficult temperaments, diagnosis could possibly be improved if the sample was given a temperament screening test to distinguish the two subtypes (those who have a temperament problem and those who do not). Further improvements in diagnosis would arise if age of onset for the children with poor temperament was different from the age of onset for the children with ordinary temperament (and similarly for other risk factors that distinguish the subtypes). The impact on prognosis could be established by comparing the course of stuttering development for the two subtypes (e.g., one subtype may be more likely to be bullied than the other subtype). Behavioral treatments that have been developed for children with temperamental difficulties could be examined to see if they are effective with children who stutter. The fluency problems of adults with temperamental difficulties could be managed in a different way from adults who stutter who are not from this subtype.

The idea that there are different subtypes of speakers who stutter has a long history and it maintains its popularity. Two reviews on subtyping in the stuttering area appeared recently (Hubbard Seery, Watkins, Mangelsdorf, & Shigeto, 2007; Yairi, 2007). This chapter is not going to repeat these reviews in their entirety. Instead, the question examined will be what topics should be considered reasonable prospects for subtyping. It also will consider how the subtypes approach relates to procedures that have been used in studies in other chapters of this book. The Hubbard Seery et al. paper considers how language ability and temperament variables are relevant to subtyping issues, but does not propose any additional subtypes. Since language ability was examined in Chapter 7 and temperament was considered in Chapter 9, little is to be said about Hubbard Seery et al. Yairi's (2007) comprehensive typology of subtypes is considered. The subtype groups Yairi discussed are (1) stuttering typologies, (2) stuttering symptoms, (3) reaction to drugs, (4) biological, (5) concomitant disorders, (6) developmental course, and (7) statistical models. Some of these subtypes are not relevant to developmental issues in stuttering. Yairi's list of subtypes is critically examined: It is argued that the grounds for including some of the subtypes is questionable and some general issues about the logic behind subtyping are discussed. Subtypes are often identified on the basis of symptoms that a disorder shares with stuttering. Examples from Chapter 1 were selective mutism (Howell, 2007) and tic disorders, and from Chapter 13 was attention deficit hyperactivity disorder (Alm & Risberg, 2007; Blood et al., 2003). Cramer, Waldorp, van der Maas, and Borsboom (in press) have recently argued that subtyping is incorrect and proposed an alternative approach to subtyping (network analysis). Brief details of their reasons for dismissing comorbidity based on shared symptoms and their alternative are given. This work challenges recent research on subtyping and stuttering.

14.2   WORK ON SUBTYPING ONSET TO AGE 8

The broad aim of subtyping research is, according to Hubbard Seery et al. (2007, p. 200), "the valid and reliable characterization of individuals (according to specified variables) such that those within their subtype have more in common with each other than with those outside that subtype."

Yairi's taxonomy of subtypes was mentioned in the introduction. The seven categories of subtypes he indicated were:

1. Stuttering typologies (general etiologies)
2. Stuttering symptoms
3. Reaction to drugs
4. Biological
5. Concomitant disorders
6. Developmental course
7. Statistical models

It was also stated in the introduction to this chapter that this list would be reduced. The two main reasons for making this reduction include, first, categories 1, 3, and 5 all involve comorbid disorders according to Yairi's description. To be able to subtype them properly, stuttering and the comorbid disorder both need to be easily and reliably identifiable. This is not the case with stuttering where experts often disagree about the classification of cases (Kully & Boberg,

1988) nor for psychological and other language disorders where similar things apply (Stott, Merricks, Bolton, & Goodyer, 2002). Necessarily, comorbid cases are harder to identify than is either class alone. Thus, if two disorders can each be identified with 90% accuracy, cases with both disorders could only be identified with 81% accuracy (90% of 90%). In practice, this reduces case sensitivity and makes identification of groups with more and less in common problematic. To put it another way, subtyping comorbid disorders makes the classes fuzzier than dealing with pure cases of either class, and this would reduce the chances of identifying common features in the subtype that contrast with those outside the subtype. Arguably, then, subtyping should not be applied to Yairi's classes: 1 (etiology based), 3 (reaction to drugs), and 5 (concomitant disorders), given the stated intention behind subtyping research. Section 14.3 discusses further issues about using comorbidity for identifying subtypes.

Second, a clear idea is needed about how the data will be coded and analyzed. Subtyping should not be done merely as a way of tidying up patterns in results; there needs to be a principled reason for the subtyping. Based on a single study with six variables, there are six opportunities for the subtyping variable and five variables remain to be investigated once a subtype has been selected. Making many comparisons is problematic statistically because the more comparisons that are made, the greater the chance of obtaining a spurious result. Some principles that govern what selection should be made are needed. One basis for selection could be whether the resulting subtypes can be used to address practical important issues (diagnosis, prognosis, treatment, fundamental understanding of the disorder). At least one category that has been considered a subtype is arguably better treated as a potential risk factor. Thus, it seems more appropriate to consider biological characteristics (category 4) as a risk factor rather than as a subtype. A strong argument for this view is that much research has used characteristics in this class as risk factors, including work by Yairi's own group.

Subtyping has implications for how the data are analyzed. It is revealing that Yairi (2007) has a separate category of statistical models. The illustrative work in this category tends to involve multivariate techniques like those discussed in Chapter 13 (e.g., Andrews and Harris', 1964, work is included, which used factor analysis). Studies in many of the remaining subtype classes use analyses with single dependent variables. These are simpler to perform than multivariate analyses and may make the results appear clearer. However, they can give an inflated impression about the importance of the variables examined. This is apparent in the reports of Ajdacic-Gross et al. (2009) and Reilly et al. (2009) that were discussed in the previous chapter. In both of these reports, significant differences were reported when risk factors were examined as single dependent variables in analyses, whereas these same factors had very little influence on risk of stuttering in multivariate analyses.

In summary, categories 1, 3, and 5 were ruled out based on the fact that combined categories are less distinct than categories based on a single feature. Category 4 was ruled out on the grounds that the biological factors are better treated as risk factors rather than subtypes. Category 7 is an analysis method rather than a subtype proposal; there are reasons to employ using such techniques in all subtype analyses.

A stronger case can be made for subtyping people who stutter based on prominent stuttering phenomena (category 2) and developmental course (category 6). Examples of subtypes in Yairi's category 2 are disfluency class (the clonic/tonic distinction of Froeschels, 1943, and Wingate, 2002) and severity (Watson & Alfonso, 1987). Clonic/tonic symptoms and severity were discussed in Chapter 3 of this book; it is a concept Wingate, among others, employed). Developmental course involves tracks that different authors have deduced, based mainly on their clinical experience (Van Riper, 1971) or single studies (Ambrose, Cox, & Yairi, 1997). The proposals in this category need further empirical support, though this should not necessarily be used as grounds for dismissing them as bases for subtyping.

14.3   LATENT VARIABLE MODELING, DISORDERS THAT ARE COMORBID WITH STUTTERING AND SUBTYPES

This is a short chapter and I considered leaving it out. However, recent work by Cramer, Waldorp, van der Maas, and Borsboom (in press) persuaded me that there are issues about comorbidity that need airing that have a bearing on subtype work with people who stutter (Yairi's 2007 subtypes often involve comorbidity as indicated in the previous section). Cramer et al. (in press) also present a new perspective that should be examined by those interested in subtyping.

Cramer et al. argue that if comorbidity is genuine, it should be independent of the diagnostic criteria, measurement scales, and measurement models used to assess the state. If people adhere to the comorbidity model, this implies underlying latent variables exist that lie behind the comorbid states (see Chapter 4 for a discussion of latent variable modeling in connection with structural equation modeling). In this case, there should not be direct relations between symptoms of the comorbid states. Most work on stuttering fails to take account of this. For instance, social phobia, tic disorder, selective mutism, ADHD, and others have all been considered to be comorbid with stuttering because they show similar symptoms. Cramer et al. go on to comment that, in a strict psychometric sense, latent variable models do not allow for many direct relations because the majority of covariance between symptoms needs to be explained by the common cause behind the two states. As such, psychometric latent variable models imply that correlations between observable indicators are spurious.

An example they use is "sleep disturbances" and "fatigue," both of which are *Diagnostic and Statistical Manual of Mental Disorders–IV* (DSM-IV) symptoms of major depressive disorder. If the common cause hypothesis is adopted, a high positive correlation between these symptoms would be entirely due to the common influence of the latent variable major depressive disorder. However, this is questionable since a direct causal relationship between those symptoms seems likely to hold. Namely, if you do not sleep, then you get tired. A hypothetical example from stuttering would be that a child who stutters may experience anxiety and this leads to difficulty in concentrating. In turn, difficulties in concentrating lead to ADHD. The link between ADHD and stuttering could arise from this causal path, so it is not necessary to postulate a latent construct to account for high rates of comorbidity between the disorders.

This leads directly to Cramer et al.'s own network proposal. The essential idea they adopt is to define and analyze relationships between symptoms without assuming a priori that such relationships arise due to an underlying common cause. As they put it, a disorder is conceptualized as a cluster of directly related symptoms. They go on to detail application of this analysis to comorbid disorders. (Interested readers are referred to Cramer et al.'s paper). This approach seems to have more in common with what people interested in subtyping stuttering have in mind. For example, the work of Conture and his students discussed in Chapter 10 looked at how phonological disorder might have an impact on measured symptoms of stuttering. The network proposal ought to be examined in connection with proposed subtypes of stutterers.

Examining the relationships between symptoms also seems to be a goal of successful therapeutic interventions, such as cognitive therapy, that is currently popular in the field of stuttering (see Chapter 15). As Cramer et al. characterize their network approach, the purpose of cognitive therapy is to lessen the impact of cognitions on relationships between symptoms. For instance, a hypothetical example from stuttering might be: "If I stutter, I am a worthless person and it is better for everyone if I kept silent." They argue that therapeutic interventions that attempt to break such links may not naturally arise from a latent variable perspective. This challenges notions about exactly what underlying structure are being treated in therapies. whether there is a basic underlying cause as in a latent variable perspective or a network of directly related symptoms that potentially lead to new approaches to intervention.

Finally, an interesting set of ways of examining comorbidity between disorders that has implications for subtypes of stuttering is raised in the network approach. Direct links between symptoms may not be established synchronously, one disorder may develop before another, the order of development of disorders may differ between individuals and so on. Such issues would merit investigation in people who stutter and help establish the network of symptoms and, possibly, how best to intervene.

14.4 SUMMARY

Caution should be exercised when proposing subtypes, and the status of some subtypes that have been proposed seems questionable. These points are not arguments for the position that stuttering should be considered as a unitary phenomenon. However, they are reasons for being critical about different types of stuttering that have been proposed. Subtyping that involves combining two disorders makes the classes less distinct. Multivariate techniques should be more widely adopted, and closer attention should be paid to whether variables should be considered subtypes or risk factors; they should not have both roles. The network approach should be examined in connection with stuttering.

14.5 EXERCISES

1. Chapter 13 described studies that used logistic regression to estimate the relative importance of risk factors in predicting stuttering onset or course. Some of the risk factors in that chapter are used to subtype groups of stutterers in this chapter. Examine these two approaches and consider which approach you think is most appropriate.

2. Take an example of a disorder that has been hypothesized to be comorbid with stuttering. Examine this disorder from a latent variable and network perspective. Indicate what differences there are, what problems were encountered, and which approach you would choose to examine stuttering.

15 Application to Treatment and General Issues About Recovery

One point of view that could be taken about treatment is that it should mimic recovery. That is, a person should have speech after treatment that is similar to a person who has recovered naturally. Consistent with this point of view, protagonists of some treatments see loss of overt symptoms as the primary goal, although, as is evident in other chapters in this volume, it is not clear precisely what this means. Sometimes loss of symptoms is linked with the view that if speech is corrected, affect will automatically become normal (e.g., they might also experience anxiety within normal limits and so on). Some practitioners working with cognitive behavior therapy (and personal construct theory before that) with adults, consider that the affective aspects of stuttering should be the primary goal of therapy, not treatment of speech symptoms. This chapter considers the adequacy of these alternative positions about treatment: whether or not it is necessary to lose symptoms, acceptability of treatments to clients, whether treatment improves characteristics other than speech, etc.

15.1 INTRODUCTION

This book is not about treatment. It has used the methods of the research laboratory, which cannot be transferred directly for routine use in clinics because this would be impractical. However, the results are not devoid of relevance to clinical practice by any means. Many elements of the research that have been discussed now should be adopted in well-funded clinics, selected procedures can be transferred in part to general-purpose clinical settings, and other procedures can be adopted in modified form. For a speech pathologist or a parent, simply understanding how research studies are designed, what the findings indicate, and their limitations is important in order for them to judge what treatments are likely to be effective. In this chapter, an attempt is made to identify those aspects from the discussion in earlier parts of this book that are applicable in clinics, and to identify some research requirements more specific to clinical practice, which have not been covered in the volume so far.

This chapter starts with a résumé (section 15.2) and expansion of those aspects from previous chapters that are relevant to clinical practice. There are two main ways this could have been approached: (1) by identifying those issues that are discussed in several chapters (often at several points) that are of particular clinical concern, and (2) by taking a conventional clinical perspective (research provides a service to support existing clinical practice). The first approach was adopted, but it should be noted that it is not the intention to propose research agendas to clinicians. Hopefully, clinicians should be able to take some of the ideas and adopt them in their own investigations. The agenda set out in this book from a research point of view has its biases, blind spots, and limitations, too, both relative to clinical work and the perspectives of other researchers. Perhaps the most notable area where the biases apply, which is relevant both to clinicians and other researchers, is the emphasis on language and motor research evidence. The emphasis on language and speech in this volume is not exclusive of other factors (genetic, CNS, affective, and cognitive processes have all been considered). This chapter also partly redresses the imbalance that arose due to the emphasis on language and speech motor processes. Some of the treatments do not specifically address speech and language factors.

Section 15.3 discusses application of these ideas to specific treatments. However, before this, some essential background information on randomized control trials is given. The treatments are then considered. They were chosen to contrast in various ways and all have been the subject of research investigations. Section 15.4 covers some issues about recovery that have not been discussed so far. Finally, section 15.5 pulls the work together and draws some conclusions about treatment.

15.2   TOPICS FROM OTHER CHAPTERS RELEVANT TO TREATMENT

Eight topics from earlier chapters are discussed. These include:

1. Speech symptomatology at admission and completion of treatment
2. Assessment methods and instruments for onset and their application at admission to treatment
3. Assessment methods and instruments for application to treatment outcome
4. Digital data archiving
5. Nonspeech variables as onset (pretreatment) and outcome measure (posttreatment)
6. Theory
7. Leads and warnings from risk and subtyping
8. Ethics and treatment (with subtopic of client selection, client expectations, and client rights)

15.2.1   SPEECH SYMPTOMATOLOGY AT ADMISSION AND COMPLETION OF TREATMENT

One concern is whether or not whole-word repetitions should be considered as symptoms of stuttering. This topic has been discussed in several previous chapters of this volume. Up to now, a neutral stance has been taken about the role of whole-word repetitions. Studies have been documented with respect to whether they use whole-word repetitions as an inclusion factor for case designation, and/ or for assessing the course into persistence, etc., but without further comment. However, when evaluating treatments, it is necessary to adopt a specific position about their role. There are two perspectives with regard to whether or not whole-word repetitions should be considered stutters, and a third option is offered after these have been described.

The first option is to include whole-word repetitions as symptoms of stuttering. Probably the most popular current scheme of this type is the SLD/OD scheme of Yairi and Ambrose (2005), which was discussed in Chapters 1 and 3. Yairi and Ambrose include whole-word repetitions in the stuttering-like disfluency class (SLD) and the remaining, or other, disfluencies (OD) are discarded. This measure is used as part of their procedure for diagnosing early stuttering and establishing its subsequent course. Several authors have used stuttering assessments that include whole-word repetitions and a particular threshold of SLD (3% SLD) for assessing stuttering.

For example, Boey, Wuyts, van de Heyning, Heylen, and de Bodt (2009) reported an application of similar symptom counts to diagnosis of stuttering. They examined 80 fluent participants and 431 older children and adults who self-reported that they stuttered. Stuttering was defined as including repetitions of monosyllabic words repeated three or more times as well as within-word disfluencies (sound and syllable repetitions, sound prolongations, and blocks). In addition to inclusion of selected whole-word repetitions in their stuttering counts, some further details of their methods are important for the later discussion. Their assessment methods were demanding, as the clinician made and noted the following in real time: (1) a running count of the number of words (to obtain a sample that was 100 words long), (2) individual disfluency types and their durations, (3) the number of words repeated in the case of monosyllabic words, (4) disfluencies in SLD and OD categories, and (5) secondary features (similar to Riley's, 1994, physical concomitants). The authors reported that a criterion of 3% stuttered words applied to conversational speech made it possible to distinguish stuttering from nonstuttering individuals with high sensitivity (0.9345) and perfect specificity (1.0000). The absence of permanent recordings makes it impossible to check these claims. Reilly et al. (2009) and other studies by Onslow's group also include whole-word repetitions in their assessment of stuttering.

The second option is that whole-word repetitions should not be considered stutterings. This is Wingate's (2002) view as well as others (Bernstein Ratner & Sih, 1987; Dejoy & Gregory, 1985; Gaines, Runyan, & Meyers, 1991; Jayaram, 1981; Kloth, Kraimaat, Janssen, & Brutten, 1999; Riley, 1994; Wall, Starkweather, & Harris, 1981). Wingate maintained that studies that did include whole-word repetitions (such as Yairi and Ambrose's) led to people being erroneously diagnosed as stutterers. Furthermore, he mentioned that the inclusion of misdiagnosed cases in treatment studies would inflate claims about treatment efficacy

Following are two further observations about the role of whole-word repetitions that lead to the third option. First, whole-word repetitions are not primary symptoms of stuttering, as Anderson's (2007) and Howell's (2007) data show (whole-word repetitions are not affected by the same variables as other disfluencies in Yairi and Ambrose's SLD category). This is consistent with Wingate's position. Second, although whole-word repetitions are not in the class of primary stuttering symptoms, they do have a role in maintaining fluency; they are used to stall rather than advance (Howell, Bailey, & Kothari, 2010), and it is important to document them so that the dominant strategy a speaker uses can be determined. Retention of other disfluencies is not consistent with Wingate's view. To be explicit, the third option classifies whole-word repetitions as other disfluencies, but the class of other disfluencies is not discarded as in Yairi and Ambrose's work. Wingate would also advocate discarding other disfluencies, which would include whole-word repetitions in his case.

15.2.2   Assessment Methods and Instruments for Onset and Their Application at Admission to Treatment

As mentioned, Yairi and Ambrose (2005) use a criterion of 3% SLD stuttering symptoms to classify a child as a stutterer. They do not treat the participants they work with, so 3% SLD stutterings is not being used by them as a criterion for admission to treatment or for judging outcome of treatment. Others have used similar stuttering measures to Yairi and Ambrose for differential diagnosis (Boey et al., 2009; Reilly et al., 2009) and for assessing outcome of treatment (Onslow, Packman, Stocker, van Doorn, & Siegel, 1997). Three percent SLD stutterings is a low threshold and is highly dependent on how the assessments are made. Studies that have used this criterion differ with regards to how the assessments were conducted, which would affect the absolute level; precise details of how Yairi and Ambrose made their assessments are not given. Our assessments are made from digital recordings using a wave editor. This has been found to be the most sensitive and reliable procedure (Howell, Soukup-Ascencao Davis & Rusbridge, submitted, 2010). Thus, stuttering rates for the same material are higher and produce reproducible results compared to listening and making the judgments in real time. The speech assessments are not the only criterion that Yairi and Ambrose (2005) use in their assessments, they also use ratings. These, as well as the speech assessments, have lenient criteria that would classify fluent children at the margins as stutterers, as discussed in Chapter 1.

15.2.3   Assessment Methods and Instruments for Course of Stuttering and Their Application to Treatment Outcome

As described in Chapter 1, Yairi and Ambrose (2005) use a criterion of less than 3% SLD stutters to determine whether a child had recovered from stuttering, although no specification of stuttering rate was made for the children who persisted. A sustained rate of 3% SLD stutters might be used to determine treatment outcome if it is considered that achieving a recovered status for speech is a goal for treatment. Howell and Davis (in press) have used stuttering severity instrument-3 (SSI-3) as a threshold for determining persistence/recovery (see Chapter 13). It is possible for this to be used as a criterion for treatment outcome as has Yairi and Ambrose's percent stuttering threshold. The advantages in doing this are that SSI-3 assessment procedures are specified precisely and SSI-3 has been evaluated statistically (Riley, 1994).

15.2.4 Digital Data Archiving

While there is no agreed assessment method, it seems imperative to archive the data. It has been pointed out that different assessment methods give different results. Thus, again this emphasizes that it is essential that a permanent record is kept. The most efficient way of doing this is to store material digitally; this applies to speech and questionnaire information. As the data ought to be archived in this way, the speech assessments also ought to be made on these records using a waveform editor, which is fast and convenient to perform. Digitally archived material can be examined by ethics auditors. Arguably, this should be part of funding decisions because it is the most efficient method for clinics with large numbers of clients.

Digital data records allow results to be checked, which is an advantage, and, in some cases, a requirement, in scientific work. Some further advantages include, first, reclassifying disfluencies (as suggested in Chapter 13, section 13.2.1) is relatively straightforward if the speech data are stored as digital records and a standard coding convention is used to mark the stutters. Thus, if the balance of the evidence swings away from including whole-word repetitions, or if new classification schemes are proposed, recomputations could easily be made. The method used in Boey et al.'s (2009) study, which used real-time assessment, does not allow such recalculations.

A further point about Boey et al.'s methods is that they do not look to be very sensitive. The same applies to some extent with assessments made in real time using Onslow's hand-held counter device, which users employ to simultaneously count all syllables with one hand and stuttered ones with the other, a form of which is included in SSI-4. The assessments based on digital recordings and investigated with a wave editor give more sensitive and more reliable results than real-time methods (Howell et al., in press).

15.2.5 Nonspeech Variables as Onset (Pretreatment) and Outcome (Posttreatment) Measure

Venkatagiri (2009) recently asked people who stuttered whether factors other than speech should be targeted in treatment. He ran a web-based survey asking people who stutter whether they wanted fluency (reduction of stuttering symptoms) or freedom (reduction of maladaptive behaviors that speakers who stutter use to attempt to minimize the occurrence and expectation of stutters). There are treatment programs that target reduction of speech disfluencies (see section 15.3.3 about the Lidcombe program that attempts this). There are also treatments that focus primarily on the reduction or elimination of these maladaptive behaviors and the outlook that produced them (Ham, 1986; Sheehan, 1970; Van Riper, 1973). People who focus on fluency consider that once the person who stutters is trained to speak without a significant amount of stutters, the maladaptive behaviors and the outlook that led to them would be effectively eliminated (Guitar & Peters, 1980).

The survey showed that there were four groups of people who stuttered: (1) those who consistently seek fluency, (2) those who consistently seek freedom, (3) those who seek fluency but with some ambivalence, and (4) those who seek freedom but with some equivocation. The result showed that the respondents were split about equally between these four groups, although fluency was primarily important for over 50% of the participants. This finding fits well with a recent paper on these kind of issues using fluency and other data on different treatment approaches (Huinck et al., 2006). The Venkatagiri (2009) study has obvious limitations that the author discusses (e.g., the sample was self-selected). However, it shows that the goals of improved speech control in some speakers who stutter does not focus on symptom reduction.

Affectual problems could influence stuttering early (temperament is partly genetically determined and would be present early) or late in life (anxiety). Clinicians have stressed the importance of taking these factors into account in treatment. For example, Menzies, Onslow, Packman, and O'Brian (2009) raised the question of whether anxiety should be the target for treatment when cognitive behavior therapy is used in treatment (discussed in section 15.3.5). This is a proposal that uses affect as an outcome factor. The proposal contrasts with the view that anxiety is an epiphenomenon of stuttering whereby once speech symptoms are treated, the anxiety disappears (see Davis, Shisca, & Howell, 2007, for a discussion of this view about anxiety).

15.2.6 THEORY

Elsewhere in this volume, theories of the etiology of stuttering have been discussed. Here theory refers to proposals outside stuttering that suggest why treatment works, how they could be improved, etc., and that could offer new suggestions about ways to approach the treatment of stuttering. This contrasts with some of the less theory-based, more pragmatic approaches to stuttering; it may not be known why a treatment works, but use it if you believe it helps. Examples of frameworks for treatment that do not submit to particular theories include ones designed to be flexible, that are not testable, but that do allow clinical management (e.g., demands and capacities) or where the central focus is clinical management (OASES).

There are justifications for why formal theory should be applied to stuttering. Everyone who has worked with altered auditory feedback is asked why it works (i.e., effectively, what your theory is). Several different explanations of the auditory feedback effect were considered in Chapter 11, some of which were developed outside the domain of stuttering. In some cases, the theoretical alternatives have suggested other manipulations that also should have similar effects (nonspeech rhythms). Another example where there is a well-developed body of psychological theory that could be useful is operant conditioning. The theories in this area could be used to augment existing treatments or enhance them (Reed, Howell, Davis, & Osborne, 2007). These developments may help inform and improve approaches to treatment (see 15.6 Exercise, no. 3).

A second point is that theories can be tested and this may assist by preventing investigators spending time on fruitless ideas. For instance, the example of whether anxiety is a cause or effect of stuttering could be addressed empirically. There may be reasonable grounds for the view that treating anxiety can be backed up by experimental results. Alternatively, treating anxiety may be a way of indirectly treating speech symptoms. Models of whether anxiety is a cause or effect of stuttering could be represented in structural equations and modeled and the possibilities tested to establish which alternative is favored (Levine, Petrides, Davis, Jackson, & Howell, 2005).

15.2.7   LEADS AND WARNINGS FROM RISK AND SUBTYPING

It was pointed out in the discussion of risk modeling and stuttering in Chapter 13 that classifiers do not work well when there is a big imbalance between the two classes used. In particular, it was shown that attempting to classify which children stutter and which are fluent is difficult when there is only a small proportion of stutterers in a sample (at most, around 1 in 20). The imbalance problem also applies when trying to determine whether a treatment is effective with very young children who stutter because 80% of these children recover spontaneously anyway (Yairi & Ambrose, 2005).

It was argued that subtyping was not a good way of distinguishing groups of stutterers. The basis point was that combining subgroups gives a less clear segregation of cases with the joint disorder than segregating either of the disorders alone. In the light of this, it would be difficult to select specific subgroups (e.g., children who stutter and who have phonological problems) for specific forms of treatment. Nevertheless, clinicians face the dilemma of what to do if a child displays symptoms that may be classified under both aspects: what is the best treatment for these children, when to apply treatment, etc. Cramer, Waldorp, Van der Maas, and Borsboom's (in press) network approach suggests an alternative approach to comorbidity that offers exciting possibilities for stuttering.

15.2.8   ETHICS AND TREATMENT

Issues about ethics and predicting prognosis were discussed in Chapter 13. These concerned, in particular, whether speech–language pathologists wanted to know the information about a client's likely outcome (whether the child will persist or recover by his/her teens). Many of the issues raised in that discussion also apply to clinicians' expectations concerning whether a client will respond to treatment, whether or not they are backed up by empirical data (the latter was the case with Howell and Davis's prognostic predictions). Discussion of specific points about how these issues apply to treatments follows.

15.2.8.1   Client Selection

Ethical issues raised earlier by the work that showed you can predict the outcome of therapy for children who stutter were discussed in Chapter 13. There is a set of equivalent questions that arise when pathologists use their experience to decide on a client's treatment. Thus, part of the professional activity of a speech language pathologist is to assess children and decide whether they should be admitted to treatment. If it is considered that they can make this decision with a degree of accuracy, then all the ethical issues raised in connection with prognosis also apply to these decisions. One of the main issues is deciding who to treat (Huinck et al., 2006). There are also issues additional to those raised in the prognosis chapter. For instance, children who speak a language other than English in the home may be excluded from some treatments (Millard, 2002) and from some research studies (Reilly et al., 2009). Single parents cannot be enrolled on parent–child interaction therapy as it calls for the involvement of two parents.

15.2.8.2   Client Expectations

Clients' expectations about treatment outcome should be established. Do they want fewer symptoms or freedom from their stuttering (Venkatagiri, 2009), or their anxiety reduced (Menzies et al., 2009)? Their choice of therapy may depend on these decisions. This may require a pathologist to recommend that the client seeks treatment at another clinic; choice should not be constrained with respect to what treatments any one clinic can deliver.

15.2.8.3   Client Rights

Two questions associated with clients' rights were discussed in Chapter 13. These included:

1. Clients have a right to know their chance of recovery. Although this was discussed with respect to natural (not treatment-dependent) recovery, the same applies to clinicians' views about the treatment they or others can offer. An important aspect of the estimates of treatment efficacy is how to discount the argument that the effects could be due to natural recovery, not treatment. There is no ideal way of making these estimates and this should be made clear to clients.

2. Speech–language pathologists want to know the chance of recovery. It was pointed out in Chapter 13 that if pathologists know a client's estimate of natural recovery, this may pose a dilemma for them as it could affect the approach they take to the client. The same point applies

to pathologist's views about treatment-assisted recovery. Again, the extra issue arises when considering treatment about whether reported improvements are due to natural recovery or the treatment itself.

15.3   APPLICATION TO SELECTED FORMS OF TREATMENT

As said, this is not a book about treatment per se. It does not attempt, therefore, to review treatments comprehensively. Its primary goal is to see what lessons can potentially be learned from the research reviewed in earlier chapters. The treatments were selected to illustrate specific points raised in these previous chapters or because they represent good models for further work. Altered auditory feedback devices are considered. The main issue with them is what sort of trial design is appropriate for this treatment as opposed to those used with more standard forms of treatment. The other treatments that are considered are Lidcombe (a form of treatment that attempts symptom reduction), pharmacological agents (if these work, they would offer some support for biological factors behind stuttering), and cognitive behavior therapy (that could be effective at reducing anxiety rather than symptoms). Before these treatments are considered, background information on the phases of trials used to investigate treatments are given. This allows some estimate of how far the proposed forms of treatment have progressed to date.

15.3.1   RANDOMIZED CONTROL TRIALS, TECHNIQUES, AND EXPLANATIONS

Randomized control trials (RCTs) are widely used in clinical assessment and are often referred to as the gold standard. With people who stutter, RCTs are infrequent and even when studies are reported, they usually have small numbers of participants.

RCTs are typically classified into four phases. All are considered essential to scientific assessment of the treatment. Each of the four phases is designed to answer different research questions.

15.3.1.1   Phase 1

Phase 1 trials involve small sample sizes, usually fewer than 30 participants. They are exploratory studies that assess the nature of the intervention, how it is administered, potential side effects, patient reactions, and so forth. A typical research question addressed in phase 1 trials is how the treatment should be given. Trials are the first steps in transforming laboratory data into clinical care, and are conducted with therapeutic intent. A phase 1 trial on stuttering might involve assessing behavior with statistical measures, and establishing the amount of therapy needed and the techniques for its administration as information for future trials. A possible risk is that unpredictable side effects would occur.

15.3.1.2   Phase 2

Phase 2 trials into stuttering are usually correlational studies of effectiveness and a typical research question might concern how the treatment affects the individual.

Larger group of participants, but still usually under 100, are employed and the information from phase 1 trials is used to justify the expense involved in setting up the phase 2 trials. On the basis of phase 1 trials, researchers often focus phase 2 trials on those clients who are most likely to show a response to therapy (if, for example, subtyping information is shown to be useful, it might be employed at this phase). It is desirable to take effective alternative treatments into account. In most phase 2 trials, all participants undergo the same intervention. The new treatment is assessed for effectiveness. Even if the new treatment seems effective, it usually requires further testing before being put into widespread use. Because the treatment has not been compared to any other therapy or technique, its relative value is as yet unclear, and it is impossible to rule out other factors that may have influenced its effectiveness. In addition, phase 2 trials are often too short to determine long-term benefits; larger and longer phase 3 trials are more suited to this purpose. There is some risk that unpredictable side effects may occur (e.g., with drug treatments into stuttering).

15.3.1.3   Phase 3

Phase 3 trials are typically randomized experiments designed to establish whether the treatment has good internal validity. One important question they can address is whether the new treatment is better than ones used in current practice. Phase 3 trials are large-scale trials, usually involving more than 100 participants, that are typically conducted at multiple institutions within a country. They ask a broader range of questions than trials at previous phases because the results are intended to guide healthcare professionals and other people in making treatment decisions. Classically, participants in phase 3 trials are assigned at random to a group that is given the new treatment, or a control group, or one which receives the current standard treatment. This is not possible with stuttering as there is no standard treatment. Also, it is not possible to have treatment/nontreatment groups with respect to stuttering because of ethical issues associated with withholding information. Some studies defer treatment and observe the effects during deferral as a form of no-treatment group (see reports of the Lidcombe and cognitive behavior therapy in sections 15.3.3 and 15.3.5).

There are several possible risks during phase 3 trials. For instance, the new treatments under study are not always better than, or even as good as, standard treatments. Sometimes new treatments may have side effects that are worse than those of standard treatment. Even though phase 1 and 2 testing has been conducted, there may be unexpected side effects. If the new treatment has benefits, it may still not work for every participant (e.g., this may also apply to drug treatments for stuttering, as discussed below).

15.3.1.4   Phase 4

Phase 4 trials explore the amount of therapy hours needed, potential unintended effects, generalizability issues, and new uses for the treatment. They seek to answer the question of what effects result from the treatment, which is usually officially approved by this phase. Phase 4 trials are intended to further evaluate the long-term safety and effectiveness of a treatment.

Phase 4 trials often involve randomized experiments that address causal assessment and internal validity considerations. The latter topics play a major role, but are not in themselves sufficient for scientific assessment. They would not typically be funded without rigorous phase 1 and 3 assessments. Phase 4 trials usually take years to accomplish. The previous phases other than phase 3 address issues of critical importance in scientific assessment, including construct and external validity. All four phases are necessary to carry out scientifically based assessment in medicine. Most new treatments do not survive past the phase 2 clinical trials.

15.3.2 ALTERED AUDITORY FEEDBACK PROSTHETIC DEVICES

It was a straightforward step to create a portable frequency shifted feedback (FSF) device, by producing a miniature digital in-the-ear device, after the fluency enhancing effects of FSF had been reported in a digital implementation (Howell, El-Yaniv, & Powell, 1987). This was done by Stuart et al. (2003).

Since the manufacture of the SpeechEasy® device, it has been the subject of two phase 1 RCTs. Molt (2006) studied 20 adults who stutter who used SpeechEasy devices over one year. He found a "pattern of initial improvement with the SpeechEasy followed by gradual relapse ... that improvements in fluency scores and on qualitative measures held for the majority of participants after three months of SpeechEasy use, but were less pronounced at 6 and 12 months postfitting" (Pollard, Ellis, Finan, & Ramig, 2009, p. 529).

Another phase 1 trial was reported by Pollard et al. (2009). They followed 11 adults who stutter who used SpeechEasy devices at least five hours per day over a period of four months. Participants were tested in three speaking situations: reading aloud (low stress), conversation (medium stress), and asking strangers questions in a public place (high stress). For the reading aloud task, the researchers found 58% less stuttering when using the devices, and 27% carryover of fluency during the month after use of the device was discontinued; for conversations, the devices reduced stuttering 15%, with 7% carryover; for questioning strangers, the devices reduced stuttering 2%, with 2% carryover.

These two studies suggest that further phase 1 work is warranted before phase 2 trials are embarked on. For instance, poor carryover might be due to using low voice amplitude over time while wearing the device (Howell & Archer, 1984, discussed in Chapter 8, section 8.2.5). If this proved to be the case, conceivably carryover would be improved by inclusion of an automatic gain control to obviate such tendencies.

Additionally, both of these phase 1 trials use conventional procedures designed to test behavioral treatments for stuttering, but it is not clear whether these procedures are appropriate for assessing a prosthetic device. An alternative view is that procedures used for assessing hearing aids might be more appropriate. A model for such a study is the RCT for assessing hearing aid use reported by Yueh et al. (2001).

15.3.3 LIDCOMBE

Other techniques for treating stuttering have their roots in the area of conditioning. Onslow, Andrews, and Lincoln (1994) describe the technique as follows:

> [It] is an operant treatment that incorporates parental verbal contingencies for stuttered speech and stutter-free speech. The contingencies for stutter-free speech are praise and tangible reinforcement, and the contingencies for stuttering are that the parents identify a stuttered utterance and request the child to correct the utterance.

Jones et al. (2005) reported a phase 3 RCT of the Lidcombe program. Fifty-four participants aged between 3 and 6 years were used. Twenty-nine underwent the Lidcombe program and 25 were assigned to the no-treatment control condition. All children showed at least 2% stuttered syllables. The outcome measures were frequency of stuttering measured as the proportion of syllables stuttered, from audiotaped recordings of participants' conversational speech outside the clinic. The parents collected speech samples in three different speaking situations before random allocation to treatment group and at three, six, and nine months after assignment to treatment group. The mean proportion of syllables stuttered at nine months after the trial started was 1.5% (SD 1.4) for the treatment group and 3.9% (SD 3.5) for the control group. The authors concluded that the Lidcombe program was an efficacious treatment for stuttering in children of preschool age.

In many respects this is the most extensive and comprehensive phase 3 investigation of any treatment for stuttering. Nevertheless, some limitations still need to be noted. First, there is no indication of what syllables were considered stutterings. As mentioned earlier, depending on what symptoms were used, children who do not stutter may have been included, which would inflate apparent recovery rate (Wingate, 2002). Second, the assessments were made in real time and this is not the most sensitive or reliable method. Third, Weidig (2005) performed a Monte Carlo simulation that included expected natural recovery rates and reported that Jones et al.'s (2005) results could have been obtained by chance. Finally, Lidcombe treatment is a particular area that would probably benefit from consideration of new theoretical work in operant procedures (Reed, Howell, Davis, & Osborne, 2007).

15.3.4 PHARMACOLOGICAL AGENTS

Pharmacological agents are important as they may support the genetic and imaging work that pointed to a biological basis for stuttering. If there is a biological basis, then if, say, specific brain sites could be targeted by an appropriate pharmacological agent, stuttering symptoms might be alleviated.

One such site was indicated by Alm (2004) who suggested that the basal ganglia are implicated in stuttering. Part of his evidence was that 40% of his sample of speakers who stuttered reported that they had had head traumas. Alm argued these could have led to basal ganglia damage, which could have precipitated the onset of stuttering. The observation that 40% of his sample had experienced head injury has been treated with caution and the question raised of why, if this is true, no associations between stuttering and contact sports have been reported. Nevertheless, his subsequent argument for basal ganglia damage merits attention.

Basal ganglia function can be modified by antipsychotic dopamine antagonists, such as risperidone. Risperidone was included in the comprehensive assessment of pharmacological agents examined in connection with stuttering in a recent review by Bothe et al. (2006). The complete list of substances that have been applied with stuttering individuals and they included in their review are as follows:

Anticonvulsant agents
Antidepressants (selective serotonin reuptake inhibitors)
Antidepressants (tricyclic antidepressants)
Antipsychotic agents (conventional)
Antipsychotic agents (atypical–risperidone)
Cardiovascular agents: alpha receptor agonists
Cardiovascular agents: beta receptor blockers
Cardiovascular agents: calcium channel blockers
Dopamine antagonists

The authors noted that, from a methodological perspective: "With respect to treatment recommendations, some previous reviews have concluded that some drugs, such as haloperidol [an antipsychotic agent], may have 'some efficacy, but poor patient acceptance and unacceptable risks' (Brady, 1991, p. 1312) as treatments for stuttering. The results of this systematic review with trial quality assessment, however, are uniformly negative: Problems were identified not only with side effects and other risks, but also with the effectiveness of the pharmacological agents tested" (Bothe et al., 2006, p. 350).

Bothe et al. went on to conclude that none of the pharmacological agents tested for stuttering have been shown in methodologically sound reports either to improve stuttering frequency to below 5%, or to reduce stuttering by at least half, or to improve relevant social, emotional, or cognitive variables. They argued that their findings raise questions about the logic supporting the continued use of current pharmacological agents for stuttering. In many ways, the lack of effects of pharmacological agents is disappointing insofar as it might have provided a further way of exploring the biological basis of stuttering. In another way, though, drug treatment does have the drawback that these agents cannot be given to children and most stuttering happens in childhood. So, drug studies offer little indication about what leads to stuttering onset, its persistence, and its effective treatment.

15.3.5 Cognitive Behavior Therapy

During the 1980s and 1990s, cognitive and behavioral techniques (CBT) merged to become cognitive behavioral therapy. The CBT model proposed that what people think can affect how they feel and how they behave. During times of mental distress, people think differently about themselves and what happens to them. Thought processes become distorted, which worsens how a person feels. The individual may then behave in a way that prolongs their distress. Cognitive interventions use a style of questioning that stimulates alternative viewpoints or ideas. This is called "guided discovery" and involves exploring and reflecting on the style of reasoning and thinking in order to develop more helpful and positive outcomes. On the basis of these alternatives, people carry out "behavioral experiments" to test out the accuracy of these alternatives and, therefore, adopt new ways of perceiving and acting. Overall, the intention is to move away from more extreme and unhelpful ways of seeing things and toward more helpful and balanced perspectives. CBT also aims to help the person to gradually test out their assumptions and fears and change their behaviors, such as reducing avoidance.

In a tutorial on CBT, Menzies et al. (2009) argued that stuttering in adults is less responsive to speech therapy than has been reported with children (Craig & Hancock, 1995). However, these same adults can have disabling levels of social anxiety. As support, they cited Stein, Baird, and Walker (1996) who reported that 44% of adults who sought treatment for stuttering warranted the co-morbid diagnosis of social phobia. A question raised is whether treatment of anxiety should be the primary target of treatment (Menzies et al., 2009). Four studies, have reported the effects of CBT on social phobia in adults who stutter (Ezrati-Vinacour, Gilboa-Schechtman, Anholt, Weizman, & Hermesh, 2007; McColl, Onslow, Packman, & Menzies, 2001; Menzies et al., 2008; St. Clare et al., 2009) and may shed light on this question.

McColl et al. (2001) used a CBT package based on the cognitive restructuring program for social phobia of Mattick, Peters, and Clarke (1989), with 11 adults who stuttered who were referred for anxiety-related problems. All 11 had reportedly failed to successfully apply speech-restructuring skills in everyday situations despite being fluent in the clinic. After 12 weekly one-hour sessions of CBT, the participants showed significant reductions in: (1) STAI Form Y-1 scores, which measures state anxiety levels, and (2) Global Self-Rating of Stuttering Severity Scores (GSS). GSS is a 9-point, self-report measure of stuttering severity over the previous week. Problems with the study were that it lacked a no-CBT comparison group and did not include follow-up measures at different points in time. Importantly, however, it did not combine speech and psychological procedures. Ezrati-Vinacour et al. (2007) and St. Clare et al. (2009) also did not follow-up participants and did not include a control group, therefore, there will be no more discussion of these studies.

Menzies et al. (2008) recently published an experimental phase 2 clinical trial that examined the rate of social phobia among adults who stutter, the effects of speech restructuring treatment on social anxiety, and the effects on anxiety and stuttering of a cognitive-behavioral therapy package for social anxiety. Thirty-two adults were randomly assigned to either a speech restructuring and CBT group (experimental) or a speech restructuring only group (control). The experimental group had a 10-week CBT program immediately after they were assigned to this group. This was followed by 14 hours of speech restructuring treatment.

The control group received no treatment for approximately 10 weeks after randomization, paralleling the CBT treatment, and then began a speech restructuring program identical to that provided to the experimental group.

Data were obtained on a range of appropriate, well-validated, and reliable speech and psychological measures at pretreatment, post-CBT program, post-speech restructuring, and at the 12-months follow-up. At the start of the trial, 60% of the cohort were diagnosed with social phobia; a significantly higher proportion than in previous studies (Stein, Baird, & Walker, 1996).

While the speech restructuring only (control) group experienced improvements on some anxiety-related measures, their social phobia diagnoses remained throughout the trial. In contrast, at 12 months posttreatment, none of the participants who received the CBT treatment were diagnosed with social phobia by a clinical psychologist. Additionally, those who received the CBT package showed much improvement and sustained global functioning scores, indicating greater engagement in everyday tasks, with fewer psychiatric difficulties and less anxiety and avoidance. Outcome measures of the experimental group also indicated less avoidance of daily speaking situations, a reduction in unhelpful "self talk," and sustained improvements on a range of psychological measures of depression and anxiety. However, it is important to note that the CBT treatment had no impact on stuttering frequency in those with (or without) social phobia.

Menzies et al.'s (2008) research has a number of strengths. Crucially, the design was such that the CBT program was administered before the speech restructuring program, enabling the researchers to assess the effectiveness of CBT alone. Other best-practice techniques included using a speech therapist who was blind to the purpose of the study to administer the speech treatment to all participants. Also, the clinical psychologist, who assessed participants for social phobia at each assessment period, remained blind to the experimental/control group status of each participant throughout the trial.

Clear participant details were provided regarding prior speech and psychological treatment: age, gender, socioeconomic background, trial inclusion and exclusion criteria, and attrition. Both the CBT and speech restructuring programs were described in some detail and care was taken to ensure that the latter contained only techniques for the control of stuttered speech and was free from the cognitive interventions.

The small sample size is the study's main shortcoming. Due to withdrawals, of the original 32 participants, only 13 were retained (eight in the experimental group and five in the control group) by the end of 12 months follow-up. The authors acknowledged that small numbers remained at follow-up, yet since the research is methodologically sound, it seems appropriate to accept the researchers' conclusions that the CBT treatment had no impact on stuttering frequency, and that speech restructuring alone did not improve social phobia, but that the CBT program was highly effective in treating social phobia and improving general functioning. It also should be noted that, statistically speaking, failure to find any significant difference is not evidence that there is no difference between treatment conditions.

Menzies et al. (2009) considered that CBT can be used with any adult who stutters and has raised levels of anxiety, whether or not they meet the DSM criteria for social phobia. Overall, it should be noted that the evidence base that supports this conclusion is limited.

15.4   OTHER ISSUES CONCERNING RECOVERY AFTER TREATMENT AND RECOVERY AFTER CHILDHOOD

The patient age groups that the treatments considered in this chapter focus on are late adolescence and adulthood, except for Lidcombe, which is applied to children. Nothing has been said about natural recovery during later life. However, a small minority of people who stutter recover unassisted even in adulthood (Ingham, Finn, & Bothe, 2005). Recovery in adulthood is unpredictable. It does not seem to be heritable and is not associated with a consistent recovery strategy (Finn, 1996; Finn, Howard, & Kubala, 2005; Ingham et al., 2005; Howell et al., 2008).

Many of the adults who recover have had intervention in the past and this raises the question of when it can be said that recovery is not due to an intervention. There is also the issue of remission to take into account, both in adulthood and in childhood, where a client has a period of fluency and then relapses. Again, this raises the question of how long a period of recovery has to last for it to be considered permanent. A further problem for recovery is that some parents report that they sought therapy for their child, but the offspring reports not to have known about it.

Contemporary writing on stuttering also discusses to the notion of covert stuttering (not to be confused with the covert repair hypothesis). Covert stuttering refers to people who do not stutter overtly, although they still consider themselves to be stutterers and feel anxious in speaking situations. The notion of covert stuttering is based on casual reports and has not been investigated thoroughly. The main issue is whether the feelings of anxiety about fluency of people who report covert symptoms are different from those that speakers who have always regarded themselves as fluent experience in stressful communication situations.

Finally, onset and recovery is rare, but can occur outside the teenage years. In our own cohort, we have developmental cases (no history of brain injury) who do recover after their teens. On the other hand, some cases of stuttering start in adulthood and these may have different symptoms (Jokel, de Nil, & Sharpe, 2007; Van Borsel & Taillieu, 2001). It is often thought that more adult cases have a neurogenic origin than is the case for children (although neurogenic onset also can occur in developmental stuttering as Alm, 2004, noted). However, some of the adults do not have identifiable neurological causes. I do not know any study that assesses and reports such cases and considers whether the course is similar to developmental stuttering.

15.5   SUMMARY AND CONCLUSIONS

This chapter started by reviewing some methodological issues that have relevance to determining the nature of therapy outcome in speakers who stutter. It was shown that many of the issues discussed in earlier chapters apply to this topic. Selected treatments were then examined to see to what phase their assessment had progressed and what results have been reported for stuttering. Although there are a few notable exceptions, the phase at which treatment research has reached at present is disappointing and worrying.

15.6   EXERCISES

1. A major point of this chapter was to bring the approaches established in earlier chapters to bear on selected treatments that have some evidence to back them up (many do not). Obvious limitations of scope are in terms of the range of topics discussed in this volume that are relevant to clinical issues, and the limited number of treatments that have been considered in this chapter. Indicate what issues you think should have received more attention and illustrate the importance of these issues with respect to a form of treatment not covered in this chapter.

2. Should a person who has been successfully treated have speech that is similar to that of a person who has recovered naturally? Are there other aspects of behavior that should be checked to establish that they are within normal limits?

3. There is a large body of theoretical work on operant procedures that has been applied to learning disorders that has had relatively little impact on stuttering. Read some of this literature and discuss its relevance to operant procedures applied to stuttering.

4. Is it satisfactory to solely treat speech symptoms in adults who stutter?

5. Scientific studies using groups of individuals who stutter allow the reader to understand whether treatments are effective or not. However, the information is impersonal. Case study methods are an alternative to investigate treatments. Compare these two approaches giving the pros and cons of each for studying treatment efficacy in stuttering.

6. Why are randomized control trials referred to as the "gold standard"?

References

Abbs, J. H., & Gracco, V. L. (1984). Control of complex motor gestures: Orofacial muscle responses to load perturbations of lip during speech. *Journal of Neurophysiology, 51,* 705–723.

Accordi, M., Bianchi, R., Consolaro, C., Tronchin, F., DeFilippi, R., Pasqualon, L., Ugo, E., & Croatto, L. (1893). The pathogenesis of stuttering: A statistical study of 2802 cases. *Acta Phoniatrica Latina, 5,* 171–180.

Ackermann, H., & Riecker, A. (2010). Cerebral control of motor aspects of speech production: Neurophysiological and functional imaging data. In B. Maasen & P. H. H. M. van Lieshout (Eds.). *Speech motor control: New developments in basic and applied research* (pp.117–134). Oxford, U.K.: Oxford University Press.

Ajdacic-Gross, V., Vetter, S., Muller, M., Kawohl, W., Frey, F., Lupi, ... & Rossler, W. (2009). Risk factors for stuttering: A secondary analysis of a large data base. *European Archives of Psychiatry and Clinical Neuroscience, 260,* 279–286.

Alfonso, P. J., & Van Lieshout, P. H. H. M. (1997). Spatial and temporal variability in obstruent gestural specification by stutterers and controls: Comparisons across sessions. In W. Hujstijn, H. F. M. Peters, & P. H. H. M. Van Lieshout (Eds.), *Speech production: Motor control, brain research and fluency disorders* (pp. 1151–1602). Amsterdam, The Netherlands: Elsevier Publishers.

Alm, P. A. (2004). Stuttering and the basal ganglia circuits: A critical review of possible relations. *Journal of Communication Disorders, 37,* 325–369.

Alm, P. A. (2005). Copper in developmental stuttering. *Folia Phoniatrica et Logopaedica, 57,* 216–222.

Alm, P. A., & Risberg, J. (2007). Stuttering in adults: The acoustic startle response, temperamental traits, and biological factors. *Journal of Communication Disorders, 40,* 1–41.

Ambrose, N. G., Yairi, E., & Cox, N. (1993). Genetic aspects of early childhood stuttering. *Journal of Speech and Hearing Research, 36,* 701–706.

Ambrose, N. G., Cox, N. J., & Yairi, E. (1997). The genetic basis of persistence and recovery in stuttering. *Journal of Speech, Language, and Hearing Research, 40,* 567–580.

American Psychiatric Association. (2000). Stuttering. In M. B. First (Ed.), *Diagnostic and statistical manual of mental disorders: DSM-IV-TR* (4th ed.) (pp. 67–69). Arlington, VA: American Psychiatric Association.

Anderson, A., Lowit, A., & Howell, P. (2008). Temporal and spatial variability in speakers with Parkinson's disease and Friedreich's ataxia. *Journal of Medical Speech-Language Pathology, 16,* 173–180.

Anderson, J. D. (2007). Phonological neighborhood and word frequency effects in the stuttered disfluencies of children who stutter. *Journal of Speech, Language, and Hearing Research, 50,* 229–247.

Anderson, J. D., & Conture, E. G. (2000). Language abilities of children who stutter: A preliminary study. *Journal of Fluency Disorders, 25,* 283–304.

Anderson, J. D., & Conture, E. G. (2004). Sentence-structure priming in young children who do and do not stutter. *Journal of Speech, Language, and Hearing Research, 47,* 552–571.

Anderson, J. D., Pellowski, M. W., Conture, E. G., & Kelly, E. M. (2003). Temperamental characteristics of young children who stutter. *Journal of Speech, Language, and Hearing Research, 46,* 1221–1233.

Andrews, G., & Cutler, J. (1974). Stuttering therapy—relation between changes in symptom level and attitudes. *Journal of Speech and Hearing Disorders, 39,* 312–319.

Andrews, G. & Harris, M. (1964). *The syndrome of stuttering. Clinics in developmental medicine (No. 17).* London, U.K.: William Heineman Medical Books Ltd.

Andrews, G., Craig, A., Feyer, A. M., Hoddinott, S., Howie, P., & Neilson, M. (1983). Stuttering: A review of research findings and theories circa 1982. *Journal of Speech and Hearing Disorders, 48,* 226–246.

Andrews, G., Morris-Yates, A., Howie, P., & Martin, N. G. (1991). Genetic factors in stuttering confirmed. *Archives of General Psychiatry, 48,* 1034–1035.

Arcuri, C. F., Osborn, E., Schiefer, A. M., & Chiari, B. M. (2009). Speech rate according to stuttering severity. *Pro-Fono, 21,* 46–50.

Armson, J., & Stuart, A. (1998). Effect of extended exposure to frequency altered feedback on stuttering during reading and monologue. *Journal of Speech, Language, and Hearing Research, 41,* 479–490.

Arnold, H. S., Conture, E. G., & Ohde, R. N. (2005). Phonological neighborhood density in the picture naming of young children who stutter: Preliminary study. *Journal of Fluency Disorders, 30,* 125–148.

Au-Yeung, J., Gomez, I. V., & Howell, P. (2003). Exchange of disfluency with age from function words to content words in Spanish speakers who stutter. *Journal of Speech, Language, and Hearing Research, 46,* 754–765.

Au-Yeung, J., Howell, P., & Pilgrim, L. (1998). Phonological words and stuttering on function words. *Journal of Speech, Language, and Hearing Research, 41,* 1019–1030.

Australian Bureau of Statistics. (2001). *Socio-economic indexes for areas.* Canberra, Australia: Australian Bureau of Statistics.

Bajina, K. (1995). Covert aspects associated with the "stuttering syndrome": Focus on self-esteem. In M. Fawcus (Ed.), *Stuttering from theory to practice.* London, U.K.: Whurr Publishers.

Bardrick, R. A., & Sheehan, J. G. (1965). Emotional loading as a source of conflict in stuttering. *American Psychologist, 11,* 391.

Barker, J. (1973). *Arizona articulation proficiency scale.* Los Angeles, CA: Western Psychological Association.

Battle, J. (1992). *Culture-free and self-esteem inventories: Examiner's manual* (2nd ed.). Austin, TX: Pro-ed.

Bauer, A., Jäncke, L., & Kalveram, K. T. (1997). Mechanical perturbation of the jaw during speech in stutterers and nonstutterers. In W. Hulstijn, H. F. M. Peters, & P. H. H. M. Van Lieshout (Eds.), *Speech production: Motor control, brain research and fluency disorders* (pp. 191–196). Amsterdam, The Netherlands: Elsevier Publishers.

Beach, H. R. & Fransella, F. (1968). *Research and experiment in stuttering.* New York, NY: Pergamon.

Beauchamp, T. L., & Childress, J .F. (1994). *Principles of biomedical ethics* (4th ed.). New York: Oxford University Press.

Bernstein, N. A. (1967). *The co-ordination and regulation of movements.* Oxford, U.K.: Pergamon Press.

Bernstein, N. E. (1981). Are there constraints on childhood disfluency. *Journal of Fluency Disorders, 6,* 341–350.

Bernstein Ratner, N. (1997). Stuttering: A psycholinguistic perspective. In R. F. Curlee & G. Siegel (Eds.), *Nature and treatment of stuttering: New directions* (2nd ed.) (pp. 99–127). Needham, MA: Allyn & Bacon.

Bernstein Ratner, N. (1998). Linguistic and perceptual characteristics of children at stuttering onset. In E. Charles Healey & H. F. M. Peters (eds.) *Proceedings of the Second World Congress on Fluency Disorders.* Nijmegen, The Netherlands: Nijmegen University Press (3-6).

Bernstein Ratner, N. (2005). Evidence-based practice in stuttering: Some questions to consider. *Journal of Fluency Disorders, 30,* 163–188.

Bernstein Ratner, N., & Sih, C. C. (1987). Effects of gradual increases in sentence length and complexity on children's dysfluency. *Journal of Speech and Hearing Disorders, 52,* 278–287.

Bernstein Ratner, N., & Silverman, F. H. (2000). Parental perceptions of children's communicative development at stuttering onset. *Journal of Speech, Language, and Hearing Research, 43,* 1252–1263.

Bernstein Ratner, N., & Wijnen, F. (2007). The vicious cycle: Linguistic encoding, self-monitoring and stuttering. In J. Au-Yeung (Ed.), *Proceedings of the 5th world congress of fluency disorders* (pp. 84–90). Dublin, Ireland: International Fluency Association.

Blackmer, E. R., & Mitton, J. L. (1991). Theories of monitoring and timing of repairs in spontaneous speech. *Cognition, 39,* 173–194.

Blakemore, S. J., Frith, C. D., & Wolpert, D. M. (2001). The cerebellum is involved in predicting the sensory consequences of action. *Neuroreport, 12,* 1879–1884.

Blood, G. W., Blood, I. M., Bennett, S., Simpson, K. C., & Susman, E. J. (1994). Subjective anxiety measurements and cortisol responses in adults who stutter. *Journal of Speech and Hearing Research, 37,* 760–768.

Blood, G. W., Blood, I. M., Tellis, G. M., & Gabel, R. M. (2003a). A preliminary study of self-esteem, stigma, and disclosure in adolescents who stutter. *Journal of Fluency Disorders, 28,* 143–159.

Blood, G. W., Ridenour, V. J., Qualls, C. D., & Hammer, C. S. (2003b). Co-occurring disorders in children who stutter. *Journal of Communication Disorders, 36,* 427–448.

Bloodstein, O. (1974). Rules of early stuttering. *Journal of Speech and Hearing Disorders, 39,* 379–394.

Bloodstein, O. (1987). *A handbook on stuttering* (4th ed.). Chicago, IL: National Easter Seal Society.

Bloodstein, O. (1995). *A handbook on stuttering* (5th ed.). San Diego, CA: Singular Publishing Group.

Bloodstein, O. (2006). Some empirical observations about early stuttering: A possible link to language development. *Journal of Communication Disorders, 39,* 185–191.

Bloodstein, O. & Bernstein Ratner, N. (2007). *A handbook on stuttering* (6th ed.), Clifton Park, NY: Thomson Delmar.

Bloodstein, O., & Gantwerk, B. F. (1967). Grammatical function in relation to stuttering in young children. *Journal of Speech and Hearing Research, 10,* 786–789.

Bloodstein, O., & Grossman, M. (1981). Early stutterings: Some aspects of their form and distribution. *Journal of Speech and Hearing Research, 24,* 298–302.

Bloom, L. (1970). *Language development: Form and function in emerging grammars.* Cambridge, MA: MIT Press.

Boberg, E., & Kully, D. (1994). Long term results of an intensive treatment program for adults and adolescents who stutter. *Journal of Speech and Hearing Research, 37,* 1059.

Boey, R. A., Wuyts, F. L., Van de Heyning, P. H., De Bodt, M. S., & Heylen, L. (2007). Characteristics of stuttering-like disfluencies in Dutch-speaking children. *Journal of Fluency Disorders, 32,* 310–329.

Boey, R. A., Wuyts, F. L., Van de Heyning, P. H., Heylen, L., & De Bodt, M. S. (2009). Characteristics of stuttering in Dutch-speaking individuals. *Clinical Linguistics Phonetics Journal, 23,* 241–254.

Bond, Z. S. (1999). Morphological errors in casual conversation. *Brain and Language, 68,* 144–150.

Bonelli, P., Dixon, M., & Onslow, M. (2000). Child and parent speech and language following the Lidcombe Programme of early stuttering intervention. *Clinical Linguistics &
Phonetics, 14,* 427–446.

Borden, G. J. (1979). Interpretation of research on feedback interruption in speech. *Brain
and Language, 7,* 307–319.

Bosshardt, H. G. (1999). Effects of concurrent mental calculation on stuttering, inhalation
and speech timing. *Journal of Fluency Disorders, 24,* 43–72.

Bosshardt, H. G. (2002). Effects of concurrent cognitive processing on the fluency of
word repetition: Comparison between persons who do and do not stutter. *Journal of
Fluency Disorders, 27,* 93–113.

Bosshardt, H. G., Ballmer, W., & de Nil, L. F. (2002). Effects of category and rhyme decisions on sentence production. *Journal of Speech, Language, and Hearing Research,
45,* 844–857.

Bothe, A. K., Davidow, J. H., Bramlett, R. E., & Ingham, R. J. (2006). Stuttering treatment
research 1970–2005: I. Systematic review incorporating trial quality assessment of
behavioral, cognitive, and related approaches. *American Journal of Speech-Language
Pathology, 15,* 321–341.

Boutsen, F. & Brutten, G. (1989). *Stutterers and nonstutterers: A normative investigation
of children's speech associated attitudes.* Unpublished manuscript, Southern Illinois
University, Carbondale, IL.

Brady, J. P. (1991). The pharmacology of stuttering: A critical review. *American Journal of
Psychiatry, 148,* 1309–1316.

Braun, A. R., Varga, M., Stager, S., Schulz, G., Selbie, S., Maisog, J. M., Carson, R. E.,
& Ludlow, C. L. (1997). Altered patterns of cerebral activity during speech and
language production in developmental stuttering. An H2(15)O positron emission
tomography study. *Brain, 120,* 761–784.

Brosch, S., Haege, A., Kalehne, P., & Johannsen, H. S. (1999). Stuttering children and the
probability of remission: The role of cerebral dominance and speech production.
International Journal of Pediatric Otorhinolaryngology, 47, 71–76.

Brown, R. (1973). *A first language: The early stages.* Cambridge, MA: Harvard
University Press.

Brown, S., Ingham, R. J., Ingham, J. C., Laird, A. R., & Fox, P. T. (2005). Stuttered and
fluent speech production: An ALE meta-analysis of functional neuroimaging studies.
Human Brain Mapping, 25, 105–117.

Brown, S. F. (1937). The influence of grammatical function on the incidence of stuttering.
Journal of Speech Disorders, 2, 207–215.

Brown, S. F. (1945). The loci of stutterings in the speech sequence. *Journal of Speech
Disorders, 10,* 181–192.

Brown, S. F., & Hull, H. C. (1942). A study of some social attitudes of a group of 59 stutterers. *Journal of Speech Disorders, 7,* 153–159.

Brutten, G. J. (1973). Behavior assessment and the strategy of therapy. In J. Lebrun & R.
Hoops (Eds.), *Neurolinguistic approaches to stuttering* (pp. 66–75). The Hague, The
Netherlands: Mouton.

Brutten, G. J. (1985). *Communication attitude test.* Unpublished manuscript, Department of
Communication Disorders and Sciences, Southern Illinois University, Carbondale, IL.

Brutten, G. J., & Dunham, S. (1989). The communication attitude test. A normative study
of grade school children. *Journal of Fluency Disorders, 14,* 371–377.

Bryngelson, B. (1938). Prognosis of stuttering. *Journal of Speech Disorders, 3,* 121–123.

Bryngelson, B., & Rutherford, B. (1937). A comparative study of laterality of stutterers and
non-stutterers. *Journal of Speech Disorders, 2,* 15–16.

Caprara, G. V., & Cervone, D. (2000). *Personality: Determinants, dynamics, and potentials*. New York, NY: Cambridge University Press.

Caramazza, A., & Berndt, R. (1985). A multicomponent deficit view of agrammatic Broca's aphasia. In M. L. Kean (Ed.), *Agrammatism* (pp. 27–63). Orlando, FL: Academic Press.

Caruso, A. J., Abbs, J. H., & Gracco, V. L. (1988). Kinematic analysis of multiple movement coordination during speech in stutterers. *Brain, 111,* 439–456.

Caruso, A. J., Chodzko-Zajko, W. J., Bidinger, D. A., & Sommers, R. K. (1994). Adults who stutter: Responses to cognitive stress. *Journal of Speech and Hearing Research, 37,* 746–754.

Caruso, A. J., Gracco, V. L., & Abbs, J. H. (1987). A speech motor control perspective on stuttering: Preliminary observations. In H. F. M. Peters and W. Hulstijn (Eds.), *Speech motor dynamics in stuttering* (pp. 245–258). Vienna, Austria: Springer-Verlag.

Cattell, R. B., & Scheier, I. H. (1961). *The meaning and measurement of neuroticism and anxiety*. New York, NY: Ronald Press.

Chang, S. E., Erickson, K. I., Ambrose, N. G., Hasegawa-Johnson, M. A., & Ludlow, C. L. (2008). Brain anatomy differences in childhood stuttering. *Neuroimage, 39,* 1333–1344.

Chang, S.-E., & Ludlow, C. L. (2010). Brain imaging in children. In B. Maasen & P. H. H. M. van Lieshout (Eds.). *Speech motor control: New developments in basic and applied research* (pp. 71–94). Oxford, U.K.: Oxford University Press.

Cherry, C., & Sayers, B. M. (1956). Experiments upon the total inhibition of stammering by external control, and some clinical results. *Journal of Psychosomatic Research, 1,* 233–246.

Chiarello, C., & Nuding, S. (1987). Visual field effects for processing content and function words. *25,* 539–548.

Clark, H. & Clark, E. (1977). *Psychology and language: An introduction to psycholinguistics*. New York, NY: Harcourt Brace.

Coady, J. A., & Aslin, R. N. (2003). Phonological neighbourhoods in the developing lexicon. *Journal of Child Language, 30,* 441–469.

Conture, E. G. (1982). *Stuttering* (1st ed.). Englewood Cliffs, NJ: Prentice-Hall.

Conture, E. G. (1990). *Stuttering* (2nd ed.). Englewood Cliffs, NJ: Prentice Hall.

Conture, E. G. (2001). *Stuttering: Its nature, diagnosis and treatment*. Boston, MA: Allyn & Bacon.

Conture, E. G., & Kelly, E. M. (1991). Young stutterers' non-speech behaviors during stuttering. *Journal of Speech and Hearing Research, 37,* 279–294.

Cordes, A. K., & Ingham, R. J. (1995). Stuttering includes both within-word and between-word disfluencies. *Journal of Speech and Hearing Research, 38,* 382–386.

Costa, P. T., & McCrae, R. R. (1990). Personality disorders and the five-factor model of personality. *Journal of Personality Disorders, 4,* 362–371.

Costello-Ingham, J. C. (1993). Current status of stuttering and behavior modification – 1. Recent trends in the application of behavior application in children and adults. *Journal of Fluency Disorders, 18,* 27–44.

Cox, M. D. (1982). The stutterer and stuttering: Neuropsychological correlates. *Journal of Fluency Disorders, 7,* 129–140.

Cox, N., Kramer, P., & Kidd, K. (1984). Segregation analyses of stuttering. *Genetic Epidemiology, 1,* 245–253.

Craig, A., & Hancock, K. (1995). Self-reported factors related to relapse following treatment for stuttering. *Australian Journal of Human Communication Disorders, 23,* 48–60.

Craig, A., Hancock, K., Tran, Y., & Craig, M. (2003). Anxiety levels in people who stutter: A randomized population study. *Journal of Speech, Language, and Hearing Research, 46,* 1197–1206.

Cramer, A. O. J., Waldorp, L. J., van der Maas, H. L .J., & Borsboom, D. (in press). Comorbidity: A network perspective. *Behavioral and Brain Sciences*.

Curlee, R. F. (1993). Identification and management of beginning stuttering. In R. F. Curlee (Ed.), *Stuttering and related disorders of fluency* (pp. 1–22). New York, NY: Thieme Medical Publishers.

Cutler, A. (1982). *Slips of the tongue and language production*. The Hague, The Netherlands: Mouton.

Danzger, M., & Halpern, H. (1973). Relation of stuttering to word abstraction, part of speech, word length, and word frequency. *Perceptual and Motor Skills, 37,* 959–962.

Davis, S., Howell, P., & Cook, F. (2002). Sociodynamic relationships between children who stutter and their non-stuttering classmates. *Journal of Child Psychology and Psychiatry, 43,* 939–947.

Davis, S., Shisca, D., & Howell, P. (2007). Anxiety in speakers who persist and recover from stuttering. *Journal of Communication Disorders, 40,* 398–417.

Dayalu, V. N., & Kalinowski, J. (2002). Pseudofluency in adults who stutter: The illusory outcome of therapy. *Perceptual and Motor Skills, 94,* 87–96.

Dayalu, V. N., Kalinowski, J., Stuart, A., Holbert, D., & Rastatter, M. P. (2002). Stuttering frequency on content and function words in adults who stutter: A concept revisited. *Journal of Speech, Language, and Hearing Research, 45,* 871–879.

de Andrade, C. R., Cervone, L. M., & Sassi, F. C. (2003). Relationship between the stuttering severity index and speech rate. *Sao Paulo Medical Journal, 121,* 81–84.

de Joy, D. A., & Gregory, H. H. (1985). The relationship between age and frequency of disfluency in preschool children. *Journal of Fluency Disorders, 10,* 107–122.

de Marco, G., Vrignaud, P., Destrieux, C., de Marco, D., Testelin, S., Devauchelle, B., & Berquin, P. (2009). Principle of structural equation modeling for exploring functional interactivity within a putative network of interconnected brain areas. *Magnetic Resonance Imaging, 27,* 1–12.

De Moor, W., Ghyselinck, M., & Brysbaert, M. (2001). The effects of frequency of occurrence and age-of-acquisition in word processing. In: Columbus, F., Editor. *Advances in psychology research* Vol. 5, Nova Science, Huntington, NY, pp. 71–84.

de Nil, L., & Bosshardt, H. G. (2000). Dual-task language processing in persons who stutter: An fMRI study. *Journal of Fluency Disorders, 25,* 172–182.

de Nil, L., & Brutten, G. (1991). Speech-associated attitudes of stuttering and nonstuttering children. *Journal of Speech and Hearing Research, 34,* 60–66.

de Nil, L., Kroll, R. M., & Houle, S. (2001). Functional neuroimaging of cerebellar activation during single word reading and verb generation in stuttering and nonstuttering adults. *Neuroscience Letters, 302,* 77–80.

de Nil, L. F., Kroll, R. M., Kapur, S., & Houle, S. (2000). A positron emission tomography study of silent and oral single word reading in stuttering and nonstuttering adults. *Journal of Speech Language and Hearing Research, 43,* 1038–1053.

de Nil, L. F., Kroll, R. M., Lafaille, S. J., & Houle, S. (2003). A positron emission tomography study of short- and long-term treatment effects on functional brain activation in adults who stutter. *Journal of Fluency Disorders, 28,* 357–379.

de Nil, L. F., Beal, D. S., Lafaille, S. J., Kroll, R. M., Crawley, A. P., & Gracco, V. L. (2008). The effects of simulated stuttering and prolonged speech on the neural activation patterns of stuttering and nonstuttering adults. *Brain and Language, 107,* 114–123.

de Saussure, F. (1916). *Course in general linguistics*. New York, NY: McGraw-Hill.

de Saussure, F. (1966). *Course in general linguistics*. New York, NY: McGraw-Hill.

Dell, G. S. (1986). A spreading-activation theory of retrieval in sentence production. *Psychological Review, 93,* 283–321.

Dell, G. S. (1990). Effects of frequency and vocabulary type on phonological speech errors. *Language and Cognitive Processes, 5,* 313–349.

Dell, G. S., & Reich, P. A. (1981). Stages in sentence production—An analysis of speech error data. *Journal of Verbal Learning and Verbal Behavior, 20,* 611–629.

Demuth, K., & McCullough, E. (2009). The prosodic (re)organization of children's early English articles. *Journal of Child Language, 36,* 173–200.

Desmurget, M., & Grafton, S. (2000). Forward modeling allows feedback control for fast reaching movements. *Trends in Cognitive Sciences, 4,* 423–431.

DiLollo, A., Manning, W. H., & Neimeyer, R. A. (2003). Cognitive anxiety as a function of speaker role for fluent speakers and persons who stutter. *Journal of Fluency Disorders, 28,* 167–186.

Donath, T. M., Natke, U., & Kalveram, K. T. (2002). Effects of frequency-shifted auditory feedback on voice F0 contours in syllables. *Journal of the Acoustical Society of America, 111,* 357–366.

Dow, R. S. & Moruzzi, G. (1958). *The physiology and pathology of the cerebellum.* Minneapolis, MN: University of Minnesota Press.

Dworzynski, D., Remington, A., Rijksdijk, F., Howell, P., & Plomin, R. (2007). Genetic and environmental etiology in cases of recovered and persistent stuttering in unselected longitudinal sample of young twins. *American Journal of Speech Language Pathology, 16,* 169–178.

Dworzynski, K., & Howell, P. (2004). Cross-linguistic factors in the prediction of stuttering across age groups—The case of German. In A. Packman, A. Meltzer, & H. F. M. Peters (Eds.), *Theory, research and therapy in fluency disorders* (pp. 382–388). Montreal, Canada: International Fluency Association.

Dworzynski, K., Howell, P., Au-Yeung, J., & Rommel, D. (2004). Stuttering on function and content words across age groups of German speakers who stutter. *Journal of Multilingual Communication Disorders, 2,* 81–101.

Edwards, M. L. & Shriberg, L. (1983). *Phonology: Applications in communicative disorders.* San Diego, CA: College-Hill.

Elman, J. L. (1981). Effects of frequency-shifted feedback on the pitch of vocal productions. *Journal of the Acoustical Society of America, 70,* 45–50.

Embrechts, M., Ebben, H., Franke, P., & van de Poel, C. (2000). Temperament: A comparison between children who stutter and children who do not stutter. In H. G. Bosshardt, J. S. Yaruss, & H. F. M. Peters (Eds.), *Proceedings of the 3rd world congress of fluency disorders: Theory, research, treatment and self-help* (pp. 557–562). Nijmegen, The Netherlands: University of Nijmegen Press.

Erikson, R. L. (1969). Assessing communication attitudes among stutterers. *Journal of Speech and Hearing Research, 12,* 711–724.

Eysenck, S. B. G., & Eysenck, H. J. (1963). On the dual nature of extraversion. *British Journal of Social and Clinical Psychology, 2,* 46–55.

Ezrati-Vinacour, R., & Levin, I. (2004). The relationship between anxiety and stuttering: A multidimensional approach. *Journal of Fluency Disorders, 29,* 135–148.

Ezrati-Vinacour, R., Gilboa-Schechtman, E., Anholt, G., Weizman, A., & Hermesh, H. (2007). *Effectiveness of cognitive behaviour group therapy (CBGT) for social phobia (SP) in people who stutter (PWS) with social phobia (SP).* Paper presented at the 5th World Congress of Behavioral and Cognitive Therapies, Barcelona, Spain.

Fairbanks, G. (1955). Selective vocal effects of delayed auditory feedback. *Journal of Speech and Hearing Disorders, 20,* 333–346.

Fattapposta, F., Pierelli, F., My, F., Mostarda, M., Del Monte, S., Parisi, L. … Amabile, G. (2002). L-dopa effects on preprogramming and control activity in a skilled motor act in Parkinson's disease. *Clinical Neurophysiology, 113,* 243–253.

Fawcett, A. J., Nicolson, R. I., & Dean, P. (1996). Impaired performance of children with dyslexia on a range of cerebellar tasks. *Annals of Dyslexia, 46,* 259–283.

Felsenfeld, S., Kirk, K. M., Zhu, G., Statham, D. J., Neale, M. C., & Martin, N. G. (2000). A study of the genetic and environmental etiology of stuttering in a selected twin sample. *Behaviour Genetics, 30,* 359–366.

Fenson, L., Dale, P. S., & Reznick, J. S. (1993). *The MacArthur communicative development inventories: User's guide and technical manual.* San Diego, CA: Singular Publishing Group.

Fenson, L., Pethick, S. J., Renda, C., Cox, J. L., Dale, P. S., & Reznick, J. S. (2000). Short-form versions of the MacArthur communicative development inventories. *Applied Psycholinguistics, 21,* 95–116.

Ferreira, F. (1993). Creation of prosody during sentence production. *Psychological Review, 100,* 233–253.

Few, L. R., & Lingwall, J. B. (1972). A further analysis of fluency within stuttered speech. *Journal of Speech and Hearing Research, 15,* 356–363.

Fiez, J. A., & Petersen, S. E. (1998). Neuroimaging studies of word reading. In *Proceedings of the National Academy of Sciences of the United States of America* (95th ed, pp. 914–921). Washington, DC: NAS.

Finn, P. (1996). Establishing the validity of recovery from stuttering without formal treatment. *Journal of Speech Hearing Research, 39,* 1171–1181.

Finn, P. (1998). Recovery without treatment: A review of conceptual and methodological considerations across disciplines. In A. K. Cordes & R. J. Ingham (Eds.), *Treatment efficacy for stuttering: A search for empirical bases* (pp. 3–26). San Diego, CA: Singular Publishing Group.

Finn, P., Howard, R., & Kubala, R. (2005). Unassisted recovery from stuttering: self-perceptions of current speech behavior, attitudes, and feelings. *Journal of Fluency Disorders, 30,* 281–305.

Fisher, S. E. (2006) Tangled webs: Tracing the connections between genes and cognition. *Cognition, 101,* 270–297

Fisher, S. E., Vargha-Khadem, F., Watkins, K. E., Monaco, A. P., & Pembrey, M. E. (1998). Localisation of a gene implicated in a severe speech and language disorder. *Nature Genetics, 18,* 168–170.

Fletcher, H., Raff, G. M., & Parmley, F. (1918). *Study of the effects of different sidetones in the telephone set.* (Report No. 19412, Case No. 120622). Chicago, IL: Western Electrical Company.

Flick, S. N. (1988). Managing attrition in clinical research. *Clinical Psychology Review, 8,* 499–515.

Folkins, J. W., & Zimmermann, G. N. (1981). Jaw-muscle activity during speech with the mandible fixed. *Journal of the Acoustical Society of America, 69,* 1441–1445.

Folkins, J. W., & Zimmermann, G. N. (1982). Lip and jaw interaction during speech: Responses to perturbation of lower-lip movement prior to bilabial closure. *Journal of the Acoustical Society of America, 71,* 1225–1233.

Foundas, A. L., Bollich, A. M., Corey, D. M., Hurley, M., & Heilman, K. M. (2001). Anomalous anatomy of speech-language areas in adults with persistent developmental stuttering. *Neurology, 57,* 207–215.

Fowler, C. A., & Turvey, M. T. (1980). Immediate compensation in bite-block speech. *Phonetica, 37,* 306–326.

Fowlie, G. M., & Cooper, E. B. (1978). Traits attributed to stuttering and non-stuttering children by their mothers. *Journal of Fluency Disorders, 3,* 233–246.

Fox, P. T., Ingham, R. J., Ingham, J. C., Hirsch, T. B., Downs, J. H., Martin, C. ... & Lancaster, J. L. (1996). A PET study of the neural systems of stuttering. *Nature, 382,* 158–162.

Fox, P. T., Ingham, R. J., Ingham, J. C., Zamarripa, F., Xiong, J. H., & Lancaster, J. L. (2000). Brain correlates of stuttering and syllable production: A PET performance-correlation analysis. *Brain, 123,* 1985–2004.

Fransella, F., & Beech, H. R. (1965). An experimental analysis of the effect of rhythm on the speech of stutterers. *Behaviour Research and Therapy, 3,* 195–201.

Fransella, F., & Beech, H. (2009). An experimental analysis of the effect of rhythm on the speech of stutterers. *Behavior Research and Therapy, 3,* 195–201.

Fritzell, B. (1976). The prognosis of stuttering in school children: A 10-year longitudinal study. In *Proceedings of the 16th Congress of the International Society of Logopedics and Phoniatrics* (pp. 186–187). Basel, Switzerland: Karger.

Froeschels, E. (1943). Pathology and therapy of stuttering. *Nervous Child, 2,* 148–161.

Fromkin, V. A. (1971). The non-anomalous nature of anomalous utterances. *Language, 47,* 27–52.

Furnham, A., & Davis, S. (2004). Involvement of social factors in stuttering: A review and assessment of current methodology. *Stammering Research, 1,* 112–122.

Gaines, N. D., Runyan, C. M., & Meyers, S. C. (1991). A comparison of young stutterers' fluent versus stuttered utterances on measures of length and complexity. *Journal of Speech and Hearing Research, 34,* 37–42.

Garnham, A. R. C., Shillcock, G. D. A., Brown, A. I., Mill, D., & Cutler, A. (1981). Slips of the tongue in the London-Lund corpus of spontaneous conversation. *Linguistics, 19,* 805–817.

Gee, J. P., & Grosjean, F. (1983). Performance structures: A psycholinguistic and linguistic appraisal. *Cognitive Psychology, 15,* 411–458.

German, D. J., & Newman, R. S. (2004). The impact of lexical factors on children's word-finding errors. *Journal of Speech, Language, and Hearing Research, 47,* 624–636.

German National Ethics Council (2004). Biobanks for research. Opinion Berlin: Nationaler Ethikrat; available at http://www.ethikrat.org/_english/publications/Opinion_Bio banks-for-research.pdf

Gershkoff-Stowe, L., & Smith, L. B. (1997). A curvilinear trend in naming errors as a function of early vocabulary growth. *Cognitive Psychology, 34,* 37–71.

Gilhooly, K. J., & Logie, R. H. (1980). Age of acquisition, imagery, concreteness, familiarity and ambiguity measures for 1944 words. *Behaviour Research Methods & Instrumentation, 12,* 395–427.

Giraud, A. L., Neumann, K., Bachoud-Levi, A. C., von Gudenberg, A. W., Euler, H. A., Lanfermann, H., & Preibisch, C. (2008). Severity of dysfluency correlates with basal ganglia activity in persistent developmental stuttering. *Brain and Language, 104,* 190–199.

Goffman, L. (2010). Dynamic interaction of motor and language factors in normal and disordered development. In B. Maasen & P. H. H. M. van Lieshout (Eds.). *Speech motor control: New developments in basic and applied research* (pp. 137–152). Oxford, U.K.: Oxford University Press.

Goldberg, G. (1991). Microgenetic theory and the dual premotor systems hypothesis: Implications for rehabilitation of the brain-damaged subject. In R. E. Hanlon (Ed.). *Cognitive microgenesis: A neuropsychological perspective* (pp. 32–52). New York, NY: Springer.

Goldfarb, R. (2006). *Ethics: A case study from fluency.* San Diego, CA: Plural Publishing.

Goldman-Eisler, F. (1968). *Psycholinguistics. Experiments in spontaneous speech.* London, U.K. and New York, NY: Academic Press.

Goldman, R. & Fristoe, M. (1986). *Goldman-Fristoe test of articulation.* Circle Pines, MN: American Guidance Service, Inc.

Goldsmith, H. H., Buss, A. H., Plomin, R., Rothbart, M. K., Thomas, A., Chess, S., Hinde, R. A., & McCall, R. B. (1987). Roundtable: What is temperament? Four approaches. *Child Development, 58,* 505–529.

Goldstein, L. (2003). Emergence of discrete gestures. In M. J. Solé, D. Recasens, & J. Romero, *Proceedings of the 15th International Congress of Phonetic Sciences* (pp. 85–88), Barcelona, Spain.

Goldstein, L. M. & Fowler, C. (2003). Articulatory phonology: A phonology for public language use. In A. S. Meyer, N. O. Schiller & (Eds.), *Phonetics and phonology in language comprehension and production: Differences and similarities* (pp. 159–207). Berlin: Mouton de Gruyter.

Gordon, B., & Caramazza, A. (1985). Lexical access and frequency sensitivity: Frequency saturation and open/closed class equivalence. *Cognition, 21,* 95–115.

Gordon, E. J., & Daugherty, C. K. (2003). 'Hitting you over the head': Oncologists' disclosure of prognosis to advanced cancer patients. *Bioethics, 17,* 142–168.

Gordon, P. A., Luper, H. L., & Peterson, H. A. (1986). The effects of syntactic complexity on the occurrence of disfluencies in 5-year-old nonstutterers. *Journal of Fluency Disorders, 11,* 151–164.

Gracco, V. L., & Lofqvist, A. (1994). Speech motor coordination and control: Evidence from lip, jaw, and laryngeal movements. *Journal of Neuroscience, 14,* 6585–6597.

Grunwell, P. (1982). *Clinical phonology.* Rockville, MD: Aspen Publishers.

Guenther, F. H. (1994). A neural network model of speech acquisition and motor equivalent speech production. *Biological Cybernetics, 72,* 43–53.

Guenther, F. H. (2001). Neural modeling of speech production. In B. Maassen, W. Hulstijn, R. Kent, & H. F. M. Peters (Eds.), *Proceedings of the 4th International Speech Motor Conference: Speech motor control in normal and disordered speech* (pp. 12–15). Nijmegen, The Netherlands: Uitgeverij Vantilt.

Guitar, B. (1976). Pretreatment factors associated with the outcome of stuttering therapy. *Journal of Speech and Hearing Research, 19,* 590–600.

Guitar, B. (2006). *Stuttering: An integrated approach to its nature and treatment* (3rd ed.). Baltimore, MD: Lippincott Williams Wilkins.

Guitar, B. & Peters, T. J. (1980). *Stuttering: An integration of contemporary therapies.* Memphis, TN: Speech Foundation of America.

Guntupalli, V., Kalinowski, J., Saltuklaroglu, T., & Nanjundeswaran, C. (2005). The effects of temporal modification of second speech signals on stuttering inhibition at two speech rates in adults. *Neuroscience Letters, 385,* 7–12.

Ham, R. (1986). *Techniques of stuttering therapy.* Englewood Cliffs, NJ: Prentice-Hall.

Hamilton, A., Plunkett, K., & Schafer, G. (2000). Infant vocabulary development assessed with a British communicative development inventory. *Journal of Child Language, 27,* 689–705.

Hannah, E. P., & Gardner, J. G. (1968). A note on syntactic relationships in nonfluency. *Journal of Speech and Hearing Research, 11,* 853–860.

Harris, M. M. (1970). Stuttering learned and unlearned. *British Journal of Disorders of Communication, 5,* 92.

Hartmann, R. R. K., & Stork, F. C. (1972). *Dictionary of language and linguistics.* London, U.K.: Applied Science.

Hartsuiker, R. J., Kolk, H. H. J., & Lickley, R. J. (2001). Stuttering on function words and content words: A computational test of the covert repair hypothesis. In B. A. M. Maassen, W. Hulstijn, R. Kent, H. F. M. Peters, & P. H. H. M. Van Lieshout (Eds.), *Proceedings of the 4th International Speech Motor Conference: Speech motor control in normal and disordered speech* (pp. 65–69). Nijmegen, The Netherlands: Uitgeverij Vantilt.

Hartsuiker, R. J., Pickering, M. J., & de Jong, N. H. (2005). Semantic and phonological context effects in speech error repair. *Journal of Experimental Psychology: Human Learning and Memory, 31,* 921–932.

Haynie, D. L., Nansel, T., Eitel, P., Crump, A. D., Saylor, K., Yu, K., & Simons-Morton, B. (2001). Bullies, victims, and bully/victims: Distinct groups of at-risk youth. *Journal of Early Adolescence, 21,* 29–49.

Healey, E. C., & Howe, S. W. (1987). Speech shadowing characteristics of stutterers under diotic and dichotic conditions. *Journal of Communication Disorders, 20,* 493–506.

Hegde, M. N. (1972). Stuttering, neuroticism and extraversion. *Behaviour Research and Therapy, 10,* 395–397.

Hepper, P. G., Wells, D. L., & Lynch, C. (2005). Prenatal thumb sucking is related to postnatal handedness. *43,* 313–315.

Hill, P. R., Hogben, J. H., & Bishop, D. M. V. (2005). Auditory frequency discrimination ability in children with specific language impairment: A longitudinal study. *Journal of Speech, Language, and Hearing Research, 48,* 1136–1146.

Hodges, E. V. E., & Parry, D. G. (1996). Victims of peer abuse: An overview. *Journal of Emotional and Behavioural Problems, 5,* 23–28.

Hodson, B. W. (1986). *The assessment of phonological processes—Revised.* Austin, TX: Pro-Ed.

Hood, L., Lahey, M., Lifter, K., & Bloom, J. (1978). Observational descriptive methodology in studying child language: Preliminary results on the development of complex sentences. In G. P. Sackett (Ed.), *Observing behavior: Vol. 1: Theory and application in mental retardation* (pp. 239–263). Baltimore, MD: University Park Press.

Horlick, R. S., & Miller, M. H. (1960). A comparative personality study of a group of stutterers and hard of hearing patients. *Journal of General Psychology, 63,* 259–266.

Houde, J. F., & Jordan, M. I. (1998). Sensorimotor adaptation in speech production. *Science, 279,* 1213–1216.

Howell, P. (1990). Changes in voice level caused by several forms of altered feedback in fluent speakers and stutterers. *Language and Speech, 33,* 325–338.

Howell, P. (2002). The EXPLAN theory of fluency control applied to the treatment of stuttering by altered feedback and operant procedures. In E. Fava (Ed.), *Current issues in linguistic theory series: Pathology and therapy of speech disorders* (pp. 95–118). Amsterdam, The Netherlands: John Benjamins.

Howell, P. (2004a). Assessment of some contemporary theories of stuttering that apply to spontaneous speech. *Contemporary Issues in Communication Science and Disorders, 31,* 122–139.

Howell, P. (2004b). Comparison of two ways of defining phonological words for assessing stuttering pattern changes with age in Spanish speakers who stutter. *Journal of Multilingual Communication Disorders, 2,* 161–186.

Howell, P. (2007a). Signs of developmental stuttering up to age 8 and at 12 plus. *Clinical Psychology Review, 27,* 287–306.

Howell, P. (2007b). A model of serial order problems in fluent, stuttered and agrammatic speech. *Human Movement Science, 26,* 728–741.

Howell, P. (2007c). The effects of gated speech on the fluency of speakers who stutter. *Folia Phoniatrica et Logopaedica, 59,* 250–255.

Howell, P. (2010). Language processing in fluency disorders. In J. Guendouzi, F. Loncke, & M. Williams (Eds.). *The handbook on psycholinguistics and cognitive processes: Perspectives on communication disorders.* London, U.K.: Taylor & Francis.

Howell, P. (in press). Phonological neighborhood and word frequency effects in the stuttered disfluencies of children who stutter: Comments on Anderson (2007). *Journal of Speech, Language and Hearing Research.*

Howell, P. Predicting Stuttering Onset/ [E-letter], *Pediatrics* (January 17, 2009), http:// pediatrics.aappublications.org/cgi/eletters/123/1/270 (accessed January 17, 2009).

Howell, P., & Akande, O. (2005). Simulations of the types of disfluency produced in spontaneous utterances by fluent speakers, and the change in disfluency type seen as speakers who stutter get older. In J. Veronis & E. Campione (Eds.), *Disfluency in spontaneous speech. ISCA Tutorial and Research Workshop* (pp. 93–98).

Howell, P., Anderson, A. J., Bartrip, J., & Bailey, E. (2009). Comparison of acoustic and kinematic approaches to measuring utterance-level speech variability. *Journal of Speech, Language, and Hearing Research, 52,* 1092–4388.

Howell, P., Anderson, A., & Lucero, J. (2010). Motor timing and fluency. In B. Maasen, & P. H. H. M. Van Lieshout (Eds.). *Speech motor control: New developments in basic and applied research* (pp. 215–225). Oxford, U.K.: Oxford University Press.

Howell, P., & Archer, A. (1984). Susceptibility to the effects of delayed auditory feedback. *Perception & Psychophysics, 36,* 296–302.

Howell, P., & Au-Yeung, J. (1995). Syntactic determinants of stuttering in the spontaneous speech of normally fluent and stuttering children. *Journal of Fluency Disorders, 20,* 317–330.

Howell, P., & Au-Yeung, J. (2002). The EXPLAN theory of fluency control and the diagnosis of stuttering. In E. Fava (Ed.), *Pathology and therapy of speech disorders* (pp. 75–94). Amsterdam, The Netherlands: John Benjamins.

Howell, P., & Au-Yeung, J. (2007). Phonetic complexity and stuttering in Spanish. *Clinical Linguistics Phonetics, 21,* 111–127.

Howell, P., Au-Yeung, J., & Pilgrim, L. (1999). Utterance rate and linguistic properties as determinants of speech dysfluency in children who stutter. *Journal of the Acoustical Society of America, 105,* 481–490.

Howell, P., Au-Yeung, J., & Rustin, L. (1997). Clock and motor variance in lip tracking: A comparison between children who stutter and those who do not. In W. Hulstijn, H. F. M. Peters, & P. H. H. M. Van Lieshout (Eds.), *Speech production: Motor control, brain research and fluency disorders* (pp. 573–578). Amsterdam, The Netherlands: Elsevier.

Howell, P., Au-Yeung, J., & Sackin, S. (1999). Exchange of stuttering from function words to content words with age. *Journal of Speech, Language, and Hearing Research, 42,* 345–354.

Howell, P., Au-Yeung, J., & Sackin, S. (2000). Internal structure of content words leading to lifespan differences in phonological difficulty in stuttering. *Journal of Fluency Disorders, 25,* 1–20.

Howell, P., Au-Yeung, J., Yaruss, S., & Eldridge, K. (2006). Phonetic difficulty and stuttering in English. *Clinical Linguistics and Phonetics, 20,* 703–716.

Howell, P., Bailey, E., & Kothari, N. (2010). Changes in the pattern of stuttering over development for children who recover or persist. *Clinical Linguistic and Phonetics, 24,* 556–575.

Howell, P. & Davis, S. (in press). Predicting persistence and recovery from stuttering at teenage based on information gathered at age eight. *Journal of Developmental and Behavioral Pediatrics.*

Howell, P., Davis, S., & Au-Yeung, J. (2003). Syntactic development in fluent children, children who stutter, and children who have English as an additional language. *Child Language Teaching and Therapy, 19,* 311–337.

Howell, P., Davis, S., & Bartrip, J. (2009). The UCLASS archive of stuttered speech. *Journal of Speech, Language, and Hearing Research,* 556–569.

Howell, P., Davis, S., Patel, H., Cuniffe, P., Downing-Wilson, D., Au-Yeung, J., & Williams, R. (2004). Fluency development and temperament in fluent children and children who stutter. In A. Packman, A. Meltzer, & H. F. M. Peters (Eds.), *Proceedings of the 4th world congress on fluency disorders: Theory, research and therapy in fluency disorders* (pp. 250–256). Nijmegen, The Netherlands: Nijmegen University Press.

Howell, P., Davis, S., & Williams, S. M. (2006). Auditory abilities of speakers who persisted, or recovered, from stuttering. *Journal of Fluency Disorders, 31,* 257–270.

Howell, P., Davis, S., & Williams, S. M. (2008). Late childhood stuttering. *Journal of Speech, Language, and Hearing Research, 51,* 669–687.

Howell, P., Davis, S., & Williams, R. (2009). The effects of bilingualism on stuttering during late childhood. *Archives of Disease in Childhood, 94,* 42–46.

Howell, P., & Dworzynski, K. (2005). Planning and execution processes in speech control by fluent speakers and speakers who stutter. *Journal of Fluency Disorders, 30,* 343–354.

Howell, P., & El-Yaniv, N. (1987). The effects of presenting a click in syllable-initial position on the speech of stutterers: Comparison with a metronome click. *Journal of Fluency Disorders, 12,* 249–256.

Howell, P., El-Yaniv, N., & Powell, D. J. (1987). Factors affecting fluency in stutterers when speaking under altered auditory feedback. In H. Peters & W. Hulstijn (Eds.), *Speech motor dynamics in stuttering* (pp. 361–369). New York, NY: Springer Press.

Howell, P., Hamilton, A., & Kyriacopoulos, A. (1986). *Automatic detection of repetitions and prolongations in stuttered speech. Speech input/output: Techniques and applications.* London, UK: IEE Publications.

Howell, P., & Huckvale, M. (2004). Facilities to assist people to research into stammered speech. *Stammering Research, 1,* 130–242.

Howell, P., Marchbanks, R. J., & El-Yaniv, N. (1986). Middle ear muscle activity during vocalization in normal speakers and stutterers. *102,* 396–402.

Howell, P., & Powell, D. J. (1984). Hearing your voice through bone and air: Implications for explanations of stuttering behaviour from studies of normal speakers. *Journal of Fluency Disorders, 9,* 247–264.

Howell, P., & Powell, D. J. (1987). Delayed auditory feedback with delayed sounds varying in duration. *Perception and Psychophysics, 42,* 166–172.

Howell, P., Powell, D. J., & Khan, I. (1983). Amplitude contour of the delayed signal and interference in delayed auditory feedback tasks. *Journal of Experimental Psychology: Human Perception and Performance, 9,* 772–784.

Howell, P., Rosen, S., Hannigan, G., & Rustin, L. (2000). Auditory backward-masking performance by children who stutter and its relation to dysfluency rate. *Perceptual & Motor Skills, 90,* 355–363.

Howell, P., & Sackin, S. (2000). Speech rate modification and its effects on fluency reversal in fluent speakers and people who stutter. *Journal of Developmental and Physical Disabilities, 12,* 291–315.

Howell, P., & Sackin, S. (2001). Function word repetitions emerge when speakers are operantly conditioned to reduce frequency of silent pauses. *Journal of Psycholinguistic Research, 30,* 457–474.

Howell, P., & Sackin, S. (2002). Timing interference to speech in altered listening conditions. *Journal of the Acoustical Society of America, 111,* 2842–2852.

Howell, P., Sackin, S., & Glenn, K. (1997a). Development of a two-stage procedure for the automatic recognition of dysfluencies in the speech of children who stutter: I. Psychometric procedures appropriate for selection of training material for lexical dysfluency classifiers. *Journal of Speech, Language, and Hearing Research, 40,* 1073-1084.

Howell, P., Sackin, S., & Glenn, K. (1997b). Development of a two-stage procedure for the automatic recognition of dysfluencies in the speech of children who stutter: II. ANN recognition of repetitions and prolongations with supplied word segment markers. *Journal of Speech, Language, and Hearing Research, 40,* 1085–1096.

Howell, P., Sackin, S., & Williams, R. (1999). Differential effects of frequency shifted feedback between child and adult stutterers. *Journal of Fluency Disorders, 24,* 127–136.

Howell, P., Soukup-Ascencao, T., Davis, S., & Rusbridge, S. (submitted, 2010). Comparison of alternative methods for obtaining severity scores from the speech of people who stutter.

Howell, P., & Vause, L. (1986). Acoustic analysis and perception of vowels in stuttered speech. *Journal of the Acoustical Society of America, 79,* 1571–1579.

Howell, P., & Williams, S. M. (2004). Development of auditory sensitivity in children who stutter and fluent children. *Ear and Hearing, 25,* 265–274.

Howell, P., Wingfield, T., & Johnson, M. (1988). Characteristics of the speech of stutterers during normal and altered auditory feedback. In *Proceedings Speech* 88, Vol. 3. W. A. Ainsworth & J. N. Holmes (Eds.). pp. 1069–1076. Edinburgh: Institute of Acoustics.

Hubbard, C. P., & Prins, D. (1994). Word familiarity, syllabic stress pattern, and stuttering. *Journal of Speech and Hearing Research, 37,* 564–571.

Hubbard Seery, C., Watkins, R. V., Mangelsdorf, S. C., & Shigeto, A. (2007). Subtyping stuttering II: Contributions from language and temperament. *Journal of Fluency Disorders, 32,* 197–217.

Hugh-Jones, S., & Smith, P. K. (1999). Self-reports of short and long-term effects of bullying on people who stammer. *British Journal of Educational Psychology, 69,* 141–158.

Huinck, W. J., Langevin, M., Kully, D., Graamans, K., Peters, H. F. M., & Hulstijn, W. (2006). The relationship between pre-treatment clinical profile and treatment outcome in an integrated stuttering program. *Journal of Fluency Disorders, 31,* 43–63.

Hulstijn, W., Summers, J. J., Van Lieshout, P. H. M., & Peters, H. F. M. (1992). Timing in finger tapping and speech: A comparison between stutterers and fluent speakers. *Human Movement Science, 11,* 113–124.

Hurst, J. A., Baraitser, M., Auger, E., Graham, F., & Norell, S. (1990). An extended family with a dominantly inherited speech disorder. *Developmental Medicine & Child Neurology, 32,* 352–355.

Imamizu, H., Miyauchi, S., Tamada, T., Sasaki, Y., Takino, R., Putz, B., Yoshioka, T., & Kawato, M. (2000). Human cerebellar activity reflecting an acquired internal model of a new tool. *Nature, 403,* 192–195.

Indefrey, P., & Levelt, W. J. (2004). The spatial and temporal signatures of word production components. *Cognition, 92,* 101–144.

Ingham, R. J. (1976). Onset, prevalence, and recovery from stuttering: A reassessment of findings from the Andrews and Harris study. *Journal of Speech and Hearing Disorders, 41,* 280–281.

Ingham, R. J. (1984). *Stuttering and behavior therapy: Current status and experimental foundations.* San Diego, CA: College-Hill Press.

Ingham, R. J., Finn, P., & Bothe, A. K. (2005). "Roadblocks" revisited: Neural change, stuttering treatment, and recovery from stuttering. *Journal of Fluency Disorders, 30,* 91–107.

Ingham, R. J., Fox, P. T., Ingham, J. C., Xiong, J., Zamarripa, F., Hardies, L. J., & Lancaster, J. L. (2004). Brain correlates of stuttering and syllable production: Gender comparison and replication. *Journal of Speech, Language, and Hearing Research, 47,* 321–341.

Ingham, R. J., Fox, P. T., Ingham, J. C., & Zamarripa, F. (2000). Is overt stuttered speech a prerequisite for the neural activations associated with chronic developmental stuttering? *Brain and Language, 75,* 163–194.

Ingham, R. J., Fox, P. T., Ingham, J. C., Zamarripa, F., Martin, C., Jerabek, P., & Cotton, J. (1996). Functional-lesion investigation of developmental stuttering with positron emission tomography. *Journal of Speech and Hearing Research, 39,* 1208–1227.

Ingham, R. J., Montgomery, J., & Ulliana, L. (1983). The effect of manipulating phonation duration on stuttering. *Journal of Speech and Hearing Research, 26,* 579–587.

Ivry, R. (1997). Cerebellar timing systems. *International Review of Neurobiology, 41,* 555–573.

Jakielski K. J. (1998). *Motor organization in the acquisition of consonant clusters* (Doctoral dissertation: UMI Dissertation Services). University of Texas at Austin, Austin, TX.

Jancke, L., Kaiser, P., Bauer, A., & Kalveram, K. T. (1995). Upper lip, lower lip, and jaw peak velocity sequence during bilabial closures: No differences between stutterers and nonstutterers. *Journal of the Acoustical Society of America, 97,* 3900–3903.

Janssen, P., Kloth, S., Kraaimaat, F., & Brutten, G. (1996). Genetic factors in stuttering: A replication of Ambrose, Yairi and Cox's (1993) study with adult probands. *Journal of Fluency Disorders, 21,* 105–108.

Janssen, P., Kraaimaat, F., & Brutten, G. (1990). Relationship between stutterers genetic history and speech-associated variables. *Journal of Fluency Disorders, 15,* 39–48.

Jayaram, M. (1981). Grammatical factors in stuttering. *Journal of the Indian Institute of Science, 63,* 141–147.

Jennische, M., & Sedin, G. (1999). Speech and language skills in children who required neonatal intensive care: Evaluation at 6.5 y of age based on interviews with parents. *Acta Paediatrica, 88,* 975–982.

Johnson, M. & Associates (1959). *The onset of stuttering.* Minneapolis, MN: University of Minnesota Press.

Johnson, N. F. (1965). The psychological reality of phrase-structure rules. *Journal of Verbal Learning and Verbal Behavior, 4,* 469–475.

Johnson, W., Darley, F. L., & Spriestersbach, D. C. (1963). *Diagnostic methods in speech pathology.* New York, NY: Harper and Row.

Johnson, W., & Rosen, P. (1937). Studies in the psychology of stuttering: VII. Effect of certain changes in speech pattern upon stuttering frequency. *Journal of Speech and Hearing Disorders, 2,* 105–109.

Jokel, R., de Nil, L. F., & Sharpe, K. (2007). Speech disfluencies in adults with neurogenic stuttering associated with stroke and traumatic brain injury. *Journal of Psychosomatic Research, 15,* 243–261.

Jones, M., Onslow, M., Packman, A., Williams, S., Ormond, T., Schwarz, I., & Gebski, V. (2005). Randomised controlled trial of the Lidcombe programme of early stuttering intervention. *British Medical Journal, 331,* 659.

Jurgens, U. (2002). Neural pathways underlying vocal control. *Neuroscience and Biobehavioral Review, 26,* 235–258.

Kadi-Hanifi, K., & Howell, P. (1992). Syntactic analysis of the spontaneous speech of normally fluent and stuttering children. *Journal of Fluency Disorders, 17,* 151–170.

Kalinowski, J., Armson, J., & Stuart, A. (1995). Effect of normal and fast articulatory rates on stuttering frequency. *Journal of Fluency Disorders, 20,* 293–302.

Kalinowski, J., Stuart, A., Rastatter, M. P., Snyder, G., & Dayalu, V. (2000). Inducement of fluent speech in persons who stutter via visual choral speech. *Neuroscience Letters, 281,* 198–200.

Kalinowski, J. S. & Saltuklaroglu, T. (2006). *Stuttering.* San Diego, CA: Plural Publishing.

Kalveram, K. T. (2001). Neurobiology of speaking and stuttering. In H. G. Bosshardt, J. S. Yaruss, & F. M. Peters (Eds.), *Proceedings of the 3rd world congress of fluency disorders: Theory, research, treatment and self-help* (pp. 59–65). Nijmegen, The Netherlands: Nijmegen University Press.

Kalveram, K. T., & Jancke, L. (1989). Vowel duration and voice onset time for stressed and nonstressed syllables in stutterers under delayed auditory feedback condition. *Folia Phoniatrica, 41,* 30–42.

Kamhi, A., Lee, R., & Nelson, L. (1985). Word, syllable, and sound awareness in language-disordered children. *Journal of Speech and Hearing Disorders, 50,* 207–212.

Kang, C., Riazuddin, S., Mundorff, J., Krasnewich, D., Friedman, P., Mullikin, J. C., & Drayna, D. (2010). Mutations in the lysosomal enzyme-targeting pathway and persistent stuttering, *The New England Journal of Medicine, 362,* 677–685. Retrieved from http://www.nejm.org doi: 10.1056/NEJMoa0902630

Karrass, J., Walden, T., Conture, E., Graham, C., Arnold, H., Hartfield, K., & Schwenk, K. (2006). Relation of emotional reactivity and regulation to childhood stuttering. *Journal of Communication Disorders, 39,* 402–423.

Kawato, M., Furukawa, K., & Suzuki, R. (1987). A hierarchical neural-network model for control and learning of voluntary movement. *Biological Cybernetics, 57,* 169–185.

Kelly, E. M., & Conture, E. G. (1992). Speaking rates, response time latencies, and interrupting behaviors of young stutterers, nonstutterers, and their mothers. *Journal of Speech and Hearing Research, 35,* 1256–1267.

Kelso, J. A. S., Vatikiotis-Bateson, E., Tuller, B., & Fowler, C. A. (1984). Functionally specific articulatory cooperation following jaw perturbations during speech: Evidence for coordinative structures. *Journal of Experimental Psychology-Human Perception and Performance, 10,* 812–832.

Kessler, R. & Mroczek, D. (1994). *Final version of our non-specific psychological distress scale [memo].* Ann Arbor, MI: Institute for Social Research.

Kidd, K. (1983). Recent developments in the genetics of stuttering. In C. Ludlow & J. Cooper (Eds.), *The genetic aspects of speech and language disorders.* New York, NY: Academic Press.

Kidd, K. (1984). Stuttering as a genetic disorder. In R. Curlee & W. Perkins (Eds.), *Nature and treatment of stuttering: New directions.* London, UK: Taylor & Francis.

Kidd, K., Heimbuch, R. C., & Records, M. A. (1981). Vertical transmission of susceptibility to stuttering with sex-modified expression. *Proceedings of the National Academy of Sciences of the United States of America-Biological Sciences, 78,* 606–610.

Kidd, K., Kidd, J., & Records, M. A. (1978). The possible causes of the sex ratio in stuttering and its implications. *Journal of Fluency Disorders, 3,* 13–23.

Kitamura, T., Takemoto, H., Honda, K., Shimada, Y., Fujimoto, I., Syakudo, Y., Masaki, S., Kuroda, K. … Senda, M. (2005) Difference in vocal tract shape between upright and supine postures: Observation by an open-type MRI scanner. *Acoustical Science and Technology, 5,* 465–468.

Klassen, T. R. (2001). Perceptions of people who stutter: Re-assessing the negative stereotype. *Perceptual and Motor Skills, 92,* 551–559.

Klima, E., & Bellugi, U. (1966). Syntactic regularities in the speech of children. In J. Lyons & R. Wales (Eds.), *Psycholinguistic papers* (pp. 183–208). Edinburgh: Edinburgh University Press.

Kloth, S. A. M., Kraimaat, F. W., Janssen, P., & Brutten, G. (1999). Persistence and remission of incipient stuttering among high risk children. *Journal of Fluency Disorders, 24,* 253–265.

Kolk, H. H. J., & Postma, A. (1997). Stuttering as a covert-repair phenomenon. In R. F. Curlee & G. Siegel (Eds.), *Nature and treatment of stuttering: New directions* (pp. 182–203). Boston, MA: Allyn & Bacon.

Kozhevnikov, V. A., & Chistovich, L. A. (1965). *Speech, articulation and perception*. Washington, DC: Joint Publications Research Service.

Kraaimaat, F. W., Vanryckeghem, M., & Van Dam-Baggen, R. (2002). Stuttering and social anxiety. *Journal of Fluency Disorders, 27*, 319–331.

Kroll, R. M., de Nil, L. F., Kapur, S., & Houle, S. (1997). A positron emission tomography investigation of post treatment brain activation in stutterers. In H. F. M. Peters, W. Hulstijn, & P. H. M. Van Lieshout (Eds.), *Speech production: Motor control, brain research and fluency disorders* (pp. 307–319). Amsterdam, The Netherlands: Elsevier.

Kucera, H., & Francis, W. M. (1967). *Computational analysis of present-day American English*. Providence, RI: Brown University.

Kugler, P. N., Kelso, J. A. S., & Turvey, M. T. (1982). On the control and coordination of naturally developing systems. In J. A. S. Kelso & J. E. Clark (Eds.), *The development of movement control and coordination* (pp. 5–78). Chichester, UK: John Wiley.

Kully, D., & Boberg, E. (1988). An investigation of interclinic agreement in the identification of fluent and stuttered syllables. *Journal of Fluency Disorders, 13*, 309–318.

Kuniszyk-Jozkowiak, W., Smolka, E., & Adamczyk, B. (1996). Effect of acoustical, visual and tactile echo on speech fluency of stutterers. *Folia Phoniatrica et Logopaedica, 48*, 193–200.

Labelle, M. (2005). The acquisition of grammatical categories: A state of the art. In H. Cohen & C. Lefebvre (Eds.), *Handbook of categorization in cognitive science* (pp. 433–457). New York, NY: Elsevier.

Lamont, E. B., & Christakis, N. A. (2001). Prognostic disclosure to patients with cancer near the end of life. *Annals of Internal Medicine, 133*, 1096–1105.

Landgraf, J. M., Abetz, L., & Ware, J. E. (1999). *The CHQ user's manual* (2nd ed.). Boston, MA: HealthAct.

Lane, H., & Tranel, B. (1971). The Lombard sign and the role of hearing in speech. *Journal of Speech and Hearing Research, 14*, 677–709.

Lanyon, R. I., Goldsworthy, R. J., & Lanyon, B. P. (1978). Dimensions of stuttering and relationship to psychopathology. *Journal of Fluency Disorders, 3*, 103–113.

Largo, R. H., Molinari, L., Kundu, S., Lipp, A., & Duc, G. (1990). Intellectual outcome, speech and school performance in high risk preterm children with birth weight appropriate for gestational age. *European Journal of Pediatrics, 149*, 845–850.

Lee, B. (1950). Effects of delayed speech feedback. *Journal of the Acoustical Society of America, 22*, 824–826.

Levelt, W. J. (1983). Monitoring and self-repair in speech. *Cognition, 14*, 41–104.

Levelt, W. J. (1989). *Speaking: From intention to articulation*. Cambridge, MA: MIT Press.

Levine, S. Z., Petrides, K. V., Davis, S., Jackson, C. J., & Howell, P. (2005). The use of structural equation modeling in stuttering research: Concepts and directions. *Stammering Research, 1*, 344–363.

Levis, B., Ricci, D., Lukong, J., & Drayna, D. (2004). Genetic linkage studies in a large West African kindred. *American Journal of Human Genetics, 75*, S20–S26.

Limber, J. (1973). The genesis of complex sentences. In T. Moore (Ed.), *Cognitive development and acquisition of language* (pp. 169–185). New York, NY: Academic Press.

Lincoln, M., Packman, A., & Onslow, M. (2006). Altered auditory feedback and the treatment of stuttering: A review. *Journal of Fluency Disorders, 31*, 71–89.

Logan, K. J., & Conture, E. G. (1995). Length, grammatical complexity, and rate differences in stuttered and fluent conversational utterances of children who stutter. *Journal of Fluency Disorders, 20*, 35–61.

Logan, K. J., & Conture, E. G. (1997). Selected temporal, grammatical, and phonological characteristics of conversational utterances produced by children who stutter. *Journal of Speech, Language, and Hearing Research, 40,* 107–120.

Lombard, E. (1911). Le signe de l'elevation de la voix. *Annales des Maladies de l'Oreille et du Larynx, 37,* 101–199.

Löser, H. (1995). *Alkoholembryopathie und Alkoholeffekte.* Stuttgart, Germany: G. Fischer.

Lotto, A. J., Hickok, G. S., & Holt, L. L. (2009). Reflections on mirror neurons and speech perception. *Journal of Psychosomatic Research, 13,* 110–114.

Louko, L., Edwards, M., & Conture, E. (1990). Phonological characteristics of young stutterers and their normally fluent peers: Preliminary findings. *Journal of Fluency Disorders, 15,* 121–191.

Love, L. R., & Jeffress, L. A. (1971). Identification of brief pauses in the fluent speech of stutterers and non stutterers. *Journal of Speech and Hearing Disorders, 14,* 229–240.

Lu, C., Chen, C., Ning, N., Ding, G., Guo, T., Peng, D. et al. (2010). The neural substrates for atypical planning and execution of word production in stuttering. *Experimental Neurology, 221,* 146–156.

Lu, C., Ning, N., Peng, D., Ding, G., Li, K., Yang, Y., & Lin, C. (2009). The role of large-scale neural interactions for developmental stuttering. *Neuroscience, 161,* 1008–1026.

Lu, C., Peng, D., Chen, C., Ning, N., Ding, G., Li, K., Yang, Y., & Lin, C. (2010). Altered effective connectivity and anomalous anatomy in the basal ganglia-thalamocortical circuit of stuttering speakers. *Cortex, 46,* 49–57.

Luce, P. A., & Pisoni, D. B. (1998). Recognizing spoken words: The neighborhood activation model. *Ear and Hearing, 19,* 1–36.

Lucero, J. C. (2005). Comparison of measures of variability of speech movement trajectories using synthetic records. *Journal of Speech, Language, and Hearing Research, 48,* 336–344.

Ludlow C. L., & Loucks, T. (2003). Stuttering: A dynamic motor control disorder. *Journal of Fluency Disorders, 28,* 273–295.

Luper, H. L., & Mulder, R. L. (1964). *Stuttering: Therapy for children.* Englewood Cliffs, NJ: Prentice-Hall, Inc.

MacFarlane, W. B., Hanson, M., & Walton, W. (1991). Stuttering in five generations of a single family: A preliminary report including evidence supporting a sex-modified mode of transmission. *Journal of Fluency Disorders, 16,* 117–123.

Maclay, H., & Osgood, C. E. (1959). Hesitation phenomena in spontaneous English speech. *Word, 15,* 19–44.

MacNeilage, P., & Davis, B. (1990). Acquisition of speech production: Frames, then content. In M. Jeannorod (ed.), *Attention and performance XIII: Motor representation and control.* Hillsdale: Lawrence Erlbaum.

MacWhinney, B., & Osser, H. (1977). Verbal planning functions in children's speech. *Child Development, 48,* 978–985.

Maguire, G. A., Riley, G. D., Franklin, D. L., Maguire, M. E., Nguyen, C. T., & Brojeni, P. H. (2004). Olanzapine in the treatment of developmental stuttering: A double-blind, placebo-controlled trial. *Annals of Clinical Psychiatry, 16,* 63–67.

Mahl, G. F. (1981). Normal disturbances in speech. In R. L. Russell (Ed.), *Spoken interaction in psychotherapy: Strategies of discovery.* New York, NY: Irvington.

Manning, W. H., Dailey, D., & Wallace, S. (1984). Attitude and personality characteristics of older stutterers. *Journal of Fluency Disorders, 9,* 207–215.

Mansson, H. (2000). Childhood stuttering: Incidence and development. *Journal of Fluency Disorders, 25,* 45–57.

Marge, D. K. (1966). The social status of speech-handicapped children. *Journal of Speech and Hearing Research, 9,* 165–177.

Marshall, C. (2005). The impact of word-end phonology and morphology on stuttering. *Stammering Research, 1,* 375–391.

Mattick, R. P., Peters, L., & Clarke, J. C. (1989). Exposure and cognitive restructuring for social phobia: A controlled study. *Behavior Therapy, 20,* 3–23.

Max, L., & Caruso, A. J. (1997). Contemporary techniques for establishing fluency in the treatment of adults who stutter. *Contemporary Issues in Communication Sciences and Disorders, 24,* 45–52.

Max, L., Guenther, F. H., Gracco, V. L., Ghosh, S. S., & Wallace, M. E. (2004). Unstable or insufficiently activated internal models and feedback-biased motor control as sources of dysfluency: A theoretical model of stuttering. *Contemporary Issues in Communication Sciences and Disorders, 31,* 105–122.

Max, L., & Yudman, E. M. (2003). Accuracy and variability of isochronous rhythmic timing across motor systems in stuttering versus nonstuttering individuals. *Journal of Speech, Language, and Hearing Research, 46,* 146–163.

McClean, M. D., & Runyan, C. M. (2000). Variations in the relative speeds of orofacial structures with stuttering severity. *Journal of Speech, Language, and Hearing Research, 43,* 1524–1531.

McColl, T., Onslow, M., Packman, A., and Menzies, R.G. (2001). A cognitive behavioral intervention for social anxiety in adults who stutter., *Paper presented at the proceedings of the 2001 speech pathology Australia national conference,* Melbourne, Australia.

McDevitt, S. C., & Carey, W. B. (1978). The measurement of temperament in 3-to-7 year old children. *Journal of Child Psychology and Psychiatry, 19,* 245–253.

McManus, I. C. (2002). *Right hand, left hand.* London, UK: Weidenfeld & Nicolson.

Melnick, K. S., & Conture, E. G. (2000). Relationship of length and grammatical complexity to the systematic and nonsystematic speech errors and stuttering of children who stutter. *Journal of Fluency Disorders, 25,* 21–45.

Melnick, K. S., Conture, E. G., & Ohde, R. N. (2003). Phonological priming in picture naming of young children who stutter. *Journal of Speech, Language, and Hearing Research, 46,* 1428–1443.

Menyuk, P. (1969). *Sentences children use.* Cambridge: MIT Press.

Menyuk, P., & Anderson, S. (1969). Children's identification and reproduction of /w/, /r/ and /l/. *Journal of Speech and Hearing Research, 12,* 39–52.

Menzies, R. G., O'Brian, S., Onslow, M., Packman, A., St, C. T., & Block, S. (2008). An experimental clinical trial of a cognitive-behavior therapy package for chronic stuttering. *Journal of Speech, Language, and Hearing Research, 51,* 1451–1464.

Menzies, R. G., Onslow, M., Packman, A., & O'Brian, S. (2009). Cognitive behavior therapy for adults who stutter: A tutorial for speech-language pathologists. *Journal of Fluency Disorders, 34,* 187–200.

Meyers, S. C., & Freeman, F. J. (1985). Interruptions as a variable in stuttering and disfluency. *Journal of Speech Hearing Research, 28,* 428–435.

Miall, R. C., Weir, D. J., Wolpert, D. M., & Stein, J. F. (1993). Is the cerebellum a Smith predictor? *Journal of Motor Behavior, 25,* 203–216.

Miles, S., & Ratner, N. B. (2001). Parental language input to children at stuttering onset. *Journal of Speech, Language, and Hearing Research, 44,* 1116–1130.

Millard, S. (2003). Stammering. *Royal College of Speech Language Therapists Bulletin, 611,* 17.

Miller, S., & Watson, B. C. (1992). The relationship between communication attitude, anxiety and depression in stutters and nonstutters. *Journal of Speech and Hearing Research, 55,* 789–798.

Molt, L. (2006). *SpeechEasy AAF device long term clinical trial: Speech fluency and naturalness measures.* Poster presented in the Annual Convention of the American Speech–Language–Hearing Association, Miami, FL.

Molt, L., & Guilford, A. M. (1979). Auditory processing and anxiety in stutterers. *Journal of Fluency Disorders, 4,* 255–267.

Mooney, S., & Smith, P. K. (1995). Bullying and the child who stammers. *British Journal of Special Education, 22,* 24–27.

Moreno, J. L. (1960). *The sociometry reader.* Glencoe, IL: Free Press.

Motluk, A. (1997). Cutting out stuttering. *New Scientist, 153,* 32–35.

Mouradin, M. S., Paslawski, T., & Sluaib, A. (2000). Return of stuttering after stroke. *Brain and Language, 73,* 120–123.

Namasivayam, A. K., & Van Lieshout, P. H. H. M. (2008). Investigating speech motor practice and learning in people who stutter. *Journal of Fluency Disorders, 33,* 32–51.

Namasivayam, A. K., Van Lieshout, P. H. H. M., & de Nil, L. (2008). Bite-block perturbation in people who stutter: Immediate compensatory and delayed adaptive processes. *Journal of Communication Disorders, 41,* 372–394.

Namasivayam, A. K., van Lieshout, P. H. H. M., McIlroy, W. E., & de Nil, L. (2009). Sensory feedback dependence hypothesis in persons who stutter. *Human Movement Science, 28,* 688–707.

Natke, U., Grosser, J., & Kalveram, K. T. (2001). Fluency, fundamental frequency, and speech rate under frequency shifted auditory feedback in stuttering and nonstuttering persons. *Journal of Fluency Disorders, 26,* 227–241.

Neilson, M. D., & Neilson, P. D. (1991). Adaptive model theory of speech motor control and stuttering. In H. F. Peters, W. Hulstijn, & C. W. Starweather (Eds.), *Speech motor control and stuttering* (pp. 149–156). Amsterdam, The Netherlands: Excerpta Medica.

Neumann, K., Euler, H. A., von Gudenberg, A. W., Giraud, A. L., Lanfermann, H., Gall, V., & Preibisch, C. (2003). The nature and treatment of stuttering as revealed by fMRI A within- and between-group comparison. *Journal of Fluency Disorders, 28,* 381–409.

Newman, R. S., & Bernstein Ratner, N. (2007). The role of selected lexical factors on confrontation naming accuracy, speech, and fluency in adults who do and do not stutter. *Journal of Speech, Language, and Hearing Research, 50,* 196–213.

Newman, R. S., & German, D. J. (2002). Effects of lexical factors on lexical access among typical language-learning children and children with word-finding difficulties. *Language and Speech, 45,* 285–317.

Nippold, M. A. (1990). Concomitant speech and language disorders in stuttering children: A critique of the literature. *Journal of Speech and Hearing Disorders, 55,* 51–60.

Nippold, M. A. (2001). Phonological disorders and stuttering in children: What is the frequency of co-occurrence? *Clinical Linguistics and Phonetics, 15,* 219–228.

Nippold, M. A. (2002). Stuttering and phonology: Is there an interaction? *American Journal of Speech-Language Pathology, 11,* 99–110.

Nishitani, N., & Hari R. (2000). Temporal dynamics of cortical representation for action. *Proceedings on the National Academy of Sciences of the United States of America. 97,* 913–918.

Niven, N. (1994). *Health psychology.* London, UK: Churchill Livingstone.

Nooteboom, S. G. (2005). Lexical bias revisited: Detecting, rejecting and repairing speech errors in inner speech. *Speech Communication, 47,* 43–58.

Noth, E., Niemann, H., Haderlein, T., Decher, M., Eysholdt, U., Rosanowski, F., & Wittenberg, T. (2000). Automatic stuttering recognition using hidden Markov models. In *Proceedings of the 4th international conference on spoken language processing (ICSLP)* (IV ed.) (pp. 65–68). Beijing, China.

Nusbaum, H.C., Pisoni, D. B., & Davis, C. K. (1984). *Sizing up the Hoosier mental lexicon: Measuring the familiarity of 20,000 words (Research on Speech Perception, Progress Report No. 10)*. Bloomington, IN: Indiana University, Psychology Department, Speech Research Laboratory.

Okasha, A., Bishry, Z., Kamel, M., & Hassam, M. (1974). Psychosocial study of stammering in Egyptian children. *British Journal of Psychiatry, 124,* 531–533.

Onslow, M. (1994). The Lidcombe programme for early stuttering intervention: The hazards of compromise. *Australian Communication Quarterly,* Supplementary Issue, 11–14.

Onslow, M., Andrews, C., & Lincoln, M. (1994). A control/experimental trial of an operant treatment for early stuttering. *Journal of Speech and Hearing Research, 37,* 1244–1259.

Onslow, M., Packman, A., Stocker, S., & Siegel, G. M. (1997). Control of children's stuttering with response-contingent time-out: Behavioral, perceptual, and acoustic data. *Journal of Speech, Language, and Hearing Research, 40,* 121–133.

Ooki, S. (2005). Genetic and environmental influences on stuttering and tics in Japanese twin children. *Twin Research and Human Genetics, 8,* 69–75.

Packman, A., Code, C., & Onslow, M. (2007). On the cause of stuttering: Integrating theory with brain and behavioral research. *Journal of Neurolinguistics, 20,* 353–362.

Packman, A., & Onslow, M. (1997). Linguistic stress and the rhythm effect in stuttering. In H. M. Peters, W. Hulstijn, & P. H. H. M. van Lieshout (Eds.), *Speech motor production and fluency disorders* (pp. 473–478). New York, NY: Elsevier.

Packman, A., Onslow, M., & Van Doorn J. (1994). Prolonged speech and modification of stuttering: Perceptual, acoustic, and electroglottographic data. *Journal of Speech Hearing Research, 37,* 724–737.

Paden, E. P. (2005). Development of phonological ability. In E. Yairi & N. Ambrose (Eds.), *Early childhood stuttering* (pp. 197–234). Austin, TX: Pro-Ed.

Paden, E. P., & Yairi, E. (1996). Phonological characteristics of children whose stuttering persisted or recovered. *Journal of Speech Hearing Research, 39,* 981–990.

Paden, E. P., Yairi, E., & Ambrose, N. G. (1999). Early childhood stuttering II: Initial status of phonological abilities. *Journal of Speech, Language, and Hearing Research, 42,* 1113–1124.

Palen, C., & Peterson, J. M. (1982). Word frequency and children's stuttering: The relationship to sentence structure. *Journal of Fluency Disorders, 7,* 55–62.

Panconcelli-Calizia, G. (1955). Die bedingtheit des Lombardschen versuches in der stimm- und-spracheilkunde. *Acta Oto-Laryngolical, 45,* 244–251.

Parker, J. G., & Asher, S. R. (1987). Peer relations and later personal adjustment: Are low-accepted children at risk? *Psychological Bulletin, 102,* 357–389.

Pearl, S. Z., & Bernthal, J. E. (1980). Effect of grammatical complexity upon disfluency behavior of non-stuttering preschool-children. *Journal of Fluency Disorders, 5,* 55–68.

Pellowski, M. W., & Conture, E. G. (2005). Lexical priming in picture naming of young children who do and do not stutter. *Journal of Speech, Language, and Hearing Research, 48,* 278–294.

Perkins, W. H. (1975). Articulatory rate in the evaluation of stuttering treatments. *Journal of Speech Hearing Research, 40,* 277–278.

Perkins, W. H. (1992a). Stuttering prevention. 1: Academic exercise or clinical relevance. *Journal of Fluency Disorders, 17,* 33–38.

Perkins, W. H. (1992b). Stuttering prevention. 2: Plaudits with problems. *Journal of Fluency Disorders, 17,* 89–93.

Perkins, W. H., Kent, R. D., & Curlee, R. F. (1991). A theory of neuropsycholinguistic function in stuttering. *Journal of Speech Hearing Research, 34,* 734–752.

Perry, D. G., Bussey, K., & Fischer, J. (1980). Effects of rewarding children for resisting temptation on attitude change in the forbidden toy paradigm. *Australian Journal of Psychology, 32,* 225–234.

Peters, H. F. M., Hulstijn, W., & Van Lieshout, P. H. H. M. (2000), Recent developments in speech motor research in stuttering. *Folia Phoniatrica, 52,* 103–119.

Peters, T. J., & Guitar, B. (1991). *Stuttering: An integrated approach to its nature and treatment.* Baltimore, MD: Williams & Wilkins.

Pihan, H., Altenmuller, E., Hertrich, I., & Ackermann, H. (2000). Cortical activation patterns of affective speech processing depend on concurrent demands on the subvocal rehearsal system: A DC-potential study. *Brain, 123,* 2338–2349.

Pindzola, R. H., Jenkins, M. M., & Lokken, K. J. (1989). Speaking rates of young children. *Language, Speech, and Hearing Services in Schools, 20,* 133–138.

Pinker, S. (1995). Language acquisition. In L. R. Gleitman, M. Liberman, & D. N. Osherson (Eds.), *An invitation to cognitive science* (2nd ed.). Cambridge, MA: MIT Press.

Pisoni, D. B., Nusbaum, H. C., Luce, P. A., & Slowiacek, L. M. (1985). Speech perception, word recognition, and the structure of the lexicon. *Speech Communication, 4,* 75–95.

Pollard, R., Ellis, J. B., Finan, D., & Ramig, P. R. (2009). Effects of the SpeechEasy on objective and perceived aspects of stuttering: A 6-month, phase I clinical trial in naturalistic environments. *Journal of Speech, Language, and Hearing Research, 52,* 516–533.

Postma, A. (2000). Detection of errors during speech production: A review of speech monitoring models. *Cognition, 77,* 97–132.

Postma, A., & Kolk, H. (1993). The covert repair hypothesis: Prearticulatory repair processes in normal and stuttering dysfluencies. *Journal of Speech and Hearing Research, 36,* 472–487.

Preibisch, C., Neumann, K., Raab, P., Euler, H. A., von Gudenberg, A. W., Lanfermann, H., & Giraud, A. L. (2003). Evidence for compensation for stuttering by the right frontal operculum. *Neuroimage, 20,* 1356–1364.

Preus, A. (1972). Stuttering in Down's syndrome. *Scandinavian Journal of Educational Research, 16,* 89–104.

Preus, A. (1993). Stuttering in Down's syndrome. In Y. Lebrun & R. Hoops (Eds.), *Neurolinguistic approaches to stuttering* (pp. 90–100). The Hague, The Netherlands: Mouton.

Prins, D. (1972). Personality, stuttering severity and age. *Journal of Speech and Hearing Research, 15,* 148–154.

Prior, M., Sanson, A., & Oberklaid, F. (1989). The Australian temperament project. In G. A. Kohnstamm, J. E. Bates, & M. K. Rothbart (Eds.), *Temperament in childhood* (pp. 537–554). Chichester,UK: John Wiley.

Prosek, R. A., Walden, B. E., Montgomery, A. A., & Schwartz, D. M. (1979). Some correlates of stuttering severity judgments. *Journal of Fluency Disorders, 4,* 215–222.

Pukacova, M. (1973). Psychological characteristics of stuttering children. *Psychologia a patopsychologia dietata (Checo-Slovakia), 8,* 233–238.

Pulvermüller, F. (1999). Words in the brain's language. *Behavioural and Brain Sciences, 22,* 253–336.

Quirk, R., Greenbaum, S., Leech, G., & Svartvik, J. (1985). *A comprehensive grammar of the English language* (2nd ed.). London, UK and New York, NY: Longman.

Radford, A. (2009). *Syntactic theory and the structure of English.* UK: Cambridge, Blackwell.

Ramsay, J. O., Munhall, K. G., Gracco, V. L., & Ostry, D. J. (1996). Functional data analyses of lip motion. *Journal of the Acoustical Society of America, 99,* 3718–3727.

Ravikumar, K. M., Rajagopal, R., & Nagaraj, H. C. (2009). An approach for objective assessment of stuttered speech using MFCC features. *DSP Journal, 9,* 19–24.

Reed, P., Howell, P. C., Davis, S., & Osborne, L. A. (2007). Development of an operant treatment for content word dysfluencies in persistent stuttering children: Initial experimental data. *Journal of Stuttering Therapy, Advocacy and Research, 2,* 1–13.

Reilly, S., Onslow, M., Packman, A., Wake, M., Bavin, E. L., Prior, M., Eadie, P. ... Ukoumunne, O. C. (2009). Predicting stuttering onset by the age of 3 years: A prospective, community cohort study. *Pediatrics, 123,* 270–277.

Reilly, S., Wake, M., Bavin, E. L., Prior, M., Williams, J., Bretherton, L., Eadie, P., Barrett, Y., & Ukoumunne, O. C. (2007). Predicting language at 2 years of age: A prospective community study. *Pediatrics, 120,* e1441–e1449.

Riaz, N., Steinberg, S., Ahmad, J., Pluzhnikov, A., Raizuddin, S., Cox, N., & Drayna, D. (2005). Genomewide significant linkage to stuttering on chromosome 12. *American Journal of Human Genetics, 76,* 647–651.

Richardson, D. (1985). *Speaking, stuttering, and distfluency rates of preschool stutterers and their mothers.* Unpublished master's thesis. California State University, Long Beach.

Rijsdijk, F., & Sham, P. (2002). Analytic approaches to twin data using structural equation models. *Briefings in Bioinformatics, 3,* 119–133.

Riley, G. D. (1980). *Stuttering severity instrument for children and adults.* Tigard, OR: C.C. Publications.

Riley, G. D. (1981). *Stuttering prediction instrument* (Revised ed.). Austin, TX: Pro-Ed.

Riley, G. D. (1994). *Stuttering severity instrument for children and adults (SSI-3)* (3rd ed.) Austin, TX: Pro Ed.

Rispoli, M. (2003). Changes in the nature of sentence production during the period of grammatical development. *Journal of Speech, Language, and Hearing Research, 46,* 818–830.

Rispoli, M., & Hadley, M. (2001). The leading edge: The significance of sentence disruptions in the development of grammar. *Journal of Speech, Language, and Hearing Research, 44,* 1131–1143.

Rizzolatti, G., & Craighero, L. (2004). The mirror-neuron system, *Annual Review of Neuroscience, 27,* 169–192.

Robbins, S. D. (1935). The role of rhythm in the correction of stammering. *Quarterly Journal of Speech, 21,* 331–343.

Roelofs, A. (2004). Error biases in spoken word planning and monitoring by aphasic and non-aphasic speakers: Comments on Rapp and Goldrick (2000). *Psychological Review, 111,* 561–572.

Rommel, D., Hage, A., Kalehne, P., & Johannsen, H. (1999). Developmental, maintenance, and recovery of childhood stuttering: Prospective longitudinal data 3 years after first contact. In K. Baker, L. Rustin, & K. Baker (Eds.), *Proceedings of the 5th Oxford disfluency conference* (pp. 168–182). Windsor, Berkshire, UK: Chappell Gardner.

Ronson, I. (1976). Word frequency and stuttering: The relationship to sentence structure. *Journal of Speech and Hearing Research, 19,* 813–819.

Rosenberg, M. (1965). *Society and the adolescent self-image.* Princeton, NJ: Princeton University Press.

Rowland, C. F., & Theakston, A. L. (2009). The Acquisition of Auxiliary Syntax: A Longitudinal Elicitation Study. Part 2: The Modals and Auxiliary DO. *Journal of Speech Language and Hearing Research, 52,* 1471–1492.

Russ, R., Rickards, F., Poulaki, Z., Barke, M., Saunders, K., & Wake, M. (2002). Six year effectiveness of a population based two tier infant hearing screening programme. *Archives of Disease in Childhood, 86,* 245–250.

Rutter, M. (2005). *Genes and behaviour: Nature-nurture interplay explained.* Oxford, UK: Blackwell Publishing.

Ryan, B. P. (1974). *Programmed therapy for stuttering children and adults.* Springfield, IL: Charles C Thomas.

Ryan, B. P. (1984). Treatment of stuttering in school children. In W. Perkins (Ed.), *Current therapy of communication disorders: Stuttering disorders* (pp. 95–106). New York, NY: Thieme.

Ryan, B. P. (1992). Articulation, language, rate, and fluency characteristics of stuttering and nonstuttering preschool children. *Journal of Speech Hearing Research, 35,* 333–342.

Ryan, B. P. (2001). A longitudinal study of articulation, language, rate and fluency of 22 pre-school children who stutter. *Journal of Fluency Disorders, 26,* 107–127.

Ryan, B. P., & Van Kirk, R. B. (1995). Programmed stuttering treatment for children: Comparison of two establishment programs through transfer, maintenance, and follow-up. *Journal of Speech Hearing Research, 38,* 61–75.

Salmelin, R., Schnitzler, A., Schmitz, F., & Freund, H. J. (2000). Single word reading in developmental stutterers and fluent speakers. *Brain, 123,* 1184–1202.

Saltuklaroglu, T., & Kalinowski, J. (2006). The inhibition of stuttering via the presentation of natural speech and sinusoidal speech analogs. *Neuroscience Letters, 404,* 196–201.

Saltzman, E., Nam, H., Goldstein, L., & Byrd, D. (2006). The distinctions between state, parameter and graph dynamics in sensorimotor control and coordination. In M. L. Latash & F. Lestienne, (Eds.). *Motor control and learning* (pp. 63–73). New York, NY: Springer Publishing.

Saltuklaroglu, T., Dayalu, V. N., & Kalinowski, J. (2002). Reduction of stuttering: The dual inhibition hypothesis. *Medical Hypotheses. 58,* 67–71.

Sander, E. K. (1972). When are speech sounds learned? *Journal of Speech and Hearing Disorders, 37,* 55–63.

Savage, C., & Howell, P. (2008). Lexical priming of function words and content words with children who do, and do not, stutter. *Journal of Communication Disorders, 41,* 459–484.

Savage, C., & Lieven, E. (2004). Can the usage-based approach to language development be applied to analysis of developmental stuttering? *Stammering Research, 1,* 83–100.

Schindler, M. D. (1955). A study of educational adjustments of stuttering and non-stuttering children. In W. Johnson & R. R. Leutenegger (Eds.), *Stuttering in children and adults.* Minneapolis, MN: University of Minnesota Press.

Schlesinger I., Forte, M., Fried B., & Melkman R. (1965). Stuttering information load and response strength. *Journal of Speech and Hearing Disorders, 30,* 32–36.

Schneider, M., Retz, W., Coogan, A., Thome, J., & Rosler, M. (2006). Anatomical and functional brain imaging in adult attention-deficit/hyperactivity disorder (ADHD): A neurological view. *European Archives of Psychiatry and Clinical Neuroscience, 256,* 32–41.

Schwenk, K. A., Conture, E. G., & Walden, T. A. (2007). Reaction to background stimulation of preschool children who do and do not stutter. *Journal of Communication Disorders, 40,* 129–141.

Selkirk, E. (1984). *Phonology and syntax: The relation between sound and structure.* Cambridge, MA: MIT Press.

Sermas, C. E., & Cox, M. D. (1982). The stutterer and stuttering: Personality correlates. *Journal of Fluency Disorders, 7,* 141–158.

Shaiman, S., & Gracco, V. L. (2002). Task-specific sensorimotor interactions in speech production. *Experimental Brain Research, 146,* 411–418.

Shames, H. & Rubin, R. (1986). *Stuttering, then and now.* Columbus, OH: Merrill Publishing Co.

Shearer, W. M. (1966). Speech: Behavior of middle ear muscle during stuttering. *Science, 152,* 1280.

Sheehan, J. G., & Martyn, M. M. (1966). Spontaneous recovery from stuttering. *Journal of Speech and Hearing Research, 9,* 121–135.

Sheehan, J. G. (1970). *Stuttering: Research and therapy.* New York, NY: Harper and Row.

Shriberg, L. D., & Kwiatkowski, J. (1982). Phonological disorders III: A procedure for assessing severity of involvement. *Journal of Speech and Hearing Research, 25,* 256–270.

Shriberg, L. D., Tomblin, J. B., & McSweeny, J. L. (1999). Prevalence of speech delay in 6-year-old children and comorbidity with language impairment. *Journal of Speech, Language, and Hearing Research, 42,* 1461–1481.

Shugart, Y. Y., Mundorff, J., Kilshaw, J., Doheny, K., Doan, B., Wanyee, J., Green, E. D., & Drayna, D. (2004). Results of a genome-wide linkage scan for stuttering. *American Journal of Medical Genetics, 124A,* 133–135.

Silverman, F. H. (1996). *Stuttering and other fluency disorders* (2nd ed.). Needham, MA: Allyn & Bacon.

Small, L. H. (2005). *Fundamentals of phonetics: A practical guide for students.* Boston, MA: Allyn & Bacon.

Smith, A., & Goffman, L. (2004). Interaction of motor and language factors in the development of speech production. In B. Maasen, R. Kent, H. Peters, P. H. H. M. Van Lieshout, & W. Hulstijn (Eds.), *Speech motor control in normal and disordered speech* (pp. 227–252). Oxford, UK: Oxford University Press.

Smith, A., Goffman, L., Zelaznik, H. N., Ying, G. S., & Mcgillem, C. (1995). Spatiotemporal stability and patterning of speech movement sequences. *Experimental Brain Research, 104,* 493–501.

Smith, A., & Kleinow, J. (2000). Kinematic correlates of speaking rate changes in stuttering and normally fluent adults. *Journal of Speech, Language, and Hearing Research, 43,* 521–536.

Smith, A., & Zelaznik, H. N. (2004). Development of functional synergies for speech motor coordination in childhood and adolescence. *Developmental Psychobiology, 45,* 22–33.

Smits-Bandstra, S., & de Nil, L. (2009). Speech skill learning of persons who stutter and fluent speakers under single and dual task conditions. *Clinical Linguistics & Phonetics, 23,* 38–57.

Smits-Bandstra, S., de Nil. L., & Rochon, E. (2006). The transition to increased automaticity during finger sequence learning in adult males who stutter. *Journal of Fluency Disorders, 31,* 22–42.

Soderberg, G. A. (1966). Relations of stuttering to word length and word frequency. *Journal of Speech and Hearing Research, 9,* 584–589.

Soderberg, G. A. (1967). Linguistic factors in stuttering. *Journal of Speech Hearing Research, 10,* 801–810.

Sommer, M., Knappmeyer, K., Hunter, E. J., Gudenberg, A. W., Neef, N., & Paulus, W. (2009). Normal interhemispheric inhibition in persistent developmental stuttering. *Movement Disorders, 24,* 769–773.

Sommer, M., Koch, M. A., Paulus, W., Weiller, C., & Buchel, C. (2002). Disconnection of speech-relevant brain areas in persistent developmental stuttering. *Lancet Neurology, 360,* 380–383.

Spielberger, C. D., Gorsuch, R. L., & Lushene, R. E. (1970). *Manual for the state-trait anxiety inventory.* Palo Alto, CA: Consulting Psychologists Press.

Spohr, H. L., Willms, J., & Steinhausen, H. C. (2007). Fetal alcohol spectrum disorders in young adulthood. *Journal of Pediatrics, 150,* 175–179.

St. Clare, T., Menzies, R. G., Onslow, M., Packman, A., Thompson, R., & Block, S. (2009). Unhelpful thoughts and beliefs linked to social anxiety in stuttering: Development of a measure. *International Journal of Language & Communication Disorders, 44,* 338–351.

Stager, S. V., Jeffries, K. J., & Braun, A. R. (2003). Common features of fluency-evoking conditions studied in stuttering subjects and controls: An H(2)15O PET study. *Journal of Fluency Disorders, 28,* 319–335.

Starkweather, C. W. (1985). The development of fluency in normal children. In H. Gregory (Ed.), *Stuttering therapy: Prevention and intervention with children* (pp. 9–42). Memphis, TN: Speech Foundation of America.

Starkweather, C. W., Gottwald, S. R., & Halfond, M. M. (1990). *Stuttering prevention: A clinical method.* Englewood Cliffs, NJ: Prentice-Hall.

Stein, M. B., Baird, A., & Walker, J. R. (1996). Social phobia in adults with stuttering. *American Journal of Psychiatry, 153,* 278–280.

Steinhausen, H. C., & Spohr, H. L. (1998). Long-term outcome of children with fetal alcohol syndrome: Psychopathology, behavior and intelligence. *Alcoholism-Clinical and Experimental Research, 22,* 334–338.

Stemberger, J. P. (1984). Structural errors in normal and agrammatic speech. *Cognitive Neuropsychology, 1,* 281–313.

Stephenson, H., & Haggard, M. (1992). Rationale and design of surgical trials for otitis media with effusion. *Clinical Otolaryngology, 17,* 67–78.

Stoel-Gammon, C. & Dunn, C. (1985). *Normal and disordered phonology in children.* Baltimore, MD: University Park Press.

Storkel, H. L. (2009). Developmental differences in the effects of phonological, lexical and semantic variables on word learning by infants. *Journal of Child Language, 36,* 291–321.

Stott, C. M., Merricks, M. J., Bolton, P. F., & Goodyer, I. M. (2002). Screening for speech and language disorders: The reliability, validity and accuracy of the general language screen. *International Journal of Language and Communication Disorders, 37,* 133–151.

Stow, C., & Dodd, B. (2003). Providing an equitable service to bilingual children in the UK: A review. *International Journal of Language and Communication Disorders, 38,* 351–377.

Strenstrom, A.-B., & Svartvik, J. (1994). Imparsable speech: Repeats and other nonfluencies in spoken English. In N. Oostdijk & P. de Hann (Eds.), *Corpus-based research into language.* Atlanta, GA: Rodopi Amsterdam.

Stuart, A., Frazier, C. L., Kalinowski, J., & Vos, P. W. (2008). The effect of frequency altered feedback on stuttering duration and type. *Journal of Speech, Language, and Hearing Research, 51,* 889–897.

Stuart, A., Xia, S. X., Jiang, Y. N., Jiang, T., Kalinowski, J., & Rastatter, M. P. (2003). Self-contained in-the-ear device to deliver altered auditory feedback: Applications for stuttering. *Annals of Biomedical Engineering, 31,* 233–237.

Suresh, R., Ambrose, N., Roe, C., Pluzhnikov, A., Wittke-Thompson, J. K., Maggie, C. Y. Ng., Wu, X., Cook, E. H. ... Cox, N. J. (2006). New complexities in the genetics of stuttering: Significant sex-specific linkage signals. *American Journal of Human Genetics, 78,* 554–563.

Suri, R. E., Bargas, J., & Arbib, M. A. (2001). Modeling functions of striatal dopamine modulation in learning and planning. *Neuroscience, 103,* 65–85.

Szczurowska, I., Kuniszyk-Józkowiak, W., & Smolka, I. (2009). Speech nonfluency detection using Kohonen networks. *Neural Computing & Applications, 18,* 677–687.

Theakston, A. L., & Rowland, C. F. (2009). The Acquisition of Auxiliary Syntax: A Longitudinal Elicitation Study. Part 1: Auxiliary BE. *Journal of Speech Language and Hearing Research, 52,* 1449–1470.

Throneburg, R. N., Yairi, E., & Paden, E. P. (1994). Relation between phonologic difficulty and the occurrence of disfluencies in the early stage of stuttering. *Journal of Speech and Hearing Research, 37,* 504–509.

Trager, G. L. & Smith, H. L. (1962). *An outline of English structure.* Washington, DC: American Council of Learned Societies.

Tremblay, S., Shiller, D. M., & Ostry, D. J. (2003). Somatosensory basis of speech production. *Nature, 423,* 866–869.

Treon, M., Dempster, L., & Blaesing, K. (2006). MMPI-2/A assessed personality differences in people who do and do not stutter. *Social Behavior and Personality, 34,* 271–294.

Trouton, A., Spinath, F. M., & Plomin, R. (2002). Twins early development study (TEDS): A multivariate, longitudinal genetic investigation of language, cognition and behavior problems in childhood. *Twin Research, 5,* 444–448.

Van Borsel, J., & Taillieu, C. (2001). Neurogenic stuttering versus developmental stuttering: An observer judgment study. *Journal of Communication Disorders, 34,* 385–395.

Van Lieshout, P. H. H. M. (2004). Dynamical systems theory and its application in speech. In B. Maassen, R. Kent, H. F. M. Peters, P. H. H. M. Van Lieshout, & W. Hulstijn (Eds.), *Speech motor control in normal and disordered speech* (pp. 51–82). Oxford, UK: Oxford University Press.

Van Lieshout, P. H. H. M., Hulstijn, W., Alfonso, P. J., & Peters, H. F. M. (1997). Higher and lower order influences on the stability of the dynamic coupling between articulators. In H. F. M. Peters, W. Hulstijn, & P. H. H. M. Van Lieshout (Eds.), *Speech production: Brain research, motor control, and fluency disorders* (pp. 161–170). Amsterdam, The Netherlands: Elsevier Science.

Van Lieshout, P. H. H. M., Hulstijn, W., & Peters, H. F. M. (2004). Searching for the weak link in the speech production chain of people who stutter: A motor skill approach. In B. Maassen, R. Kent, H. F. M. Peters, P. H. H. M. Van Lieshout, & W. Hulstijn (Eds.), *Speech motor control in normal and disordered speech* (pp. 313–356). Oxford, UK: Oxford University Press.

Van Lieshout, P. H. H. M., & Moussa, W. (2000). The assessment of speech motor behaviors using electromagnetic articulography. *The Phonetician, 81,* 9–22.

Van Lieshout, P. H. H. M., & Namasivayam, A. K. (2010). Speech motor variability in people who stutter. In B. Maasson, & P. H. H. M. Van Lieshout, *Speech motor control: New developments in basic and applied research* (pp. 191–214). Oxford, UK: Oxford University Press.

Van Lieshout, P. H. H. M., Rutjens, C. A. W., & Spauwen, P. H. M. (2002). The dynamics of interlip coupling in speakers with a repaired unilateral cleft-lip history. *Journal of Speech, Language, and Hearing Research, 45,* 5–19.

Van Riper, C. (1971). *The nature of stuttering.* Englewood Cliffs, NJ: Prentice-Hall.

Van Riper, C. (1973). *The treatment of stuttering.* Englewood Cliffs, NJ: Prentice-Hall.

Van Riper, C. (1982). *The nature of stuttering* (2nd ed.). Englewood Cliffs, NJ: Prentice-Hall.

Van Riper, C. (1992). *The nature of stuttering* (3rd ed.). Prospect Heights, IL: Waveland Press.

Vanryckeghem, M. (1995). The communication attitude test: A concordancy investigation of stuttering and nonstuttering children and their parents. *Journal of Fluency Disorders, 20,* 191–203.

Vanryckeghem, M., & Brutten, G. J. (1992). The communication attitude test: A test-retest reliability investigation. *Journal of Fluency Disorders, 17,* 109–118.

Venkatagiri, H. S. (2009). What do people who stutter want: Fluency or freedom? *Journal of Speech, Language, and Hearing Research, 52,* 500–515.

Viswanath, N. S. (1989). Global-temporal and local-temporal effects of a stuttering event in the context of a clausal utterance. *Journal of Fluency Disorders, 14,* 245–269.

Viswanath, N. S., Lee, H. S., & Chakraborty, R. (2004). Evidence for a major gene influence on persistent developmental stuttering. *Human Biology, 76,* 401–412.

Viswanath, N. S., & Neel, A. T. (1995). Part-word repetitions by persons who stutter: Fragment types and their articulatory processes. *Journal of Speech and Hearing Research, 38,* 740–750.

Vitevitch, M. S. (1997). The neighborhood characteristics of malapropisms. *Language and Speech, 40,* 211–228.

Vitevitch, M. S. (2002). The influence of onset-density on spoken word recognition. *Journal of Experimental Psychology: Human Perception and Performance, 28,* 270–278.

Viviani, P., & Terzuolo, C. (1980). Space-time invariance in learned motor skills. In: G.E. Stelmach and J. Requin, (eds), *Tutorials in motor behavior*, North-Holland, Amsterdam (pp. 525–533).

Viviani, P., & Terzuolo, C. (1983). The organization of movement in handwriting and typing. In B. Butterworth (Ed.), *Language production* (pp. 103–146). London, UK: Academic Press.

Von Bekesy, G. (1960). *Experiments in hearing.* New York, NY: McGraw Hill.

Wakaba, Y. (1998). Research on temperament of children who stutter with early onset. In E. C. Healey & H. F. M. Peters (Eds.), *Proceedings of the 2nd world congress on fluency disorders* (pp. 84–87). Nijmegen, The Netherlands: University of Nijmegen Press.

Wall, M. J. (1980). A comparison of syntax in young stutterers and nonstutterers. *Journal of Fluency Disorders, 5,* 345–352.

Wall, M. J., Starkweather, C. W., & Cairns, H. S. (1981a). Syntactic influences on stuttering in young child stutterers. *Journal of Fluency Disorders, 6,* 283–298.

Wall, M. J., Starkweather, C. W., & Harris, K. S. (1981b). The influence of voicing adjustments on the location of stuttering in the spontaneous speech of young child stutterers. *Journal of Fluency Disorders, 6,* 299–310.

Ward, D. (1997). Intrinsic and extrinsic timing in stutterers' speech: Data and implications. *Language and Speech, 4,* 289–310.

Ward, D., & Arnfield, S. (2001). Linear and nonlinear analysis of the stability of gestural organization in speech movement sequences. *Journal of Speech, Language, and Hearing Research, 44,* 108–117.

Watkins, R. V. (2005). Language abilities of young children who stutter. In E. Yairi & N. Ambrose (Eds.), *Early childhood stuttering* (pp. 235–252). Austin, TX: Pro-Ed.

Watkins, K. E., Patel, N., Davis, S., & Howell, P. (2005). Brain activity during altered auditory feedback: An fMRI study in healthy adolescents. In *Proceedings of the 11th annual conference of the Organization for Human Brain Mapping.* Toronto, Canada. Available on CD-ROM in Neuroimage 26 (Suppl. 1).

Watkins, K. E., Smith, S. M., Davis, S., & Howell, P. (2008). Structural and functional abnormalities of the motor system in developmental stuttering. *Brain, 131,* 50–59.

Watkins, R. V., Yairi, E., & Ambrose, N. G. (1999a). Early childhood stuttering. II: Initial status of expressive language abilities. *Journal of Speech and Hearing Research, 42,* 1125–1135.

Watkins, R. V., Yairi, E., & Ambrose, N. G. (1999b). Early childhood stuttering. III: Initial status of expressive language abilities. *Journal of Speech and Hearing Research, 42,* 1125–1135.

Watson, B. C., & Alfonso, P. J. (1987). Physiological bases of acoustic LRT in nonstutterers, mild stutterers, and severe stutterers. *Journal of Speech Hearing Research, 30,* 434–447.

Watson, C. S., & Love, L. (1965). Distribution of silent periods in speech: Stutterers versus nonstutterers. *Journal of the Acoustical Society of America, 38,* 935.

Watson, D., & Gibson, E. (2004). The relationship between intonational phrasing and syntactic structure in language production. *19,* 713–755.

Webster, R. L., & Dorman, M. F. (1970). Decreases in stuttering frequency as a function of continuous and contingent forms of auditory masking. *Journal of Speech and Hearing Research, 14,* 307–311.

Webster, R. L., & Lubker, B. B. (1968a). Masking of auditory feedback in stutterers' speech. *Journal of Speech Hearing Research, 11,* 221–223.

Webster, R. L., & Lubker, B. B. (1968b). Interrelationships among fluency producing variables in stuttered speech. *Journal of Speech Hearing Research, 11,* 754–766.

Weidig, T. (2005). The statistical fluctuation in the natural recovery rate between control and treatment group dilutes their results. Rapid response to "Randomised controlled trial of the Lidcombe programme of early stuttering intervention" by Jones, Onslow, Packman, Williams, Ormond, Schwarz & Gebski (2005). *British Medical Journal,* Retrieved from: http://bmj.bmjjournals.com/cgi/eletters/331/7518/659#115238 (November 27, 2009).

Weiss, A. L., & Jakielski, K. J. (2001). Phonetic complexity measurement and prediction of children's disfluencies: A preliminary study. In B. Maassen, W. Hulstijn, R. Kent, H. F. M. Peters, & P. H. H. M. Van Lieshout (Eds.), *Proceedings of the 4th conference on speech motor control and stuttering.* Nijmegen, The Netherlands: Uitgeverij Vantilt.

Wells, G. (1985). *Language development in the pre-school years.* Cambridge: Cambridge University Press.

Wells, G. B. (1979). Effect of sentence structure on stuttering. *Journal of Fluency Disorders, 4,* 123–129.

Wetherby, A., & Prizant, B. (2002). *Communication and symbolic behaviour scales.* Baltimore, MD: Paul H. Brookes Publishing Company.

Wijnen, F. (2006). Begrijpen wat je niet hoort. Stem-, Spraak-, en. *Taalpathologie, 14,* 3–15.

Wing, A. M., & Kristofferson, A. B. (1973). Response delays and timing of discrete motor responses. *Perception & Psychophysics, 14,* 5–12.

Wingate, M. (1964). A standard definition of stuttering. *Journal of Speech Hearing Disorders, 29,* 484–489.

Wingate, M. (1976). *Stuttering: Theory and treatment.* New York, NY: Irvington.

Wingate, M. (1984). Stutter events and linguistic stress. *Journal of Fluency Disorders, 9,* 295–300.

Wingate, M. (1988). *The structure of stuttering.* New York, NY: Springer-Verlag.

Wingate, M. (2001). SLD is not stuttering. *Journal of Speech, Language, and Hearing Research, 44,* 381–383.

Wingate, M. (2002). *Foundations of stuttering.* San Diego, CA: Academic Press.

Wingate, M. (2009). Early position and stuttering occurrence. *Journal of Fluency Disorders,* *7,* 243–258.

Wittke-Thompson, J. K., Ambrose, N., Yairi, E., Roe, C., Cook, E. H., Ober, C., & Cox, N. J. (2007). Genetic studies of stuttering in a founder population. *Journal of Fluency Disorders, 32,* 33–50.

Wolk, L., Edwards, M. L., & Conture, E. G. (1993). Coexistence of stuttering and disordered phonology in young children. *Journal of Speech and Hearing Research, 36,* 906–917.

Wolpert, D. M., Miall, R. C., & Kawato, M. (1998). Internal models in the cerebellum. *Trends in Cognitive Sciences, 2,* 338–347.

Woods, C. E., & Williams, D. E. (1976). Traits attributed to stuttering and normally fluent males. *Journal of Speech and Hearing Research, 19,* 267–278.

World Health Organization. (1992). *International statistical classification of diseases and related health problems* (10th revision: ICD-10). Geneva, Switzerland: World Health Organization.

Wright, B. A., Lombardino, L. J., King, W. M., Puranik, C. S., Leonard, C. M., & Merzenich, M. M. (1997). Deficits in auditory-temporal and spectral resolution in language-impaired children. *Nature, 387,* 176–178.

Wu, J. W., Riley, G., Maguire, G., Najafi, A., & Tang, C. (1997). PET scan evidence of parallel cerebral systems related to treatment effects: FDG and FDOPA PET scan findings. In W. Hulstijn, H. F. M. Peters, & P. H. H. M. Van Lieshout (Eds.), *Speech production: Motor control, brain research and fluency disorders* (pp. 329–339). Amsterdam, The Netherlands: Elsevier.

Yairi, E. (2007). Subtyping stuttering. I: A review. *Journal of Fluency Disorders, 32,* 165–196.

Yairi, E., & Ambrose, N. (1992). Onset of stuttering in pre-school children: Selected factors. *Journal of Speech and Hearing Research, 35,* 782–788.

Yairi, E., & Ambrose, N. G. (1999). Early childhood stuttering. I: Persistency and recovery rates. *Journal of Speech and Hearing Research, 42,* 1097–1112.

Yairi, E. & Ambrose, N. G. (2005). *Early childhood stuttering.* Austin, TX: Pro-Ed.

Yairi, E., Ambrose, N., & Cox, N. (1996). Genetics of stuttering: A critical review. *Journal of Speech Hearing Research, 39,* 771–784.

Yairi, E., Ambrose, N. G., Paden, E. P., & Throneburg, R. N. (1996). Predictive factors of persistence and recovery: Pathways of childhood stuttering. *Journal of Communication Disorders, 29,* 51–77.

Yaruss, J. S. (1998). Describing the consequences of disorders: Stuttering and the international classification of impairments, disabilities, and handicaps. *Journal of Speech, Language, and Hearing Research, 41,* 249–257.

Yaruss, J. S., & Conture, E. G. (1992). Relationship between mother–child speaking rates in adjacent fluent utterances. *American Speech-Language-Hearing Association, 34,* 210.

Yaruss, J. S., & Conture, E. (1995). Mother and child speaking rates and utterance lengths in adjacent fluent utterances: Preliminary observations. *Journal of Fluency Disorders, 20,* 257–278.

Yaruss, J. S., & Conture, E. G. (1996). Stuttering and phonological disorders in children: Examination of the covert repair hypothesis. *Journal of Speech and Hearing Research, 39,* 349–364.

Yaruss, J. S., LaSalle, L. R., & Conture, E. G. (1998). Evaluating stuttering in young children: Diagnostic data. *American Journal of Speech-Language Pathology, 7,* 62–76.

Yovetich, W. S., Leschied, A. W., & Flicht, J. (2000). Self-esteem of school-age children who stutter. *Journal of Fluency Disorders, 25,* 143–153.

Yueh, B., Souza, P. E., McDowell, J. A., Collins, M. P., Loovis, C. F., Hedrick, S. C., Ramsey, S. D., & Deyo, R. A. (2001). Randomized trial of amplification strategies. *Archives of Otolaryngology-Head & Neck Surgery, 127,* 1197–1204.

Zebrowski, P. M. (1991). Duration of the speech disfluencies of beginning stutterers. *Journal of Speech and Hearing Research, 34,* 483–491.

Zebrowski, P. M. (1994). Duration of sound prolongation and sound/syllable repetition in children who stutter. *Journal of Speech and Hearing Research, 37,* 254–263.

Zebrowski, P. M., & Conture, E. G. (1998). Influence of non-treatment variables on treatment effectiveness for school-age children who stutter. In A. Cordes & R. Ingham (Eds.), *Treatment efficacy for stuttering: A search for empirical bases* (pp. 293–310). San Diego, CA: Singular Publishing Group, Inc.

Zebrowski, P. M., Conture, E. G., & Cudahy, E. A. (1985). Acoustic analysis of young stutterers' fluency: Preliminary observations. *Journal of Fluency Disorders, 10,* 173–192.

Zelaznik, H. N., Spencer, R. M., & Ivry, R. B. (2002). Dissociation of explicit and implicit timing in repetitive tapping and drawing movements. *Journal of Experimental Psychology: Human Perception and Performance, 28,* 575–588.

Zerbin, R. W. (1973). Erfassung der symptomatik stotternder. *Die Sprachheilarbeit, 18,* 174–185.

Zuckerman, M. (2006). *Psychology of personality.* Cambridge, UK: Cambridge University Press.

Author Index

Subject Index